The Senator from New England

The Senator from New England

The Rise of JFK

SEAN J. SAVAGE

excelsior editions
State University of New York Press
Albany, New York

Cover photo of John F. Kennedy courtesy of Getty Images (taken from the LIFE Images Collection). Photographer: Verner Reed.

Published by State University of New York Press, Albany

© 2015 State University of New York

All rights reserved

Printed in the United States of America

No part of this book may be used or reproduced in any manner whatsoever without written permission. No part of this book may be stored in a retrieval system or transmitted in any form or by any means including electronic, electrostatic, magnetic tape, mechanical, photocopying, recording, or otherwise without the prior permission in writing of the publisher.

Excelsior Editions is an imprint of State University of New York Press

For information, contact State University of New York Press, Albany, NY
www.sunypress.edu

Production, Diane Ganeles
Marketing, Kate R. Seburyamo

Library of Congress Cataloging-in-Publication Data

Savage, Sean J., 1964–
  The senator from New England : the rise of JFK / Sean J. Savage.
      pages cm
  Includes bibliographical references and index.
  ISBN 978-1-4384-5703-1 (hardcover : alk. paper)
  ISBN 978-1-4384-5704-8 (e-book)
  1. Kennedy, John F. (John Fitzgerald), 1917–1963. 2. Legislators—Massachusetts—Biography. 3. United States. Congress. Senate—Biography. 4. New England—Politics and government—20th century. 5. Presidents—United States—Election—1960. 6. United States—Politics and government—1945–1989.
7. New England—Biography. I. Title.

E842.1.S28 2015
973.922092—dc23
[B]   2014030986

10 9 8 7 6 5 4 3 2 1

*This book is dedicated to
Harry Savage and Truman "Buddy" Savage*

Contents

Abbreviations		ix
Preface		xi
Chapter 1	JFK and Massachusetts Politics	1
Chapter 2	JFK and New England Economics	41
Chapter 3	JFK and the St. Lawrence Seaway	75
Chapter 4	JFK and the Politics of 1956	103

photo gallery follows page 138

Chapter 5	JFK and the 1958 Elections	139
Chapter 6	JFK and the Politics of 1959	193
Chapter 7	From New England to the Nation: 1960	215
Epilogue		247
Notes		249
Selected Bibliography		305
Photographic Credits		321
Index		325

Abbreviations

ADA	Americans for Democratic Action
BC	Boston College
BPL	Boston Public Library
BTC	Bates College
BU	Boston University
CHC	College of the Holy Cross
CQ	*Congressional Quarterly*
DAC	Democratic Advisory Council
DDE	Dwight D. Eisenhower
DDEL	Dwight D. Eisenhower Library
DNC	Democratic National Committee
DTC	Dartmouth College
EMK	Edward M. Kennedy
FDR	Franklin D. Roosevelt
GF	General Files
GPO	Government Printing Office
HST	Harry S. Truman
HSTL	Harry S. Truman Library
JFK	John F. Kennedy
JFKL	John F. Kennedy Library
JPK	Joseph P. Kennedy
LBJ	Lyndon B. Johnson
LBJL	Lyndon B. Johnson Library
LOC	Library of Congress
MCSL	Margaret Chase Smith Library
MHS	Massachusetts Historical Society

MSL	Massachusetts State Library
NYT	*New York Times*
OF	Office Files
OH	Oral History transcript
PC	Providence College
POF	President's Office Files
PPP	Pre-Presidential Papers
RFK	Robert F. Kennedy
RNC	Republican National Committee
SC	Stonehill College
TPO	Thomas P. O'Neill, Jr.
UCT	University of Connecticut
UPI	United Press International
URI	University of Rhode Island
UVM	University of Vermont
WHCF	White House Central File

Preface

I developed the idea for writing *The Senator from New England: The Rise of JFK* while I was researching my third book, *JFK, LBJ, and the Democratic Party*. While researching secondary sources, I read *John Kennedy: A Political Profile* by James MacGregor Burns and *Jack: The Struggles of John F. Kennedy* by Herbert S. Parmet. Each book includes a chapter entitled "The Senator from New England." I then realized that the aspect of John F. Kennedy's Senate career that focused on regional policy issues merited a book-length survey and analysis. In particular, *The Senator from New England: The Rise of JFK* explores how and why JFK changed from a senator emphasizing bipartisan, centrist, and eclectically conservative policy proposals to solve or ameliorate policy problems unique to, or especially prominent in, New England to a more liberal, partisan Democratic senator and presidential candidate who connected and subordinated the policy needs of Massachusetts and New England to those of the nation in general.

The primary sources used in this book include not only those of the Kennedy, Johnson, Truman, and Eisenhower presidential libraries. They also include those of Assumption College, Stonehill College, Boston College, Boston University, Bates College, Providence College, Dartmouth College, the College of the Holy Cross, the state universities of Massachusetts, Connecticut, Vermont, and Rhode Island, the Boston Public Library, the Massachusetts Historical Society, the Massachusetts State Library, the Margaret Chase Smith Library, the Catholic Diocese of Worcester, and the Library of Congress. I am grateful for research grants from Saint Mary's College and the foundations of the John F. Kennedy and Margaret Chase Smith libraries. I am also grateful for the typing skills of Sophia Schrage in preparing the manuscript of this book.

1

JFK and Massachusetts Politics

On January 9, 1961, President-elect John F. Kennedy delivered an address to the Massachusetts state legislature, officially known as the General Court of the Commonwealth of Massachusetts, at the State House in Boston. As he prepared to be inaugurated president, JFK assured his fellow Bay Staters, "The enduring qualities of Massachusetts—the common threads woven by the Pilgrim and the Puritan, the fisherman and the farmer, the Yankee and the immigrant—will not be and could not be forgotten in this nation's executive mansion."[1] He also quoted John Winthrop's famous reference to the Puritans' determination to make their colony "a city upon a hill—the eyes of all the people are upon us."[2] In concluding his brief yet poignant speech, JFK identified courage, judgment, integrity, and dedication as "the historic qualities of the Bay Colony and the Bay State" and hoped that they "will characterize our government's conduct in the four stormy years that lie ahead."[3]

Theodore C. Sorensen, JFK's chief speech writer and future White House special counsel, helped JFK to prepare this speech. He wrote, "Kennedy the President-elect was not unmindful of his inability to be proud of all the politicians of Massachusetts as Massachusetts was of him."[4] Sorensen added that, in January 1961, few states exceeded Massachusetts in "repeated disclosures of official wrongdoing" and that JFK "could neither avoid that issue nor deliver a self-righteous lecture about it."[5]

In his classic study of the 1960 presidential election, journalist Theodore H. White, a Boston native and Harvard graduate, claimed that Massachusetts was one of the four most politically corrupt states in the nation.[6] In his account of the Kennedy presidency, historian and White House aide Arthur M. Schlesinger, Jr., quoted JFK as telling him in 1960, "If I were knocked out of the Presidential thing, I would put Bobby into the Massachusetts picture to run for governor. It takes someone with Bobby's nerve and his investigative experience to clean up the mess in the Legislature and the Governor's Council."[7]

The contrast between the lofty, sentimental tone of JFK's "Farewell to Massachusetts" speech and his private comments about his home state's embarrassing national reputation for its politics was analogous to historian Perry Miller's earlier observation in *The New England Mind: From Colony to Province*. In this book, Miller wrote that even as John Winthrop and other Puritans sought to build a "city upon a hill" in Massachusetts, they knew that it "was going to be the old, familiar world of sin and struggle."[8]

Shortly after JFK's death, *Boston Globe* reporter John Harris wrote an article detailing much of the petty corruption, clannish factionalism, and Machiavellian maneuvering in Massachusetts politics during the 1950s and 1960s. Nevertheless, he optimistically concluded, "That the puritan ideal should be permitted permanently to languish in the state and city of its most perfect development seems unthinkable" because "the spirit and determination which once blazed the way to the establishment of a republic, are still in the New England air."[9]

Despite his frequent, private expressions of exasperation with politics in Massachusetts, JFK needed to appeal to the Puritan ideal of a "city upon a hill" in his rhetoric and some of his policy behavior while adapting to the unseemly aspects of Massachusetts politics that pressured and motivated him to develop the political skills necessary to progressively succeed in state, regional, and national politics. Kennedy was a Catholic and the great-grandson of Irish immigrants as well as the grandson of a state senator and mayor of Boston. Thus, JFK could understand and shrewdly participate in the Irish-dominated, so-called "immigrant ethos" which included machine politics, the use of government resources to benefit one's family, friends, and political supporters, and an emphasis on social welfare and labor reforms in public policy.[10] Meanwhile, JFK's inherited wealth, Harvard education, and father's determination to instill in his sons the Brahmin values of *noblesse oblige* toward public service also enabled JFK to understand and apply the so-called "Yankee ethos." In addition to the achievement of a morally and intellectually superior public good derived from the Puritans' concept of a "city upon a hill," the "Yankee ethos" within New England's political culture included an emphasis on honesty and efficiency in government spending, a distaste for patronage jobs and other ethically questionable uses of government resources, professionalism in policy making and implementation, and a scholarly, idealistic political style, especially in campaign rhetoric.[11]

In analyzing Kennedy's successful combination and embodiment of these two political value systems, political scientists James MacGregor Burns, Edward C. Banfield, and James Q. Wilson described JFK as a "Green Brahmin."[12] Banfield and Wilson further contended that, by the mid-1960s and partially because of the precedent set by JFK's political career and presidency, "The perfect candidate, then, is of Jewish, Polish, Italian, or Irish extraction and has the speech, dress, manner, and public virtues—honesty, impartiality, and devotion to the public interest—of the upper-class Anglo Saxon."[13] Likewise, historian David Hackett Fischer, in his study of the enduring "folkways" of New England and other regional cultures, stated that, while JFK "was raised within a distinctive Irish Catholic culture and acquired many of its values," he "was also a New Englander" and "combined ethnic and regional elements."[14]

JFK's Senate career and presidency coincided with a renewed interest in political science in studying both the concept and application of political culture. Gabriel Almond's groundbreaking 1956 article distinguished political culture from ideology in the study of comparative political systems.[15] Almond and Sidney Verba later coauthored *The Civic Culture: Political Attitudes and Democracy in Five Nations*, published in 1963.[16] While Almond and Verba were primarily concerned with studying the political cultures of other nations, Yale political scientist Robert A. Dahl partially and implicitly used political culture in his study of pluralism in the local politics and government of New Haven, Connecticut during the 1950s.[17]

The increasing interest of political scientists in studying and comparing the politics of the New England states was evident in Duane Lockard's book, *New England State Politics*, published in 1959. Lockard analyzed and compared the six New England states within a framework similar to that of V. O. Key, Jr.'s book, *Southern Politics in State and Nation*, first published in 1949. In his 1966 book, *American Federalism: A View from the States*, Daniel J. Elazar analyzed and categorized state and local politics throughout the nation according to three types of political subcultures: moralistic, individualistic, and traditionalistic.[18] According to Elazar, Massachusetts combined a moralistic subculture, similar to the "Yankee ethos," and an individualistic subculture, similar to the "immigrant ethos."[19] In his 1965 book, *The Political Cultures of Massachusetts*, Edgar Litt argued that, after World War II, the political cultures of Massachusetts were influenced more by differences in education, occupation, and income and less by ancestry, ethnicity, religion, and party affiliation. In particular, Litt categorized and defined four political cultures in Massachusetts: patricians, yeomen, workers, and managers.[20] Thus, JFK shared more of the patrician political culture of Senator Leverett Saltonstall, his Republican colleague from Massachusetts, than the worker political culture of an Irish Catholic taxi driver from South Boston.

If political culture is an important prism for understanding and analyzing the politics of Massachusetts during the 1950s and JFK's participation in it, exactly how should political culture be defined for the purpose of studying its relationship to JFK's Senate career? Political scientists and historians generally agree that a political culture is a distinctive pattern of behavior and set of values within a political community, regardless of whether it is national, state, or local, that are influenced by historical, ethnic, religious, economic, and social factors.[21] In their study of local politics, which used Boston politics of the 1950s and early 1960s as their primary example, Banfield and Wilson stated that a participant in a political culture "acquires a more or less stable set of beliefs about who runs things, how to get things done, whom to see, who wants what, and where 'the bodies are buried.'"[22]

The political environment that JFK entered shortly after World War II was often perceived nationally as one of economic decline, political corruption, stagnant population growth, and a rigid class system based on ancestry. Journalists of the late-1940s promoted this perception. The subtitle of Louis M. Lyons's 1947 article on Boston was a "Study in Inertia."[23] Journalist William V. Shannon characterized the few local Democratic committees of Massachusetts as "the private preserves of dead beats and stuffed shirts."[24] In their tabloid-style, investigatory book, *U.S.A. Confidential*, Jack Lait and Lee Mortimer dismissed New England as "an anachronism decadent and broke" and Massachusetts and Boston as "venal and corrupt— miniature Washingtons."[25] Providing a more favorable assessment, John Gunther wrote, "More than any other American region, New England owes its present to its past."[26]

The election of James Michael Curley to his fourth term as mayor of Boston in 1945 seemed to confirm the most sardonic and dismissive appraisals of Boston politics. By 1945, Curley was a 71-year-old congressman who had previously served as mayor of Boston and governor of Massachusetts. In the national press, he had become famous and notorious as colorfully corrupt, eloquent yet demagogic, and popular among Boston's oldest and poorest Catholic voters. In 1946, Curley was convicted of federal mail fraud charges, yet he continued to serve as mayor while imprisoned in Danbury, Connecticut.[27]

Curley's decision to run for mayor instead of reelection to the U.S. House of Representatives left an open congressional seat that JFK won in the 1946 congressional elections. Was it merely a coincidence that Curley's election as mayor in 1945 created an opportunity for JFK to run for Congress? Probably not. According to several sources, Joseph P. Kennedy (JPK) paid Curley to vacate his congressional seat and began negotiations with him in late 1944.[28] In his memoir, Edward M. Kennedy (EMK) claimed, however, that all of the Kennedys, including his father, were surprised by JFK's decision to run for Congress. "Jack's initial interest in elective office registered as a mild surprise to our family. He had never to my knowledge talked about political ambitions . . . Not even Dad saw this coming."[29] EMK further elaborated that their father thought that JFK's health was too fragile for the rigors of political life and that he would continue his budding career as a journalist focusing on international relations.

It is unlikely that JFK's decision to run for elective office was even a "mild surprise" for Joseph P. Kennedy (JPK). JPK had encouraged and financed the 1942 Senate campaign of his father-in-law, John F. "Honey Fitz" Fitzgerald. Fitzgerald ran against Joseph Casey, a congressman favored by the Roosevelt administration, in the Democratic primary.[30] Although Fitzgerald lost the primary, the incumbent Republican senator, Henry Cabot Lodge, Jr., easily defeated Casey, partially by using tape recordings of some of Fitzgerald's most caustic anti-Casey speeches.[31] JPK's apparent purposes in opposing Casey were to express his anti-Roosevelt sentiment and develop a political base in Massachusetts for his family.[32]

In a March 9, 1944 letter, JPK thanked his cousin Joe Kane, who was active and experienced in political campaigns in Massachusetts, for discussing future political opportunities with JFK. JPK noted that JFK had spent "a most interesting four hours" with Kane and asked Kane to "drop me a line on what you see for the future of these youngsters in Massachusetts."[33] By "youngsters," JPK meant both of his oldest sons, Joseph P. Kennedy, Jr., and JFK. JFK probably would not have had a four-hour conversation with Kane if he were not already considering a future political career and if JPK was not already contemplating political careers for both JPK, Jr., and JFK.[34] This and similar letters contradict the conventional perception that JFK reluctantly and unexpectedly entered elective politics as a substitute for his older brother, who died in August 1944 while serving as a navy pilot in Europe.[35]

Despite JPK's negotiations with Curley, it was uncertain whether JFK would run for Congress or lieutenant governor in 1946. In 1945, Governor Maurice Tobin asked JPK to travel throughout Massachusetts for the purposes of assessing problems in the state's economy, proposing solutions for them, and justifying Tobin's recommendation that a state department of commerce be created.[36] Accepting Tobin's appointment as chairman of this special commission, JPK used his position to promote the Kennedy name on a state-wide level and to test the political waters for JFK.[37]

Tobin was especially eager to have JFK run for lieutenant governor because he expected a large infusion of campaign funds from

JPK if JFK was his running mate.[38] JPK, a Florida resident, was notorious in Massachusetts politics for contributing little or nothing to Democratic campaigns that did not include his family members. For a while in 1945 and early 1946, JPK seemed increasingly attracted to the idea of his son running for lieutenant governor.[39]

Joe Kane speculated that JPK was considering Tobin's offer. There was a remote possibility that both Tobin and Democratic Senator David I. Walsh would be reelected in 1946; the ailing, elderly Walsh would then either die or resign; Tobin would appoint himself to Walsh's Senate seat; and JFK would succeed Tobin as governor.[40] In addition, Kane warned JPK, "Jack's candidacy for Lieut. Gov., would cause a howl, that Kennedy was interested in making his son Lieut. Gov., not helping Massachusetts."[41]

By early 1946, JPK agreed with Kane's advice and JFK's preference to run for Congress.[42] Ever since he was a college student, JFK preferred to study, write about, and involve himself in international rather than state and local issues.[43] He greatly admired both the speaking style and worldview of Winston Churchill, evident in his published college thesis, *Why England Slept*. Furthermore, he covered the British parliamentary elections for the Hearst newspapers in 1945 and gave several speeches in Boston on veterans' and foreign policy issues.[44] As a congressional candidate, JFK could speak regularly about his ideas on foreign policy and how he wanted the United States to influence the post-war world.

There were also more political, calculating reasons for JFK to run for Congress.[45] The Republican Party in Massachusetts was strong enough to win elections to major statewide offices. A significant minority of Democratic voters were likely to split their tickets and vote Republican for governor and lieutenant governor in order to express their frustration with and grievances against the Tobin administration and about such current state and local issues as high taxes, the decline in industrial employment since World War II, and problems with mass transit in Boston.[46] In addition to being forced to subordinate his campaign to Tobin's record and reelection needs, JFK's candidacy would be vulnerable to the disunited, factionalized nature of the Massachusetts Democratic Party.[47]

A poll financed by JPK finally convinced him that JFK should run for Congress.[48] JFK established his residency in the district by renting a room at the Bellevue Hotel where John F. Fitzgerald, his maternal grandfather, also lived.[49] Besides having been mayor of Boston, Fitzgerald had previously been a congressman in this district. "Honey Fitz" regularly campaigned with, or on behalf of, JFK in order to attract the support of the district's older voters.[50] Although Curley and Fitzgerald had once been bitter political enemies, Curley publicly predicted that JFK would win the highly contested Democratic congressional primary, partially because JFK's middle name was Fitzgerald. Curley stated that JFK "doesn't need to campaign. He can go to Washington now and forget the primary and election."[51]

Because the eleventh congressional district of Massachusetts was overwhelmingly Democratic in its voting behavior, the Democratic nominee was assured of winning the general election in November, regardless of how well the Republicans performed nationally in the 1946 congressional elections. With the Democratic nomination for this congressional seat so desirable, JFK was one of ten candidates competing in the primary. The candidate who was initially expected to win the primary was Michael Neville, a state representative, former city councilor, and future mayor of Cambridge. Thomas P. "Tip" O'Neill, Jr., a Neville supporter, noticed how JFK became increasingly popular in Cambridge through his personal door-to-door campaigning, publicity, and tea parties sponsored by his mother, Rose Kennedy. O'Neill wrote, "If Jack Kennedy could get people excited in Cambridge, which was Neville's own backyard, there wasn't much hope for Mike in the rest of the district."[52]

In their account of JFK's 1946 primary campaign, Kenneth P. O'Donnell and David F. Powers noted that the accusation by Kennedy's opponents that JFK was a carpetbagger mattered little to the voters since Curley had not lived in the eleventh district.[53] According to Powers, JFK's most effective campaign publicity was a brochure entitled *Survival*. It was an account of JFK's decorated bravery in the South Pacific involving his PT boat.[54]

There were few, if any, significant issue differences among the Democratic candidates. They all ran as New Deal liberals favorable to labor unions, national health insurance, improvement in the wages and working conditions of dock workers, and public housing.[55] The voters were also unlikely to be dazzled by JFK's speeches. Joseph A. DeGuglielmo, who served as mayor of Cambridge from 1952 to 1953, later claimed that the "biggest fault" in JFK's 1946 campaign was "his lack of oratorical polish. He would fumble his words."[57]

Hired to help JFK write and deliver his speeches for radio, Mark Dalton stated that JPK was the "real campaign manager." JPK kept a low public profile while directing the campaign from a room at the Ritz Carlton hotel. According to journalist Francis Russell, JPK wanted "a spectacular win that would make his son's name familiar all over the state."[58]

With seemingly unlimited funds, the Kennedy campaign spent lavishly on advertising and paid women in the district for the costs of hosting receptions for JFK in their homes.[59] The Kennedy campaign also offered to pay families in the district $50 each to work at the polls on primary day. In his autobiography, Tip O'Neill wrote that JPK reputedly spent $300,000 on his son's congressional primary campaign, approximately six times as much as O'Neill spent in the same district in his 1952 congressional campaign.[60]

JFK won the June 18th primary with 40.5 percent of the votes, nearly double the percentage of votes received by Michael Neville, his closest rival.[61] In November, he easily defeated his Republican opponent with almost 72 percent of the votes.[62] Meanwhile, the Democrats lost fifty-five U.S. House seats and control of Congress.[63] Walsh, Tobin, and Paul Dever, the Democratic nominee for lieutenant governor, also lost.

After JFK took his seat in Congress in 1947, he soon became bored and restless with his duties and status as a member of the U.S. House of Representatives. JFK's position was further weakened and obscured by the fact that he was a freshman member of the minority party and that his state's Democratic delegation was dominated by Representative John W. McCormack from South Boston. McCormack was minority whip and eventually became Speaker of the U.S. House of Representatives. McCormack disliked JFK's lackadaisical approach to his duties, especially his committee assignments, his casual apparel on the House floor, and his refusal to follow McCormack's leadership.[64]

Although *Look* magazine referred to JFK as a "fighting conservative," he generally voted the same as other northern liberal Democrats on domestic policy issues.[65] While he privately believed that tougher federal laws were needed to rid labor unions of Communists, racketeers, and abuses of power, JFK voted against the Taft-Hartley Act. He gained national attention by debating Republican Congressman Richard M. Nixon of California on this issue.[66]

JFK also distinguished himself as a hawkish critic of the Truman administration's Cold War policies, especially after China fell to Communism in 1949.[67] In a speech delivered on January 30, 1949, in Salem, Massachusetts, i.e., outside of his district, JFK denounced how the Truman administration treated the anti-Communist Chinese nationalists. He referred to the Communist victory in China as "the tragic story of China whose freedom we once fought to preserve. What our young men had saved, our diplomats and our President have frittered away."[68]

While developing his own Cold War policy ideas, JFK was careful to maintain an efficient, highly responsive system of constituency service in his Washington and district offices.[69] He had no trouble in being reelected. He was unanimously reelected in 1948 and won with 82 percent of the votes in 1950.[70]

As early as 1948, JFK was considering his candidacy for the Senate in 1952.[71] His desire to become a senator while he was still a freshman representative partially resulted from his feeling of insignificance on foreign and defense policy issues. JFK later complained that he and other representatives "were just worms over in the House—nobody pays much attention to us nationally."[72]

Kennedy also disliked his subordinate relationship with McCormack. With the Democrats regaining control of Congress in 1948, McCormack became House majority leader, further enhancing his power. JFK alienated McCormack further when he distinguished himself as the only Democratic congressman from Massachusetts who refused to sign McCormack's petition asking President Harry S. Truman to commute the sentence of James Michael Curley, the imprisoned mayor of Boston.[73]

By late 1947, there were already rumors in Massachusetts that JFK might run for governor in 1948.[74] JFK found the prospect of running for governor, whether in 1948 or later, only marginally more attractive than that of lieutenant governor in 1946. JFK remarked to historian Arthur M. Schlesinger, Jr., "I hate to think of myself in that corner office deciding on sewer contracts."[75]

As governor, Kennedy would be forced to deal with the distribution of state contracts and patronage jobs, a periodically uncooperative executive council on judicial appointments, and squabbles with the state legislature over budgets and taxes. With a two-year term as governor, JFK would also be forced to frequently run for reelection while trying to position himself for a future senatorial, vice presidential, or presidential campaign.[76] Since 1940, most incumbent governors of Massachusetts who ran for reelection were either defeated or reelected very narrowly.[77] A governor's chances for reelection were always vulnerable to voter discontent about taxes, corruption, traffic delays on highways, and chronic financing and service problems with the Boston area's mass transit system, the Massachusetts Transit Authority (MTA).[78]

Before he formally announced his candidacy for the U.S. House of Representatives on April 25, 1946, JFK had spent several months visiting the eleventh congressional district and making several speeches in Boston in order to promote his name recognition without revealing that he was a candidate for any office. JFK used this same tactic on a statewide level for four years in order to develop a constituency for a campaign for either governor or senator in 1952. As early as October of 1947, a Massachusetts resident warned Governor Robert Bradford, a fellow Republican, that, among Democratic politicians, "the only man we have to watch very carefully is young Kennedy, who is conducting himself in a sane and sober manner, and in addition to his father's great wealth, will have a youthful appeal to the voters."[79]

It was possible, though, that Democratic Governor Paul Dever might want to run for the Senate in 1952 instead of for reelection. As attorney general of Massachusetts during the late 1930s, Dever developed an impressive record of cracking down on loan sharks and improving the collection of funds owed to the state.[80] Dever's corpulent appearance and jovial personality masked a shrewd political mind. In 1948, he was elected governor with 59 percent of votes against the Republican incumbent. In 1950, when the Democrats lost twenty-nine U.S. House seats and six Senate seats in the midst of an increasingly unpopular Truman administration, rising inflation, and the Korean War, Dever was reelected with 56 percent of the votes.[81]

Dever's first election as governor benefited from the Democratic landslide in Massachusetts in 1948. Massachusetts was one of the two northeastern states that President Truman carried in his upset victory.[82] For the first time in history, the Democrats won control of the state house of representatives and elected Thomas P. "Tip" O'Neill, Jr., as speaker.[83] The state ballot in 1948 included Republican-sponsored referenda that wanted to repeal a ban on contraceptive information and adopt a right-to-work law. Consequently, the Catholic church and labor unions intensified their voter mobilization efforts among mostly Democratic, blue-collar Catholic voters.[84]

The only prominent Republican electoral success in Massachusetts in 1948 was the election of Senator Leverett Saltonstall to a full six-year term with 53 percent of the votes.[85] Both Republican businessmen and Democratic dock workers appreciated Saltonstall's staunch opposition to the St. Lawrence Seaway.[86] During Saltonstall's victorious 1938 campaign for governor, James Michael Curley, his Democratic opponent, derided Saltonstall for having "a South Boston face and a Back Bay name."[87] Curley's sneering remark backfired. The Yankee Brahmin developed a friendly relationship with Irish Democratic voters who were willing to split their tickets for "Old Salty."

JPK, therefore, was not surprised when he commissioned a poll which revealed that his son would have a better chance of defeating Senator Henry Cabot Lodge, Jr., in 1952 than Saltonstall in 1954.[88] Lodge was the grandson of the legendary Senator Henry Cabot Lodge of Massachusetts who led Republican efforts to reject American membership in the League of Nations and ratification of the Treaty of Versailles following World War I.[89] The Kennedys and Fitzgeralds always remembered that the senior Lodge defeated "Honey Fitz" by approximately 33,000 votes in his 1916 Senate race. "Honey Fitz" then lost the 1942 Democratic senatorial primary in his bid to run against the junior Lodge.[90]

First elected to the Senate in 1936 at the age of 34 and reelected in 1942, Henry Cabot Lodge, Jr., resigned from the Senate in 1944 and resumed full-time active duty in the army. He served with distinction in Europe and North Africa and was decorated for bravery. He was again elected to the Senate in 1946 by defeating Democratic Senator David I. Walsh.[91] In all three of his successful Senate campaigns, Lodge benefited from the split ticket voting of Democrats and independents.[92]

Unfortunately for JFK, Dever did not inform him until April of 1952 whether he would run for the Senate or for reelection as governor. Consequently, the content of JFK's speeches in Massachusetts typically focused on either foreign and defense policies, useful in a Senate campaign, or the state's economy, more appropriate for a gubernatorial campaign. In February 1951, JFK returned to Boston after a trip to Europe. He went there to survey economic and military conditions concerning the threat of Communist aggression against Western Europe. He broadcast a radio address in Boston about his findings on February 6.[93] On August 6, 1951, JFK delivered a speech in Worcester blaming inflation on the Truman administration's policies.[94] Earlier, in a 1948 speech in Roxbury, JFK criticized Franklin D. Roosevelt for selling out Poland to the Soviet Union.[95]

In addition to his public speaking agenda, JFK used his position as a congressman to broaden and diversify his statewide, multiethnic appeal by introducing legislation focusing on the policy interests of Jews, Italians, and eastern European ethnics.[96] In a speech delivered on the House floor on April 9, 1951, JFK denounced the 1947 Italian peace treaty as "harshly restrictive," "unfair," and "a dangerous treaty for the whole free world."[97] JFK then introduced a joint resolution asking the president to negotiate a new peace treaty. JFK also supported legislation to liberalize immigration laws in order to allow more displaced persons into the United States, especially Jews, Italians, and Poles.[98]

JFK's foreign policy trip to the Middle East and Asia in 1951 included a meeting with David Ben-Gurion, the prime minister of

Israel. In a very close election for either governor or senator in 1952, Jewish voters could be essential to a Kennedy victory.[99] In the past, though, Jews had shown a willingness to vote for Yankee Brahmin Republicans like Lodge and Saltonstall. They were especially active in the Americans for Democratic Action (ADA), a liberal organization which JFK disliked and avoided.[100] His maverick streak as a representative had irked House Majority Leader John W. McCormack. McCormack was influential among rabbis and other Jewish community leaders in Massachusetts.[101]

JFK's greatest liability in attracting Jewish voters was his father's reputation as an anti-Semite who was a pro-Nazi appeaser and an isolationist while serving as U.S. Ambassador to Great Britain. JFK found it difficult to convince Jews that his father was not anti-Semitic. Instead, he patiently and persuasively reminded Jewish audiences that he, not his father, was running for the Senate and that his policy views were different than JPK's.[102] Nevertheless, JFK needed the intervention of McCormack to explain his vote to cut American aid to Israel.[103] In a December 2, 1951 interview on the television program *Meet the Press*, JFK mostly discussed his opinion of American foreign and defense policies based on his fact finding trip to the Middle East and Asia. He was asked, however, if he would run for the Senate in 1952. JFK replied, "I would like to go to the Senate. I'm definitely interested in it . . . I'm not sure yet . . . I'll come to a final decision after the first of the year."[104]

Two months later, Leland Bickford, a broadcast news executive in Boston, told JPK how impressed he was with JFK's telegenic appearance and speaking skills and that they would increase bipartisan electoral appeal for the congressman. Bickford wrote, "I think that eventually even you will be surprised at certain Republican support which I believe I am quietly drumming up for Jack. He is easy to sell, Mr. Kennedy."[105]

Although Governor Paul Dever had not yet announced whether he would run for the Senate in 1952, JPK increasingly assumed that JFK would run for the Senate. In February, JPK was busy corresponding with his political contacts in Massachusetts and JFK's campaign operatives from his estate in Palm Beach, Florida. The elder Kennedy told David F. Powers, a veteran of JFK's 1946 congressional race who was now helping to prepare JFK for a statewide campaign, that he was confident that his son could defeat Lodge, especially if Dwight D. Eisenhower was not the Republican presidential nominee. JPK concluded that "the only thing for Jack" to do would be "to continue speaking to as many people as he can and organizing all his friends to put a couple hundred thousand votes on the list, and then we'll be home nice and comfortable."[106]

Mark J. Dalton, a politically active Boston attorney, had worked in JFK's 1946 campaign and would briefly serve as manager of his Senate campaign. In a February 14th letter, JPK acknowledged receipt of "the outline of the organization" and expressed his opinion that Eisenhower's "campaign will break in the seams in the next six weeks."[107] Less than two weeks later, JPK told Dalton that, unfortunately, President Harry S. Truman would receive the Democratic presidential nomination of 1952 if he wanted it. Meanwhile, he believed that Senator Robert A. Taft of Ohio was increasingly likely to become the Republican presidential nominee "and, frankly I have a very high regard for him as a man and as a candidate."[108] JPK then mentioned that his son's 1952 campaign "is extremely likely to be against Henry Cabot Lodge for the U.S. Senate."[109]

Anxious to get a definite answer from Governor Paul Dever, JFK met Dever on Sunday, April 6, 1952. Dever revealed that he would seek reelection as governor. Kennedy's campaign advisers and operatives sensed that Dever's decision partially resulted from his fear that he could not defeat Lodge and his hope that his reelection campaign would benefit from JPK's wealth and sophisticated publicity efforts.[110] In publicly announcing his Senate candidacy on Monday, April 7, 1952, JFK emphasized foreign and defense policy issues centering on "the threat of Communist aggression." JFK connected these Cold War issues with the need to improve the industrial economy of Massachusetts in order for Bay State residents to be better able to contribute to the fight against Communism. JFK stated, "For entirely too long the representatives of Massachusetts in the United States Senate have stood by helplessly while our industries and jobs disappear."[111] JFK faced no opposition for the Democratic nomination for the Senate but the primary would not be held until September. In order to recruit campaign volunteers and keep them busy during the spring and summer, the Kennedy campaign decided to break all historical records for the number of signatures obtained in nomination papers for entering a senatorial primary in Massachusetts. State law required the signatures of only 2,500 registered voters, but the Kennedy campaign managed to obtain 262,324.[112]

Mark J. Dalton spent nearly four months as JFK's campaign manager.[113] Dalton resigned after JPK criticized how he was managing the campaign's money. JPK immediately replaced Dalton with one of his younger sons, Robert F. Kennedy (RFK).[114] RFK had accompanied JFK and their sister Patricia in the congressman's 1951 foreign policy trip to Europe, the Middle East, and Asia. He had recently resigned from his position with the U.S. Department of Justice in order to manage JFK's campaign.[115]

RFK, however, knew little about Massachusetts politics and nothing about how to manage a successful statewide campaign. Thus, he recruited the help of Kenneth P. O'Donnell, who had played football with RFK at Harvard, and was a native of Worcester in central Massachusetts. JFK previously enlisted the help of Lawrence F. O'Brien, a native of Springfield in western Massachusetts. Both O'Donnell and O'Brien were knowledgeable about the local politics of their home towns. O'Brien's family owned a bar and restaurant that was a popular hangout for Springfield politicians. O'Brien had also managed successful campaigns for Foster Furcolo, Springfield's congressman.[116] Furcolo was now running for state treasurer.

In order to avoid entangling this campaign in local Democratic factional disputes, the Kennedys appointed a so-called "secretary" to lead each local campaign organization. The title of "chairman" might have insulted and alienated local Democratic committee chairmen.[117] In heavily Republican small towns in the Berkshires of western Massachusetts and in the Cape Cod area, the Kennedy campaign sometimes appointed Republicans or independents as "secretaries."[118]

Although JFK promised to coordinate his Senate campaign with Dever's gubernatorial campaign in Massachusetts, he increasingly ran an independent campaign that emphasized the celebrity status of his family. Kennedy's claims that the economy of Massachusetts was declining and that the state needed a senator who would successfully advocate its policy needs with the federal government conflicted with Dever's assertion that the state's economy had improved during his governorship. JFK also needed to have enough partisan and ideological flexibility to attract the votes of pro-Taft, anti-Lodge Republicans and conservative independents who were unlikely to vote for Dever or Stevenson.[119]

JFK seemed more eager to challenge and debate Lodge on the Cold War. He wanted to highlight those issues in which Lodge supported Truman's policies while JFK opposed them, especially regarding China.[120] Nonetheless, the Kennedy campaign decided to emphasize the domestic policy needs of Massachusetts by coining the slogan, "Kennedy Will Do More for Massachusetts." Most of the policy information and advice that the Kennedys had accumulated since JPK's tour of Massachusetts in 1945 concerned the Bay State's economy. Ralph Coghlan, a journalist who had previously worked for the *Saint Louis Post-Dispatch*, and James Landis, a former dean of the Harvard law school, were two members of the "brains trust" hired by JPK to work in his son's Senate campaign. Coghlan suggested to Landis that JFK deliver a speech in which he not only expresses his desire to use his Senate seat to fight for the policy interests of the state but also those of the entire region of New England.[121]

Emphasizing state and local economic issues also worked with the regional and chronological aspects of JFK's campaign strategy. To maximize voter turnout in Boston, JFK relied on John E. Powers, a state senator from South Boston, to chair a joint Kennedy-Dever organization there and to prevent or reconcile any factional disputes with Dever supporters. Meanwhile, from the spring of 1952 until early September, JFK concentrated his campaign visits in central, western, southeastern, and northeastern Massachusetts, especially in areas where Lodge had done well in the 1946 election. JFK wanted to reduce Lodge's expected level of electoral strength in cities and towns in these regions.[122] Two days after JFK publicly announced his candidacy, Walter French, a Massachusetts voter, wrote a letter to Kennedy stating, "You'll convince the people who are out of work in Lawrence, Haverhill, Fall River, [and] New Bedford that all their troubles are due to Lodge's failure to act."[123]

The economic problems of the textile industry provided an especially useful campaign issue for JFK. Textile mills were located throughout Massachusetts but were especially concentrated in regions where he wanted to weaken Lodge's electoral support. The textile industry of New England had experienced gradual, relative decline for decades while that of the South grew. However, its problems in Massachusetts had been especially severe and noticeable since the end of World War II with strikes, wage freezes and cuts, layoffs, factory closings, and losses of federal contracts.[124]

In some of his speeches, JFK blamed federal tax, labor, electrification, contracting, and trade policies for accelerating the decline of the textile industry in Massachusetts and its rise in the South. In Lenox, a town near Pittsfield in western Massachusetts, the Kennedys held a tea party in September, 1952. During it, JFK asserted that Massachusetts paid more federal taxes than it received in federal spending while the South received proportionately more federal spending than it paid in federal taxes.[125] At an October Democratic rally in Worcester, JFK stated that Lodge "has done very little for Massachusetts" and specified that Lodge's inadequate constituency service had contributed to the movement of the state's textile and shoe industries to the South.[126]

JFK more specifically criticized Lodge's record on labor issues by citing the Republican senator's votes for the Taft-Hartley Act and against a minimum wage increase in 1947.[127] The Taft-Hartley Act included a provision to allow states to make right-to-work laws which kept labor unions weak and wages low in southern textile mills. In an October 1952 press release, JFK promised, "In the U.S. Senate I will work for the repeal of these labor laws which have fostered unfair Southern competition for our textile and shoe industries."[128]

Lodge defended his record by citing his votes in the Senate benefiting Massachusetts, such as a higher tariff on imported fish and different formulas for calculating and allocating federal funds for highways and public school construction in order to provide more funds for Massachusetts.[129] He also began to regularly attack JFK's relatively high rate of absenteeism for roll call votes.[130] Newspapers friendly to Lodge published editorials criticizing JFK's high rate of absenteeism. The *Boston Herald* noted that JFK missed 29 percent of his roll call votes during his nearly six-year congressional career while Lodge only missed 5 percent in the Senate during the same period.[131] The *North Adams Transcript* revealed that JFK missed most of the House roll call votes from January to July of 1952 and concluded, "Obviously, he hasn't been tending very closely to the business of legislating."[132]

The Kennedy campaign generally ignored the attacks of Lodge and several newspapers on JFK's absenteeism. Instead, JFK carefully selected a few major Senate votes for which Lodge was absent. In particular, JFK criticized Lodge for being absent when the Senate voted on the McCarran-Walter bill. This bill, which was enacted over Truman's veto on June 27, 1952, restricted immigration from southern and eastern Europe.[133] This law proved to be especially unpopular among Jewish, Italian, Portuguese, and Polish voters in Massachusetts. In his opposition to this law and criticism of Lodge, JFK stated, "Massachusetts needs a United States senator who will protect the rights of its minority groups on the floor of the United States Senate, not one who votes by remote control."[134]

In an August 22, 1952 televised interview on a CBS political talk show, *Longines Chronoscope*, JFK referred to his earlier request that Congress hold a special session to pass more effective legislation on price controls, especially rent controls which affected working-class people in Massachusetts. He added that Lodge's allegedly ineffective, negligent constituency service was partially caused by "the leading role that Senator Lodge has played in securing General Eisenhower's nomination."[135] Concerning Truman's currently unpopular foreign policy, JFK stated, "Senator Lodge's record is stronger in support of the administration's policy than mine is."[136]

Both of these comments were implicit appeals to pro-Taft, anti-Eisenhower Republicans in Massachusetts. The Kennedy campaign assumed that these voters were more likely to either vote for JFK or not vote at all in the Senate election if it regularly told them that Lodge's occasional absenteeism from the Senate was mostly caused by his leading role in helping to defeat Senator Robert A. Taft for the Republican presidential nomination.[137] In a letter to a campaign volunteer, R. Sargent Shriver, JFK's future brother-in-law, wrote, "We want factual information to give Mass. Republicans who are fighting Lodge."[138] Ideologically, Taft Republicans tended to be either "Fortress America" isolationists similar to JPK or supporters of more aggressive policies against both international and domestic Communism compared to the bipartisan containment policy represented by Truman, Eisenhower, and Lodge.[139] Thus, JFK's occasional attacks on the Truman administration for being too soft and ineffective in fighting Communism and his father's reputation as a conservative friendly to Taft made JFK more attractive to pro-Taft Republicans and independents in Massachusetts.[140]

The most prominent Taft supporter who endorsed JFK was Basil Brewer, publisher of the *New Bedford Standard Times*. In his editorial endorsing JFK, Brewer claimed that the respective voting records of JFK and Lodge in Congress proved that JFK had a better record in opposing Communist aggression, especially in Asia.[141] John J. Fox, the publisher of the *Boston Post*, endorsed JFK without criticizing Lodge. Like Brewer, Fox was an admirer of Senator Joseph R. McCarthy of Wisconsin and praised JFK's record on fighting Communism.[142] Fox later received a $500,000 loan from JPK for his financially struggling newspaper.[143]

As the Kennedy-Lodge race became more competitive according to the polls, both campaigns wondered how the intervention of Senator Joseph R. McCarthy, if he chose to visit Massachusetts, would affect the outcome of the election.[144] In a memo to RFK, campaign aide Edward J. Dunn stated, "It has been printed that Lodge wants to bring Senator McCarthy here to help him. Whether McCarthy comes here, our speakers should be coached to keep driving home the fact that Jack moved in on the Communists and really did something about it before McCarthy and others."[145]

According to historian Thomas L. Reeves, Lodge repeatedly telephoned McCarthy's office in order to ask the Wisconsin senator to personally campaign with him in Massachusetts. McCarthy required conditions which he knew Lodge would not accept.[146] However, McCarthy's endorsement of JFK could lose the Democratic congressman the votes of Jewish liberals and ADA members who questioned the sincerity of JFK's liberalism.[147] McCarthy had socialized with the Kennedys and received a campaign contribution from JPK.[148] The Wisconsin senator stayed out of Massachusetts.[149]

Meanwhile, newspapers throughout Massachusetts noted that Republican presidential nominee Dwight D. Eisenhower attracted larger, more enthusiastic crowds during his campaign tour of the state in late October than President Truman and Democratic presidential nominee Adlai Stevenson had.[150] One poll revealed that, while the Republicans would probably win the presidential and gubernatorial elections in Massachusetts, the Kennedy-Lodge race was a toss-up.[151] Lodge made a joint televised appearance with Eisenhower at Boston Garden on the night before the 1952 election. Unfortunately for Lodge, the popular general received such prolonged, loud applause that the senator's prepared introduction of Eisenhower was canceled.[152]

JFK defeated Lodge with 51.4 percent of the votes and by a margin of 70,737 votes. For the first time since 1924, a Republican carried Massachusetts in a presidential election. Eisenhower received 54.2 percent of the votes and by a margin of 208,800 votes.[153] Republican gubernatorial nominee Christian Herter defeated Governor Paul Dever with 49.9 percent of the votes to Dever's 49.3 percent and by a margin of 14,456 votes.[154] The Republicans won control of the state legislature, and Joseph W. Martin, Jr., a Republican congressman from southeastern Massachusetts, was expected to become the next speaker of the U.S. House of Representatives.[155]

A few days before the 1952 presidential election, Dwight D. Eisenhower stated in a televised interview in New York City that a top priority of his administration would be "to solve the economic problems created in New England by the migration of textile factories to the South."[156] In his 1953 State of the Union message to Congress, Eisenhower did not recommend special legislation for the economic problems of New England. Instead, he called for the elimination of deficit spending and the achievement of a balanced budget. In particular, the Republican president suggested cuts in agricultural programs, especially the Truman administration's price support policies.[157]

During his first two years in the Senate, JFK was one of the few Democrats to support Eisenhower's proposed budget cuts in agricultural, rural electrification, and flood control programs.[158] JFK's voting behavior on these spending items was a continuation of the eclectic fiscal conservatism that he had expressed through several roll call votes as a congressman. It also highlighted his frequent complaint that the taxpayers of New England were being forced to accelerate their industrial decline and aggravate their economic problems by financing federal programs that subsidized and favored agriculture and industries in the South and West. In particular, because of federal electrification programs, industries in the South and West paid far less for electricity than those in New England.[159] Meanwhile, JFK's policy agenda to help New England's textile and fishing industries included protective tariffs, stronger federal efforts to research and market American fish products, and the development of hydroelectric and nuclear power in New England.[160]

In order to help him research, articulate, and promote an economic policy agenda to benefit New England in general and Massachusetts in particular, JFK hired Theodore C. Sorensen as a legislative assistant. Sorensen, a Nebraskan, noted in his memoir that he "knew little about economics and nothing about New England" but enjoyed the challenge of this task.[161] With Sorensen's help, JFK's articles and speeches about the economic problems of New England and his policy proposals to solve or alleviate them included more current statistics and case studies compared to his previous speeches as a congressman and senatorial candidate.[162]

JFK also developed a cooperative, bipartisan relationship on these issues with Senator Leverett Saltonstall of Massachusetts. He and his Republican colleague cosponsored legislation to benefit Massachusetts, especially its textile and fishing industries.[163] In a 1964 interview, Saltonstall stated that his relationship with JFK "was very pleasant and became a helpful one, I think, to both of us."[164] Later, in his memoir, Saltonstall fondly recalled that "the most worthwhile project that John Kennedy and I sponsored was the Cape Cod National Seashore Park."[165]

The Republican landslide of 1952 yielded a one-seat Republican majority in the Senate. The GOP's majority status enabled Saltonstall to chair the Senate Armed Services Committee.[166] Consequently, the Democrats at the national level especially wanted to defeat Saltonstall in the 1954 mid-term elections.

JFK, however, did not want Saltonstall defeated for reelection. He wanted to continue his mutually beneficial legislative relationship with Saltonstall regarding their shared policy goals for Massachusetts. Furthermore, JFK's political influence in Massachusetts and the Senate might be weakened if Massachusetts had two Democratic senators.

Kennedy's reluctance and eventual refusal to actively oppose Saltonstall's reelection were partially based on the fact that Foster Furcolo was Saltonstall's Democratic opponent.[167] Furcolo had been a congressman from a Springfield-based Massachusetts district. Governor Paul Dever appointed Furcolo state treasurer when this position became vacant in 1952 and encouraged him to campaign for a full term for this office in order to balance the Democratic state ticket regionally and ethnically.[168] Like JFK's election to the Senate, Furcolo's election as state treasurer was one of the few statewide electoral successes for Massachusetts Democrats in 1952.

In a 1964 interview, Furcolo stated that he and JFK "had a very cordial relationship."[169] Most of the observers of the relationship between JFK and Furcolo, however, claim that it was one of mutual distrust and hostility.[170] The best published source on the Kennedy-Furcolo relationship is the autobiography of Lawrence F. O'Brien. O'Brien had managed Furcolo's congressional campaigns and briefly managed Furcolo's office in Washington, DC.

Shortly after Furcolo's reelection in 1950, O'Brien informed Furcolo that he did not want to continue living and working in Washington, DC, and wanted to remain in Springfield. The congressman felt betrayed and abruptly ended their friendship. After O'Brien helped to organize a speaking engagement for JFK in Springfield in early 1952, JFK did not previously inform Furcolo that he would speak in Furcolo's district. In addition, Kennedy had rejected O'Brien's earlier requests that he campaign for Furcolo in 1948 and cosponsor legislation with him.[171]

In recalling his 1954 Senate campaign, Saltonstall tactfully stated that JFK "was not opposing me as strenuously as he might."[172] The Massachusetts Republican further explained how his staff and

JFK's staff collaborated on how to defeat Furcolo. Throughout 1954, Saltonstall's office periodically announced new bills cosponsored by Saltonstall and JFK while Furcolo attacked the Republican senator's record.[173]

Despite the acknowledgment of John Jackson, a Saltonstall supporter in northeastern Massachusetts, that Kennedy was "more favorable" toward Saltonstall than Furcolo, Jackson and other Republicans who submitted campaign reports to Saltonstall feared that Furcolo would defeat him. They noted several factors favoring a Furcolo victory. Bay State residents of Italian ancestry or immigration comprised the second largest Catholic ethnic group in Massachusetts after the Irish. They presumably would be much more likely to vote for Furcolo because of his Italian surname. Some Republican farmers disliked Eisenhower's agricultural policies, and an increase in industrial unemployment in Massachusetts made blue-collar workers even more likely to vote Democratic.[174]

The turning point of this increasingly close Senate race was the joint television appearance of JFK, Furcolo, and Robert Murphy, the Democratic nominee for governor, in October 1954.[175] Suffering from severe back pain and hobbling on crutches, JFK joined Furcolo and Murphy at a Boston television studio. Shortly before air time, Furcolo asked JFK to attack Saltonstall's record and specifically endorse him by name. Kennedy was angry that Furcolo wanted to suddenly change the script and wording of JFK's endorsement of the Democratic ticket that he, Furcolo, and Murphy had previously discussed and accepted. Only the intervention of Murphy prevented the senator from boycotting the broadcast.[176] At the conclusion of the 15-minute program, JFK stated to Furcolo that he wanted to "wish you, Bob Murphy, and the entire Democratic ticket every success in November."[177]

The controversy was further inflamed by Francis X. Morrissey, JFK's office manager in Boston. Morrissey told reporters that JFK "definitely will not give Furcolo a personal endorsement."[178] JFK had recently entered a New York City hospital for back surgery, so RFK issued a public statement prepared by JFK. RFK said, "In view of conflicting statements regarding the Senator's positions, I am authorized to say my brother stands by his original statement which he made on a TV program that he is a Democrat and supports the entire Democratic ticket."[179]

Unfortunately for the Kennedys, this statement did not end or mitigate the controversy. The Kennedy-Furcolo rift was further aggravated by the closeness of the election results in the 1954 Senate race in Massachusetts. Saltonstall won reelection with 50.5 percent of the votes to Furcolo's 49 percent.[180] While Saltonstall defeated Furcolo by a margin of approximately 29,000 votes, Republican Governor Christian Herter defeated Murphy more easily by a margin of 4 percent and approximately 75,000 votes.[181] There also seemed to be an ethnic pattern in split-ticket voting behavior. Boston neighborhoods and communities with high concentrations of Italians were more likely to vote for Furcolo and Herter while those with high concentrations of Irish residents were more likely to vote for Saltonstall and Murphy.[182] On the day after the 1954 elections, the *Boston Globe* stated, "The independence or non-partisanship of a large bloc of Massachusetts voters was demonstrated by the outcome of the state-wide contests."[183] The newspaper also revealed that "Democratic leaders freely admitted that the poor Boston showing of Murphy and Furcolo probably cost these candidates the election."[184]

Two days after the 1954 elections, Furcolo told the *Springfield Daily News*, "We've analyzed the election returns and we know we were knifed, but I'm not going to have any comment."[185] Furcolo did not specifically mention JFK as the cause of being "knifed." Earlier in 1954, Wilton Vaugh, a reporter for the *Boston Post*, wrote about how the Kennedy family was organizing a campaign event that included Murphy, but not Furcolo. Vaugh observed, "This is the first time that the young Democratic senator has asked his political chieftains in every city, town, hamlet, village and voting district of the Commonwealth to get out and work for any other candidate but himself."[186]

While his constituents sympathized with JFK's long recuperation from spinal surgery, more Democrats in Massachusetts were complaining that JFK's aloof independence from other Democratic politicians had become selfish opportunism that was detrimental to the electoral welfare of other Democratic candidates. Three weeks after the 1954 elections, Francis X. Kelly, a Boston lawyer who ran unsuccessfully for the Democratic nomination for governor, asked Representative John W. McCormack to unite and assume unofficial leadership of the Democratic Party in Massachusetts. In his letter to McCormack, Kelly wrote, "I do not blame Bob Murphy or Foster Furcolo because this was their first important state-wide election campaign. The blame belongs on others who no doubt realize their many tragic political mistakes in refusing the aid and active support of a number of experienced leaders with large personal followings who brought disaster to the Democratic Party of Massachusetts."[187]

During JFK's long recuperation and work on his book *Profiles in Courage*, a power struggle developed for control of the Democratic state committee in 1955. Through the influence of Governor Paul Dever, John Carr was elected Democratic state chairman in 1952.[188] Carr quickly adjourned a disruptive committee meeting that challenged the legitimacy of his election as chairman. Anti-Carr committee members held a rump session and elected William "Onions" Burke as Democratic state chairman. Burke was a farmer and tavern owner from western Massachusetts and a political ally of John W. McCormack and his brother, Edward "Knocko" McCormack. After Carr challenged Burke's election, the state courts ruled in favor of Burke.[189]

Garrett H. Byrne was elected district attorney of Suffolk County in 1952. He later remarked that "Jack Kennedy always felt as though he represented all the people of the Commonwealth of Massachusetts, and he didn't think that his function should become the leader of the Democratic Party."[190] Byrne added, "This isn't an organizational state . . . It's every man for himself."[191]

By late 1955, JFK became interested in electing a pro-Kennedy Democratic state chairman in order to help the senator control that state's delegates to the 1956 Democratic national convention. If JFK failed to do this, his national political status among his fellow Democratic senators would be diminished and any ambition to be nominated for vice president or president would be jeopardized.[192] JFK enlisted the help of Lawrence F. O'Brien and Kenneth P. O'Donnell to elect a pro-Kennedy chairman and majority of committee members in the Massachusetts Democratic presidential primary of 1956.[193] The newly elected chairman and committee members would then choose the state's delegates to the Democratic national convention.

On March 8, 1956, JFK announced at a press conference in Washington, DC, that he endorsed Adlai Stevenson for the Democratic presidential nomination. The Democratic senator from Massachusetts stated that he would "exert every effort" for Stevenson's nomination. He also expressed confidence that the former governor of Illinois "would be nominated and had a good chance of being elected."[194]

JFK's endorsement of Stevenson for the Democratic presidential nomination further complicated the task of O'Brien and O'Donnell. John W. McCormack and other Democratic politicians were not enthusiastic about Stevenson becoming the presidential nominee again.[195] Some of them believed that Stevenson's presidential nomination in 1952 contributed to Democratic losses in that election. In his study of voting behavior in Boston in the 1952 and 1956 presidential elections, political scientist Lawrence H. Fuchs found that Stevenson was especially unpopular among older, working-class Irish voters. Particularly in the 1952 presidential election, these voters who were interviewed expressed their dislike of Stevenson's cerebral rhetoric, sophisticated wit, divorced status, and perceived softness on Communism.[196]

Pro-McCormack Democrats promoted McCormack as a write-in, favorite son presidential candidate. In the April 24, 1956, Democratic presidential primary in Massachusetts, John W. McCormack received 47.9 percent of the votes to Adlai Stevenson's 34.9 percent.[197] Despite these disappointing results for Stevenson supporters, JFK managed to influence the election of Democratic state committee members who were mostly loyal to him. With the help of Paul Dever, JFK was able to influence the replacement of William "Onions" Burke with John M. "Pat" Lynch, the former mayor of Somerville, as the new Democratic state chairman in May.[198]

JFK returned to Massachusetts politics with his power and reputation among Bay State Democrats greatly enhanced by the events of the 1956 Democratic national convention. JFK received favorable national publicity for his eloquent narration of a film about the Democratic Party, his nominating speech for Stevenson, and his dramatic, narrow defeat in the race for the vice presidential nomination.[199] The Massachusetts senator also succeeded in delivering thirty-two of his state's forty delegate votes to Stevenson on the first ballot at the convention.[200]

While JFK spoke and traveled throughout the nation to campaign for Stevenson, Democrats in Massachusetts expected another Eisenhower landslide in the 1956 presidential election. They wanted to generate high enough voter turnout and split-ticket voting in order to win the governorship, retain their majority status in the state house of representatives, and continue control of half of the state's fourteen congressional seats.[201] Foster Furcolo easily defeated former state auditor Thomas Buckley in the primary for the Democratic nomination for governor. JFK was careful to specifically endorse Furcolo by name.[202]

In his platform, Furcolo expressed his commitment "to the task of attracting new industry to Massachusetts for more jobs and greater security for our people."[203] If elected, Furcolo's major policy goals were to aid economic development in depressed areas, save textile jobs, promote tourism in Massachusetts through better parks and beaches, increase federal aid, and improve public education, especially in higher education through the creation of community colleges.[204] Furcolo's Republican opponent was Sumner Whittier, currently the lieutenant governor. Whittier accused Furcolo of being a "pious fraud" and associated him with the corruption and policy problems of Paul Dever's governorship.[205]

Electorally, Dwight D. Eisenhower performed better in Massachusetts in 1956 than in 1952. He received 59.3 percent of the popular votes and 445,007 more votes than Stevenson, despite some evidence that Stevenson was slightly more attractive to Irish and Jewish voters in the Boston metropolitan area in 1956 compared to 1952.[206] Meanwhile, Furcolo defeated Whittier with 52.8 percent of the votes and by a margin of 137,859 votes.[207] The Democrats also added three seats to their majority in the state house of representatives while the Republicans retained their narrow majority in the state senate with no partisan change in seats. All of the incumbent

U.S. representatives, seven Democrats and seven Republicans, were reelected.[208] In an editorial, the *Boston Globe* stated, "While the state, like 41 others, was giving the President a ride on the magic carpet at the highest level, Foster Furcolo, the Democratic aspirant for governor, was spreading his coattails wide to help transport almost the entire state ticket of that party into state offices whence the Republicans were ousted."[209]

One week after the 1956 elections, Robert X. Tivnan, a state representative, wrote a letter to JFK providing his analysis of why Eisenhower won overwhelmingly in Massachusetts, despite JFK's highly publicized advocacy of Stevenson's candidacy and the success of Democratic nominees for state offices. Of the one hundred absentee ballots that Tivnan submitted for elderly constituents, one of them voted straight Republican while the rest voted for Eisenhower and then Democratic for all other offices, mostly because they disliked Stevenson's personality. Tivnan facetiously noted that another John F. Kennedy, the Democratic nominee for state treasurer, was especially popular among these voters. He concluded, "I think there is great sentiment in Massachusetts for Kennedy for President."[210]

While the residents of Massachusetts increasingly discussed the possibility of JFK running for president in 1960, Governor Furcolo was confronted with the largest budget deficit in the state's history.[211] In addition to needing more revenue to end this deficit and balance budgets throughout his governorship, Furcolo needed more revenue to finance his policy goals, especially in public higher education. Massachusetts excessively depended on a state income tax and local property taxes for state and local revenue. Furcolo, therefore, proposed a sales tax, a tax which most states had already enacted. Although the state house of representatives had a Democratic majority, almost half of the Democrats joined nearly two-thirds of the Republicans to reject Furcolo's sales tax bill.[212] During the remainder of Furcolo's two-term governorship, economic growth in Massachusetts generated higher than expected revenue for state income and local property taxes.[213] This unexpected revenue increase enabled the state government to balance its budgets and appropriate funds needed for Furcolo's spending priorities in higher education. The improved revenue situation undermined Furcolo's persistent contention that the state still needed a limited sales tax.[214]

Furcolo was politically wounded by the sales tax defeat and continued to experience a contentious relationship with fellow Democrats in the state legislature. Nonetheless, JFK needed to be at least superficially friendly with Furcolo during his 1958 reelection campaign. This year was the first time since 1952 that JFK and Furcolo were listed together on a statewide ballot. In order to achieve a record-breaking, overwhelming margin of victory, JFK needed to attract the votes of virtually all Democrats, most independents, and a substantial minority of Republicans. In his book, *Ballots Anyone?*, Furcolo noted that he and JFK discussed running a joint campaign.[215] Photographs of JFK and Furcolo's names and photographs appeared together on several campaign billboards and leaflets.[216]

JFK's reason for including Furcolo in shared campaign publicity seemed to be limited to trying to avoid antagonizing voters of Italian ancestry who were perceived to be enthusiastic about Furcolo yet ambivalent or hostile toward JFK.[217] JFK chose his youngest brother, Edward M. Kennedy, to manage his 1958 campaign. In his memoir, EMK noted why he and the Kennedy's campaign's advertising consultants changed JFK's campaign slogan from "Make Your Vote Count. Vote Kennedy." to "Kennedy. He has served Massachusetts with distinction."[218] EMK revealed that the Kennedy campaign dropped its first campaign slogan because political leaders of Italian ancestry claimed that it was an anti-Italian slur against Vincent J. Celeste, JFK's Republican opponent.[219] They argued that the first slogan implied that a person's vote would "count" for an Irish candidate, but not for an Italian candidate.[220]

In addition to his greater sensitivity to Italian voters, JFK also wanted to improve his status among black voters in Massachusetts. The Democratic senator needed to counteract the growing belief among African Americans and white liberals that he was either weak or insincere on civil rights. Recent evidence substantiating this perception was the surprising degree of support that JFK received from southern delegates in his bid for the vice presidential nomination at the 1956 Democratic national convention and two of JFK's votes regarding the Civil Rights Act of 1957. JFK was one of the few northern Democrats to vote with southern Democrats and the most conservative Republicans in the Senate to reject a motion that would have allowed this legislation to bypass the Senate Judiciary Committee, chaired by segregationist James Eastland of Mississippi, and to require a jury trial amendment.[221] Roy Wilkins, executive secretary of the NAACP, delivered a speech in Pittsfield, Massachusetts, in April of 1958, denouncing these two votes by JFK and his friendly relationships with segregationist southern politicians.[222] In order to help him improve his relationships with black voters and civil rights activists, JFK consulted Marjorie Lawson, an African-American attorney from Washington, DC, on civil rights issues.[223]

Despite some special attention to voters of Italian and African ancestry, JFK's speeches, press releases, and campaign materials portrayed JFK as a non-partisan centrist who had diligently and effectively represented and advocated the policy interests of Massachusetts, especially by cosponsoring legislation with Senator Leverett Saltonstall.[224] In May 15, 1958, in Lawrence, Massachusetts, JFK cited the chronically high unemployment in that city as a major reason for the Senate's passage of legislation to assist and revitalize economically depressed areas.[225] In a speech delivered at Boston College, JFK criticized the inadequacy of the amount of federal funds appropriated for Boston's Logan International Airport compared to the federal funds for the airports of other major East Coast cities.[226] Vincent J. Celeste, the Republican nominee for the Senate in 1958, argued that JFK would use his father's immense wealth to "buy" reelection to the Senate, so the Kennedy campaign wanted to limit the use of television advertising and emphasize personal campaigning by JFK and his wife, Jacqueline.[227] Because of her fluency in Romance languages, Jacqueline Kennedy was especially an asset in campaigning among voters whose first or second language was French, Spanish, Portuguese, or Italian.[228]

Besides the decision to limit television advertising, the Kennedy campaign was also burdened by JFK's frequent absences from Massachusetts as he campaigned for Democratic candidates throughout the nation.[229] The Kennedy campaign's staff and volunteers found it to be useful, rather than detrimental, to frequently tell voters that voting for JFK's reelection in 1958 would help him to be elected president in 1960.[230] An editorial in the *Worcester Telegram* expressed befuddlement that this tactic was not being used by Celeste and other Republicans to criticize JFK for not being sincere about wanting to serve another six-year term as a senator. Using the pseudonym "the Bay Stater," it concluded, "The thought of having Massachusetts represented on a national ticket in 1960 doubtless is a glamorous and appealing notion to thousands of Bay State voters."[231]

Through the Joseph P. Kennedy, Jr. Foundation, the Kennedys increased their donations to Catholic institutions. One major beneficiary of this foundation was Assumption College, a Catholic college in Worcester popular among New Englanders of French-Canadian ancestry. Assumption College was destroyed by a tornado in 1953, and a large donation from the Kennedy foundation helped to relocate and rebuild it.[232] In a letter to JPK referring to JFK's recent visit to the college during his 1958 campaign, the Rev. Armand H. Desautels, the president of Assumption College, wrote, "The invited guests included not only the French elite of the Worcester area but some of Worcester's very finest from the banks, insurance companies, industries, and businesses."[233] Desautels added that JFK made "many friends on the occasion."[234] In a similar letter, the Most Reverend John J. Wright, the bishop of the Catholic diocese of Worcester, informed JPK that a Worcester banker who was a prominent Republican "ran the breakfast for Jack here in Worcester."[235]

Some of Kennedy's campaign aides were alarmed when Furcolo received more votes than JFK in September's Democratic primary. Furcolo performed better than JFK in Boston, especially in heavily Italian neighborhoods. JFK's response to these primary results was to include more joint appearances with Furcolo in Massachusetts than he had originally expected or wanted.[237] JFK could not bear to listen to Furcolo's campaign song, which was sung to the tune of "The Colonel Bogey March" popularized in the movie, *The Bridge on the River Kwai*.[238]

Edward J. McCormack, Jr., whom Furcolo appointed attorney general in 1958, recalled that JFK did not want former president

Harry S. Truman to campaign in Massachusetts. JFK feared that Truman's partisan rhetoric would cost JFK votes from independents and Republicans.[239] Likewise, the senator asked McCormack to persuade his uncle, Representative John W. McCormack, to reduce the partisanship of his campaign rhetoric.[240] This was part of JFK's campaign strategy to receive, according to campaign worker John H. Treanor, Jr., "the largest plurality in the history of the state and he was to get it."[241]

Earlier, Meade Alcorn, the chairman of the Republican National Committee (RNC), stated in a speech in Newton, Massachusetts, "I believe that Senator John Kennedy can be defeated and I believe, moreover, that he deserves defeat on the basis of the very record he has made and is making in the United States Senate."[242] Senator Leverett Saltonstall, however, passively provided only the most perfunctory endorsement of Vincent J. Celeste, JFK's Republican opponent. Republican campaign workers also tended to focus their efforts on the gubernatorial election instead of the Senate race. George Fingold, the Republican attorney general, had proven to be an attractive vote getter among independents and Democrats. He was the GOP's presumed nominee for governor until he died two weeks before the September primary. After the Republicans nominated Charles Gibbons, an obscure candidate, for governor, Furcolo's chances of reelection greatly improved.[243]

In announcing its endorsements shortly before the 1958 elections, the *New Bedford Standard Times* endorsed JFK for senator and Gibbons for governor. It praised JFK's legislative record for serving Massachusetts well and concluded, "It would be poetic justice if the voters should see fit to give Kennedy an all-time high record vote, reserving for his opponent the booby prize of an all-time low."[244] This newspaper also criticized Furcolo's record as governor, especially on spending and job creation, and Furcolo's attempt to "ride the Kennedy coattails to victory."[245]

In the 1958 Senate election in Massachusetts, JFK won 73.2 percent of the votes and a margin of 874,608 votes against Celeste.[246] In his reelection as governor, Foster Furcolo received 56.2 percent of the votes and a margin of 248,557 votes against Gibbons.[247] JFK and

Furcolo, like Democratic nominees in other states, benefited from the lingering effects of the 1957–1958 recession, the declining popularity of Eisenhower, and an unusually high turnout among Democratic voters in a mid-term election.[248] Another advantage for JFK was a 1957 state law which moved the placement of the names of U.S. Senate candidates from last place to first place on the ballot, thereby locating JFK's name above Furcolo's. In their history of the Massachusetts state legislature, Cornelius Dalton and James J. Dobbins wrote, "This was done to help John F. Kennedy roll up a big vote in the 1958 Senate election to aid his campaign for President in 1960."[249]

For his electoral victory, Furcolo depended more than JFK on votes from the state's largest cities. JFK not only received more votes from these cities than Furcolo but he also received more votes from small towns and suburbs.[250] For example, JFK received 878 votes to Celeste's 392 votes in Douglas, a small town south of Worcester. By contrast, Furcolo received 623 votes to Gibbons's 653 votes in Douglas.[251] In Wilbraham, a town near Springfield and within Furcolo's home region, JFK received 1,558 votes compared to Furcolo's 850 votes.[252] In analyzing JFK's widespread and overwhelming electoral success, the *Springfield Daily News* stated, "Kennedy, who was supported by the traditionally-Republican *Boston Herald*, stumped every part of the state but never once mentioned the name of his opponent."[253]

While JFK was busy preparing for his 1960 presidential campaign, he was reluctantly drawn into a bitter Democratic conflict in the Boston mayoral election of 1959.[254] With Boston's mayoral election being non-partisan, the two mayoral candidates who opposed each other in the run-off election were both Democrats, John E. Powers and John F. Collins. Powers was a state senator from South Boston. He became president of the state senate following the 1958 elections.[255] Powers was favored to win the mayoral election and his supporters included JFK, the McCormacks, Leverett Saltonstall, Richard Cardinal Cushing, and Garrett H. Byrne, the district attorney of Suffolk County.[256] Collins previously served in the state legislature and on the Boston city council. He was currently serving as register of probate for Suffolk County.[257] While Furcolo and John B. Hynes, the current, outgoing mayor, were publicly neutral in the mayoral election, associates of both of them were active in the Collins campaign.[258]

Furcolo may have implicitly backed Collins because Collins supported a state sales tax and Powers did not.[259] Also, many of Boston's leading bankers and investors assumed that Collins would continue the honest, efficient administration demonstrated by Hynes and would be more likely than Powers to lead a vigorous urban renewal program that would benefit their interests.[260] The Collins campaign repeatedly warned voters that the election of Powers as mayor would return Boston to the fiscal mismanagement, corruption, and cronyism of Hynes's predecessor, the now deceased James Michael Curley.

The supporters of Collins also told voters that their candidate had not received any contributions from "bookies," i.e., operators of illegal gambling activities, and implied that Powers had. On October 30, a few days before the mayoral election, federal agents raided several bookie joints in East Boston, including that of a prominent backer of Powers.[261] Collins defeated Powers by approximately 24,000 votes.[262] Historian Thomas H. O'Connor characterized Collins's unexpected victory as "perhaps the biggest upset in Boston's political history."[263]

In their 1960 study of Boston politics, political scientists Edward C. Banfield and Martha Derthick wrote, "There are built-in antagonisms which prevent the Mayor of Boston, the Governor, and the leading Boston Democrat in the legislature from getting along together."[264] While Collins was busy launching an ambitious urban renewal program, Furcolo continued to clash with the state legislature, especially with Powers and John Thompson, the Democratic speaker of the state house of representatives. As the Democratic Party of Massachusetts became larger in its voter base, more electorally successful in local and congressional elections, and more dominant in the state legislature, it experienced more conflicts among factions and personal followings, more difficulty in uniting behind gubernatorial and senatorial nominees other than JFK, and more corruption during the late 1950s and early 1960s.[265] Edward J. McCormack, Jr., who ran against EMK in the Democratic senatorial primary of 1962, later commented that the Massachusetts Democratic Party during this era was merely "a federation of the followers of individual office holders or candidates."[266]

With JFK busy seeking to win the Democratic presidential nomination and presidency in 1960, he needed to avoid becoming entangled in the increasingly fractious, turbulent Democratic politics of Massachusetts. At the very least, JFK wanted to ensure that there was enough unity behind his presidential candidacy so that all of the delegates from Massachusetts would definitely vote for him on the first ballot. Part of the strategy that JFK, his staff, and his allies, developed in 1959 was to ensure that all 114 delegate votes from New England would be cast for JFK's nomination for president on the first ballot at the 1960 Democratic national convention.[267]

Democratic governors, like Paul Dever in 1952, often led their states' delegates at Democratic national conventions.[268] JFK, however, was determined that Representative John W. McCormack, instead of Governor Foster Furcolo, would lead the Massachusetts delegation at the 1960 convention. Besides the fact that JFK continued to distrust Furcolo, the governor was embroiled in a highly contested primary for the Democratic senatorial nomination of 1960. Also, JFK had steadily improved his relationship with McCormack since their 1956 conflict over control of the Democratic state chairmanship. He valued and respected McCormack's ability to deliver the votes of all of the Massachusetts delegates on the first ballot.[270]

While the Kennedy campaign struggled to win a very narrow first ballot victory at the 1960 Democratic national convention, politics in Massachusetts became more turbulent and divisive than usual because of intense intraparty competition for the Democratic gubernatorial and senatorial nominations. A 1953 state law required the Democratic and Republican parties to hold state conventions that endorsed candidates before the primaries.[271] The effect of this law on the Massachusetts Republican Party was that it increased intraparty cohesion and motivated party leaders to use convention endorsements to promote ethnic and religious diversity among preferred Republican candidates for statewide offices. The effect of this law on the state's Democratic Party, however, was the opposite. Democratic candidates who narrowly lost endorsements at the summer conventions were more likely to wage expensive, divisive campaigns against the endorsed candidates in the September primaries.[272] Also, Democratic state tickets determined by the primaries were less likely to be ethnically diverse and balanced.

This contrast between the two parties was especially true in 1960. The convention-endorsed Republican candidates included John Volpe, a former federal highway administrator of Italian ancestry, for governor, and Edward Brooke, an African-American attorney, for secretary of state. Volpe's three opponents for the nomination ended their candidacies at the convention, so he ran unopposed in the primary. By contrast, Joseph Ward, the current secretary of state and an Irish Catholic, received the Democratic state convention's endorsement and faced six opponents in the Democratic primary. Ward's two most formidable opponents were Lieutenant Governor Robert Murphy and Endicott "Chub" Peabody, a former member of the executive council. Murphy was a more popular and experienced vote-getter than Ward, especially among lower income Irish voters in Boston. Peabody, a Yankee Protestant whose family was as distinguished as those of Henry Cabot Lodge, Jr., and Leverett Saltonstall, proved to be attractive to liberal activists, "good government" reformers, suburbanites, and Jewish voters. Ward won the primary with only 30.23 percent of the votes.[273]

The Democratic contest for the nomination for U.S. senator was even more vitriolic. Governor Foster Furcolo received the endorsement of the state convention; but he was opposed in the Democratic primary by Thomas O'Connor, the mayor of Springfield, and Edmund Buckley, the register of deeds for southern Middlesex County.[274] O'Connor ran a vigorous campaign against Furcolo by stridently criticizing the record of his administration throughout the state. O'Connor won the primary and defeated Furcolo by a wide margin with 48.33 percent of the votes to Furcolo's 39 percent.[275] In commenting on the results of the Democratic gubernatorial and senatorial primaries, Claude E. Welch, Jr., wrote in the *Harvard Crimson*, "Massachusetts politics often resembles a Punch and Judy show with no one pulling the strings backstage."[276]

JFK, of course, had no reason to worry that he would fail to carry Massachusetts in the 1960 presidential election. He received

60.2 percent of the popular votes in his home state while Republican gubernatorial nominee John Volpe won 52.5 percent of the votes and Republican Senator Leverett Saltonstall was reelected with 56.2 percent of the votes.[277]

During and shortly after JFK's presidency, the problems of corruption and mismanagement in Massachusetts politics and government became better known, not only to Bay Staters but also to the general public throughout the United States.[278] Published in 1965, the report of the Massachusetts Crime Commission concluded that much of the corruption, such as police collusion with gamblers, bribery, favoritism, excessive spending by the state government on construction, insurance, and bonds, and patronage jobs that violated or evaded civil service laws, partially resulted from "the now deeply ingrained view of government jobs and government business as a private preserve for taking care of those with political connections."[279] After analyzing these scandals, political scientists Murray B. Levin and George Blackwood wrote, "In Massachusetts, however, the evidence indicates that the exchange of personal favors between influential individuals has all but replaced government by parties."[280]

JFK's January 9, 1961 speech to the Massachusetts state legislature reflected the ideals and purposes of John Winthrop and other founders of the Massachusetts Bay colony. The president-elect encouraged his fellow Bay Staters and public servants to regard the Puritan founders as role models of integrity and devotion to public service. JFK asserted that he and the state legislators must measure their decisions according to four moral criteria, including whether they were "truly men of dedication—with an honor mortgaged to no single individual or group, and compromised by no private obligation or aim, but devoted solely to serving the public good and the national interest."[281]

Between the day of the 1960 presidential election and JFK's January 9th speech, the Massachusetts state legislature voted itself pay raises and bonuses as well as salary increases of approximately $7.5 million for other state employees, despite the howls of protests from an enraged public. It was then called into special session by outgoing Governor Foster Furcolo to solve a commuter railroad problem, but it rejected his proposals and adjourned after three days.[282] After assessing examples of similar political arrogance and self-indulgence in Massachusetts, journalist Edward R. F. Sheehan wrote that "it remains evident that many of the present problems of Massachusetts, and particularly of its Democratic Party, are attributed to the detachment of John F. Kennedy."[283]

Sheehan's judgment of JFK is too harsh and unrealistic. JFK was astute and prescient in his aversion to running for lieutenant governor or governor. By developing an independent political base, JFK was often able to avoid the internecine conflicts of his state party while successively being elected to both houses of Congress and then the presidency.[284] He was also able to develop and project an image of centrist, bipartisan leadership and regional cooperation for progress in public policy for not only Massachusetts but for all of New England.

2

JFK and New England Economics

JOHN F. KENNEDY'S 1952 CAMPAIGN theme of wanting to improve the economy of New England in general and Massachusetts in particular was not unusual or surprising. His father publicly reentered Massachusetts politics in 1945 for the official purpose of studying economic conditions in the state at the request of Governor Maurice Tobin. Tobin wanted to create a department of commerce. Ralph Coghlan, a former journalist and a member of the "brains trust" organized by JPK for JFK's Senate campaign, suggested that JFK's campaign speeches should emphasize that he wanted to become a senator in order "to organize a powerful task force to fight the battle of New England."[1]

During the late 1940s and early 1950s, local newspapers, the *Harvard Business Review*, and, increasingly, the national media published articles and front page headlines detailing the problems of the New England economy, especially in its sharply declining textile industry. A 1945 memo to JPK warned that "Massachusetts may well be the first American state to have to project a course within a static or declining economy instead of within a dynamic economy. The implications of such a possibility are truly cataclysmic."[2]

With an equally alarming tone, journalist William V. Shannon wrote in 1949 that "the American South and West may one day find it necessary to provide Massachusetts and her neighbors with a Marshall Plan." He added, "What Massachusetts lacks is a leader to inspire a broad forward movement, a man to strike from her giant resources the shackles of the past."[3]

Recent studies of the region's economic problems and how to solve them were conducted by Harvard University economists Seymour Harris and John Kenneth Galbraith, the Federal Reserve Bank in Boston, President Truman's Council of Economic Advisers, and the National Planning Association. They bolstered the nonpolitical, intellectual legitimacy of JFK's intention to use his Senate seat to protect and advance the economic interests of his state and region. During JFK's Senate campaign, Galbraith delivered a speech to the New England Council in Boston. In it, he stated that "there is a small but flourishing statistical industry which sometimes shows that New England is doing well and sometimes shows that it is going to the dogs."[4]

In 1952, Seymour Harris's book, *The Economics of New England*, was published. In its conclusion, Harris wrote, "New England will have to reconsider its attitude towards the federal government."[5] He warned, "If it does not accept a stronger federal government and seek a fair share of federal outlays, it will suffer continued drains of cash, which will be used in part to strengthen the competitive position of areas attracting our industries, capital, and managerial talent."[6]

During his Senate campaign, JFK asserted that he would be the type of advocate for New England with the federal government that Harris recommended. Fulfilling this ambitious campaign promise, however, would be difficult. When JFK ran for the Senate in 1952, only two of New England's twelve senators were Democrats. With Democrats controlling the presidency for twenty consecutive years and Congress for eighteen of those years, the federal government's policies on taxes, agriculture, hydroelectric power, flood control, social welfare, highway construction, defense industries, and international trade had disproportionately benefited the South the most and New England the least.[7]

The Republican victories in the presidential and congressional elections of 1952 actually improved JFK's potential to become an effective spokesman for New England's economy in its relationship with the federal government. The end of Democratic control of Congress, however temporary, actually benefited JFK. With no southern Democratic control of committee chairmanships, there would be less of a southern bias in federal economic policies. Also, New England Republicans who shared JFK's concern with the economic plight of their region assumed influential positions in the Eisenhower administration and the Republican-controlled Congress. Joseph W. Martin, Jr., a congressman from southeastern Massachusetts, became Speaker of the House. Leverett Saltonstall, JFK's Republican colleague from Massachusetts, became chairman of the Senate Armed Services Committee. Saltonstall's chairmanship facilitated JFK's joint efforts with Saltonstall to direct more defense contracts to Massachusetts and extra federal funds for repairing and improving the Army Pier in Boston.[8]

New Englanders also held key positions in the Eisenhower administration. Sherman Adams, a former governor of New Hampshire, was the White House chief of staff. Max Rabb, a Bostonian, was secretary to the cabinet. Sinclair Weeks, the secretary of commerce, had recently chaired the Republican state committee in Massachusetts.[9] While JFK was a Democrat who still had important policy differences with these Republicans, especially concerning labor unions, he shared some empathy and understanding with these New England Republicans regarding the economic problems of their home region.

Of these New England Republicans, Sherman Adams was the most influential. He soon distinguished himself as an especially powerful White House chief of staff.[10] During his nearly six-year tenure in this position, Adams shrewdly and eclectically advised Eisenhower to only support policy proposals of JFK which were compatible with Eisenhower's policy agenda and those of moderate New England Republican senators like Saltonstall and Margaret Chase Smith of Maine.[11]

With the GOP having achieved only a one-seat majority in the Senate as a result of the 1952 elections, Eisenhower understood the need to co-opt the votes of a few maverick northern Democratic senators like JFK on such administrative goals as budget cuts to agricultural subsidies and rural electrification that disproportionately benefited the South.[12] In a 1953 letter to Speaker of the House Joseph W. Martin, Jr., the president wrote, "Moreover, because of the thinness of our Party margin, we will more than once in the days ahead be dependent upon some Democrat voting strength. Consequently, we should take care our offer of cooperative work is genuine and proffered before the other side could make some capital out of a sudden Republican need."[13]

Sherman Adams previously served as chairman of the New England Governors' Conference while he was governor of New Hampshire. This organization's major purposes were to promote discussion and cooperation among the region's governors regarding shared economic problems and policy issues and to increase New England's potential influence with the federal government.[14] In a 1951 speech to the New York–New England Inter-Agency Committee in Hanover, New Hampshire, Adams stated, "In their conception of the Federal-State relationship, it is my opinion that most of our people do not regard the financial assistance which is received from the Federal government as either a hand-out or a subsidy. Rather, they feel it is an inadequate dividend on a very substantial investment."[15]

JFK communicated a similar regional perspective in several speeches, articles, legislative proposals, and through his establishment of the New England Senators' Conference. Like Adams, JFK claimed that he simply wanted New England to receive its fair share of appropriations and attention from the federal government for its economic needs. Furthermore, just as Adams used his chairmanship of the New England Governors' Conference to organize delegate support for Eisenhower's nomination for president among New England's Republican politicians, JFK later used his leadership of the New England Senators' Conference to organize delegate support for his presidential nomination among New England's Democratic politicians.[16]

As a freshman senator from the minority party in the Senate, JFK shrewdly offered the chairmanship of his proposed New England Senators' Conference to Senator Margaret Chase Smith of Maine. Smith politely declined Kennedy's offer. She agreed with JFK that such "an organization of the New England delegation" with a "hard-hitting New England team" was needed. However, she was busy with her committee assignments and preparations for her 1954 reelection campaign.[17]

JFK was elected chairman of this conference following a series of speeches in the Senate and nationally published articles that documented the economic problems that were either unique to New England or more severe there compared to the nation in general. This was especially true during the 1948–1949 recession. While the national unemployment rate increased from 3.8 percent in 1948 to 5.9 percent in 1949, local unemployment rates in Massachusetts in 1949 ranged from 12 percent in Lowell and Fall River to 18 percent in New Bedford and 26 percent in Lawrence.[18] From 1947 to 1954, the number of jobs in New England textile mills declined from approximately 280,000 to 170,000.[19] In its 1951 report on the so-called "New England Problem" to President Harry S. Truman, the Council of Economic Advisors wrote, "Its problem is no longer one of shifting from the primary industries such as agriculture, fisheries, and forestry to manufacturing, but rather one of adapting its existing manufacturing industries to changing technologies and new products and diverting industries which involve a high ratio of value-added to value-shipped."[20]

In May of 1953, JFK delivered three speeches on the Senate floor detailing the economic problems of New England and proposing legislation. In his first speech, delivered on May 18, 1953, the Democratic senator from Massachusetts emphasized that he was not seeking preferential treatment for New England at the expense of other regions. Instead, he contended that the economic problems of New England were harbingers of similar problems which would soon plague states and communities in other regions. "In short, although I shall use the needs of the New England economy to point up the needs of the economics of our Nation and other great regions and States, these are not matters of interest to New Englanders alone."[21] His legislative proposals in this speech included a bill to establish regional industrial development corporations, tax incentives to encourage investment in new industrial technologies, job training, an independent federal agency to help small businesses to expand and attract federal contracts, and appropriate federal funds to help the commercial fishing industry to market its products domestically and internationally.[22]

JFK's second speech, delivered on May 20, 1953, focused on the labor costs of New England compared to other regions and Puerto Rico, especially in the textile industry. In order to reduce this disparity and discourage the exploitation of cheaper labor in the South and Puerto Rico, JFK recommended an increase in the federal minimum wage from 75 cents to $1 per hour. For businesses that received federal contracts, he suggested that the Walsh-Healey Act of 1936 be amended and interpreted to require prevailing wages according to national instead of local standards. JFK also specifically referred to an earlier study by the New England Governors' Conference when Sherman Adams chaired it. This study criticized the Taft-Hartley Act of 1947, especially its right-to-work provision, for "freezing" an advantage to the South in labor costs by helping that region to discourage stronger labor unions, especially in the textile industry.[23] In the remaining sections of this second speech, JFK recommended changes in federal policies in unemployment compensation, Social Security payroll taxes, government contracts, and transportation rates which had the effect, however unintentional, of discriminating against New England compared to other regions.[24]

In his third speech, delivered on May 25, 1953, JFK cited areas of surplus labor and higher than average unemployment throughout the United States but especially in New England. He suggested new legislation to extend unemployment insurance payments, increase Social Security benefits, subsidize the development of middle-income housing, and reform antitrust and international trade laws according to how they affect the local economics of distressed areas. In the conclusion of this speech, JFK stated, "As I have stressed throughout, although many of the recommendations I have made are of special importance to New England, nevertheless, none is contrary to the national interest, but rather would, if enacted, be of benefit to all people wherever they may live."[25]

With the help of legislative aide and speech writer Theodore C. Sorensen, JFK also explained the plight of New England's economy to a national audience through several magazine articles published in 1953 and 1954. In a November 1953 article for the *New York Times Magazine* entitled, "What's the Matter with New England?," JFK asserted that his proposed 40-point program for federal action for areas of surplus labor and economic distress in New England and other regions "provides instead a basic framework within which our regional economics can take full advantage of their own resources, their own initiative and their own enterprise and free themselves from the burdens that unfair competition these days that presses down upon them."[26]

Two months later, JFK's article "New England and the South" was published in *Atlantic Monthly*. In it, he specified how federal tax, labor, and electrification policies accelerated the movement of textile mills and jobs from New England to the South. However, he also explained that these newly industrialized southern communities often experienced such economic problems as inadequate tax revenues from these factories and underpaid, exploited labor forces. The junior senator from Massachusetts wrote, "The elimination of unfair competition of this character will benefit the South as it will benefit New England. The proposals I have made should not be regarded as posing an antagonistic issue between North and South."[27]

In his speeches and articles, JFK repeatedly and carefully stated that he was not being hostile toward the South or trying to change federal policies in order to provide preferential treatment for New England at the expense of other regions and the national good. However, several southern Democratic senators interpreted JFK's proposed policy changes to be detrimental to their region's economic interests. In particular, Senator J. William Fulbright of Arkansas, a state that had been successful in attracting northern textile industries, opposed JFK's proposal to amend the Walsh-Healey Act in order to reduce the South's labor cost advantages in attracting federal contracts.[28] Fulbright also disagreed with Senator Richard B. Russell of Georgia on awarding more defense contracts to areas of high unemployment in New England.[29]

It was unlikely, therefore, that JFK could expect much support from southern Democrats in Congress for passage of his economic development policies that could be applied to depressed, also known as distressed, areas throughout the nation, if they were tailored for New England. Determined to deliver tangible legislative accomplishments reflecting his campaign promises to his constituents, JFK focused on co-sponsoring legislation with Senator Leverett Saltonstall during his first two years as a senator. In particular, JFK and Saltonstall co-sponsored legislation to secure federal funds to repair and improve the Army Pier in Boston, impose higher tariffs on imported frozen fish, and provide federal loans to help rebuild communities in central Massachusetts damaged by a tornado in 1953.[30] Sorensen later wrote that JFK and Saltonstall "took turns taking the lead in joint measures for Massachusetts, with the wholly unspoken understanding that they would all be known as Saltonstall-Kennedy bills in the senior Senator's 1954 and 1960 campaigns and as Kennedy-Saltonstall bills in 1958."[31]

Saltonstall readily agreed with JFK's suggestion to establish the New England Senators' Conference, which held its first meeting on March 5, 1954. In a joint press release issued on September 5, 1954, Saltonstall and JFK concluded, "Looking back over the activities and achievements of the Conferences initiated last March, we believe that a highly worthwhile and constructive start has been made toward building closer cooperation between the New England Senators."[32]

JFK relied on Sorensen to organize meetings of the New England Senators' Conference, develop topics for discussion, and research policy proposals.[33] Besides serving the policy purposes of increasing the possibility of Congress and the president enacting legislative proposals intended to benefit New England, this organization also had the potential to improve the 1954 reelection chances of senators who could further publicize their efforts to serve their constituents on a bipartisan, regional basis. This potential was especially important for Saltonstall in the general election and for Margaret Chase Smith, who faced a tough primary campaign against Robert Jones, a conservative, pro-McCarthy Republican.[34]

Of course, partisan policy differences remained among the New England senators. JFK joined the other Democratic senators from New England, Theodore F. Green and John O. Pastore, both from Rhode Island, in voting for labor and minimum wage legislation opposed by their Republican colleagues. Most of New England's senators, including JFK, eventually voted for the St. Lawrence Seaway. Saltonstall and both of Connecticut's Republican senators, Prescott Bush and William Purtell, opposed it, despite the Eisenhower administration's vigorous advocacy of the Seaway.[35]

JFK also found that Eisenhower and Adams were more receptive to his legislative proposals if they were endorsed by most or all of New England's Republican senators and could help deflect any Democratic charges that the Eisenhower administration was insensitive to the region's economic needs during the 1954 mid-term elections.[36] Henry Cabot Lodge, Jr., now serving as U.S. Ambassador to the United Nations, warned Eisenhower about the possible impact of unemployment on Republican electoral prospects in 1954, especially in New England. Lodge wrote, "The greatest single danger is unemployment. I have heard rumblings of discontent in New England, and I note some in those reports from industrial centers in other places."[37]

The policy advocacy and public concerns of the New England Senators' Conference were further enhanced by its collaboration and coordination with the New England Governors' Conference. Such cooperation between these two organizations was especially evident in their efforts to have the Senate investigate and the Interstate Commerce Commission (ICC) change what they regarded as discriminatory, unfair freight rates in New England by railroads and trucking companies.[38] Donald W. Campbell, an insurance company executive from Massachusetts, chaired a committee on public transportation created by the New England Governors' Conference. In 1956, Campbell submitted this committee's study to Governor Dennis J. Roberts of Rhode Island, the chairman of the New England Governors' Conference. Acknowledging the cooperative efforts of New England's governors and senators, Campbell optimistically stated that he and his fellow committee members "are happy to note that New England railroads and other railroads of the Northeast have joined in an effort to remove the present rail rate differential that discriminates against New England ports in favor of Philadelphia and Baltimore. The potential gains that could accrue to New England from this effort are very great."[39]

The efforts of JFK, the New England Senators' Conference, the New England Governors' Conference, and the New England Council, a private, nonprofit organization, to improve New England's economy were further legitimized by the National Planning Association's Committee of New England. This committee's extensive, highly detailed study of New England's economy was entitled, *The Economic State of New England*, and published in 1954.[40] This study's general tone and content were less pessimistic and alarmist than those of JFK's earliest speeches and articles on this subject. New England had the oldest industrial economy in the nation and was too dependent on the lower paying, less skilled, and labor-intensive textile and shoe industries. Therefore, it was natural and inevitable that New England would gradually lose these industries, as it had since 1919. New England now needed new policies to adapt its economy and labor force to more service jobs and more highly skilled manufacturing jobs in such modern industries as aircraft engines in Connecticut and electronics in Massachusetts.

The Economic State of New England generally agreed with JFK on how the federal government should treat New England better regarding defense contracts, freight rates, unemployment compensation, taxes, and international trade.[41] Unlike JFK, however, this report's analysis and recommendations assigned greater responsibilities to state and local governments, research universities, industrial managers, and bankers in New England as well as to this region's chronically unemployed factory workers' willingness and ability to relocate and be trained for different types of jobs.[42] In its conclusion, *The Economic State of New England* urged the development and encouragement of a more visionary, creative, and entrepreneurial culture in New England. "We urge upon every New Englander the value of the economic vision that will both reveal avenues of industrial advancement and induce widespread support of those who are actively seeking to provide jobs at good wages for the population."[43]

In a speech delivered at Trinity College in Hartford, Connecticut, on December 15, 1954, Alfred C. Neal, the first vice president of the Federal Reserve Bank of Boston, emphasized unique characteristics of New England which contributed to its economic advantages as well as its disadvantages.[44] He noted that there had been relatively little growth in manufacturing in New England during the past twenty years. However, this region remained a "high income economy" where 191,000 jobs were gained in durable goods industries, such as machine tools and metal work, while 173,000 jobs were lost in non-durable goods industries, such as textiles and shoes, from 1919 to 1953.[45] In this speech's conclusion, he asserted that federal policies intended to benefit the entire nation's economy, such as lower tariffs to increase American exports and the construction of the St. Lawrence Seaway, would benefit rather than harm New England's economy. Neal stated, "In expanding its foreign trade by increasing its exports, New England will be working not only for its own interest but for the national interest, which depends upon an expansion of world trade as one of the means of combating Communism abroad."[46]

In addition to studies and rhetoric which differed from JFK's diagnosis of New England's economic problems and policy proposals to address them, JFK was also vulnerable to charges that he was exaggerating or distorting his region's economic problems for political gain. Although *The Economic State of New England* did not name JFK in this context, it warned its readers, "Solutions to New England's economic problems may be addressed for political motives, for motives of advanced personal gain, or for narrow interests rather than for the wider interests which must be considered in any measures involving the federal taxing and spending powers."[47]

The *Worcester Gazette*, a newspaper in central Massachusetts which often endorsed Republican candidates, challenged JFK's statistics and dire warnings about New England's economy as well as his policy agenda. An editorial expressing this challenge was published under the confident headline, "Jobs in Massachusetts: No Need for Confusion."[48] In an extensive reply to the *Worcester Gazette*'s managing editor, JFK wrote, "Instead, I have cited such statistics to indicate the need for action on legislation I have introduced to raise the minimum wage and otherwise reduce the North-South wage differential; reduce New England's power and transportation costs; strengthen our old age and unemployment benefit systems; close tax loopholes encouraging industrial migration; and in other ways assisting our textile, ship building, fishing and other hard-hit industries."[49]

The congressional elections of 1954 yielded Democratic majorities in both houses of Congress, although by a margin of only one seat in the Senate. The Senate Armed Services Committee would now be chaired by Senator Richard B. Russell of Georgia instead of

Leverett Saltonstall. Saltonstall's chairmanship of this committee and position as Republican majority whip during the 1953–1954 sessions of Congress helped JFK to direct more defense spending to Massachusetts and attract more attention from the White House to his policy agenda for New England.[50] Southern Democrats, who had been either indifferent or hostile to the economic policy proposals of JFK and the New England Senators' Conference, now chaired major committees in Congress. Throughout the remainder of Eisenhower's presidency, southern and midwestern Democrats in Congress remembered that JFK had supported Eisenhower's changes in farm price support payments and budget cuts in flood control and rural electrification programs that benefited their constituents.[51] Also, Eisenhower was more likely to have an antagonistic relationship with a Democratic Congress on budgetary issues and was less likely to be receptive to the more expensive items on JFK's economic policy agenda, such as new programs and extended unemployment compensation for chronically depressed, or distressed, areas that the Republican president regarded as too expensive or excessive.[52]

JFK's position relative to Eisenhower, Saltonstall, and the New England Senators' Conference also changed during the 1955–1956 sessions of Congress. JFK was now a member of the majority party in the Senate. The Senate majority leader was Lyndon B. Johnson, a Texan, and the chairmen of the two committees on which JFK served, Government Operations and Labor and Public Welfare, were southern Democrats. JFK's legislative behavior and speeches on the Senate floor and articles in national publications became less likely to advocate major economic policy changes opposed by southern Democrats, such as amendments to the Walsh-Healey Act and the Taft-Hartley Act. After his narrowly defeated bid for the Democratic vice presidential nomination received a significant amount of southern delegate votes at the Democratic national convention of 1956, JFK continued to nurture more cooperative relationships with southern Democratic senators. Meanwhile, JFK also developed a more partisan, antagonistic relationship with Eisenhower as his national ambition and rising status within the Democratic Party became more evident.[53]

Flood control in New England, however, was a policy issue in which JFK and the other senators from New England were able to achieve quick, effective cooperation from Congress and the Eisenhower administration. Since textile mills were often built along major rivers in New England, they often suffered severe damage from floods. Political factors, such as opposition to the dislocation caused by the construction of flood control projects in Vermont and New Hampshire, the fear of private utility companies that federally subsidized electric power plants would be built in New England, disagreements among state governments, and insufficient attention and funding by the federal government contributed to New England having the weakest flood control system of any region by the early 1950s.[54]

The inadequacy of federal authority and funding for flood control and disaster relief in New England was apparent during the first few months of the Eisenhower administration. After Saco, Maine, was severely damaged by a flood in the spring of 1953, Senator Margaret Chase Smith asked the Eisenhower administration for emergency federal funds for Saco. Wilton Persons, Eisenhower's liaison with Congress, replied to Smith, "Certainly we readily understand your and Mayor Warren's interest in the problems faced by the city of Saco, but lacking specific authority for Federal participation in a flood control operation, it is, of course, impossible at this time to make the necessary funds available."[55]

Severe hurricanes and floods that devastated southern New England in 1954 and 1955 contributed to the Bush-McCormack Act of 1956.[56] On March 19, 1956, the New England Senators' Conference asked Representative Clarence Cannon, chairman of the House Appropriations Committee, to expedite the appropriation of additional federal funds for flood control projects. In this letter's conclusion, the members of the New England Senators' Conference stated, "In the past, the people of New England have contributed very heavily to this work in other areas of the country, and will do so in the future. We do not begrudge our aid to our sister states, but do feel strongly that our own needs, so tragically demonstrated in the 1955 disaster, now demand sympathetic and effective action."[57]

The above quotation reflects the perspective that JFK repeatedly expressed in his speeches on the New England economy and in the establishment of the New England Senators' Conference. Despite partisan, constituency, and policy differences among themselves, the senators from New England were not seeking preferential treatment from the federal government compared to other regions or federal policy changes that conflicted with the national interest. Instead, they sought and expected what they perceived to be fair and effective policy responses from the federal government. This message was communicated earlier to Eisenhower by the New England Governors' Conference. In a September 23, 1955 letter to Eisenhower, the New England governors stated that immediate, effective federal intervention following the hurricanes and floods was necessary partially because "New England is a highly industrialized and important part of the national economy and the national defense, with the consequence that the disruption of its production and commerce adversely affects the entire nation."[58]

The Bush-McCormack Act of 1956 was the most quickly enacted legislation that the New England Senators' Conference advocated. Cosponsored by Republican Senator Prescott Bush of Connecticut and Democratic Representative John W. McCormack of Massachusetts, this law not only increased federal funds for flood control projects and disaster relief in New England and research on hurricanes. The Bush-McCormack Act also granted discretionary authority for the U.S. Army Corps of Engineers to make modest changes, repairs, and improvements in the nation's flood control projects without acts of Congress.[59]

JFK regularly issued press releases and delivered speeches in Massachusetts which updated his constituents on the progress of the New England Senators' Conference. In his address to the Rotary Club in Springfield, Massachusetts, JFK stated that since the creation of this regional association of senators, "The members of our delegation have exchanged information, opinions and viewpoints, without regard to party affiliation, on issues of common interest to the six states of New England."[60] The Democratic senator listed ten economic problems confronting New England and the current status of legislative efforts by the New England Senators' Conference to solve or alleviate them. He mentioned the conference's successes regarding tariffs and international trade, executive branch decisions beneficial to the woolen textile and fishing industries, the future generation of cheaper, more abundant electricity for New England from nuclear power plants and hydroelectric power from the St. Lawrence River, and flood control projects and flood insurance.

However, he also informed the Springfield Rotary Club of his and his New England colleagues' frustrations, disappointments, and defeats in trying to influence legislation and administrative decisions in other policy areas, such as labor reform, federal aid to distressed areas, and a formula for distributing federal highway funds that would benefit New England. Nonetheless, JFK confidently concluded that "there has been a desirable improvement in the attitude of the Federal Government toward New England—and in the attitude of New England toward the Federal Government. If each will continue to recognize the importance and the proper role of the other in the solution of these problems, we may look forward to a better, a newer New England in the years that lie ahead."[61]

Two of the more challenging problems confronting the New England Senators' Conference in 1956 and 1957 were federal highway funds and a quota on imported oil. Both issues drew JFK and the other New England senators into conflict with members of Congress from other regions, especially the South. During the spring of 1956, Congress needed to resolve major differences in the distribution of federal highway funds to the states between a formula proposed by Senator Albert A. Gore, Sr., of Tennessee and one proposed by Representative George Fallon of Maryland.[62] All of the New England states would receive fewer federal highway funds under the Gore formula compared to the Fallon formula.[63] This disparity was especially significant for Massachusetts, which would receive approximately $893.4 million under the Fallon formula compared to $528.4 million under the Gore formula.[64] Partially because of the lobbying efforts of the New England Senators' Conference, the Gore formula was rejected, and Congress passed a compromised version of the Fallon formula in the Federal Aid Highway Act of 1956.[65]

In his previous speeches and articles, JFK cited the high cost of energy in New England as one of this region's economic problems. This problem included the fact that New England depended more on imported oil for its heating and electricity than other regions. The price of oil increased after the quota on imported oil was reduced in order to increase the price and supply of domestically produced oil. Oil prices also rose and fluctuated during the Suez crisis of 1956.[66] Eisenhower's veto of a natural gas bill, which was strongly backed by members of Congress from oil and gas producing states and lobbyists representing these interests, also made energy prices a more prominent issue for the New England Senators' Conference in 1956 and 1957.[67]

The New England Senators' Conference held a special meeting in early 1957 to discuss the high price of oil in their states. At this time, domestic oil production and reserves increased while American oil companies continued to try to further restrict the importation of oil. In a letter to JFK, Senators George Aiken of Vermont and Margaret Chase Smith of Maine wrote, "In view of the gravity of this situation, we believe that a meeting of the New England delegation should be held to discuss this problem and decide upon a course of action to protect the consumers of New England."[68]

The increase in fuel oil prices, therefore, was the top priority of the February 6, 1957 meeting of the New England Senators' Conference. Other issues included a survey of water resources, the need for more federal aid for flood and hurricane damage, lobbying the Interstate Commerce Commission (ICC) for lower freight rates for railroads in New England, favorable tariff decisions on imported wool and cotton textile goods from Japan, and federal funds for forestry research in New England.[69] The New England senators also chose Margaret Chase Smith to represent them at a meeting of the Senate Committee on Interior and Insular Affairs regarding the oil price issue.

Testifying before this committee on February 21, 1957, Smith stated, "The only appreciable element of competition which has acted to provide some degree of protection for New England fuel oil consumers in the past has been foreign imports of oil. And on that score we of New England have had to wage a continuing fight against attempts of domestic producers to have restrictive quotas and other restrictions placed on foreign imports of oil."[70] She dismissed the idea that the sharp increase in fuel oil prices in New England was mostly or entirely a result of the Suez crisis. Instead, she asserted that domestic oil producers "have failed to make a plausible case for themselves and to remove the suspicion that New England fuel oil consumers have of their motives."[71]

At the May 16, 1957 meeting of the New England Senators' Conference, the senators agreed to further pursue the issue of quotas on imported oil by having JFK and Senator Norris Cotton of New Hampshire meet with Gordon Gray, the director of the Office of Defense Mobilization (ODM). They also planned to meet with Gray regarding whether woolen-worsted imports threatened national security by contributing to the decline of the domestic woolen textile industry.[72] In his memoir, Cotton explained how Gray rejected the request of the New England Senators' Conference to increase the quota on imported oil. After their meeting with Gray, Cotton wrote that JFK "cussed all the way back to the Capitol, damning the policy which forced New England to pay more than any other section of the country for oil to heat its homes and schools and to turn the wheels of many of its industries."[73]

The agenda for the January 30, 1958 meeting of the New England Senators' Conference included imported oil as one of the five issues for discussion. It noted that the Eisenhower administration's policy of asking American oil companies to voluntarily restrict oil imports "has not had a significant cost or supply impact in New England. However, there have been recent indications that pressure will be applied to make this program mandatory."[74] Despite the policy preferences and lobbying efforts of JFK and the other senators from New England, the Eisenhower administration imposed mandatory restrictions on oil imports on March 10, 1959.[75] Eisenhower did this as a response to the declining oil prices and profits experienced by domestic oil producers, partially caused by the growing supply of imported oil and the effects of the 1957–1958 recession.[76]

While the New England Senators' Conference's efforts on oil imports exerted little or no influence on the decisions of the

Eisenhower administration on this issue, they brought JFK into conflict with Senate Majority Leader Lyndon B. Johnson. The Texas Democrat outlined and promoted a mostly liberal policy agenda for the Senate in 1956 entitled "Program with a Heart" but included the deregulation of oil and natural gas prices.[77] Through Johnson's influence, JFK received a seat on the Senate Foreign Relations Committee in 1957, an especially prestigious and coveted committee assignment for a freshman senator.[78] During the 1957–1958 sessions of Congress, JFK used his seats on the Senate Foreign Relations Committee and Labor and Public Welfare Committee to focus his rhetoric and legislative behavior more on international and national issues and less on regional issues.

Instead, JFK carefully selected and actively pursued those policy goals of the New England Senators' Conference which coincided with the national policy priorities of most Democrats and moderate Republicans in Congress and the Eisenhower administration and were also beneficial to the development of JFK's future presidential candidacy. Federal aid to distressed, or depressed, areas satisfied the above political criteria more than any other policy goal of the New England Senators' Conference.[79] The higher unemployment rates caused by the 1957–1958 recession made federal aid to distressed areas more of a national issue and less of a regional issue.[80] Johnson had included passage of a distressed areas bill as one of his policy priorities for the Senate in his 1956 "Program with a Heart." Eisenhower expressed his willingness to sign a distressed areas bill, but only if it specifically targeted chronically high unemployment in urban, industrial areas, instead of becoming a broader, more expensive anti-poverty program that included rural, agricultural areas as much as urban, industrial areas.[81]

In his first speech to the Senate about New England's economic problems, JFK stated, "As a Senator's responsibility is not only to his State but to his Nation, I think that it is proper to point out that even though many of the recommendations I have made are of special importance to New England, nevertheless, none is contrary to the national interest, but rather would, if enacted, be of benefit to all people wherever they may live."[82] In his speeches and policy proposals of 1953 and 1954, the Democratic senator from Massachusetts initially emphasized and specified the economic problems of New England and then used them as a regional example of national economic problems. He believed that some of them partially could be solved or alleviated through a resumption, improvement, and expansion of the distressed areas policy of the Truman administration.[83]

During JFK's third speech on the economic problems of New England, he received favorable, encouraging comments and questions from Senator Paul Douglas of Illinois, a fellow Democrat. Douglas was an economist who had taught at the University of Chicago. After visiting distressed areas of rural, southern Illinois in February, 1954, Douglas either researched or personally visited distressed areas in New Hampshire, Maine, Michigan, Wisconsin, and Arizona. The Illinois Democrat made federal aid to distressed areas a major issue in his 1954 reelection campaign.[84]

JFK's approach to developing and promoting legislation in distressed areas was incremental, consensual, and bipartisan. Especially from 1953 to 1955, he focused on more modest items in this policy agenda for distressed areas that the New England Senators' Conference, the Eisenhower administration, and most members of Congress were more likely to support, such as distributing more defense contracts and more federal spending on highways, hospitals, and other public works in distressed areas and providing tax incentives to encourage economic development there. Meanwhile, JFK carefully separated these aspects of his economic policy agenda from those which were more controversial and divisive and less likely to be enacted, namely, policy changes that favored the interests of labor unions.[85]

Unlike JFK, Douglas immediately involved labor union officials in developing a comprehensive bill on federal aid to distressed areas.[86] While JFK usually enjoyed a friendly, cooperative relationship with Senator Lyndon B. Johnson, Douglas was a frequent, outspoken critic of Johnson's party leadership and legislative tactics.[87] He already alienated the Eisenhower administration on the issue of distressed areas by publicly asserting in 1954 that the nation was suffering from a recession, which the White House denied.

Like JFK, Douglas was a member of the Senate Labor and Public Welfare Committee. In 1955, Senator Lister Hill of Alabama, this committee's chairman, appointed Douglas chairman of a subcommittee with jurisdiction over distressed areas legislation. Douglas held hearings and reported a bill out of his subcommittee in 1956.[88] Concerned that a Democratic bill on distressed areas would inevitably be broader in its purposes and applicability and more expensive than Eisenhower would accept, the White House began restructuring and formulating an alternative distressed areas policy as early as 1954.

Eisenhower's Council of Economic Advisers used Lawrence, Massachusetts, with its chronically high unemployment rates and declining textile and shoe industries, as a microcosm for the economic problems of distressed areas nationally. In his report on Lawrence, Roy Williams, vice president of the Associated Industries of Massachusetts, stated that, despite its 1954 unemployment rate of 20 percent, "the fact that the President has indicated his firm interest in assisting Lawrence, and since the situation is very much on the minds of the members of the Administration in Washington, a complete revitalization of the area development programs has been set in motion."[89] Robert H. Ryan was a Boston businessman consulted by the White House about Lawrence and other distressed areas of Massachusetts. He was more pessimistic and skeptical than Williams about the ability of federal intervention to solve or even ameliorate the economic problems of Lawrence and similar communities. Ryan wrote, "I am sure you are familiar with the permanency of the problem, particularly in the older textile communities which are suffering all the problems of age, including congestion, out-moded facilities and deep-seated feelings."[90]

Eisenhower eventually decided to develop a policy for distressed areas, but it was mostly a revival of Truman's program for "areas of surplus labor."[91] Unlike Truman's program, which was implemented by the U.S. Department of Labor, Eisenhower wanted a distressed areas program to be implemented by the U.S. Department of Commerce. He also wanted to ensure that any distressed areas program did not conflict with his administration's principles and policy goals of cutting taxes, limiting spending, and balancing budgets.[92]

A new policy idea that Douglas wanted to include in his distressed areas legislation was a job training program. William L. Batt was one of the labor experts whom Douglas consulted. Batt previously served as assistant secretary of labor in the Truman administration and helped to develop a state distressed areas program for Pennsylvania.[93] Batt and others informed Douglas that factories which required highly skilled labor were unlikely to move to or originate in a distressed area unless the local work force already had the necessary job skills. Douglas also believed that unemployed workers should receive extended unemployment benefits while being trained. As these and other new items were added to his bill, Douglas realized, as he later stated, "that each new provision we added would make it harder to get the bill passed."[94]

After Douglas's bill died in the House of Representatives at the end of the 1956 legislative session, he reintroduced it through the Senate Banking and Currency Committee at the beginning of the 1957 session. Unfortunately for Douglas, Senator J. William Fulbright of Arkansas, the chairman of this committee, was hostile to Douglas's bill because its criteria for defining distressed areas did not apply to many rural, agricultural areas of the South.[95] In order to increase bipartisan support for his bill, Douglas cosponsored it with Senator Frederick Payne of Maine, a Republican member of this committee.[96] Payne was motivated to assume a leading role on distressed areas legislation because he faced a tough reelection campaign in 1958 against Democratic Governor Edmund S. Muskie.[97]

With distressed areas now renamed area redevelopment, the Douglas-Payne legislation was also influenced by proposals from a report of the Joint Economic Committee chaired by Senator John Sparkman, a Democrat from Alabama, and a bill focusing on the economic problems of depressed coal mining areas that was sponsored by Representative Daniel Flood of Pennsylvania.[98] Meanwhile, JFK was busy with developing and promoting labor reform legislation that influenced the content and purposes of the Landrum-Griffin Act of 1959.[99] William L. Batt, however, later commented that JFK remained influential in the content, direction, and legislative progress of Douglas's bill. In a 1966 interview, Batt stated, "I must say that you'd run into Senator Kennedy, though, on any bill of any significance in this field. Everybody tried to get him to sponsor the bills in which they were interested because he had a great deal of influence, far beyond his seniority, in getting bills adopted and getting backing for them from both wings of the Democratic party."[100]

By 1958, the most novel content of the Douglas-Payne bill was the creation of an Area Redevelopment Administration (ARA). Communities that satisfied this bill's criteria as "industrial redevelopment areas" could receive grants and loans to attract new industries. In order to attract broad, bipartisan support, the content and criteria of the Douglas-Payne bill ensured that most states had areas that qualified for ARA help.[101]

Douglas's intuitive fear had been that, as he accepted more compromises and added new provisions to his original bill in order to broaden support in Congress, he made it less likely that Eisenhower would sign his distressed areas bill into law.[102] On September 6, 1958, Eisenhower vetoed the Douglas-Payne bill, formally known as S.3683. In his veto message, the president stated that his objections to S.3683 included its costs, the eligibility of rural, agricultural areas, excessive federal control, and its failure to locate the ARA within the U.S. Department of Commerce.[103] In his memoir, Eisenhower wrote, "I resisted this congressional effort to distort a proposal designed specifically to help urban areas characterized by unemployment which was both substantial and persistent."[104]

With larger Democratic majorities in Congress generated by the 1958 congressional elections, Douglas redesigned his distressed areas legislation and attracted thirty-eight cosponsors. JFK had been one of seven Democratic cosponsors of Douglas's original bill.[105] The compromised version of Douglas's bill reduced the initial appropriation for an area redevelopment program in order to make the bill more acceptable to Eisenhower. Nevertheless, Eisenhower vetoed this distressed areas bill, officially named S.722, on May 13, 1960. He specified six major defects in this bill in his veto message. The president stated, "The most striking defect of S.722 is that it would make eligible for federal assistance areas that don't need it—thus providing less help for communities in genuine need than would the Administration's proposal."[106]

Almost one year later, on May 1, 1961, President John F. Kennedy signed the Area Redevelopment Act into law.[107] During his first two years as a senator and as the founder and first chair of the New England Senators' Conference, JFK's ideas and perspective on legislation for distressed areas were more similar to than different from those of Eisenhower. Like Eisenhower, he initially perceived a distressed areas program to be limited to a combination of defense contracts, public works projects, technical assistance, and federally guaranteed, long-term, low-interest loans for industrial development that applied to a few urban, industrial areas that suffered from unusually and chronically high unemployment rates.[108]

By the end of his Senate career and during his presidential campaign, JFK agreed with Paul Douglas and other liberal Democrats that an area redevelopment program should include job training and extended unemployment benefits and should be one part of a comprehensive anti-poverty policy that applied equally to urban, industrial areas and rural, agricultural, and mining areas.[109] JFK delivered a speech on the Senate floor on May 13, 1958, urging his colleagues to pass Douglas's distressed areas bill. The tone and content of JFK's speech sharply contrasted with those of Eisenhower's 1958 and 1960 veto messages and, to some extent, with those of JFK's May 1953 speeches on New England's economic problems. In his speech, JFK asserted that Douglas's bill, S.3683, "is not a temporary solution to a temporary problem. It is a permanent recipe for relief of chronic unemployment wherever it may occur."[110]

While JFK assumed an early, prominent role in distressed areas legislation during the Eisenhower administration, he played a more passive, supplemental role in urban renewal, originally known as urban redevelopment. There were several reasons for this contract. First, JFK's seat on the Senate's Labor and Public Welfare Committee did not provide him with committee jurisdiction over federal housing and slum clearance policies. Second, Senator Joseph Clark of Pennsylvania was a former mayor of Philadelphia who immediately emerged as the leading Democratic senator on urban renewal after he entered the Senate in 1957.[111] Third, while members of the New England Senators' Conference generally agreed about the importance of Boston for New England's economy, it would be difficult for JFK to develop a bipartisan consensus and public position within the conference for federal policies affecting urban renewal in Boston. Even JFK and Leverett Saltonstall disagreed on the impact of the construction of the St. Lawrence Seaway on Boston's economy.[112]

The fourth and most important reason was the fact that Boston's urban renewal program began before JFK's election to the Senate in 1952. After Pittsburgh began its urban renewal program in 1949, Boston was the second major city to begin a comprehensive urban renewal program following the election of John B. Hynes as mayor in 1949.[113] Pittsburgh developed its urban renewal program with little consideration of federal policies. Hynes, however, was elected mayor in the same year that Congress passed the Housing Act of 1949.[114] Consequently, Hynes developed and implemented Boston's urban renewal program with the intention of using federal funds and authority from the Housing Act of 1949 for slum clearance and the construction of public housing.[115]

Until the election of John F. Collins as mayor of Boston in 1959, Boston experienced mixed results in its urban renewal program. Hynes failed to develop the same degree of cooperation and support from Republican business and civic leaders that Mayor David L. Lawrence had achieved in Pittsburgh.[116] Nevertheless, Hynes began slum clearance projects in the West End of Boston, facilitated the construction of the Prudential Center, and established the Boston Redevelopment Authority (BRA).[117]

Collins proved to be more effective than Hynes in coalescing with business leaders and lobbying the state legislature on behalf of Boston's urban renewal program.[118] Shortly after his election, Collins recruited Edward Logue as the director of the BRA.[119] Logue had previously served as the director of the nationally praised urban renewal program in New Haven, Connecticut.[120] During the eight years of Collins's mayoral administration, Boston's economic redevelopment also benefited from the political influence of the Kennedys and Speaker of the House John W. McCormack and the sharp increase in the number, variety, and funding of federal programs applied to the economic and social needs of cities during the Kennedy and Johnson administrations.[121]

From 1958 to 1960, JFK increasingly referred to the need for more federal spending and new programs to address the economic and social conditions of cities.[122] The Democratic senator from Massachusetts, however, rarely mentioned Boston as an example when speaking in other states. Instead, JFK was rhetorically adapting to the fact that after the 1956 elections liberal Democrats made urban renewal and proposals for new federal urban policies higher priorities. The Democratic Advisory Council (DAC), an appendage of the Democratic National Committee (DNC), created a committee on urban affairs and appointed Mayor Richard Lee of New Haven as its chairman.[123] Furthermore, when JFK ran for reelection to the Senate in 1958 and as he prepared for his presidential campaign, he made urban renewal part of his increasingly liberal ideology and policy agenda.[124] JFK was determined to assure liberal activists of the sincerity and efficacy of his liberalism as he sought the Democratic presidential nomination of 1960. His determination included a promise to establish a cabinet-level Department of Urban Affairs if elected president.[125]

Although a well-funded, comprehensive federal policy on distressed areas remained a higher priority than urban renewal for JFK, he joined other liberal Democrats in the Senate in proposing more spending on urban renewal and public housing than he knew Eisenhower would approve.[126] In addition to his presidential campaign strategy, JFK's more outspoken position on urban renewal was also influenced by the political and economic effects of the 1957–1958 recession, the larger, more liberal Democratic majorities elected to Congress in 1958, and the increasingly antagonistic relationship between Eisenhower and the Democrats in Congress on budgetary issues.[127] Despite the Republican president's 1959 veto of $900 million in urban renewal funds for two years, JFK proposed that Congress spend $600 million annually on urban renewal.[128] In a 1960 speech given at the Urban Affairs Conference in Pittsburgh, JFK characterized the Eisenhower administration's record on urban renewal and other urban issues as "shameful."[129]

The growing conflicts over urban renewal between Eisenhower and liberal Democrats by the late 1950s were also a result of the Eisenhower administration's interpretation and implementation of the Housing Act of 1954. In his study of the Housing Act of 1954, political scientist Richard M. Flanagan wrote, "The Housing Act of 1954 transcended the occasional divide between liberals and conservatives, forging a new consensus that emphasized commercial redevelopment instead of public housing as the answer to central city decline."[130] This "consensus," however, developed locally instead of nationally as mostly Democratic mayors and city councilors cooperated with mostly Republican business leaders in urban renewal projects. New Haven, Connecticut was the classic case study of such a local consensus.[131]

Nationally, there were significant differences between Eisenhower's perception of the appropriate federal role in urban renewal and that of JFK and other liberal Democrats in Congress. The Truman-approved Housing Act of 1949 envisioned and authorized the construction of 135,000 units of public housing per year for a total of 810,000 units, over a six-year period, strict federal oversight of local urban renewal projects, and a matching fund formula in which the federal government provided two-thirds of the funding for approved projects.[132] By contrast, the Eisenhower-endorsed Housing Act of 1954 greatly reduced the federal government's commitment to the construction of public housing and its regulatory supervision of urban renewal projects, encouraged the construction of affordable private housing, and emphasized the commercial redevelopment of downtown business districts through voluntary cooperation between local governments and business interests.[133] By 1958, the Republican president wanted to further limit the federal role in urban renewal by reducing the federal government's proportion of spending on urban renewal projects from two-thirds to one half.[134]

Unlike urban renewal, labor reform legislation initially seemed to be a shared policy goal in which JFK and Eisenhower could achieve a compromised, mutually satisfactory legislative solution by the end of the latter's presidency. Eisenhower, of course, never shared some of JFK's objectives in amending the Taft-Hartley Act of 1947, such as repealing its right-to-work provision.[135] In his second speech regarding New England's economic problems delivered on the Senate floor in May, 1953, JFK specifically mentioned the fact that White House chief of staff Sherman Adams chaired the New England Governors'

Conference when this organization published a report criticizing section 14(b) of the Taft-Hartley law's right-to-work provision for expediting the movement of industrial jobs from New England to the South.[136] In his memoir, however, Eisenhower referred to the retention of the right-to-work section as "wise and proper."[137]

When JFK was a more centrist Democratic senator from 1953 to 1957, he was more likely to agree with Eisenhower, southern Democrats, and moderate Republicans about the types of federal laws and amendments to the Taft-Hartley Act that were needed to purge labor unions of Communists and racketeers and protect the participation of rank-and-file union members in their relationships with their unions' officials. In January 1957, RFK became chief counsel to a select committee investigating labor racketeering and chaired by Senator John McClellan of Arkansas. RFK's investigation and the hearings of the McClellan committee increasingly focused on the Teamsters Union.[138] In December, 1957, the AFL-CIO expelled the Teamsters from membership in its organization.[139] Both of these events in 1957 made it easier for JFK to move to the left and become more consistently supportive of the interests of AFL-CIO unions, especially the United Automobile Workers (UAW), while apparently demonstrating political courage and independence through his aggressive rhetoric and legislative behavior directed at the controversial leadership of the Teamsters.[140]

In a speech delivered in Boston on October 24, 1957, JFK proudly claimed that New England in general and Massachusetts in particular benefited from "harmonious industrial relations" which were "unsurpassed in any section of the nation." He added, "For some twenty years, the total of man-days lost because of strikes, lockouts, jurisdictional disputes, violence or other labor trouble has compared most favorably with the rest of the country."[141] JFK devoted most of this speech's content to a detailed revelation of corrupt, abusive practices by the leadership of the Teamsters and examples of unethical labor-management collaboration which harmed the legitimate economic interests of rank-and-file union members. He then argued that there was a need for fair, effective amendments to the Taft-Hartley Act to prohibit and prevent such practices. JFK suggested that a new labor law protecting and promoting "union democracy" would simultaneously and symbiotically benefit further unionization of the nation's labor force, honest union officials, cooperative labor-management relations, and labor productivity.[142]

The centrist, bipartisan content of JFK's speech may have been influenced by the fact that he was addressing an audience of industrial managers, i.e., members of the Associated Industries of Massachusetts. From 1957 to 1959, JFK developed, promoted, and tried to achieve passage of labor reform legislation that would be acceptable to most Democrats and moderate Republicans in Congress, President Dwight D. Eisenhower, and the AFL-CIO. JFK needed to achieve the enactment of a major law that bore his name. He had to counteract critics and skeptics of his rumored, future presidential candidacy who claimed that he lacked the legislative skills to be qualified for the presidency.[143] JFK also wanted to cosponsor a bipartisan bill on a major, national issue in order to attract the votes of enough Republicans and independents in Massachusetts for a landslide reelection margin in 1958.[144]

In 1958, JFK cosponsored a labor reform bill with Senator Irving Ives of New York, a Republican. Major provisions of the Kennedy-Ives bill included the requirements of financial disclosure statements by unions, criminal penalties for the destruction of union records, and regular elections of union officials by secret ballots, and prohibitions of "shakedown" picketing, improper loading fees, and convicted felons holding positions as union officers.[145] The AFL-CIO reluctantly endorsed the Kennedy-Ives bill while several major business interest groups as well as the Teamsters, United Mine Workers (UMW), and United Steel Workers of America (USWA) opposed it.[146]

The Senate passed the Kennedy-Ives bill by a vote of 88 to 1 after an amendment requiring union officials to swear anti-Communist affidavits was added to it. The Kennedy-Ives bill then died in the House of Representatives. In 1959, JFK cosponsored his labor reform bill with Democratic Senator Sam Ervin of North Carolina. With JFK opposing some of the objectives of Eisenhower's 20-point program for labor reform legislation, the Senate tabled a motion to reconsider a "bill of rights" amendment opposed by JFK and union officials by a vote of 46 to 45. Vice President Richard M. Nixon cast the tie-breaking vote.[147] This vote, in effect, killed the original Kennedy-Ervin bill.

In September 1959, Congress passed the Landrum-Griffin bill, and Eisenhower signed it into the law. This alternative labor reform bill included most of what Eisenhower wanted.[148] JFK reluctantly and ambivalently voted for the Landrum-Griffin bill. Perceiving this law more favorably than his brother, RFK referred to the Landrum-Griffin Act of 1959 as being, despite some flaws and omissions, "a good law and one that is absolutely essential" in his book, *The Enemy Within*.[149]

Fortunately for JFK, the failure of his cosponsored labor reform legislation to be enacted did not prove to be a serious liability in either his 1958 Senate campaign or in the nationwide speaking engagements that were a prelude to his declared presidential candidacy. As JFK developed national name recognition and public support for the 1960 Democratic presidential nomination, the New England Senators' Conference become less important as a political vehicle for JFK and as an organization for formulating and promoting shared regional policy positions regarding the federal government.[150] In his autobiography, Leverett Saltonstall stated that he suspected that JFK voted for the St. Lawrence Seaway because his Democratic colleague was planning to run for president as early as 1954. Saltonstall wrote, "He never told me that he voted that way because he needed the Midwestern vote, but I felt this was the situation."[151]

The decline of the New England Senators' Conference was also accelerated by the increase in the number of Democratic senators from New England as a consequence of the 1958 Senate elections. In these elections, Democratic senatorial nominees Thomas J. Dodd and Edmund S. Muskie, respectively, defeated incumbent Republican Senators William Purtell of Connecticut and Frederick Payne of Maine. JFK also made more speeches and appearances in New Hampshire and Maine to endorse Democratic nominees for major offices and to improve Democratic voter appeal and organization in these states, especially New Hampshire with its "first in the nation" presidential primaries.[152] In a June 7, 1958 speech in Manchester, New Hampshire, JFK stated that "1958 represents New Hampshire's best opportunity to cast off permanently the shackles of one-party rule."[153]

Muskie later distinguished himself as the first Democratic senator in the nation to publicly endorse JFK for president.[154] Such partisan rhetoric and behavior made the remaining Republican senators from New England, especially those running for reelection, more suspicious of JFK's motives as a fellow member of the New England Senators' Conference. Ever since Muskie was elected governor of Maine in 1954, the Democratic Party in that state had become much more successful electorally.[155] Senator Margaret Chase Smith of Maine believed that JFK had betrayed their friendship by campaigning for her Democratic opponent in 1960.[156]

The creation of the Cape Cod National Seashore Park was the last major legislation that enjoyed unanimous bipartisan support from the New England Senators' Conference during JFK's last two years as a senator. As president, JFK signed the enabling legislation establishing the Great Outer Beach area of Cape Cod as a national park in 1961. According to Charles H. W. Foster, a former commissioner of natural resources in Massachusetts, the Cape Cod National Seashore Park was "the first of a new generation of national conservation projects and a pioneer in several respects.[157]

After World War II, the Cape Cod area of Massachusetts experienced sharp growth in the number of tourists and summer residents. Full-time residents and environmentalists became more concerned about how the summer population growth and commercial activities and traffic associated with it affected the natural beauty and wildlife of this area.[158] In February, 1957, the National Park Service began a field survey for a proposed Cape Cod National Seashore Park and published its report with exact boundaries in 1959.[159]

Legislation creating the Cape Cod National Seashore Park was broadly supported as a policy goal by the congressional delegation of Massachusetts and the New England Senators' Conference. However, the details of how this legislation would be implemented were hotly contested by the residents of several Cape Cod communities. Local governments were concerned about the loss of taxable private property to the federal government and increased traffic congestion, and local business interests believed that they were less likely to benefit from increased tourism because less land would be available for commercial purposes. Meanwhile, national interest groups, namely the Audubon Society, National Parks Association, and the Mellon Foundation, favored the establishment of a national seashore park and wanted it to serve as a role model for national seashore parks elsewhere in the nation.[160]

In July 1959, the Senate staffs of JFK and Leverett Saltonstall visited Cape Cod to conduct a survey. Congressional hearings were held on Cape Cod in 1959 and 1960.[161] On September 3, 1959, JFK and Saltonstall submitted enabling legislation with Representative Hastings Keith, a Republican whose district included Cape Cod. After describing the bill on the Senate floor, JFK optimistically concluded, "If we act sensibly now, while the opportunity remains, we shall have preserved for America and for her people a priceless heritage to be enjoyed many times over, not only by this generation but those which follow."[162]

This bill, however, died in the Senate. There were important differences between it and a national parks' bill sponsored by Senator Richard Neuberger of Oregon. There was also opposition by some residents of Cape Cod, especially in the town of Eastham. Unlike Neuberger's bill, the Kennedy-Saltonstall-Keith bill made boundary concessions to Eastham and created an advisory commission of Cape Cod residents to share governance of the national park with the U.S. Department of the Interior.

Despite these concessions, local opposition to a national seashore park on Cape Cod continued. The Kennedys owned houses in Hyannis Port and had vacationed there since the 1920s. Nevertheless, many full-time residents of Cape Cod towns still regarded the Kennedys as outsiders and interlopers who, according to freelance writer Leo Damore, "had never courted general popularity on Cape Cod until Jack's entry into politics."[163] Damore wrote that JFK's proposal to create a national park on Cape Cod's seashore had aroused "the bitterest controversy that had ever split the Cape."[164]

Congress held further hearings on a proposed national park for Cape Cod from December 1959 until March 1961. This issue persisted during JFK's 1960 presidential campaign. In February, 1961, Senator Benjamin A. Smith of Massachusetts, who was appointed to fill JFK's vacated Senate seat, joined Saltonstall in cosponsoring S.857, a revised bill to establish a national park on Cape Cod's seashore. In order to further reduce local opposition, the Saltonstall-Smith bill removed two of the three areas that the town government of Eastham wanted to be removed form a future national park.[165] In his testimony before a Senate subcommittee on public lands, Charles H. W. Foster, the Massachusetts commissioner of natural resources, stated that "the public interest to be served is regional and National rather than purely state or local."[166] Representative Hastings Keith testified that there was ultimately a compatibility between the national interest and "the way of Cape Cod" in protecting the natural resources of Cape Cod's seashore.[167]

On August 7, 1961, President John F. Kennedy signed S.857 into law. In his remarks, JFK elaborated on how the establishment of the Cape Cod National Seashore Park benefited not only Massachusetts but also New England and the entire nation. He added, "I must say that from personal knowledge I realize very well how useful this is going to be for the people of the Cape and Massachusetts and New England and the entire United States."[168] Four days before JFK signed S.857 into law, an editorial in the *Berkshire Eagle* referred to this bill as "the finest victory ever recorded for the cause of conservation in New England."[169]

When JFK ran for the Senate in 1952, he promised to protect and promote the economic policy interests of Massachusetts better than his opponent. Of course, it was not unusual for a Senate candidate to promise better constituency service than his opponent, especially if his opponent was an incumbent. It was unusual, though, for a newly elected senator to immediately connect his state's policy interests to those of his region in its relationship with the federal government on a bipartisan basis. JFK's establishment and chairmanship of the New England Senators' Conference helped JFK to develop both a regional and national reputation as a centrist, pragmatic senator who could work cooperatively with his fellow senators from New

England on a bipartisan basis. During his first two years as a senator, however, JFK confronted an issue which sharply divided the New England Senators' Conference, led him to break a campaign promise, and forced him to consider the differences between a senator serving the short-term interests of his state and region and the long-term interests of his nation. That issue was the St. Lawrence Seaway.

3

JFK and the St. Lawrence Seaway

DURING JOHN F. KENNEDY'S 1946 congressional campaign and 1952 Senate campaign, it seemed unlikely that the development of the St. Lawrence Seaway would become such a prominent issue in his Senate career and in his relationships with other members of Congress from New England, especially Senator Leverett Saltonstall of Massachusetts. As a congressman, JFK opposed the St. Lawrence Seaway partially because the conventional wisdom in the Boston area was that its construction threatened the jobs of longshoremen and railroad employees. During his 1952 Senate race in Massachusetts, both JFK and his Republican opponent, Senator Henry Cabot Lodge, Jr., promised to vote against the St. Lawrence Seaway because of its presumably detrimental impact on the Massachusetts economy in general and on the business and labor interests of Boston in particular. Furthermore, JFK's maternal grandfather and Lodge's paternal grandfather had distinguished themselves throughout their long political careers as persistent foes of the St. Lawrence Seaway.

Delivered on Mary 18, 1953, JFK's first Senate speech on the economic problems of New England briefly mentioned the potential of the St. Lawrence River for providing cheaper, more abundant electricity for New England's consumers and industries. He mentioned New York's recent application for a license from the Federal Power Commission (FPC) for the purpose of developing hydroelectric power with the Canadian province of Ontario. JFK concluded his statement on this topic by asserting, "It is not enough to respond that the power to be available from the proposed St. Lawrence project will only fill a small part of our area's needs; that is but further evidence of the importance of making provision for specific allocation of a sizable portion of such power output to New England, and for definite machinery giving New England its proper voice in all determinations affecting the distribution of such power."[1]

In this speech, JFK was careful to avoid elaborating on the controversial and divisive question of whether the United States government should cooperate with Canada in building a seaway that would enable large ships to navigate between the Atlantic Ocean and the Great Lakes. JFK was trying to define and promote himself as a regional advocate of New England's economic interests in the Senate. He would find it especially difficult to develop the fledgling New England Senators' Conference as an effective, cohesive organization if he immediately prioritized the St. Lawrence Seaway, which most of the region's senators opposed at that time.

Two prominent exceptions were Senator George D. Aiken of Vermont, a Republican, and Senator Theodore F. Green of Rhode Island, a Democrat. Aiken was a moderate, maverick Republican who was elected governor of Vermont in 1936 and senator in 1940. As lieutenant governor, he criticized the Roosevelt administration's proposals to build a federal highway around the Green Mountains and flood control dams along the Connecticut River in Vermont.[2] Aiken, however, was also a Republican who was influenced by Theodore Roosevelt's "Bull Moose" progressivism. He nationally criticized his fellow Republicans during the 1930s for not offering voters an attractive policy agenda as an alternative to the New Deal.[3]

During his early political career, Aiken had battled electric power companies. He accused them of giving Vermonters inadequate service at excessively and unfairly high rates. Thus, he favored the construction of the St. Lawrence Seaway. Aiken believed that the Seaway would generate enough hydroelectric power to provide cheaper, more abundant electricity to Vermonters and also provide cheaper transportation for midwestern farmers who sold grain to Vermont's dairy farmers.[4] Furthermore, Vermont is the only New England state that does not border the Atlantic Ocean. Unlike other New England senators, especially those from Massachusetts and Maine, Aiken did not face intense interest group pressure from constituents who feared major economic losses from the navigational aspect of the St. Lawrence Seaway.[5]

On September 28, 1943, Aiken submitted a bill that called for construction of the St. Lawrence Seaway with Canada after World War II.[6] Unfortunately for Aiken, his bill, an amendment to rivers and harbors legislation, was assigned to a Senate committee hostile to it. The Senate rejected it on December 12, 1944.[7]

Nevertheless, Aiken was determined to eventually achieve congressional approval of the St. Lawrence Seaway. On November 14, 1945, Aiken delivered a speech on the St. Lawrence Seaway in Boston, where it was especially unpopular. He referred to the recent economic survey of Massachusetts conducted by Joseph P. Kennedy (JPK) at the request of Governor Maurice Tobin. Like JFK's 1954 Senate speech favoring the St. Lawrence Seaway, Aiken's speech in Boston argued that the economy of New England in general and Massachusetts in particular would benefit from the construction of the St. Lawrence Seaway just as the entire nation's economy would benefit.[8] Aiken concluded, "When the St. Lawrence Seaway and Power Project is completed, we will all be proud of it for it will contribute immeasurably to our economic welfare and to our national safety."[9]

First elected to the Senate in 1936, Theodore F. Green was a member of an old, distinguished Yankee family that traced its New England roots to the colonial era. Unlike Aiken, Green did not become a vocal, major supporter of the St. Lawrence Seaway until the late 1940s and represented a state that had an extensive border on the Atlantic Ocean. Green's endorsement of the St. Lawrence Seaway was influenced by national security reasons cited by the Truman administration and the economic fact that it was unlikely that the commerce of Rhode Island's small harbors would be significantly harmed or reduced by the construction of the Seaway.[10]

By the time that JFK was elected to the Senate in 1952, American proponents of the St. Lawrence Seaway were repeatedly frustrated by their failure to achieve congressional approval of the Seaway despite the fact that every president since William H. Taft had supported it.[11] Three successive presidents, Herbert Hoover, Franklin

D. Roosevelt, and Harry S. Truman, were especially emphatic and persistent in their efforts to begin construction of the Seaway with Canada. On July 18, 1932, Hoover signed the St. Lawrence Deep Waterway Treaty with Canada.[12] This treaty did not include any provision for the development and generation of hydroelectric power, which Hoover regarded as a domestic issue. Roosevelt, then the governor of New York and Hoover's Democratic opponent in the 1932 presidential election, contended that the federal government should build and control hydroelectric power plants along the St. Lawrence River.[13]

The Seaway treaty languished in the Senate for the rest of 1932. On February 20, 1933, approximately one month before Roosevelt took office as president, Hoover urged the Senate to ratify the treaty. This was the second priority of his special message to Congress regarding pending legislation to promote economic recovery. Hoover stated, "The Great Lakes–St. Lawrence Treaty should be ratified. It not only will serve a great national purpose but is of importance now also to relieve unemployment by its construction."[14]

Busy with New Deal legislation, the Senate did not vote on ratification during its 1933 session. Roosevelt was aware that the Seaway was unpopular with southern Democratic members of Congress from coastal states, especially Texas and Louisiana. The Democratic president, therefore, waited until 1934 to publicly and formally encourage Congress to ratify the Seaway treaty. In a January 10, 1934 message to the Senate, Roosevelt detailed the economic benefits of the completion of the Seaway for cheaper, quicker transportation for agricultural, industrial, and mineral goods between the Great Lakes and the Atlantic Ocean; job creation during the Great Depression; and the future generation and distribution of cheaper, more abundant hydroelectric power. The economic claims were already familiar to Congress because of the lobbying and publicity efforts of pro-Seaway interest groups and public officials.

In this message, Roosevelt included another reason for ratification. Canada was already building dams, locks, canals, and hydroelectric plants on sections of the St. Lawrence River that it controlled exclusively. If the Senate rejected this treaty, then an "all-Canadian"

St. Lawrence Seaway would eventually be built. The United States would serve its national interests better if it cooperated with Canada in developing and regulating the international segments of the St. Lawrence River. The president stated, "I want to make it very clear that the great international highway for shipping is without any question going to be completed in the near future and that this completion should be carried out by both Nations instead of one."[15]

During a press conference on May 14, 1934, Roosevelt was asked if he thought that the Senate would ratify the Seaway treaty. Instead of answering this question directly, the president elaborated on the progress that Canada had already made on the Seaway and the inevitability of its completion. The president warned, "The thing is going through; perhaps not today, but the St. Lawrence Seaway is going to be built just as sure as God made little apples."[16] On that same day, the Senate rejected the treaty.

Because a two-thirds or greater majority in the Senate is required to ratify a treaty, it was unlikely that the Senate would eventually ratify the 1932 treaty or any similar Seaway treaty. The hydroelectric power aspect of the St. Lawrence River was also less controversial with Congress than the navigational aspect of the seaway. In his history of the St. Lawrence Seaway, Carleton Mabee wrote, "The New England manufacturing interests which hoped to use St. Lawrence power favored, but New England port interests opposed."[17] After Canada entered World War II in 1939 and the United States began its "lend lease" military aid policy, Roosevelt emphasized a national defense argument for developing more hydroelectric power along the St. Lawrence River, especially for producing aluminum for airplane manufacturing.

Despite the growing, imminent prospect of the United States entering World War II, it was still unlikely that Roosevelt could secure enough votes in the Senate to ratify a new treaty with Canada. Therefore, he signed an executive agreement with the prime minister of Canada on March 19, 1941. Since this was not a treaty, Roosevelt only needed simple majorities from both houses of Congress to authorize and finance the American role in this executive agreement. In his June 2, 1941 message to Congress, the president urged its authorization and funding to benefit the hydroelectric and navigational needs of defense manufacturing, shipbuilding in the ports of the Great Lakes, and the transportation of raw materials. Roosevelt concluded, "I know of no single project of this nature more important to this country's future in peace or war. Its authorization will demonstrate to the enemies of democracy that, however long the effort, we intend to outstrip them in the race of production."[18]

Roosevelt's request of Congress was bolstered by a survey of the economic effects of the St. Lawrence Seaway. It was published by the U.S. Department of Commerce in 1941. Part IV of this survey considered and refuted the argument that the completion and opening of the Seaway would harm the New England economy in general and that of Boston harbor in particular. In 1937, Boston harbor received only 6.4 percent of the tonnage in total U.S. imports and exports.[19] Furthermore, this 1941 study stated that, if the St. Lawrence Seaway were built, then railroad and truck traffic from the Midwest to Boston would actually increase. It confidently concluded, "Serving in this capacity as a gathering and distributing point for products using the Seaway in domestic commerce, Boston stands to gain in importance as a transportation center."[20]

After the United States entered World War II, Roosevelt used his expanded war-time powers to issue an executive order to authorize and finance construction of the St. Lawrence Seaway. The implementation of this executive order, however, was blocked by Undersecretary of War Robert Patterson and General Brehon B. Somervell. Patterson and Somervell claimed that there was not enough money in this special, discretionary fund to finance the Seaway project and that scarce, war-time construction funds, raw materials, and labor were needed for higher priority, more immediate defense projects.[21]

For the remainder of Roosevelt's presidency, the last major executive or legislative action promoting the St. Lawrence Seaway was Senator George D. Aiken's bill, which the Senate rejected in 1944. Fortunately for Aiken and other Seaway proponents, President Harry S. Truman was one of the senators who had voted for Aiken's legislation. With the implementation of the Marshall Plan, the development of collective security alliances like NATO, and the emergence of the Cold War, Truman emphasized both the short-term and long-term necessity of the St. Lawrence Seaway.[22] He also noted how World War II increased and highlighted the need for the United States and Canada to become more cooperative in their economic and defense interests. In an October 3, 1945 special message to Congress, Truman stated, "The experience of two wars and of many years of peace had shown beyond question that the prosperity and defense of Canada and of the United States are closely linked together."[23]

Legislative progress on Roosevelt's 1941 executive agreement was further complicated and delayed by partisan and campaign politics. After the Republicans won control of Congress in 1946, Representative Joseph W. Martin, Jr., of Massachusetts became Speaker of the House. In a January 26, 1948 letter to Martin urging congressional approval of Roosevelt's 1941 executive agreement, Truman concluded, "I am personally convinced of the need for this project both from the standpoint of our common economic welfare and of our national security."[24] Martin's district, however, included ports in New Bedford and Fall River. Martin's staunch opposition to the St. Lawrence Seaway was bolstered by a bipartisan coalition of northeastern Republicans and southern Democrats in Congress.

Senator Arthur H. Vandenberg of Michigan, a pro-Seaway Republican, chaired the Senate Foreign Relations Committee from 1947 to 1949. However, Senator Thomas T. Connally of Texas, an anti-Seaway Democrat, was the ranking minority member and Vandenberg's successor as chairman. In May 1947, Vandenberg introduced Senate Resolution (S.J.) 111, which focused on the use of tolls to finance the construction and maintenance of the American portion of the St. Lawrence Seaway, if Congress eventually authorized it. The Senate Foreign Relations Committee then referred S.J. 111 to a subcommittee chaired by Senator Alexander Wiley of Wisconsin, a pro-Seaway Republican.

Advocacy of the Seaway for national defense was unexpectedly undermined by the testimony of Truman's undersecretary of war, Kenneth Royal. In his testimony before Wiley's subcommittee, Royal stated that the development of the Seaway's hydroelectric power and transportation purposes would be helpful but was not essential to national defense.[25] The most powerful and persuasive arguments against the Seaway before Wiley's subcommittee were presented by Senators Leverett Saltonstall and Henry Cabot Lodge, Jr., of Massachusetts. Besides asserting that it would be unfair to expect New England tax payers to subsidize a transportation project detrimental to the port of Boston and railroads in their region, they claimed that the St. Lawrence Seaway's locks and dams would be vulnerable to enemy bombing raids, especially with the invention of atomic bombs.[26] Saltonstall suggested that national security would be better served by improving existing ports, instead of spending money on a Seaway that would often be frozen during the winter and would not be deep enough for the heaviest, most modern ships.

Saltonstall also expressed doubts that tolls would be enough to finance the Seaway and that inevitably tax revenue from the general treasury would be needed to subsidize it. He stated, "As a New England Yankee, I have always agreed with the principle of having the direct benefactors of any project pay for all of its construction costs, but I just wonder whether anyone has enough up-to-date factual knowledge of construction costs and transportation patterns in these rapidly changing times to give assurance that the St. Lawrence Seaway can be self-liquidating."[27] Likewise, Lodge testified that building the St. Lawrence Seaway and protecting it militarily would be a waste of limited defense funds and personnel.[28]

Henry Foley and Frank Davis also testified against S.J. 111. Foley was the counsel for the New England Project Conference. Foley stated, "For Boston and New England, the port's share in traffic westward is vital. If Boston and New England are to survive economically, we cannot afford to lose many thousands of tons."[29] Davis was a member of the Boston Chamber of Commerce. Davis contended that the Port of Boston had served the nation's defense well during World War II and could continue to do so if Congress appropriated enough funds for its improvement and modernization. Davis concluded, "We have many instances in New England of important approved waterways and similar projects that are not being properly maintained because the War Department is not being provided with funds to do the work."[30]

Shortly after the Wiley subcommittee's hearings on S.J. 111 ended on June 20, 1947, the Association of American Railroads published an anti-Seaway booklet entitled *The Great Delusion*. It referred to and elaborated on the testimony of the above Seaway opponents. It also provided extensive statistics to contend that the proposed tolls would be insufficient to build and maintain the Seaway.[31] *The Great Delusion* also used statistics to argue that American railroads had proven their ability to transport a sharp increase in defense-related freight during World War II. According to *The Great Delusion*, "Besides being a doubtfully justified expenditure of a huge amount of public funds, at a time when the financial state of the nation is such that the Congress has spent many weeks of intense study in trying to find ways of cutting the Federal budget, the construction of this proposed waterway would be a detriment to many segments of our national economy."[32] Released on April 15, 1947, the majority report of the Wiley subcommittee advised the Senate Foreign Relations Committee to recommend that the full Senate pass S.J. 111. This committee accepted the subcommittee's majority report and its recommendation. However, it also decided to wait until the first week of the 1948 session to report it to the Senate in order to give the minority enough time to prepare its report.[33]

After the subcommittee's majority and minority reports were filed on January 7, 1948, senators delivered speeches for or against S.J. 111 from late January until late February. Anti-Seaway speeches outnumbered pro-Seaway speeches with Senator Henry Cabot Lodge, Jr., leading the opposition with a speech that lasted nearly four hours.[34] In a January 13, 1948 letter to Senator Robert A. Taft of Ohio, Senator Leverett Saltonstall thanked Taft for "being willing to read a short statement of mine in opposition to the St. Lawrence Seaway as a navigational artery."[35]

On February 23, 1948, Saltonstall issued a press release citing his fourteen reasons for opposing the St. Lawrence Seaway in general and S.J. 111 in particular. Saltonstall specified that he opposed the navigational aspect of the Seaway but not the hydroelectric power aspect of it. Most of Saltonstall's reasons emphasized the engineering and financing of the Seaway.[36] It was only on the last page of

Saltonstall's press release that he mentioned the detrimental economic impact on the Port of Boston as his twelfth reason. "According to Boston Port Authority officials, this port, if the seaway generates the traffic claimed, may well suffer a direct seaway loss each year of over 700,000 tons of cargo and an indirect loss of 100,000 tons."[37]

Four days after Saltonstall's press release, the Senate voted to recommit S.J. 111 to the Senate Foreign Relations Committee. This action effectively buried S.J. 111 and the Seaway issue in the Senate for the rest of 1948. The hydroelectric power dimension of the Seaway issue and the upcoming 1948 presidential campaign, however, soon revived the St. Lawrence Seaway as a contentious political issue. Governor Thomas E. Dewey of New York, the presumptive and eventual Republican nominee for president in 1948, sought an agreement with the Canadian province of Ontario to develop and distribute hydroelectric power along the International Rapids section of the St. Lawrence River. In order to reduce interest group opposition from private utility companies, Dewey and the New York Power Authority were willing to allow future hydroelectric power from this source to be sold by private utility companies as long as consumers were adequately protected.[38]

Regardless of how much Dewey wanted to deal directly with Ontario, New York and Ontario needed to obtain permission from the International Joint Commission (IJC) in order to change the depth of the river in the International Rapids section. Also, New York needed to apply for and receive a license from the Federal Power Commission (FPC).[39] Despite Dewey's prompt action in seeking permission from both commissions in the spring and summer of 1948, New York's application to both commissions languished for the remainder of 1948.

During the 1948 presidential campaign, Truman announced his opposition to Dewey's hydroelectric plan and insisted that Congress pass the 1941 executive agreement with Canada so that all Americans could eventually benefit from the development of both hydroelectric power and navigation from the Atlantic Ocean to the Great Lakes. In an October 13, 1948 speech in Duluth, Minnesota, Truman implied that he sought to protect and promote the national interest in the St.

Lawrence Seaway while his Republican opponent catered to "special interests." Truman stated, "I pledge to you that as President I shall continue to fight for the development of the resources of this great area and for the full development of the St. Lawrence Seaway and Power Project. I will not compromise with special interests, as some candidates for office are doing by supporting just the electric power development of the St. Lawrence at the expense of the Seaway."[40]

Truman's combative, partisan rhetoric in criticizing Dewey's hydroelectric power proposal with Ontario, his upset victory in the 1948 presidential election, and the return of Congress to Democratic control seemed to harden Republican opposition in New England to the development of the St. Lawrence River for both electric power and navigational purposes. An exception to this political trend was the expression of support for the St. Lawrence Seaway project from George M. Putnam, the 84-year-old president of the New Hampshire Farm Bureau. Affectionately known as "Uncle George," Putnam was a Yankee Republican who was popular and influential among New Hampshire's farmers.

Two weeks after the 1948 presidential and congressional elections, Putnam issued a statement from his hospital bed in Concord, New Hampshire. He urged his fellow members of the New Hampshire Farm Bureau "to bring into reality the St. Lawrence Seaway."[41] Like Senator George D. Aiken of Vermont, Putnam emphasized the potential for cheaper electricity and midwestern grain for New Hampshire's farmers. Of New Hampshire's two Republican senators, Charles Tobey supported the Seaway project while Styles Bridges continued to oppose it.[42]

In his annual message to Congress delivered on January 5, 1949, Truman again urged Congress to approve the St. Lawrence Seaway project for both power and navigation purposes. He sardonically noted that this was the fifth time that he asked Congress to approve it.[43] Unfortunately for Truman, the Democratic-controlled 81st Congress was no more likely to authorize and finance the 1941 executive agreement than the Republican-controlled 80th Congress had been. The bipartisan majority in Congress opposing the St. Lawrence Seaway as a dual purpose project, especially in the Senate, continued.

Furthermore, Senator Thomas T. Connally of Texas, an anti-Seaway Democrat, succeeded Senator Arthur H. Vandenberg of Michigan, a pro-Seaway Republican, as chairman of the Senate Foreign Relations Committee.

One of the economic and national defense arguments that Seaway advocates had advanced was the recent discovery of large iron ore deposits in the Canadian region of Labrador and the depletion of iron ore deposits in the Mesabi region of the American Midwest. They contended that the Seaway could move large amounts of iron ore from Labrador to American steel mills in the Midwest more quickly and cheaply than railroads. Greater efficiency in the transportation of iron ore would be especially beneficial, if not essential, during wartime when steel production rapidly increased.[44]

Some New England opponents of the St. Lawrence Seaway now claimed that if the Seaway was not built then American steel companies would be motivated to relocate some of their factories to New England in order to be geographically closer to Labrador's iron ore. An article by Edward Haley in the November 18, 1949 issue of the *Harvard Crimson* expressed the hope that by the early 1950s newly built steel mills in New England could provide enough new jobs to partially compensate for the large number of jobs lost in the region's textile and shoe industries. Haley surmised, "With the steel mill proposal, will come a redoubled effort on the part of New England businessmen to block the St. Lawrence Seaway. If the ore from Labrador could travel down the St. Lawrence to the Great Lake ports, the geographical advantage of a New England steel mill would be materially diminished."[45]

By 1950, public opinion in Canada had become overwhelmingly favorable toward construction of the St. Lawrence Seaway for both hydroelectric and navigational purposes.[46] Canadians also became increasingly frustrated and impatient with either the refusal or inability of Congress to approve the 1941 executive agreement and of the Federal Power Commission (FPC) to issue a license for New York to cooperate with Ontario in a joint hydroelectric power system.[47] Public opinion in Canada was reflected in the policy behavior and public statements of national and provincial politicians in Canada.

Lionel Chevrier, Canada's minister of transport from 1945 to 1954, expressed this position in his 1959 book, *The St. Lawrence Seaway*. He wrote, "As Canadians, we were unanimous that the seaway must be built. If we determined to go ahead alone, the U.S. might be stirred into action."[48]

In several speeches from 1950 to 1951, Chevrier and Canadian prime minister Louis St. Laurent promoted the feasibility of an "all-Canadian" Seaway. American opponents of the Seaway dismissed the bold Canadian proposal as an unrealistic bluff, and the U.S. House of Representatives tabled a pro-Seaway bill during the summer of 1951. Undaunted by American opposition, the Canadian parliament passed legislation that created a St. Lawrence Seaway Authority and gave this agency the power to either build and manage an all-Canadian Seaway or cooperate with the United States in a joint Seaway project in December, 1951.[49]

A few months before this action by the Canadian parliament, St. Laurent traveled to the White House to confer with Truman on the prospect of an all-Canadian Seaway. Truman empathized with St. Laurent about his frustrations with the U.S. Congress's inability or unwillingness to approve the 1941 executive agreement and other pro-Seaway legislation. The U.S. president promised the Canadian prime minister that he was willing to support an entirely Canadian-built navigational waterway and American participation in hydroelectric power if Congress did not approve of a jointly built and managed, dual purpose Seaway in the near future.[50]

In a January 28, 1952 special message to Congress on the St. Lawrence Seaway, Truman mentioned his meeting with St. Laurent and the legislation passed by the Canadian parliament. He also repeated the reasons that he had previously stated in urging Congress to pass the 1941 executive agreement: cheaper and more abundant electricity, the need to transport iron ore more cheaply and quickly from Labrador to the Midwest, national security, and a closer, more cooperative relationship with Canada. He added new reasons, namely, the weakening of national pride if the United States did not participate in this major historic project and of national sovereignty if Canada exerted complete control over locks and tolls. The president concluded, "It seems inconceivable to me, now that this project is on the eve of accomplishment, that the Congress should allow any local or special interest to divest our country of its rightful place in the joint development of the St. Lawrence River in the interest of all the people of the United States."[51]

During the first few months of 1952, Truman fulfilled his promise to St. Laurent to support Canada's application to the International Joint Commission (IJC) for a license to develop hydroelectric power in the International Rapids section of the St. Lawrence River. Meanwhile, Congress delayed any significant action on pro-Seaway legislation until June, 1952. On June 18, 1952, the Senate approved a motion to recommit a pro-Seaway bill to the Senate Foreign Relations Committee by a vote of 43 to 40. This motion was sponsored by Senator Herbert O'Conor of Maryland, an anti-Seaway Democrat, and the Senate Foreign Relations Committee was still chaired by Senator Thomas T. Connally of Texas, an especially fervent opponent of the St. Lawrence Seaway.[52] The Senate's approval of O'Conor's motion effectively killed any possibility of congressional approval of the 1941 executive agreement for the remainder of Truman's presidency.

Nevertheless, there was some hope for Seaway supporters in the Senate vote on O'Conor's motion. The Senate rejected favorable action on a dual purpose Seaway project with Canada by a very narrow margin, and a larger proportion of Democrats supported the Seaway compared to previous Senate action on the Seaway. The increased Democratic support seemed to be generated by aggressive lobbying by Truman administration officials, including Secretary of State Dean Acheson, concern that the increased steel and aluminum production required by the Korean War proved the necessity of the Seaway for both transportation and electric power purposes, and the persuasive, pro-Seaway lobbying of N. R. Danielian, executive vice-president of the Great Lakes-St. Lawrence Association.[53] A 1951 booklet published by Danielian's organization ominously stated, "The need for the Seaway is not ordinary and the added security it promises may be even more crucial tomorrow than today. It is a necessary component of the mobilization of the Heartland for continental defense."[54]

During his 1952 presidential campaign, it was uncertain if Dwight D. Eisenhower would be as fervent and emphatic in his support of the 1941 executive agreement as Roosevelt and Truman had been. When he was army chief of staff, Eisenhower had supported the Seaway for national security reasons. As a presidential candidate, he had sent a message to Senator Edward Thye of Minnesota, a pro-Seaway Republican, stating that he preferred American participation in the Seaway to an all-Canadian Seaway. Eisenhower, however, avoided making any specific commitment on the Seaway issue in his campaign speeches.

Furthermore, Seaway opponents were heartened by Eisenhower's frequent campaign promises to reduce federal spending if elected president, especially on water and power projects.[55] Eisenhower's economic philosophy included an aversion to government-sponsored, tax-subsidized, TVA-style hydroelectric power projects that competed with private enterprise. In his study of the Dixon-Yates controversy, political scientist Aaron Wildavsky wrote, "During the presidential election campaign of 1952, candidate Eisenhower rejected any notion that the nation was dependent upon the federal government for its power needs."[56]

After Dwight D. Eisenhower became president in January 1953, some of his top advisers and incoming administration officials were New England Republicans who were either definitely or presumably opponents of the St. Lawrence Seaway.[57] They included Henry Cabot Lodge, Jr., the head of Eisenhower's transition team who soon became U.S. Ambassador to the UN, Secretary of Commerce Sinclair Weeks, and White House chief of staff Sherman Adams. Moreover, anti-Seaway New England Republicans in the Republican-controlled 83rd Congress included Speaker of the House Joseph W. Martin, Jr., Senator Leverett Saltonstall as chairman of the Senate Armed Services Committee, and Senator Styles Bridges of New Hampshire as chairman of the Senate Appropriations Committee.[58] Thus, when Senator Alexander Wiley of Wisconsin, a pro-Seaway Republican and the new chairman of the Senate Foreign Relations Committee, informed Eisenhower that he would sponsor pro-Seaway legislation, the president merely replied that he would consider it.[59]

To Congress, Canada, and the American public, the recently inaugurated president seemed evasive, indecisive, and possibly dismissive about the St. Lawrence Seaway. During a press conference on February 25, 1953, Eisenhower stated that he could not reveal his "attitude" about the Seaway to the press and was still studying the issue. He added, "There are so many controversial factors, and they seem to vary geographically as to their content, that I just think it takes a longer time than I have had to reach a decision."[60] Likewise, at his March 5, 1953 press conference, Eisenhower stated that his administration was not prepared "to give a complete blessing or to abandon" the Seaway project.[61] Two weeks later, he told the press that "if the St. Lawrence Seaway is really an economic necessity for the United States, eventually it is going to be built, and there is just nothing that my attitude for the moment could do to prevent it."[62]

The fact, however, was that Eisenhower and his cabinet had been privately conducting a vigorous debate on the St. Lawrence Seaway. Advocates of American participation in a dual purpose Seaway project included Secretary of the Treasury George Humphrey, Secretary of State John Foster Dulles, and, surprisingly, Secretary of Commerce Sinclair Weeks. Weeks had previously served as Republican state chairman in Massachusetts.[63] In a memo summarizing a March 30, 1953 cabinet meeting on the St. Lawrence Seaway, Eisenhower concluded, "If there is general concurrence with this attitude, I should like for Senator Taft and Mr. Martin, upon leaving this conference, to announce that the Administration definitely favors the general plan described in the Wiley Bill and will support it."[64]

The Wiley bill was later matched with similar pro-Seaway legislation in the House of Representatives that was sponsored by Representative George Dondero, a Republican from Michigan. After learning of Eisenhower's support for the Seaway, Speaker of the House Joseph W. Martin, Jr. politely yet firmly informed the president that he would not vote for the Dondero bill or organize support for it. Martin wrote in his autobiography, "Even when one is the President's leader in the House of Representatives, one has to consider the interests of one's own people now and then."[65]

Senator Robert A. Taft of Ohio, the Republican majority leader during the first six months of 1953, had previously opposed American participation in the Seaway project. He often cited budgetary reasons and the interests of Ohio farmers for his opposition.[66] Taft's responsibilities as Senate majority leader and as a member of the Senate Foreign Relations Committee and Wiley's contention that his bill was more likely to make the American cost of Seaway construction self-liquidating and less burdensome to American tax payers than previous pro-Seaway bills influenced Taft's decision to eventually support the Seaway.[67] Unfortunately for Seaway advocates, Taft died of cancer before Congress voted on the Wiley-Dondero legislation in 1954.

In a letter to Wiley that he publicly released on April 24, 1953, Eisenhower stated that the National Security Council (NSC) had recommended "that the United States participate in the construction of the Seaway."[68] On March 8, 1953, Eisenhower's cabinet announced that it also recommended that the United States participate in the construction and operation of the St. Lawrence Seaway. Four days later, the Federal Power Commission (FPC) ruled in favor of New York's request for a license to develop hydroelectric power on the St. Lawrence River with Canada, a decision which Eisenhower had previously and publicly discouraged.[69]

Opponents of the Seaway were aroused by Eisenhower's support of the Wiley bill. After learning that John J. Holloran, director of the Boston Port Authority, was preparing to testify against the St. Lawrence Seaway, Governor Christian A. Herter of Massachusetts, a Republican, asked Holloran to include anti-Seaway opinions. Herter told Holloran, "As a member of Congress for ten years, I have consistently taken the position that the construction of the Seaway represented a tremendous expenditure of money in which all the country would be obliged to share, including New England, and the returns from the investment were of doubtful value except to a small segment of the country."[70] Herter carefully informed Holloran that he opposed the navigational purpose of the Seaway while backing its electric power purpose. Paul T. Rothwell, president of the Boston Chamber of Commerce, however, bluntly stated in an earlier press release that his organization opposed both purposes because "the proponents of a St. Lawrence Waterway and hydro-electric power project have no case."[71]

Thomas P. "Tip" O'Neill, Jr. succeeded JFK as the U.S. representative for the eleventh congressional district of Massachusetts. His office was inundated with letters and telegrams opposing the St. Lawrence Seaway. In a 1953 letter to the president of the Boston and Maine Railroad, O'Neill wrote, "As a Representative from New England, I am violently opposed to the Seaway and you may depend upon my best efforts as a Member of the National Legislature to prevent favorable action in the House of Representatives."[72] The Boston Chamber of Commerce stated to the congressman, "We view this project as a national liability rather than an asset," and warned him that the construction of the Seaway would be "a crippling blow to the port of Boston and the economic life of the surrounding area."[73] Maurice O'Connor, one of O'Neill's constituents, told O'Neill that the St. Lawrence Seaway "would seriously damage other New England industries and the port of Boston."[74]

Of course, not all of the correspondence that Tip O'Neill received opposed the Seaway. N. R. Danielian, executive vice president of the Great Lakes–St. Lawrence Association, mailed a pro-Seaway economic analysis and expressed his hope that the congressman would not be "misled by much propaganda and inspired by unfounded fear that their jobs are in jeopardy" because "many well-meaning industrial and labor leaders, particularly those connected with the railroad, coal, and utility industries, have tried to secure commitments from members of Congress to oppose this project."[75] Likewise, James Luchini, the Washington lobbyist for a Massachusetts construction company, expressed his company's support for the Seaway. Luchini told O'Neill "that New England must shed reactionary tendencies. We are still part of a great economy, and in the past have been a major source of our nation's internal development."[76] Another Seaway supporter from Massachusetts expressed his belief to O'Neill that construction of the St. Lawrence Seaway "will induce Massachusetts, as well as the other five states in the New England bloc, to undertake the job of tackling their own resources problems which they have delayed doing for so many years."[77]

Despite such evidence that public support for the Seaway in Massachusetts grew modestly yet steadily in early 1954, Tip O'Neill remained a staunch opponent of it. In the rough draft of a speech opposing the Seaway, O'Neill stated that, besides being "a threat to the Port of Boston," the St. Lawrence Seaway would be closed five months of the year because of ice and "would be very vulnerable to attack during a war."[78] O'Neill joined eleven of the fourteen U.S. representatives from Massachusetts in voting against the pro-Seaway Dondero bill on May 6, 1954. The two Massachusetts congressmen who voted for the St. Lawrence Seaway were Democrat Edward Boland and Republican John Heselton. Boland and Heselton represented districts in western Massachusetts.[79] Boland and Heselton joined a solid majority of U.S. representatives who passed the Dondero bill by a vote of 241 to 158.[80]

Where was Senator John F. Kennedy during the prolonged, tortuous, byzantine process of the Wiley-Dondero legislation being formulated, contested, and promoted? During his first year in the Senate, JFK quietly researched and developed his own pro-Seaway position. As early as 1952 when JFK was still a congressman, a Senate candidate, and an apparent opponent of the St. Lawrence Seaway, a pro-Seaway interest group predicted that JFK would vote for pro-Seaway legislation if elected to the Senate.[81] Furthermore, Theodore C. Sorensen, who served as JFK's principal policy researcher, adviser, and speech writer in 1953 and 1954, was from Nebraska. He lacked the reflexive, innate hostility of many coastal Bay Staters toward the St. Lawrence Seaway.

While Sorensen was helping JFK to develop his series of 1953 Senate speeches and policy proposals, he told JFK that there was a contradiction between the senator's explicit advocacy of cheaper hydroelectric power for New England industries and his presumed opposition to pro-Seaway legislation. Such legislation would facilitate cooperation with Canada for providing new sources of hydroelectric power for New York and New England.[82] Although he was impressed by this argument, JFK still did not reveal to Sorensen how he would vote on the Wiley bill and directed Sorensen to continue researching the facts and arguments on both sides of the Seaway issue.[83]

In notes that he wrote to himself regarding the Seaway issue, JFK summarized various facts from federal surveys about how the opening of the Seaway would affect all U.S. ports, including Boston. He also noted lingering questions, such as "10. What could we get from the middle west that would be cheaper. [sic]" and the eventual costs to the federal government of not only building the St. Lawrence Seaway but also the deepening of ports on the Great Lakes.[84]

In these undated notes, JFK also wrote that he wanted to "9. Get Seymour Harris' statements on the St. Lawrence."[85] Harris, a Harvard economist, was a major scholarly influence on JFK's 1953 speeches on the New England economy and on *The Economic State of New England*. This report documented the fact that, even without the completion of the St. Lawrence Seaway, cargo traffic in the port of Boston had been sharply declining since the 1930s.[86] In his 1952 book, *The Economics of New England*, Harris claimed that the arguments of New England opponents of the Seaway were often exaggerated and sometimes fallacious. Harris concluded that he and his fellow New Englanders "cannot afford to be unreceptive to government projects, too large for construction by private interests, and we cannot afford to be unreceptive when the government offers the region cheaper power and transportation."[87]

Likewise, *The Economic State of New England* contended that improving the future of New England's economy depended less on seeking federal intervention to help inexorably declining industries, like textiles and shoes, or preventing completion of the St. Lawrence Seaway, and more on modernizing industrial management and making the region's economy more attractive to investors. It cited a study of New England management by a consulting firm. "Where the consultants felt New England as a whole to be deficient in some respects, the deficiency singled out was almost always excessive conservatism or lack of aggressiveness rather than administrative incompetence."[88]

Thus, elite academic and business opinion in New England by the early 1950s seemed to be either favorable to or ambivalent about the completion of the St. Lawrence Seaway. This suggested that general public opinion in Massachusetts may have become less monolithically hostile toward the St. Lawrence Seaway. In his 1965 account of his relationship with JFK, Theodore C. Sorensen noted that Kennedy seemed fatalistic about delivering a Senate floor speech revealing that he would vote for the pro-Seaway Wiley bill. Sorensen wrote, "A quiet vote of opposition would have received no attention. But he was determined to represent the national interest, and he had told his constituents that a provincial outlook would only continue their neglect by the rest of the country. Still he hesitated."[89]

In his Senate speech of January 14, 1954, JFK announced that he would vote for the construction and completion of the St. Lawrence Seaway.[90] He contended that continued American opposition to the Seaway was futile since Canada was determined to complete its construction with or without the participation of the United States. More importantly, JFK argued that he and other senators should base their votes on the Seaway according to a shared, long-term national interest in economic development and national security instead of pressures to serve immediate local and regional interests. In the conclusion of his speech, Kennedy asserted that his vote for the St. Lawrence Seaway was consistent with his 1953 speeches seeking greater national attention to and federal help for New England's economic problems. He stated that "it has been this arbitrary refusal of many New Englanders to recognize the legitimate needs and aspirations of other sections which has contributed to the neglect of, and even opposition to, the needs of our region by the representatives of other areas. We cannot continue so narrow and destructive a position."[91]

On January 20, 1954, the Senate voted 51 to 32 to pass the Wiley bill.[92] Despite speculation that most of New England's twelve senators would vote against the St. Lawrence Seaway, a narrow majority of them, by a margin of 7 to 5, voted for it. The seven supporters were JFK, Senators John Pastore and Theodore Green of Rhode Island, Senators Margaret Chase Smith and Frederick Payne of Maine, Senator Robert Upton of New Hampshire, and Senator George Aiken of Vermont. Among the five opponents, Senator Styles

Bridges of New Hampshire did not vote on the Wiley bill but was later paired in opposition to it.[93]

In explaining his vote for the Seaway, Senator Payne referred to national security and the self-liquidating formula for financing its construction.[94] By contrast, Senator Smith vaguely and evasively stated to the press that her vote "speaks for itself" and refused to elaborate.[95] Smith's vote for the St. Lawrence Seaway legislation was perhaps more surprising than JFK's. She was expected to face a tough primary campaign in 1954 because of her outspoken criticism of Senator Joseph R. McCarthy of Wisconsin.[96] In its 1952 analysis of how senators were expected to vote on the St. Lawrence Seaway, a pro-Seaway interest group noted that Margaret Chase Smith "does not feel right about her vote [in opposition] and that she is not hopeless."[97]

Senator George D. Aiken of Vermont was the earliest and most prominent advocate of the St. Lawrence Seaway among New England's senators. He stated in a 1964 interview that he was somewhat surprised and impressed by JFK's support for the Seaway. Aiken said, "When President Kennedy voted for the construction of the Seaway, and the Power Project, that, I think, was the first time I realized that he had a great deal of courage, because he was voting against the desires of influential people in his own community and his own state."[98]

Senator Leverett Saltonstall and Representative Thomas P. "Tip" O'Neill, Jr., voted against the St. Lawrence Seaway. In their autobiographies, their analyses of JFK's vote for the Seaway were far less laudatory than Aiken's. They attributed JFK's vote for the St. Lawrence Seaway to his growing national political ambition because of the overwhelming support for the Seaway among Democrats in the Midwest. Saltonstall stated that JFK "voted that way because he needed the Midwest vote."[99] Likewise, O'Neill wrote, "I knew Jack was serious about running for president back in 1954, when he mentioned that he intended to vote for the St. Lawrence Seaway project."[100]

The constituent mail that JFK received following his January 14 speech was mixed, with anti-Seaway mail slightly outnumbering pro-Seaway mail. A sales manager for a real estate office in Brockton told JFK, "By your actions you are undermining the economics of all the New England states, and more particularly the port of Boston, together with all those employed in the overland transportation and waterfront operations."[101] Another constituent wrote that "your views are disappointing to me," and an editorial in in the *Boston Post* accused JFK of "ruining New England" by voting for the Seaway.[102]

JFK and his staff, however, were surprised by the number of Massachusetts residents who supported JFK's vote for the Seaway. A man from West Roxbury wrote, "You have reason to be proud that you have placed the nation's interests above that of your state—but in so doing you have gained in stature yourself." A dentist from Waltham wrote, "As a 'very' independent Republican, I wish to congratulate you in your courage and independence of thought regarding the St. Lawrence waterway proposal."[103] Likewise, in a letter to "Tip" O'Neill, a Massachusetts man stated, "In our opinion, Senator John F. Kennedy thoroughly demolished the notion that has been drummed into the ears of New England for years by rail and utility propagandists that the Seaway would take away trade from the Port of Boston."[104]

On January 23, 1954, a few days after JFK voted for the St. Lawrence Seaway, he spoke at the Jefferson-Jackson Day dinner in Boston. James Michael Curley spoke before Kennedy did. Although the former mayor of Boston did not refer to JFK by name, Curley criticized Senate supporters of the St. Lawrence Seaway as "misguided."[105] In his remarks introducing Governor G. Mennen "Soapy" Williams of Michigan, JFK did not directly respond to Curley or mention the Seaway issue. But he did state that he and his fellow Massachusetts Democrats "are proud of our independence and we intend to maintain it regardless of what others may say or write about us."[106] JFK then quoted the eighteenth-century British statesman Edmund Burke about the need of public officials to endure "the most grievous disappointments, the most shocking results, and what is worst of all, the presumptuous judgment, of the ignorant upon their actions."[107]

Since he had been a college student and visited London during his father's ambassadorship, JFK had been attracted to British political ideas and rhetoric, especially those of Burke, John Buchan, and Winston Churchill. Buchan was a Scottish nobleman, member of Parliament, and governor-general of Canada. JFK often referred to Buchan's book, *Pilgrim's Way*, as his favorite book. In *Pilgrim's Way*, Buchan wrote, "My years in Parliament left me a more convinced believer than ever in democracy, but convinced, too, that the democratic technique wanted overhauling."[108] Like JFK, Buchan quoted Burke to substantiate his opinion.

JFK also greatly admired Winston Churchill's eloquence and political courage, especially in his speeches and writings that provided unpopular yet prescient warnings about Nazi Germany's military buildup and territorial aggression during the 1930s.[109] In the introduction of his first book, *Why England Slept*, JFK readily admitted that Churchill's book, *While England Slept*, influenced his decision to research and write about this topic for his senior thesis at Harvard.[110] Throughout *Why England Slept*, JFK periodically noted the difficulty of a democracy to significantly increase defense spending during peace time when such a policy is unpopular and controversial with voters and most elected officials. He concluded, "Any system of government will work when everything is going well. It's the system that functions in the pinches that survives."[111]

Even before JFK delivered his speech announcing his decision to vote for the St. Lawrence Seaway, he had been pondering the challenge that senators confronted in supporting legislation that they believe benefited the long-term national interest, despite the fact that most of their constituents opposed this same legislation as detrimental to their interests. In a December 2, 1953 speech at Northeastern University's convocation in Boston, JFK spoke dismissively about some senators who "vote to appease political pressures at home and stay in office."[112] He spoke more favorably about senators who, like the recently deceased Senator Robert A. Taft of Ohio, "vote according to their convictions."[113] Kennedy contended that "the only way to national survival" is for citizens to support Burke's idea that legislators should do what they believe is best for the national good, even when such a perspective conflicts with local interests.[114] JFK concluded this speech with a quote from Daniel Webster. As a famous nineteenth-century senator from Massachusetts, Webster outraged many of his constituents for supporting the 1850 compromise on slavery.

Despite the controversy over whether JFK was the exclusive or even principal author of *Profiles in Courage*, JFK had been contemplating the issues of leadership, political courage, and representation since he was a college student.[115] In the preface of *Profiles in Courage*, JFK readily expressed appreciation to several people for helping him to research, write, and prepare this book for publication. He especially thanked Theodore C. Sorensen. JFK wrote, "The greatest debt is owed to my research associate, Theodore C. Sorensen, for his invaluable assistance in the assembly and preparation of the material upon which this book is based."[116]

In a 1964 interview with historian Arthur M. Schlesinger, Jr., Jacqueline Kennedy complained that Sorensen conveyed the impression that he wrote *Profiles in Courage*. She also claimed that her husband arranged for Sorensen to receive the royalties from this book.[117] Sorensen, however, wrote in his 2008 autobiography, "Following the furor over the authorship of *Profiles in Courage*, I had been exceedingly careful never to claim authorship and always to minimize my role."[118]

Perhaps the chapter in *Profiles in Courage* that was most relevant to JFK's experiences and development as a congressman and senator was the chapter on John Quincy Adams. Like Adams, JFK had a famous, politically powerful father and was initially expected to reflect his father's political and economic beliefs and opinions. Furthermore, Joseph P. Kennedy, like John Adams, encouraged his son's increasingly independent rhetoric and voting behavior on national legislation. As a senator, John Quincy Adams became unpopular with his constituents in Massachusetts for supporting President Thomas Jefferson's policies regarding the Louisiana Purchase and a trade embargo against Great Britain. JFK wrote that Adams "resigned his seat in the Senate in order to defend the policies of the man who had driven his father from the Presidency."[119]

Historian Herbert C. Parmet conducted an exhaustive investigation of primary sources at the John F. Kennedy Library and interviews with Theodore C. Sorensen in 1977.[120] Parmet concluded that JFK was not the primary or exclusive author of *Profiles in Courage* and that he deceptively underestimated the roles of Sorensen and others in helping him to research and write the book in his public statements.[121] Especially after JFK won a Pulitzer Price for *Profiles in Courage* in 1957, the public recognition and political assets that JFK gained because of this book were "as deceptive as installing a Chevrolet engine in a Cadillac," according to Parmet.[122] He characterized JFK's role in *Profiles in Courage* as primarily that "of an overseer or, more charitably, as a sponsor and editor, one whose final approval was as important for its publication as for its birth."[123]

While providing JFK with national recognition, the best-selling, Pulitzer Prize-winning status of *Profiles in Courage* also proved to be a minor yet lingering nuisance for JFK. Columnist Drew Pearson stated in a televised interview that *Profiles in Courage* was ghostwritten. Pearson reluctantly retracted this statement only after JFK threatened a lawsuit through Clark M. Clifford, an influential Washington, DC, attorney and former White House aide in the Truman administration.[124]

Liberal critics of JFK and his increasingly apparent presidential ambition, such as Eleanor Roosevelt, charged that JFK's cautious, calculating, self-serving legislative behavior and rhetoric regarding McCarthyism and civil rights contradicted the title and theme of *Profiles in Courage*.[125] In 1959, JFK told historian and future White House aide Arthur M. Schlesinger, Jr., "that he was paying the price of having written a book called *Profiles in Courage*."[126] Even after JFK became president, journalist Arthur Krock wrote that JFK told him "that the charge made . . . that he hadn't written *Profiles in Courage* was hard to shake off, but didn't I remember seeing him writing the book at Palm Beach?"[127]

Although JFK's most enthusiastic admirers regarded his support for the St. Lawrence Seaway as a shining example of his political courage, JFK's 1954 floor speech and Senate vote favoring the Seaway were somewhat anticlimactic. The Senate passed the Wiley bill by a wide margin, 51 to 32.[128] Most of New England's senators voted for it. Of the senators representing coastal New England states, Senators Theodore F. Green and John O. Pastore of Rhode Island publicly supported the construction of the St. Lawrence Seaway before JFK did.

Of the seven New England senators who voted for the St. Lawrence Seaway, it probably took the greatest courage for Senator Margaret Chase Smith of Maine to vote for the Wiley bill. She faced a tough battle for renomination against Robert L. Jones, a pro-McCarthy conservative Republican, in Maine's June 21st primary.[129] Some of Smith's anti-Seaway critics accused her and Frederick Payne, her Senate colleague from Maine, of supporting the Seaway in exchange for a recent Senate appropriation of funds to study the feasibility of building a hydroelectric power system using the tides of Passamaquoddy Bay.[130]

JFK and his political operatives, therefore, exaggerated and dramatized the extent of his political courage in voting for the St. Lawrence Seaway. They wanted to persuade the national media and Democrats outside of New England that JFK was a national political figure who believed that the long-term national interest was more important than the immediate economic interests of his home state and region.[131] Actually, JFK devoted most of his rhetoric and legislative behavior during his first year in the Senate to economic problems that were either unique to, or especially severe in, New England in general and Massachusetts in particular.

When JFK began his second year in the Senate, he indicated in his speech on the St. Lawrence Seaway that he was simultaneously advancing both the national interest and his constituents' participation in it. He did so by helping Massachusetts and the rest of New England to become participants in a more cost-efficient transportation system that was needed to develop a more interdependent and integrated national economy for both greater prosperity and national security during the Cold War.[132] This 1954 assertion echoed JFK's statement in his first 1953 speech on New England's economic problems that the relationship between the national interest and the economic interests of New England was complementary, rather than conflicting.[133]

4

JFK and the Politics of 1956

As THE NATION PREPARED FOR THE 1956 presidential, congressional, and state elections, JFK intensified his efforts to develop a rhetorical and legislative record and national reputation as a Democratic senator. Because of two operations on his back and recuperation from them, JFK was absent from the Senate from October 11, 1954 until May 24, 1955.[1] Thus, during the remaining months of 1955, JFK was especially ubiquitous and prolific in delivering speeches and granting media interviews, especially in Massachusetts. Unlike many of his speeches in Massachusetts during his first two years in the Senate, JFK's 1955 speeches and media interviews tended to focus more on foreign policy issues. In particular, he elaborated on how to stop the spread of Communism in the Third World while respecting the independence and national self-determination of countries emerging from European colonialism.

The first speech that JFK delivered after he returned to the Senate was the commencement address at Assumption College in Worcester, Massachusetts on June 3, 1955. At the beginning of this speech, JFK noted that this was his first visit to Massachusetts in more than nine months. Assumption College is a Catholic college established by the Augustinians of the Assumption, a Catholic order of priests and brothers based in France. The senator, therefore, emphasized the roles of religious faith and French intellectual contributions in the Cold War struggle against Communism. JFK stated, "Assumption College has succeeded in carrying out this mission, so that today it stands as a bulwark on the North American continent in the battle for the preservation of Christian civilization."[2]

On June 10, 1955, JFK hosted a party in Hyannis Port for members of the Massachusetts state legislature, other state officials, and members of Congress. Although JFK's invitations were bipartisan, few Republicans attended. JFK's actual purpose in hosting this party was to appear healthy and athletic to his fellow Bay State Democrats, thereby quelling any rumors that his political power in Massachusetts was declining because of poor health.[3] On the previous day, JFK attended and addressed a Jefferson-Jackson Day dinner in Boston. He shared the dais with Foster Furcolo. Furcolo's narrow defeat in his 1954 Senate race was widely attributed to JFK's refusal to specifically endorse Furcolo by name in a television broadcast. At this Democratic "harmony dinner," Furcolo and JFK exchanged cordial remarks about each other. JFK stated, "When I came here tonight, I knew we were going to bury hatchets, but I wasn't sure just where. I think the only place to bury hatchets is in the ground."[4] Wanting to discourage further intraparty gossip or media speculation about a Kennedy-Furcolo feud, JFK added, "I hope we'll hear no more about Kennedy and Furcolo."[5]

Upon JFK's return to the Senate, he continued his somewhat maverick voting record for a northern Democrat. On May 25, 1955, JFK was the only Democratic senator who voted for an Eisenhower-backed, Republican-sponsored authorization bill for funding the construction of interstate highways. A bipartisan coalition of forty-six Democrats and thirteen Republicans easily defeated this bill.[6]

A major issue that helped Democrats to win control of Congress in the 1954 elections was the Eisenhower administration's agricultural policy of flexible price supports as a way to reduce federal spending on price supports. It was a controversial policy that many Democrats bitterly attributed to Secretary of Agriculture Ezra Taft Benson. JFK's initial endorsement of "Bensonism" in his Senate voting record later became a political liability at the Democratic national convention of 1956. However, more than one year after the 1954 elections, JFK continued to defend his vote for flexible price supports. In a November 15, 1955 speech to the Farm Bureau Federation of Massachusetts, JFK stated, "Given a choice between the present sliding-scale system of price supports and the old program of fixed supports, I shall choose—and have chosen in the past—the former, the more flexible program; not because I think it to be the ideal, final answer—and certainly not because I enjoy parting from the majority of my Democratic colleagues on the issue—but because I regard flexible supports as the less harmful of the two alternatives presented and a step in the right direction."[7]

JFK's speeches in 1955 sought to project the image of an independent-minded senator who was able to reconcile the policy interests of his home state and region with those of the nation. Unlike his speeches about New England's economic problems in 1953 and 1954, JFK's speeches on these issues in 1955 tended to be more partisan and critical of the Eisenhower administration. On October 29, 1955, JFK addressed the annual alumni association banquet of Boston College's business school. In this speech, the Democratic senator expressed his impatience with the failure of the Eisenhower administration's policies in areas of surplus labor to reduce high rates of unemployment in the cities and towns of Massachusetts. He stated, "I will say in all frankness, and without intending to exploit for partisan purposes the distress of Massachusetts businessmen and workers, that this State is growing weary of highly publicized announcements of Federal aid which, when the ballyhoo is over and the gobbledygook has been translated, boil down to little or nothing at all."[8]

The mid-term election results of 1954 and fluctuations in Eisenhower's public approval ratings emboldened JFK and other Democrats in Congress to be more combative in their rhetoric toward Eisenhower and the Republicans in Congress. For example, Eisenhower's public approval ratings in Gallup public opinion polls plummeted from 75 percent in late July 1954, to 57 percent in November 1954.[9] However, even as the Republican president's public approval ratings declined, voters who were surveyed tended to express respect for Eisenhower while blaming Secretary of Agriculture Ezra Taft Benson, other administration officials, or Republicans in Congress for economic problems or policies that they disliked.[10]

The Democrats gained nineteen seats in the U.S. House of Representatives and one seat in the Senate, thereby achieving majorities in both houses of Congress.[11] Democratic Representative Sam Rayburn of Texas succeeded Republican Representative Joseph W. Martin, Jr., of Massachusetts as Speaker of the House, and Democratic Representative John W. McCormack of Massachusetts became the next House majority leader. The one-seat Senate majority that the Democrats achieved in the 1954 elections meant that Senator Lyndon B. Johnson of Texas became the next Senate majority leader. He was now in a more powerful position to influence JFK's political career, especially concerning committee assignments in the Senate.[12]

One month after the 1954 elections, Secretary of Commerce Sinclair Weeks wrote a letter to Basil Brewer, the publisher of the *New Bedford Standard Times*. Weeks, a former Republican state chairman in Massachusetts, warned Brewer, a pro-Taft conservative who had endorsed JFK in 1952, that JFK increasingly voted in the Senate as a typical, pro-union liberal Democrat. Weeks wrote, "You were strong for Bob and for the things he stood for, so it seems highly possible that you feel the same thing about Jack's voting record."[13]

Disappointed that Johnson had not secured him a seat on the Senate Foreign Relations Committee, JFK embarked on a trip to Italy to improve his foreign policy credentials and strengthen his rapport with his constituents of Italian ancestry. While in Italy in September 1955, JFK conferred with the pope about his upcoming trip to Poland and the effects of Communist rule on religious freedom for Catholics in that country. He also consulted U.S. Ambassador to Italy Clare Booth Luce and officials of the Italian government about the need to liberalize U.S. immigration laws, especially the McCarran-Walter Act of 1952, so that more Italians could immigrate to the United States.[14] JFK arrived in Warsaw, Poland, on September 22, 1955, and spent several days observing the political, economic, and religious conditions in that city.[15]

While JFK was in Europe, Eisenhower suffered a major heart attack in Colorado on September 23, 1955.[16] During the president's long recuperation in the fall of 1955, there was growing speculation that the 65-year-old Eisenhower might choose not to run for reelection because of his health. Eisenhower did not attend another cabinet meeting until November 22, 1955, and rumors of a power struggle between Secretary of State John Foster Dulles and Vice President Richard M. Nixon circulated.[17]

At his press conference of February 29, 1956, Eisenhower stated that he was willing to be renominated by the Republican Party for a second term. However, he refused to answer questions about whether he wanted Nixon renominated for vice president.[18] Eisenhower continued to refuse to answer questions about whether he wanted Nixon to be his running mate. Privately, though, Eisenhower suggested that Nixon exchange the vice presidency for a cabinet position in order to better prepare himself for the 1960 presidential election.[19]

Nixon's prospects of being renominated were bolstered by the results of New Hampshire's Republican presidential primary held on March 13. Senator Styles Bridges of New Hampshire organized a campaign for his state's voters to write in Nixon's name for vice president. With no opponents on the ballot, Nixon received 22,202 write-in votes for vice president in New Hampshire.[20] He received approximately 30,000 write-in votes for vice president in Oregon's Republican presidential primary of May 18.

There was a resurgence of speculation that Eisenhower would not run for renomination and that Nixon would not be renominated for vice president following Eisenhower's emergency surgery for ileitis on June 9, 1956. In his memoir, White House chief of staff Sherman Adams revealed that a surgeon had told him that it was highly unlikely that a man of Eisenhower's age could recover from such an operation.[21] Eisenhower, though, impressed his doctor and White House aides with his quick recovery and rescheduled his trip to Panama for July 21.

Shortly before the president left for Panama, Harold Stassen, a special assistant on disarmament, sought an appointment with Eisenhower. Stassen urged the president to replace Nixon with Governor Christian Herter of Massachusetts as his running mate. He claimed that he had a private poll which indicated that Eisenhower would be reelected by a wider margin if Herter were nominated for vice president. Eisenhower simply told Stassen that he would not dictate the choice of a running mate to the delegates of the Republican national convention.[22] While Eisenhower was abroad, Stassen energetically promoted a pro-Herter, "dump Nixon" movement. Eisenhower's August 1 statement at a press conference that Nixon was "perfectly acceptable" to him as a running mate minimized any possibility that Nixon would not be renominated.[23] In his book *Six Crises*, Nixon wrote, "The upshot was that Chris Herter, who was embarrassed by the whole affair, placed my name in nomination, and Harold Stassen seconded it."[24]

During this prolonged period of uncertainty, intrigue, and speculation, the Democrats expected the media and the voters to focus more than usual on each party's choice of a vice presidential nominee. Since Nixon was a more partisan and divisive political figure than Eisenhower, the Democrats were more motivated than usual as the "out party" to nominate an attractive candidate for vice president as a contrast to Nixon. Also, Eisenhower's precarious health provided Democrats with a more persuasive argument that if he were reelected there was a distinct possibility that he would die in office and Nixon would succeed him. In short, according to the Democrats, reelecting Eisenhower was the same as electing Nixon president.

Furthermore, Dwight D. Eisenhower was the first president to be formally limited to two elected terms of office according to the 22nd amendment, ratified in 1951. If he were reelected in 1956, as was generally assumed, then there would be no incumbent president running for reelection in 1960. That constitutional fact and political reality made the vice presidential nominations of both parties unusually desirable as advantages for Democrats and Republicans who wanted to run for president in 1960.[25]

Joseph P. Kennedy (JPK) was certainly aware of these calculations. Shortly after the public was informed about Eisenhower's heart attack, JPK contacted Thomas G. Corcoran. Corcoran was an influential lawyer and lobbyist in Washington, DC, and had served in the Roosevelt White House. JPK asked Corcoran to visit Senator Lyndon B. Johnson at his ranch in Texas in October 1955. Johnson had suffered a severe heart attack in July. He spoke at the Dallas State Fair on October 13 in order to publicly demonstrate his improving health and encourage rumors that he was considering a presidential candidacy in 1956.[26]

Through Corcoran, JPK made the following offer to Johnson. If Johnson publicly announced his presidential candidacy soon and privately agreed to choose JFK as his running mate at the Democratic national convention, then JPK would provide substantial financial support for Johnson's campaign.[27] JPK believed that Franklin D. Roosevelt's vice presidential candidacy in 1920 had helped him to become the Democratic presidential nominee in 1932. Likewise, JPK believed that a well-financed, highly publicized vice presidential campaign for JFK in 1956 would help him to win the Democratic presidential nomination in 1960 or 1964.

Johnson politely declined JPK's offer. Corcoran met JPK and RFK in New York City and informed them of Johnson's decision. JFK did not know about his father's offer until after Johnson rejected it. He later asked Corcoran to see him in his Senate office. JFK wanted to know if Johnson planned to run for president in 1956 without him as a running mate.[28]

Adlai Stevenson and Sam Rayburn visited Johnson at his ranch in Texas from September 28 to 29, 1955.[29] On November 15, 1955, Stevenson announced his presidential candidacy in Chicago.[30] On December 3, 1955, Mayor Robert Wagner of New York City publicly stated that he would accept the Democratic vice presidential nomination if it were offered to him.[31] On that same day, JFK was visiting Stevenson at his home in Libertyville, Illinois, according to John Bartlow Martin, Stevenson's biographer and confidant. Martin, however, did not disclose if JFK and Stevenson discussed the Democratic vice presidential nomination.[32]

Unlike Wagner, JFK did not publicly announce his intention to run for vice president until after Stevenson was nominated at the Democratic national convention in August and declared an "open convention" for the purpose of allowing the delegates to freely choose his running mate. Instead, JFK and his political allies and operatives quietly encouraged Democratic politicians and journalists to promote his name for vice president. In a 1977 interview, Fletcher Knebel, a writer for *Look* magazine, recalled that in early 1956 JFK suggested to him that *Look* should publish an article about how a Catholic running mate would improve a Democratic presidential nominee's chances of winning the 1956 presidential election. Knebel also learned that JPK allegedly paid $50,000 for a study of Catholic voting power in a presidential election that was used in this article. Knebel concluded, "At any rate, the story got a hell of a lot of attention."[33]

In January 1956, Andrew Quigley, a Democratic state senator from Chelsea, Massachusetts, wrote to JFK and stated that he wanted to begin a campaign to promote JFK for vice president. In his reply, JFK did not deny that he was a candidate but informed Quigley that he did not want to publicly campaign at this time.[34] On February 4, 1956, Massachusetts Democrats held a fund raising dinner in Boston that featured former president Harry S. Truman as the guest speaker.[35] Several participants at this dinner were wearing campaign badges that included the words "Elect U.S. Sen. Kennedy Vice-President" and photographs of JFK.[36]

In a 1976 interview, Maurice Donahue, a Democratic state senator from Holyoke, Massachusetts, recalled the connection between Quigley and the campaign badges during the Democratic national convention in Chicago in August of 1956. Donahue and Quigley attended the convention as delegates from Massachusetts. Quigley brought a few of these badges with him. On the day before the balloting began for the vice presidential nomination, RFK told Quigley to have more badges sent overnight from Chelsea to Chicago.[37] Donahue concluded that "knowing the profundity of Bobby, I would expect that there was advance planning that never surfaced as such."[38]

One complication in JFK's quest for the Democratic vice presidential nomination of 1956 was that Stevenson was forced to compete for the Democratic presidential nomination. Senator Estes Kefauver of Tennessee announced his presidential candidacy on December 16, 1955.[39] Kefauver had proven to be a popular campaigner in the Democratic presidential primaries of 1952. Although he did not announce his presidential candidacy until June 9, 1956, Governor W. Averell Harriman of New York was already known to be exploring the feasibility of a presidential campaign.[40]

Theodore C. Sorensen, JFK's Senate aide and top speech writer, encouraged JFK to endorse Stevenson shortly after Stevenson announced his candidacy.[41] JFK, however, was more cautious and chose to delay the timing of his endorsement. In the 1952 presidential election, Stevenson had proven to be less popular among Catholic voters than Roosevelt and Truman had been.[42] Stevenson's lack of appeal among Catholic voters was partially attributed to his marital status as a divorced man and his perceived softness on Communism because of his association with Alger Hiss.[43] Stevenson was especially unpopular among older, working-class Irish Catholics in Massachusetts and the Irish Catholic politicians who represented them.[44]

Also, it was not definite in early 1956 that Adlai Stevenson would easily win the Democratic presidential nomination. Shortly after Senator Estes Kefauver of Tennessee announced his presidential candidacy on December 16, 1955, he made plans to enter Democratic presidential primaries, most notably those in New Hampshire, Minnesota, and California.[45] Despite Kefauver's public image as a folksy, somewhat buffoonish politician who occasionally wore a coonskin cap, he was a shrewd political tactician.[46] The senator from Tennessee developed a national reputation as a crusading reformer in 1951 through his committee's televised hearings on organized crime. Kefauver's populist, ingratiating campaign style and President Harry S. Truman's low public approval ratings helped Kefauver to defeat Truman in New Hampshire's 1952 Democratic presidential primary. Kefauver received 55 percent of the votes to Truman's 44 percent.[47] Approximately two weeks after New Hampshire's March 11 presidential primary, Truman announced that he would not seek reelection.

Most delegates sent to the 1956 Democratic national convention were not chosen and committed to presidential candidates through binding primaries. Kefauver, however, needed impressive, unexpected victories in the primaries in order to attract media coverage, campaign contributions, endorsements, and favorable public opinion polls in order to eventually influence the voting behavior of delegates at the national convention. This was quite a challenge for Kefauver since he was fiercely opposed by two major influences on delegates at Democratic national conventions: mostly Catholic urban machine politicians and his fellow white southerners.

Urban machine politicians, especially those from Chicago and New York City, believed that Kefauver's televised hearings, which exposed connections between Democratic machine politicians and organized crime, contributed to Democratic losses in state and local elections in 1952.[48] By national political standards, Kefauver was a moderate on civil rights for African Americans. He supported federal legislation to prohibit lynching and abolish poll taxes and stated that the Supreme Court's school desegregation decision in *Brown* must be implemented.[49] Kefauver, however, was a traitor and a pariah on civil rights to other southern Democratic politicians. Two days before New Hampshire's March 13, 1956 presidential primaries, Senator Walter George of Georgia announced a "Southern Manifesto" that pledged opposition to the implementation of the *Brown* decision. Kefauver distinguished himself as one of the three southern senators who refused to sign the "Southern Manifesto."[50]

Stevenson was reluctant to campaign against Kefauver in the primaries. Stevenson's strategy was to position himself as a unifying, compromise candidate to the Democratic Party's broad, diverse coalition, thereby attracting enough private pledges of delegate support to ensure his nomination at the Democratic national convention. Any embarrassing, unexpected defeats to Kefauver in the primaries could undermine this strategy.[51] Also, Stevenson's cerebral oratory and aristocratic personality might prove to be less appealing to primary voters than Kefauver's amiable, populist style.

On May 8, 1956, JFK announced his endorsement of Stevenson's presidential candidacy. JFK stated that he "wouldn't have announced for Stevenson as early as this if I didn't have confidence that he would be nominated and had a good chance of being elected." He added that Stevenson was "beholden to no group or section" and belonged "neither to a left wing nor a right wing."[52]

New Hampshire's presidential primaries were held five days later on March 13, 1956. Unlike Kefauver, Stevenson had not formally entered the New Hampshire Democratic primary or personally campaigned there. Kefauver won 85 percent of the votes in New Hampshire's Democratic presidential primary and all of its delegate votes for the Democratic national convention. Most of the remaining votes were write-in votes for Stevenson.[53] Stevenson tried to minimize the significance of Kefauver's victory by reminding reporters that it was an uncontested primary and that he was pleasantly surprised and grateful for the number of write-in votes that he received.[54]

By contrast, Stevenson filed for Minnesota's Democratic presidential primary on January 17 and had been regularly campaigning there since then. He was endorsed by Governor Orville Freeman and Senator Hubert H. Humphrey. Freeman and Humphrey assured Stevenson that he would win Minnesota and its thirty delegate votes because of their effective organization within that state's Democratic Farmer Labor (DFL) Party.[55] Therefore, Kefauver portrayed Freeman, Humphrey, and other pro-Stevenson politicians as machine bosses pressuring Minnesotans to vote for the Illinois Democrat and himself as a populist reformer. Kefauver also denounced the Eisenhower administration's flexible agricultural price support policy more unequivocally and passionately than Stevenson.

Kefauver achieved a stunning upset victory in Minnesota, winning 57 percent of the votes to Stevenson's 43 percent.[56] Some Stevenson supporters tried to minimize the importance of Kefauver's victory by claiming that many Republicans voted in Minnesota's Democratic presidential primary in order to either express opposition to flexible price supports or weaken Stevenson's candidacy.[57] Nonetheless, the results of the Minnesota primary stimulated growing speculation that if Kefauver won more primaries then he could weaken Stevenson's candidacy enough so that the Democratic national convention might nominate a still unannounced dark horse candidate for president, such as Governors W. Averell Harriman of New York or G. Mennen "Soapy" Williams of Michigan.[58]

Massachusetts would hold its presidential primaries on April 24. None of the presidential candidates' names would be listed on either the Republican or Democratic ballots. JFK was initially optimistic about Stevenson's chances in the Massachusetts Democratic primary. In a February 15, 1956 letter to William M. Blair, a Stevenson campaign aide, JFK stated that a private poll indicated Stevenson's overwhelming popularity in Massachusetts with 69 percent of likely voters surveyed choosing Stevenson and only 17 percent Kefauver.[59]

JFK's efforts to deliver his state's delegates to Stevenson were entwined with his struggle to win control of his state's Democratic committee and its chairmanship. William "Onions" Burke was the Democratic state chairman and opposed Stevenson's candidacy. Massachusetts voters could only indicate their preferences through write-in votes in the state's presidential primaries. Therefore, Burke, assisted by *Boston Post* publisher John Fox, conducted a vigorous campaign to encourage voters to support House Majority Leader John W. McCormack as a write-in presidential candidate.[60] In the April 24 Democratic presidential primary of Massachusetts, McCormack received 48 percent of the write-in votes to Stevenson's 35 percent.[61]

Fortunately for Stevenson and JFK, the *New York Times* dismissed the national significance of McCormack's victory because of the very low voter turnout in the Massachusetts primary and the favorite son status of McCormack.[62] Also, it was a non-binding primary, and the state's Democratic delegates to the national convention remained uncommitted. As explained previously, JFK's successful effort to win control of the Democratic state committee and its chairmanship enabled him to deliver most of his state's delegate votes to Stevenson at the Democratic national convention.[63]

With Massachusetts now secure for Stevenson's nomination, JFK continued to privately and indirectly convince Stevenson's advisers and staff about his assets as a running mate. He primarily did this through Sorensen as his operative.[64] Sorensen compiled and analyzed statistics regarding the influence of the Catholic vote in recent presidential elections and concluded that a Catholic running mate would help elect a Democrat as president in 1956. In particular, Sorensen's report noted that Catholics comprised anywhere from 20 percent to 60 percent of the voting-age adults of the fourteen states that held 261 of the 266 electoral votes needed to elect a president in 1956.[65] This report became known as the "Bailey Memorandum" because it was attributed to John M. Bailey, the Democratic state chairman of Connecticut and a Kennedy ally.

JFK also relied on R. Sargent Shriver, his brother-in-law and the manager of JPK's Merchandise Mart in Chicago, to lobby the Stevenson campaign. Shriver was friendly with two of Stevenson's top aides, William M. Blair and Newton Minow. After Stevenson's overwhelming victory in California's June 5th primary made him the presumptive Democratic presidential nominee, Shriver sat next to Stevenson on a flight to Chicago and promoted JFK's assets as a vice presidential nominee. In his response, Stevenson seemed skeptical. He dismissed Sorensen's statistical analysis of the Catholic vote as an "educated guess."[66] Nevertheless, Stevenson spoke positively to Shriver about JFK's attractive, articulate communication skills on television and later told reporters that both JFK and Hubert H. Humphrey would make good running mates.[67]

After Senator Lyndon B. Johnson of Texas rejected JPK's offer of financial backing for a Johnson-Kennedy ticket in 1956, JPK perceived a vice presidential nomination to be detrimental rather than beneficial to a future presidential campaign by JFK. In a May 25, 1956 letter to JFK, JPK wrote about his recent visit with U.S. Ambassador to Italy Clare Booth Luce. Luce stated that JFK should not seek or accept a vice presidential nomination because "a defeat would be a devastating blow to your prestige, which at the moment is great, and non-partisan."[68] He urged JFK to consult Luce, a prominent Republican, and follow her advice on this matter.

On May 30, 1956, the cities of Fall River and New Bedford in Massachusetts hosted an ostensibly nonpolitical, bipartisan social event for JFK and Jacqueline Kennedy. Both Democratic and Republican politicians attended. The invited senators from other states included John O. Pastore of Rhode Island, George A. Smathers of Florida, Henry M. "Scoop" Jackson of Washington, and Albert A. Gore, Sr., of Tennessee. In his speech, Gore suggested that JFK "be considered for first or second place on the national ticket."[69] Gore further stated that, regardless of whether the election year was 1956, 1960, or 1964, JFK would make an excellent presidential or vice presidential nominee for the Democratic Party.

On June 8, 1956, JFK introduced Governor Abraham Ribicoff of Connecticut as the keynote speaker of the Democratic state convention in Worcester, Massachusetts. He noted that Ribicoff was born in a "poor Jewish home" and personified the racial, ethnic, and religious diversity of the contemporary Democratic Party. JFK concluded his introduction of Ribicoff by quoting Adlai Stevenson.[70] In his speech, Ribicoff told the Massachusetts Democrats that their national party could provide the nation with its "greatest" service by nominating JFK for vice president.[71]

Furthermore, at the national Governors' Conference held in late June in Atlantic City, Ribicoff and Governor Dennis J. Roberts of Rhode Island openly lobbied their fellow Democratic governors and urged them to support JFK for vice president at the Democratic national convention in Chicago. In an interview with the *New York Times*, Ribicoff dismissed the argument that, because of Herbert Hoover's landslide victory against Governor Alfred E. Smith of New York, a Catholic, in the 1928 presidential election, a Catholic vice presidential nominee would contribute to a Democratic defeat in 1956 because of lingering religious prejudice. Ribicoff also revealed to the media that he had written a letter to Stevenson and had a discussion with James A. Finnegan, Stevenson's campaign manager, urging them to choose JFK as a vice presidential nominee.[72] Governor Raymond Gary of Oklahoma, who endorsed Harriman for president, told reporters that JFK could not be nominated for vice president because of his legislative record favoring the Eisenhower administration's flexible price supports for agriculture.

JFK was obviously not following his father's advice to end his pursuit of the Democratic vice presidential nomination. Shortly after the Governors' Conference ended, JFK wrote his father a letter on June 29, 1956. He told JPK that he was being cautious, discreet, and tactful about his vice presidential candidacy and updated his father on the efforts of Ribicoff and others on his behalf. Arthur M. Schlesinger, Jr., was working in Stevenson's campaign headquarters and was one of JFK's advocates there. John M. Bailey, the Democratic state chairman of Connecticut, had recently visited Stevenson and tried to impress him with JFK's vote getting appeal as a running mate. Finally, Senator George A. Smathers of Florida was lobbying southern governors about the advantage of JFK as a vice presidential candidate.[73]

By late June, Adlai Stevenson was ahead of Estes Kefauver in pledged delegates, but he still had not gained enough delegate votes to secure the Democratic presidential nomination. Kefauver, however, suffered a severe blow to his campaign by the end of June. Following the advice of Governor Frank Clement of Tennessee, the Democratic state convention of Tennessee decided not to pledge its delegates to Kefauver as its favorite son. Instead, Tennessee's delegates would be uninstructed when they went to the Democratic national convention. Nevertheless, Kefauver traveled to several states in July seeking delegates.[74]

A UPI poll released on July 29, 1956 disclosed the following estimates of pledged delegate votes among Stevenson, Kefauver, and Harriman. With 686½ delegate votes needed for the Democratic presidential nomination, Stevenson had 404½, Kefauver 200, and Harriman 141.[75] Harriman was making progress among delegates by positioning himself to the left of Stevenson and Kefauver on civil rights and as an attractive compromise candidate if the national convention became deadlocked.[76]

Any remote possibility that W. Averell Harriman would become the 1956 Democratic nominee for president ended on July 31, 1956. On that day, Estes Kefauver announced that he was ending his presidential candidacy and urged his supporters to back Stevenson. During his press conference, Kefauver denied that he had made a deal with Stevenson to end his presidential campaign in exchange for the Democratic vice presidential nomination. However, when a reporter asked Kefauver if the Tennessee senator would refuse the Democratic vice presidential nomination, Kefauver evasively replied, "We'll cross that bridge when we come to it, if we do, in Chicago."[77]

According to a biographer of Kefauver, the Harriman campaign previously made a similar offer to Kefauver. In negotiations between F. Joseph "Jiggs" Donohue, Kefauver's campaign manager, and George Backer, Harriman's campaign manager, the Harriman campaign offered to assume Kefauver's $75,000 campaign debt if Kefauver withdrew his presidential candidacy. Harriman, though, did not also offer to choose Kefauver as his running mate if the New Yorker became the Democratic presidential nominee.[78]

Despite the firm public denials of both Stevenson and Kefauver, rumors persisted that the two Democrats had made a "deal" for a Stevenson-Kefauver ticket. Meanwhile, JFK's public and private efforts to secure the Democratic vice presidential nomination continued unabated during the summer of 1956. On July 12, 1956, Edward

P. Grace, a former city councilor in Fall River, announced the creation of a Kennedy for Vice President Committee in that city. The purpose of this committee was to solicit delegate support for JFK's vice presidential nomination within and outside of Massachusetts. On the following day, Adlai Stevenson stated at a press conference in Burlington, Vermont, that JFK would make an "excellent" candidate for vice president.[79]

Arthur M. Schlesinger, Jr., a confidante of both JFK and Stevenson, arrived in Chicago on July 6, 1956, to begin working in Stevenson's campaign headquarters. Schlesinger found that JFK and Senator Hubert H. Humphrey of Minnesota were the most popular potential running mates among Stevenson's staff and advisers. James Finnegan, Pennsylvania's secretary of state and Stevenson's campaign manager, staunchly opposed the nomination of JFK for vice president because of the religious issue. Like Mayor David L. Lawrence of Pittsburgh, Finnegan and other older Irish Catholic politicians tended to believe that JFK's Catholicism would be a liability rather than an asset to Stevenson's voter appeal as a Democratic presidential nominee running against Eisenhower.[80]

Humphrey, however, assumed that he already had a commitment from Stevenson to become the Democratic vice presidential nominee. On July 19, 1956, he attended a Democratic fund raising dinner in Washington, DC, that also honored retiring Senator Walter F. George of Georgia.[81] In his autobiography, Humphrey wrote that he met Stevenson and Finnegan in a hotel room during this dinner. Stevenson told the Minnesota senator that he did not want Kefauver as a running mate and was considering Mayor Robert Wagner of New York City and Senators Stuart Symington of Missouri and Albert A. Gore, Sr., of Tennessee. He did not mention JFK. He then told Humphrey that the Minnesotan was the best qualified and should run for vice president. Stevenson then asked Finnegan to find some southern Democratic politicians who would endorse Humphrey for vice president.[82] Humphrey wrote, "If that happened, as I understood the conversation, Adlai would choose me as his vice-presidential running mate."[83]

On the day after this Democratic dinner and Humphrey's meeting with Stevenson, JFK resumed his role as a bipartisan, regional advocate of New England's policy interests. On July 20, 1956, JFK submitted a resolution to the Senate on behalf of all twelve of New England's senators calling for an end to discriminatory railroad freight rates in New England. JFK stated, "Now that the New England railroads have undertaken to offset the unfair advantage which for many years has been enjoyed by the South Atlantic ports, we in New England want to give every kind of encouragement to those railroads and I believe that the Congress should make it perfectly clear that there should be no discrimination in the matter of transportation rates against any area of the United States."[84]

A few days after this Senate speech, JFK traveled to Hollywood, California in order to narrate a 20-minute film, *The Pursuit of Happiness*, that chronicled the history of the Democratic Party.[85] The film was directed by Dore Schary and would be shown at the Democratic national convention.[86] *The Pursuit of Happiness* was scheduled to be shown on the first day of the Democratic national convention and had the potential to attract some delegates to JFK's vice presidential candidacy.[87]

Confident that he would be nominated for president, Adlai Stevenson conferred with his staff and advisers about the selection of a running mate. Stevenson reported that former president Harry S. Truman advised against choosing Kefauver, Humphrey, or JFK as a running mate. James A. Farley, a Catholic and former DNC chairman, contended that JFK or any other Catholic Democratic vice presidential nominee would lose more votes than he would gain for Stevenson in the general election. Sam Rayburn, the Speaker of the House, served as permanent chairman of the Democratic national convention. He asserted that, if Stevenson felt compelled to choose a Catholic running mate, then he should choose House Majority Leader John W. McCormack instead of JFK.[88] Meanwhile, Stevenson aides Schlesinger, Blair, and Minow spoke favorably about JFK.

Although Stevenson seemed disinclined toward JFK partially because of the religious issue, he still did not reveal his preferred running mate to his advisers. Theodore C. Sorensen continued to lobby Stevenson's campaign headquarters. Unlike his earlier efforts, especially through the Bailey Memorandum, Sorensen did not emphasize JFK's Catholicism as an asset. On August 1, 1956, Sorensen wrote letters to Schlesinger and John M. Bailey telling them that he was conveying JFK's desire not to have his religion mentioned in their advocacy of his vice presidential candidacy. Sorensen told Bailey, "The Senator feels that the Catholic aspect may have been over-sold and is likely to backfire. He was somewhat disturbed by the recent newspaper reports on your use of this issue, although understanding the reason you felt it was desirable."[89]

Ken Hechler, Stevenson's research director, asked Sorensen to prepare and submit a report detailing JFK's qualifications to be vice president and political assets as a running mate. In his reply to Hechler, Sorensen detailed JFK's attributes, "regardless of Governor Stevenson's need to rewin [sic] the Catholic vote," such as his political centrism, war hero status, and legislative record on labor and minority issues.[90] Sorensen also mentioned JFK's growing reputation as an author because of *Profiles in Courage*.

JFK had recently enhanced his scholarly reputation because of his well-received commencement address at Harvard University. In his June 14, 1956 speech at Harvard, JFK stated that intellectuals and politicians should realize how much they can learn from and benefit each other. He concluded that "if more politicians knew poetry and more poets knew politics, I am convinced the world would be a little better place in which to live on this commencement day of 1956."[91]

While Hubert H. Humphrey was confident in his pursuit of the vice presidential nomination, JFK seemed more tentative and cautious about his chances of being nominated a few days before the Democratic national convention began in Chicago.[92] On August 9, 1956, JFK addressed the annual convention of the Massachusetts Federation of Labor in Springfield. After his speech, JFK told the media that he was not actively seeking the Democratic vice presidential nomination. He also stated his opinion that the Democratic vice presidential nominee should be "someone from another area of the country."[93] JFK, however, did not discourage efforts by delegates and officials at this labor convention to endorse him for vice president. On that same day, Edward D. Gilgun, the treasurer of the Democratic state committee of Massachusetts, announced that he was leaving for Chicago to solicit delegate support for JFK at the Democratic national convention.[94] After JFK left Springfield, he met separately with Governors Dennis J. Roberts of Rhode Island and Abraham Ribicoff of Connecticut, the two foremost boosters of his vice presidential candidacy among Democratic governors.[95]

In their account of their relationship with JFK, Kenneth P. O'Donnell and David F. Powers wrote, "Kennedy certainly was unprepared to run for the Vice-Presidential nomination and more astonished by the Kennedy boom than any of us who were with him in Chicago."[96] Like O'Donnell and Powers, Lawrence F. O'Brien, who remained in Massachusetts during the 1956 Democratic national convention, wrote that JFK's bid for the vice presidential nomination in Chicago was "so unexpected."[97] Apparently, JFK decided not to involve O'Donnell, Powers, O'Brien, and even RFK in his undeclared candidacy for the vice presidency because of his own tentative, ambivalent attitude toward it.

In late July, JFK learned from Stevenson aide William M. Blair that JFK's health was a liability for his vice presidential candidacy because of his well-known back surgeries and extended recuperation from them. There were also rumors that he had Addison's disease. Because of Eisenhower's 1955 heart attack and 1956 surgery for ileitis, there would be more media and public scrutiny than usual regarding a presidential or vice presidential candidate's health.[98]

Vacationing on the French Riviera, JPK resigned himself to the fact that JFK would seek the Democratic vice presidential nomination regardless of his advice. In a July 23, 1956 letter to JFK, JPK urged his son to prepare for any possible, damaging publicity among his constituents in Massachusetts if Stevenson rejected JFK for the vice presidential nomination. JPK told his son to "get out a statement to the effect that representing Mass. is one of the greatest jobs in the world, and there is lots to be done for your state and her people, and while you are most grateful for the national support offered you for the vice presidency, your heart belongs to Massachusetts."[99]

Like Kefauver, JFK publicly stated that he was willing to accept the Democratic vice presidential nomination without being an active candidate as he prepared to leave for Chicago. By contrast, Hubert H. Humphrey actively campaigned for the vice presidential nomination. Humphrey publicly declared that he was "very much encouraged" about his vice presidential candidacy.[100] Although Humphrey announced that he was not running against anyone for the Democratic vice presidential nomination, Governor Orville Freeman of Minnesota publicly stated that JFK was unacceptable as a running mate for Stevenson because of his legislative record on agriculture. Humphrey also seemed to be making his vice presidential candidacy more attractive to southern delegates. In a televised interview, Humphrey projected a more moderate image on civil rights. He stated that the Supreme Court's decision on school desegregation should be "observed rather than enforced."[101] Humphrey's impassioned speech on civil rights at the 1948 Democratic national convention motivated some southern delegates to leave that convention in protest. They subsequently established the States Rights Democratic, or "Dixiecrat," Party and nominated J. Strom Thurmond for president.

While Humphrey and JFK projected contrasting public images in their vice presidential candidacies, both of them confronted the growing possibility that they might not be able to deliver their states to Stevenson. Robert Short, the chairman of the Minnesota delegation, stated that he would not support Stevenson for president unless he was assured that Kefauver would be Stevenson's running mate.[102] Because of Kefauver's victory in the Minnesota primary, Humphrey was not chosen as a delegate from Minnesota.[103]

Publicly and privately, JFK and former governor of Massachusetts Paul Dever expressed their confidence that Adlai Stevenson would be nominated for president on the second ballot. They assumed that most states, including Massachusetts, would vote for their favorite son presidential candidates on the first ballot and then vote for Stevenson on the second ballot.[104]

This assumption by JFK and other pro-Stevenson Democrats was threatened by an unexpected source, former president Harry S. Truman. On August 11, two days before the Democratic national convention began, Truman endorsed Governor W. Averell Harriman of New York for president. Truman's political allies and surrogates, such as former DNC chairmen William Boyle and Frank McKinney, were soon soliciting delegates to support Harriman. Leo Egan, a reporter for the *New York Times*, wrote, "Harriman's managers figured Mr. Truman's endorsement would add at least 100 and possibly 150 votes to the Governor's first-ballot strength. These would raise his total, according to their figures, to 500 or more votes."[105]

John W. McCormack, the House majority leader, had not endorsed Stevenson and did not disavow rumors that he favored Harriman for the Democratic presidential nomination.[106] William "Onions" Burke, a McCormack ally and delegate-at-large from Massachusetts, still resented how JFK had secured his removal as Democratic state chairman. Burke announced that he and other pro-McCormack delegates from Massachusetts would vote for Harriman. James Michael Curley, another delegate-at-large and the Democratic national committeeman from Massachusetts, also endorsed Harriman.[107]

Pro-Stevenson delegates from Massachusetts began to suspect that a favorite son candidacy for McCormack would be used by the anti-Stevenson minority in the state's delegation to deadlock the Democratic national convention and eventually nominate Harriman. John E. Powers, a Democratic state senator and delegate from South Boston, began a movement to end the agreement among Massachusetts delegates to unanimously support McCormack as a favorite son candidate on the first ballot.[108] John Shea, a pro-Stevenson delegate from Worcester, announced that he would not vote for McCormack on the first ballot. However, a later vote at a caucus meeting chaired by JFK reaffirmed the earlier decision by the delegates of Massachusetts to support McCormack's favorite son candidacy on the first ballot.[109]

As JFK struggled to control most of his state's delegate votes for Stevenson, he relied on allies, surrogates, and operatives to solicit delegate votes for his still undeclared candidacy. His brother-in-law R. Sargent Shriver was his major liaison with the Stevenson campaign, and his sister Eunice Shriver organized a reception for delegates.[110] Especially with Roberts, Ribicoff, and Dever as JFK's lobbyists, JFK's vice presidential campaign sought to unite all of New England's delegate votes behind JFK. Occasionally accompanied by Torbert Macdonald, his Harvard roommate and a U.S. representative from Massachusetts, JFK visited delegates from states outside of New England.[111]

Although briefly stimulated by Truman's endorsement, W. Averell Harriman's presidential candidacy did not prove to be a serious threat to Stevenson's nomination. After she arrived at the convention, Eleanor Roosevelt counteracted Truman's backing of Harriman by endorsing Stevenson and lobbying delegates on his behalf.[112] Estes Kefauver met with delegates who were previously pledged to his now defunct presidential candidacy and urged them to cast their votes for Stevenson. Stevenson's candidacy also experienced increased support from southern delegates who opposed Harriman's advocacy of a more liberal civil rights platform.[113] By Wednesday evening, August 15, it seemed probable that Stevenson would be easily nominated on the first ballot.

Earlier on Wednesday, JFK requested and was given an appointment with Adlai Stevenson. Stevenson asked JFK's opinion about several possible running mates, including Hubert H. Humphrey. He then offered JFK the opportunity to deliver the nominating speech for his presidential candidacy. JFK accepted Stevenson's offer and later told Theodore C. Sorensen that this may have indicated Stevenson's decision not to choose JFK as his running mate.[114] Dissatisfied with the nominating speech prepared by Stevenson's staff, JFK rewrote the speech with Sorensen's help. Refusing to use a teleprompter, JFK delivered an eloquent nominating speech for Stevenson.[115] After praising Stevenson's virtues and qualifications for the presidency, JFK concluded, "The time is ripe. The hour has struck. The man is here; and he is ready. Let the word go forth that we have fulfilled our responsibility to the Nation."[116]

After the balloting for the presidential nomination began, John S. Begley, a delegate from Massachusetts, expressed John W. McCormack's gratitude for being nominated for president. However, McCormack promptly withdrew his nomination and released all of the delegates of Massachusetts to vote as they chose on the first ballot.[117] McCormack's magnanimous gesture facilitated JFK's ability to deliver most of his state's delegates to Stevenson and prevent a pro-Harriman bandwagon effect. On the first and only ballot for the Democratic presidential nomination, the delegates from Massachusetts cast 32 votes for Stevenson, 7½ votes for Harriman, and one-half vote for Senator Lyndon B. Johnson of Texas.[118]

Despite Truman's endorsement of Harriman and the proliferation of favorite son candidates, the competition for the 1956 Democratic presidential nomination was far less intense and dramatic than expected. With 687 delegate votes needed to secure the Democratic presidential nomination, Stevenson won 905½ votes to Harriman's 210 votes on Thursday, August 16. Various other presidential candidates, including Johnson and Senator Stuart Symington of Missouri, won a total of 356 votes.[119]

With the delegates and television viewers expecting Stevenson to deliver his acceptance speech, Stevenson solemnly stated how important the office of vice president had become. He implied the recent issue of Eisenhower's precarious health, with a resulting "part-time" presidency and the growing possibility of a Nixon presidency. Stevenson, therefore, concluded that he was dispensing with the tradition of designating his running mate and then asking the delegates to nominate his choice. Instead, Stevenson stated, "I have decided that the selection of the vice presidential nominee should be made the free process of this convention, so that the Democratic Party's candidate for the office may join me before the nation not as one man's selection but as one chosen by our Party even as I have been chosen."[120] He added, "The choice will be yours. The profit will be the Nation's."[121]

The idea of having an "open convention" to choose Stevenson's running mate was not recent or entirely surprising. In February, John Sharon, a volunteer in Stevenson's campaign, prepared and submitted a memo to campaign manager James Finnegan. Sharon's memo suggested that if Stevenson became the Democratic presidential nominee then he should declare an "open convention" in order to inject drama and surprise into an otherwise dull, predictable Democratic national convention.[122]

The "open convention" idea was later secretly used by top officials of the Stevenson and Kefauver campaigns to persuade Kefauver to end his presidential candidacy and endorse Stevenson before the Democratic national convention opened. If Stevenson declared an "open convention" instead of choosing Kefauver as his running mate, then Republicans could not credibly accuse Stevenson of cynically making a "deal" with Kefauver in order to secure the Democratic presidential nomination. Kefauver, however, would presumably have the best chance of winning the Democratic vice presidential nomination in an "open convention" because he recently had 200 delegates from several states pledged to him for president.[123] In addition, James Finnegan, who also served as Pennsylvania's secretary of state, and Mayor David L. Lawrence of Pittsburgh assured Kefauver's campaign officials that they could deliver most or all of Pennsylvania's 74 delegate votes to Kefauver for vice president.[124]

On Friday, August 17, 1956, there was a frenzy of activity as representatives of Kefauver, JFK, Humphrey, and other vice presidential candidates lobbied delegates for their votes. Tennessee's delegates divided their loyalties among Kefauver, Gore, and Governor Frank Clement, who had delivered the convention's keynote address. Eleanor Roosevelt later wrote that JFK previously approached her in Chicago for her support for his vice presidential candidacy. She told JFK that she would not support his candidacy because of his failure to publicly denounce McCarthyism.[125] Furthermore, if the delegates decided to nominate a Catholic for vice president, then JFK was competing against Mayor Robert Wagner of New York City, especially for New York's delegate votes.

Kenneth P. O'Donnell had arrived in Chicago with RFK expecting to passively observe the convention and attend an all-star professional baseball game.[126] Instead, RFK recruited O'Donnell to join Shriver, EMK, Sorensen, and other JFK surrogates to lobby delegates. Bailey and Ribicoff were confident that JFK would receive virtually all of New England's delegate votes, so RFK concentrated his efforts on delegates from the South. Through his work as a Senate committee investigative counsel, RFK had developed contacts with several southern Democratic senators, especially Senator John McClellan of

Arkansas.[127] As soon as JPK learned that his son was competing for the vice presidential nomination at an "open convention," he made phone calls on JFK's behalf from his vacation home on the French Riviera for the next eighteen hours.[128]

Unlike Humphrey and other Democrats competing against Kefauver, JFK was better prepared to run for the vice presidential nomination in an "open convention." Shriver previously informed JFK about the possibility of an "open convention" because of rumors from the Stevenson campaign.[129] Furthermore, because of his friendly relationships with the Shrivers and Kennedys, JPK's ownership of the Merchandise Mart, and his antipathy toward Kefauver, Mayor Richard J. Daley of Chicago had assured Shriver that he could deliver almost all of the Illinois delegate votes to JFK on the second ballot.[130]

Abraham Ribicoff delivered the nominating speech for JFK. In his speech, Ribicoff emphasized JFK's electoral appeal among young voters, independents, and Republicans. JFK's nomination for vice president was seconded by Senator George Smathers of Florida and Representative John W. McCormack. Smathers stated that JFK "has the ability to attract the veterans' vote and other votes which our Presidential nominee may not be able to do."[131] Seconding JFK's nomination, McCormack urged his fellow Democratic delegates "to go East" to balance their national ticket.[132]

Other than Illinois and New England, JFK received significant concentrations of delegate support on the first ballot from several southern states, especially Georgia, Virginia, and Louisiana. Senator Albert A. Gore, Sr., of Tennessee received a larger number of southern votes on the first ballot, especially by receiving all fifty-six delegate votes from Texas.[133] JFK's appeal to southern delegates was enhanced by his statements to the media expressing the need for moderation on civil rights and the animosity of some southern delegates toward both Gore and Kefauver for refusing to sign the "Southern Manifesto" opposing school desegregation.[134]

In a 1967 interview, Camille Gravel, a delegate from Louisiana, recalled how he and Frank Smith, a delegate and congressman from Mississippi, lobbied other southern delegates for JFK. After Governor Frank Clement of Tennessee released Louisiana delegates from a commitment to support him for vice president, Gravel was able to deliver all twenty-four of Louisiana's delegate votes to JFK, despite the fact that Governor Earl K. Long of Louisiana backed Kefauver.[135] Gravel was surprised to hear delegates from large states, like Pennsylvania, tell him "that, regardless of anything else, Kefauver was going to do more for the local candidates on the ticket than Kennedy."[136]

After voting on the first ballot for the vice presidential nomination had been completed, the top three candidates were Kefauver with 483½ votes, JFK with 304 votes, and Gore with 178 votes.[137] Virginia cast all of its 32 delegate votes for JFK on the first and second ballots. John Battle, the vice chairman of the Virginia delegation and a former governor of that state, was the father of William Battle, who had served in the navy with JFK during World War II. JFK's close friendship with William Battle influenced the Virginia delegation's decision to unanimously vote for JFK on both ballots and lobby other southern delegates to support JFK. This effort was especially important as favorite son vice presidential candidates, such as Governor Luther Hodges of North Carolina, withdrew their candidacies during the roll call of the second ballot.[138]

JFK's chances of being nominated improved further after Robert Wagner ended his vice presidential candidacy and New York cast 96½ of its 98 delegate votes for JFK, and Texas switched its 56 votes from Gore to JFK.[139] In announcing the change of his state's votes in favor of JFK, Senator Lyndon B. Johnson of Texas dramatically bellowed, "Texas proudly casts its vote for the fighting Senator who wears the scars of battle, that fearless Senator, the next vice president of the United States, John Kennedy of Massachusetts."[140] According to their biographers, however, Johnson and Rayburn switched their state's votes to JFK because of their determination to defeat Kefauver rather than their admiration for JFK.[141] During the second ballot, the two Texans concluded that JFK had a better chance of defeating Kefauver than Gore did.

In a 1964 interview, Gore recalled that he decided to end his vice presidential candidacy after Texas switched its votes to JFK.[142] In announcing his withdrawal to the convention, Gore also stated that Tennessee was now casting all of its 32 delegate votes for Kefauver.

This announcement stunned Rayburn and other pro-JFK delegates because Kefauver was known to be unpopular among most of his state's delegates.[143]

The withdrawal of Gore's candidacy and Tennessee's switch to Kefauver initiated a bandwagon effect that eventually led to Kefauver's nomination for vice president. Hubert H. Humphrey ended his vice presidential candidacy in favor of Kefauver, thereby delivering all of Minnesota's delegates and most pro-Humphrey delegates from other states, especially Missouri, to Kefauver.[144] With 687 delegate votes needed for the Democratic vice presidential nomination, Kefauver received 755½ votes to JFK's 589 votes by the end of the second ballot.[145] During the second ballot, support for JFK's vice presidential candidacy peaked at 656 delegate votes.[146]

After the completion of the second ballot on August 17, JFK addressed the convention and asked his fellow Democrats to unanimously nominate Estes Kefauver for vice president by acclamation. JFK stated, "I want to take this opportunity first to express my appreciation to Democrats from all parts of the country, North and South, East and West, who have been so generous and kind to me this afternoon. I think that it proves as nothing else can prove how strong and united the Democratic Party is."[147]

After the Democratic national convention ended, JFK and EMK traveled to the French Riviera to visit JPK. RFK joined the Stevenson campaign as an observer in late September. In an August 24, 1956 letter to the singer Morton Downey, JPK informed Downey about JFK's recent visit and narrow defeat at the Democratic national convention. He told Downey that JFK "came out of the convention so much better than anyone could have hoped. As far as I am concerned, you know how I feel—if you're going to get licked, get licked trying for the best, not the second best. His time is surely coming!"[148]

During the general election campaign between Stevenson and Eisenhower, JFK was determined to use his recent, nationally televised bid for the vice presidency to further enhance his status as a national political figure.[149] He delivered approximately 150 major speeches in 24 states for the Stevenson campaign. Theodore C. Sorensen accompanied JFK on his speaking tour. Sorensen wrote that he and JFK were "seeking votes for Stevenson in 1956, seeking votes for Senatorial, state and local candidates in 1957–1958–1959, and seeking friends for Kennedy at every stop."[150]

The Stevenson campaign hoped that JFK and other surrogate speakers would aggressively attack Nixon and the most divisive Republican policies, such as the Dixon-Yates controversy over public power. Such attacks would enable Stevenson to maintain a lofty, high-minded tone in his speeches, especially concerning his proposals to end hydrogen bomb tests and conditionally end the peace-time draft.[151] In a televised speech on hydrogen bomb testing delivered from Chicago on October 15, 1956, Stevenson said, "People everywhere are waiting for the United States to take once more the leadership for peace and civilization."[152]

JFK, however, avoided a combative, partisan style and substance in his campaign speeches. In one speech, the Democratic senator from Massachusetts told his audience, "I'm not criticizing Richard Nixon except to say that he is a conservative."[153] In a September 21, 1956 speech in Los Angeles, JFK stated that "we cannot afford in 1956 to approach foreign policy campaign issues with partisan distortion, exaggeration or oversimplification."[154] He also urged his fellow Democrats not to speak "intemperately" about Eisenhower's leadership concerning the current Suez crisis.[155]

In several other speeches, JFK characterized the Democratic Party under Stevenson as the party of youth, new ideas, and a better future. In a speech to Young Democrats in Winston-Salem, North Carolina, he said, "Adlai Stevenson, and the young men and women who are supporting him and running for office with him, truly represent a new America."[156] Ten days later, JFK delivered a speech to the Junior Chamber of Commerce in Richmond, Virginia. He avoided explicit criticism of Eisenhower and Nixon by continuing his theme of the Democratic Party as the party of youth. JFK stated, "When Adlai Stevenson talks about the new America, he can point to the many able young leaders of the Democratic Party—including those here with me tonight—who will be able to build that New America, to meet its challenges and seize its opportunities."[157]

A more self-serving, private purpose of JFK's speaking tour for the Stevenson-Kefauver ticket was to ingratiate himself with state and local Democratic officials and party organizations throughout the nation, especially those Democrats who would probably be delegates at the 1960 Democratic national convention. After Estes Kefauver narrowly defeated JFK for the Democratic vice presidential nomination, RFK ruefully and sardonically said that Kefauver won because "he had visited people and sent out cards and this is what paid off."[158] State and local party officials submitted the names and addresses of Democratic activists to Theodore C. Sorensen.[159]

In an October 10, 1956 letter to Sorensen, Donald E. Nicoll, the executive secretary of Maine's Democratic state committee, wrote that he was providing "a list of the delegates from Maine who voted for Senator Kennedy at the national Convention."[160] In his conclusion, Nicoll wrote, "We are looking forward to seeing you in Washington and having a chance to work with you on occasion. Many thanks for your assistance in the past."[161] In referring to "We," Nicoll was including Frank M. Coffin. Coffin was the Democratic state chairman of Maine. Coffin was recently elected as a U.S. representative from Maine, the first Democrat to accomplish this since 1934. In 1956, Maine still held its gubernatorial and congressional elections in September. In that gubernatorial election, Democratic Governor Edmund S. Muskie was reelected to another two-year term. When he was elected governor in 1954, Muskie was the first Democrat to win a gubernatorial election in Maine since 1932.[162]

JFK had traveled to Maine during the 1954 mid-term elections in order to campaign for Paul Fullam, the Democratic opponent of Senator Margaret Chase Smith.[163] He hoped to politically benefit from an increasingly competitive, electorally successful Democratic Party in a previously one-party Republican state. However, at the 1956 Democratic national convention, Maine cast only 7½ of its 14 delegate votes for JFK's vice presidential candidacy on the first ballot and all of its delegate votes for Kefauver on the second ballot.[164] If JFK wanted to unite all of New England's delegates to the 1960 Democratic national convention, then he needed to cultivate political support in Maine more frequently and regularly for the next few years.[165]

The 1956 elections also provided JFK with the opportunity to improve his relationships with other Democratic politicians in Massachusetts, especially Foster Furcolo. Unlike Furcolo's 1954 senatorial candidacy, JFK actively supported Furcolo's 1956 gubernatorial candidacy and campaigned with him.[166] Because JFK was often away from Massachusetts, he relied on the so-called "secretaries" from his 1952 Senate campaign to organize the Stevenson campaign in Massachusetts.

In a 1966 interview, Richard K. Donahue, a major organizer of JFK's 1952 Senate campaign, recalled that JFK and Kenneth P. O'Donnell expected him to achieve an especially difficult objective in trying to carry Massachusetts for the Stevenson-Kefauver ticket. He recalled that many former "secretaries" from 1952 were either apathetic about Stevenson or favored Eisenhower.[167] Donahue recalled that JFK "was not here practically at all at that time. He did a staggering amount of time around the country."[168]

Meanwhile, JFK was receiving mostly positive mail from throughout the nation about his television appearances, such as his October 28, 1956 interview on *Meet the Press*.[169] JFK appeared on *Meet the Press* a few days after delivering speeches in Texas for the Stevenson campaign.[170] Because he had become well-known for his national speaking tour, JFK was asked on *Meet the Press* if he was doing enough to help Stevenson carry Massachusetts in the Electoral College. "I've been working as hard as I can. The chances look good in Massachusetts," JFK replied.[171] However, according to Richard K. Donahue, there was little enthusiastic support for Stevenson in Massachusetts, except among well-educated, affluent liberals in Boston suburbs like Newton and working-class voters living in economically struggling industrial cities like Brockton.[172]

RFK traveled throughout the United States with Stevenson's campaign for six weeks. He was dismayed by Stevenson's inability or unwillingness to communicate effectively with small groups of average voters about bread-and-butter issues, especially in small towns and working-class, urban neighborhoods. He was appalled by the disorganization and internal conflicts within Stevenson's campaign.[173] Because of this disappointing, frustrating experience, RFK voted for Eisenhower in 1956.[174]

Adlai Stevenson delivered one of the last major speeches of his presidential campaign in Boston on November 5, 1956. It was a televised speech, and JFK introduced Stevenson. In this address, Stevenson combined his more unique policy proposals, such as an end to hydrogen bomb tests, with more familiar Democratic ideas about using the federal government to reduce poverty and improve education and access to affordable health care.[175] Near the conclusion of his speech in Boston, Stevenson philosophically mused, "Man always can see further than he can reach, but let us never stop reaching. He dreams more than he can achieve, but let us never lay to rest our dreams."[176]

Stevenson's nuanced, thoughtful rhetoric and innovative policy proposals combined with his criticism of Eisenhower's allegedly lackadaisical, "part-time" presidency and controversial administration officials, especially Nixon and Dulles, persuaded the *Berkshire Eagle* to endorse Adlai Stevenson for president. The *Berkshire Eagle*, an independent-minded daily newspaper in Pittsfield, endorsed Lodge instead of JFK for senator in 1952. In its 1956 endorsement of Stevenson, the *Berkshire Eagle* concluded that members of its editorial board "firmly believe that Mr. Stevenson can serve the nation better than a President, whose record is, at best, a very mixed one and whose ability to hold the reins for four more years must—however regretfully—be considered highly uncertain."[177]

Partially to alleviate public concern about his ability to serve another term because of his health, Eisenhower engaged in a vigorous speaking tour during the last two weeks of his 1956 presidential campaign. He also wanted to refute Stevenson's criticism of his administration and policy proposals on hydrogen bomb testing and the draft in front of local audiences in various states and reassure Republican candidates that he wanted to help them attract votes. In a speech in Portland, Oregon, Eisenhower criticized his Democratic opponents for supporting "heavier government expenditures," "deficits," and "centralized government."[178] In Jacksonville, Florida, the president explained the symbiotic relationships among economic growth, military strength, and the preservation of peace. Eisenhower stated, "So I say, at this particular stage of the world's history, where we see a once proud people being trampled down by marching regiments, this is no time to stop the draft—this is no time to stop perfecting our weapons."[179]

This speech and others reminded voters of the current foreign policy crises in the Middle East over the Suez Canal and in Hungary and Poland. Especially in his press conferences and televised addresses regarding these crises, Eisenhower communicated a reassuring message of experienced, responsible diplomatic and military leadership.[180] In a televised address to the nation delivered on October 31, 1956, Eisenhower summarized recent developments in the Middle East and Eastern Europe and his administration's responses to them. He calmly and firmly concluded, "The peace we seek and need means much more than mere absence of war. It means the acceptance of law, and the fostering of justice in all the world."[181]

In winning the 1956 presidential election, Dwight D. Eisenhower defeated Adlai Stevenson by wider margins in both popular votes and electoral votes than he had in 1952. In 1956, Eisenhower won 57 percent of the popular votes and 457 electoral votes to Stevenson's 42 percent of the popular votes and 73 electoral votes.[182] The Democrats increased their majorities in Congress by two seats in the House of Representatives and one seat in the Senate.[183] In gubernatorial elections, the Democrats made a net gain of one governorship.[184]

Like the voters of most other states that Eisenhower carried in the Electoral College, the voters of Massachusetts engaged in an unusual degree of split-ticket voting.[185] In Massachusetts, Eisenhower received 59 percent of the popular votes to Stevenson's 40 percent.[186] All fourteen of the Bay State's incumbent U.S. representatives, seven Republicans and seven Democrats, were reelected.[187] In his race for the governorship of Massachusetts, Democratic nominee Foster Furcolo won with 53 percent of the votes.[188] Ralph H. Bonnell, the Republican state chairman, described Furcolo's victory as "a colossal defeat, one of the worse [sic] whippings we have ever taken."[189] The Democrats also increased their majority in the state house of representatives by five seats and were confident that, partially because of future redistricting, they would win control of the state senate in the 1958 elections.[190]

In assessing the 1956 election results in Massachusetts, journalist Charles K. Currier wrote, "Bay State voters demonstrated an overriding disposition Tuesday to keep in office most everyone who sought re-election. The election disclosed little dissatisfaction with the status quo. No one seemed mad at anyone."[191] Likewise, in an interview with the press on the day after the 1956 election, JFK stated that the continuation of divided government with a Republican president and a Democratic Congress meant that "there will be moderate progress and friendly relations between the President and Congress as in recent years."[192]

On November 8, 1956, JFK gave an off-the-record lecture at the Tavern Club in Boston. He described his recent, national speaking tour on behalf of the Stevenson campaign and Democratic senatorial candidates and the lessons that he learned from it.[193] In the quips and anecdotes that spiced his lecture, JFK stated that anyone engaging in a national political campaign must be prepared "to go from Washington, D.C. to Richmond, Virginia by way of New Orleans, Louisiana" and to include Nevada in a tour of New England.[194] He added, "In one 10-day period I heard myself introduced as Senator John B. Kennedy, Senator Wagner, Senator John Fitzgerald and the Junior Senator from Wisconsin."[195] On a more serious note, JFK concluded his lecture by asking members of the Tavern Club to "try to understand politicians, parties and political campaigns in this kindly light, and be less harsh in your future judgment upon us."[196]

After the 1956 elections, some liberal activists, especially ADA members, still perceived JFK as an opportunistic career politician who lacked a sincere commitment to liberalism.[197] In general, however, most of JFK's constituents were proud of the national name recognition that he attained because of his narration of *The Pursuit of Happiness* film, nominating speech for Adlai Stevenson, dramatic, competitive pursuit of the Democratic vice presidential nomination, nationally televised interviews, and rigorous speaking tour on behalf of Stevenson and other Democratic candidates within Massachusetts and throughout the nation.[198] The *Worcester Telegram*, a daily newspaper in central Massachusetts known for its Republican preferences, stated that JFK's vice presidential candidacy "clearly demonstrated that it is possible for a native son of New England, with its liberal civil rights tradition, to command support from the Deep South."[199] This newspaper also partially attributed Democratic gains in the state elections in Massachusetts to JFK's speeches and campaign rallies throughout the state.[200] The *Boston Globe* published a similar conclusion.[201]

The pride of many of JFK's constituents in his enhanced national name recognition and political status was evident in their encouraging remarks regarding the 1960 presidential election. During the fall campaign, J. Lincoln Ritchie wrote to JFK, "I personally dont [sic] feel at all bad about loosing [sic] out for second place at the convention . . . You made a terrific impression on the people of the nation, and why be satisfied with second place, when in 1960 you could lead the ticket."[202] One week after the 1956 elections, Robert X. Tivnan, a Democratic state representative, wrote to JFK, "I think there is a great sentiment in Massachusetts for Kennedy for President. I wish you the best of luck."[203]

Of course, not all of JFK's constituents were proud of his new status as a national celebrity within the Democratic Party and his increasingly apparent presidential ambition. As JFK's rhetoric and legislative behavior became more liberal and partisan after his first two years in the Senate, he alienated his more conservative constituents. On the day after the Democratic national convention showed its film *The Pursuit of Happiness* with JFK's narration, an irate New Bedford resident sent JFK a telegram. In his telegram, he stated, "I am completely disappointed that you chose to prostitute your intellect and popularity by narrating the filmed emotional trash shown to the American people last night."[204]

During the next two years, JFK needed to accomplish several objectives before he could begin actively and openly pursuing the Democratic presidential nomination of 1960. They included achieving a significant legislative victory in the Senate, serving as a popular speaker at Democratic fund raising dinners, state conventions, and other party functions throughout the nation, and making himself more acceptable to midwestern Democrats on agricultural issues and southern Democrats on civil rights issues. JFK's strategy, however, would also be influenced by Washington, DC's political environment of divided government and the decisions of Senate Majority Leader Lyndon B. Johnson.

PLATE 1. Joseph P. Kennedy leaving the White House in 1937.
Courtesy: Library of Congress

PLATE 2. The Kennedy family in Hyannis Port, Massachusetts during the 1940s. *Courtesy: John F. Kennedy Presidential Library and Museum, Boston*

PLATE 3. JFK and Henry Cabot Lodge, Jr. in 1952. Courtesy: *John F. Kennedy Presidential Library and Museum, Boston*

PLATE 4. JFK and Bishop John J. Wright at a church festival in Bolton, Massachusetts in 1952. *Courtesy: Catholic Diocese of Worcester*

PLATE 5. Labor union supporters of JFK's Senate candidacy in 1952. Courtesy: Department of Special Collections and University Archives, W.E.B. DuBois Library, University of Massachusetts, Amherst

PLATE 6. Harry S. Truman and Adlai E. Stevenson in the White House in 1952. *Courtesy: National Park Service, Abbie Rowe, Harry S. Truman Presidential Library and Museum*

PLATE 7. JFK examining tornado damage in Worcester, Massachusetts in 1953. *Courtesy: Catholic Diocese of Worcester*

PLATE 8. JFK at Saint Michael's College in Colchester, Vermont in 1954. *Courtesy: Saint Michael's College Archives, Saint Michael's College, Colchester, Vermont*

PLATE 9. JFK at a bill signing ceremony in the White House in 1954. *Courtesy: National Park Service and Dwight D. Eisenhower Presidential Library and Museum*

PLATE 10. JFK listening to Sr. M. Rose Isabel at Anna Maria College in Paxton, Massachusetts in 1955. *Courtesy: Anna Maria College*

PLATE 11. Leverett Saltonstall. *Courtesy: U.S. Senate Historical Office*

PLATE 12. Margaret Chase Smith. *Courtesy: U.S. Senate Historical Office*

PLATE 13. Lyndon B. Johnson in 1955. *Courtesy: Library of Congress*

PLATE 14. Joseph W. Martin, Jr. in 1956. *Courtesy: Stonehill College: Joseph W. Martin, Jr. Papers*

PLATE 15. Dwight D. Eisenhower in the White House in 1956. Courtesy: *National Park Service and Dwight D. Eisenhower Presidential Library and Museum*

Plate 16. Edmund S. Muskie voting in Waterville, Maine in 1956. *Courtesy: Edmund S. Muskie Archives and Special Collections Library, Bates College*

PLATE 17. Foster Furcolo. *Courtesy: Foster Furcolo, Jr.*

PLATE 18. JFK at Assumption College in Worcester, Massachusetts in 1958. *Courtesy: Assumption College*

PLATE 19. Grace Dodd, Thomas J. Dodd, and JFK in Hartford, Connecticut in 1958. *Courtesy: Archives and Special Collections, University of Connecticut Libraries*

PLATE 20. JFK and Jacqueline Kennedy with Merrimack College students in Andover, Massachusetts in 1958. *Courtesy: Frank Leone, Jr./Merrimack College*

PLATE 21. JFK and Bernard L. Boutin in Manchester, New Hampshire in 1958. *Courtesy: Fay Foto/Boston and New Hampshire Historical Society*

PLATE 22. JFK and campaign supporters at the Democratic state convention in Boston in 1958. *Courtesy: Department of Special Collections and University Archives, W.E.B. DuBois Library, University of Massachusetts, Amherst*

PLATE 23. JFK campaigning in Brockton, Massachusetts in 1958. *Courtesy: Stonehill College Archives and Historical Collections: Stanley A. Bauman Photograph Collection*

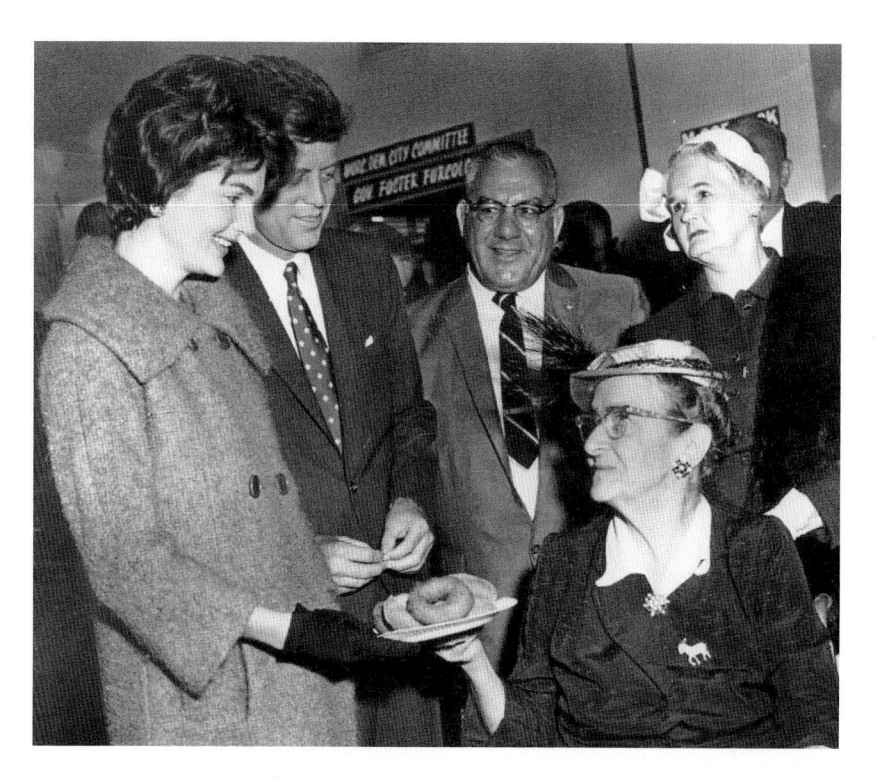

PLATE 24. JFK and Jacqueline Kennedy campaigning in Worcester, Massachusetts in 1958. *Courtesy: George P. Cocaine Collection, Worcester Historical Museum*

PLATE 25. Queen Elizabeth II and Dwight D. Eisenhower at the dedication of the St. Lawrence Seaway in 1959. *Courtesy: U.S. Navy and Dwight D. Eisenhower Presidential Library and Museum*

PLATE 26. JFK and Harry S. Truman in Independence, Missouri in 1959. *Courtesy: Harry S. Truman Presidential Library and Museum*

PLATE 27. Jacqueline Kennedy and JFK in Wisconsin in 1959, Image WHi—58661. *Courtesy: Wisconsin Historical Society*

PLATE 28. Thomas P. "Tip" O'Neill, Jr. and John W. McCormack in 1960. *Courtesy: John J. Burns Library, Boston College*

PLATE 29. Dwight D. Eisenhower and Richard M. Nixon in the White House in 1960. *Courtesy: National Park Service and Dwight D. Eisenhower Presidential Library and Museum*

PLATE 30. Abraham Ribicoff in Waterbury, Connecticut in 1960.
Courtesy: Michael Salvatore Smith

PLATE 31. JFK, Abram L. Sachar, and Eleanor Roosevelt at Brandeis University in Waltham, Massachusetts in 1960. *Courtesy: Brandeis University*

PLATE 32. JFK at Dartmouth College in Hanover, New Hampshire in 1960. *Courtesy: Dartmouth College Library*

5

JFK and the 1958 Elections

IN THE IMMEDIATE AFTERMATH OF the 1956 elections, both Democratic and Republican politicians in the nation's capital sought to develop a policymaking and publicity strategy that would benefit them in the 1958 midterm elections, either despite or because of a divided government. The headquarters of the Republican National Committee (RNC) submitted a memo to President Eisenhower explaining the difference between the president's landslide reelection and the relatively poor performance of Republican congressional and gubernatorial candidates. The RNC memo explained that while Eisenhower was popular and respected by most voters, the Republican Party suffered an image problem as the party of big business and conservatives.[1] It recommended that the Republican Party change its image, recruit more attractive congressional and gubernatorial candidates, and increase grassroots activities, "so that they touch more people and make them feel that the Party is theirs."[2]

On November 27, 1956, the executive committee of the Democratic National Committee (DNC) established the Democratic Advisory Council (DAC). The general purposes of the DAC were to research and provide policy proposals for Democratic candidates in the 1958 and 1960 elections and for the 1960 Democratic national platform. DAC members soon included such prominent Democrats as Dean Acheson, former secretary of state under Truman, and Eleanor Roosevelt.[3]

DNC chairman Paul M. Butler also invited Speaker of the House Sam Rayburn, Senate Majority Leader Lyndon B. Johnson, and JFK to join the DAC. JFK politely declined Butler's invitation in 1957 but finally joined the DAC by the end of 1959.[4] Rayburn and Johnson also declined Butler's offers of membership in the DAC.

Unlike JFK, Rayburn and Johnson were outspoken critics of Butler's chairmanship of the DNC.[5] Butler and other liberal Democrats partially attributed Adlai Stevenson's landslide defeat in 1956 to Rayburn's and Johnson's mostly cooperative, compromising relationship with Eisenhower on major legislation. Besides perceiving Butler as a divisive, controversial party leader because of his aggressive liberalism on civil rights, Rayburn and Johnson regarded Butler and the DAC as interfering rivals to their legislative leadership.[6] Although he agreed to serve on the DAC, former president Harry S. Truman generally agreed with Rayburn's and Johnson's criticisms of Butler's chairmanship.[7]

JFK wanted to remain publicly aloof from this conflict between Butler and his party's congressional leadership while privately ingratiating himself with Johnson. JFK hoped that Johnson's influence with the Democratic Steering Committee would help him to secure a seat on the Senate Foreign Relations Committee. On December 6, 1956, one day after he received Butler's invitation to join the DAC, JFK praised Johnson's leadership of the Senate and urged his fellow Democratic senators to retain Johnson as Senate majority leader during the upcoming 85th Congress. In particular, the Democratic senator from Massachusetts stated that his fellow Democrats should not blame Johnson or any other Democrat for Eisenhower's landslide victory. Instead, they should credit Johnson's legislative leadership for the increase in Democratic majorities in Congress. According to JFK, "These successes, due in considerable measure to Majority Leader Johnson's uniquely effective leadership, were largely responsible for our party's victory in last fall's Congressional elections."[8]

On January 8, 1957, the Democratic Steering Committee announced that JFK, instead of Estes Kefauver, had been selected for a seat on the Senate Foreign Relations Committee. Because of the recent retirement of Senator Walter George of Georgia, Senator Theodore F. Green of Rhode Island would chair this committee.[9] JFK would also chair the Senate Foreign Relations Committee's subcommittees on Internal Organization Affairs and African Affairs.

Rumors quickly circulated within the Senate and among journalists about why Johnson, through his domination of the Democratic Steering Committee, chose JFK instead of Kefauver, despite the Tennessean's greater seniority. Johnson's long-standing contempt for Kefauver was well-known, and the Texan had implacably opposed Kefauver's nomination for vice president.

More seriously and specifically, there was a perception that the Senate majority leader was seeking revenge on Kefauver for voting against a motion sponsored by Johnson and other southern Democrats to reject an effort to liberalize Senate rules on filibusters and invoking cloture.[10] In a January 9, 1957 letter to Johnson, Kefauver wrote, "Of course, I do not blame Jack for wanting to improve his position and I have congratulated him, but I wanted to put in the record to you my feelings about it. I am disappointed and feel I have been done very badly."[11] In his prompt reply to Kefauver, Johnson acknowledged the importance of seniority. He also wrote, "But in addition to seniority, the Steering Committee takes into account geography, political philosophy, the current status of a member desiring a change, and sometimes the estimate of a man's own colleagues toward him."[12]

With a seat on the Senate Labor and Public Welfare Committee, JFK also served on this committee's Select Committee on Improper Activities in the Labor Management Field. It became commonly known as the McClellan committee because it was chaired by Senator John McClellan of Arkansas. RFK simultaneously served as the McClellan committee's chief counsel. Meanwhile, JFK also chaired a subcommittee on labor.

In December, 1956, RFK obtained the subpoenaed files of Nathan W. Shefferman. Shefferman was a labor-management relationship consultant in Chicago who was associated with David Beck, president of the International Brotherhood of Teamsters (IBT).[13] Shefferman's files revealed that he was a "union buster" who had received $85,000 in IBT funds from Beck.[14] Further investigations and revelations regarding Beck's improper use of union funds, his expulsion from the AFL-CIO's executive council, and his repeated refusal to answer questions before the McClellan committee by resorting to the fifth amendment contributed to the end of Beck's presidency and

James R. Hoffa's succession as president of the Teamsters by October of 1957.[15]

JFK specialized in labor reform as his signature legislative accomplishment during the remainder of his Senate career for several reasons. First, JFK was aware of the fact that many of his fellow senators, especially Senate Majority Leader Lyndon B. Johnson, perceived JFK as a "show horse" instead of a "work horse."[16] The televised McClellan committee hearings provided JFK with "show horse" opportunities to join RFK in aggressively questioning labor union officials and criminals associated with them. However, labor reform's greater value for JFK's Senate career and presidential ambition was that it enabled him to demonstrate his "work horse" abilities in the legislative process to his colleagues and the media. Depending on the bill's provisions and the compromises that were made, there was a strong probability that a labor reform bill sponsored by JFK in his capacity as a subcommittee chairman would receive broad, bipartisan support in Congress and be signed into law by Eisenhower before 1960.

Second, JFK's participation in the McClellan committee hearings and his leadership in developing and advocating legislation that resulted from them offered more assets than liabilities for his 1958 reelection campaign and 1960 presidential campaign. The McClellan committee hearings focused on allegations of corrupt, unethical, and illegal activities by Teamsters' officials and criminals colluding with them in several states, but not Massachusetts.[17] JFK's rhetoric and legislative behavior moved in a more conventional direction as a northern, liberal Democratic senator on most issues after 1956. However, he needed to remind split-ticket voters in Massachusetts and later throughout the United States that he was an unconventional, independent-minded Democrat by investigating, criticizing, and seeking to reform labor union practices. In its March 1957 issue, the *American Mercury*, a magazine known for its conservative opinions, referred to JFK as "the perfect politician" and described him as "basically a moderate liberal, but with many conservative leanings."[18]

Third, the focus of JFK, RFK, and the McClellan committee in general on the Teamsters was not as bold and courageous as the general public and some journalists assumed.[19] By the time that the

McClellan committee's investigation began, most national AFL-CIO officials regarded the IBT, i.e., the Teamsters, as a troublesome, controversial member union. At the end of 1957, the executive council of the AFL-CIO expelled the IBT from its membership. The McClellan committee's investigation and the AFL-CIO's expulsion of the Teamsters were strongly endorsed by Walter Reuther, president of the United Automobile Workers (UAW). Both JFK and RFK were aware of how powerful and influential the UAW was among delegates at Democratic national conventions. Joseph L. Rauh, Jr., an attorney for the UAW and a civil rights activist, later noted how courteous and accommodating RFK and JFK were to UAW witnesses who testified before the McClellan committee.[20]

While even Republican members of the McClellan committee like Senator Barry Goldwater of Arizona were impressed by JFK's diligence in working on the details of labor reform legislation, JFK capitalized on the publicity value of this issue.[21] In a May 21, 1957 speech to the New England Publishers' Association in Boston, JFK emphasized his legislative objectives of strengthening the rights of labor union members and the power of the federal government to supervise union elections and finances and prohibit racketeering practices. He concluded this speech by urging these newspaper publishers to fulfill their responsibilities to the public concerning labor racketeering. He stated, "I know we can count on you to do your part—not for any glory or profit to yourselves, but for your state and your country, for your families and your friends, for all we believe in and all we hold dear.[22]

Two days later, JFK spoke at a Democratic dinner in Chicago. He assured his audience that the McClellan committee's investigation was "pro-labor, not anti-labor" and that the labor reform bill that resulted from it "will be in the interest of the millions of honest trade union members."[23] In a speech delivered to the annual meeting of the Associated Industries of Massachusetts on October 24, 1957, in Boston, JFK praised the relatively harmonious and cooperative relations between management and labor in Massachusetts compared to other states. Toward the end of this speech, he claimed that his work on the McClellan committee was a "discouraging, difficult task, taking the Committee into a seamy side of American life and labor that would be more pleasant to ignore, and stirring hostilities and prejudices that are politically better kept dormant."[24]

JFK's recently secured seat on the Senate Foreign Relations Committee and chairmanships of some of its subcommittees, whose jurisdictions included the United Nations and Africa, provided him with the opportunity to challenge the Eisenhower administration's foreign policy regarding Algeria. On July 2, 1957, JFK delivered a Senate speech denouncing both Soviet and European imperialism as enemies of freedom and national self-determination. He then criticized the French government's policies in Algeria and urged the Eisenhower administration to support independence for Algeria. As Americans prepared to celebrate the Fourth of July, JFK contended that they and he must realize that "our traditional and deeply felt philosophy of freedom and independence for all peoples everywhere" represented their most powerful resource in deterring the spread of Communism in the Third World.[25] In a July 8, 1957 speech on Algeria, JFK dramatically stated, "The Algerian situation is a deadly time bomb steadily ticking toward the day when another disaster to the free world—worse than Indochina—might explode."[26]

JFK's July 2nd speech on Algeria ignited immediate reactions from the Eisenhower administration and the French government. In his July 3, 1957 press conference, Eisenhower affirmed Secretary of State John Foster Dulles's earlier criticism of JFK's speech on Algeria. The president added that, in situations like the Algerian conflict, American foreign policy "means often you work behind the scenes, because you don't get up and begin to shout about such things or there will be no effectiveness."[27] On July 7, 1956, Robert Lacoste, the French minister for Algeria, dismissed JFK as "a young, ambitious Senator" who only spoke for "the old maids of the United States."[28] Lacoste also warned that if France withdrew from Algeria there would be greater turmoil in North Africa and the Middle East, eventually leading to World War III.

As a freshman senator from the opposition party, JFK, of course, could exert little immediate influence on Eisenhower's foreign policy toward Algeria. The Eisenhower administration, however, soon began to adopt a neutral position toward France regarding the Algerian situation. In his study of the Algerian war, British historian Alistair Horne wrote, "No speech on foreign affairs by Senator Kennedy attracted more attention, both at home and abroad, and under such pressure the United States official policy on Algeria now began to shift."[29]

Actually, JFK's advocacy of independence for Algeria was consistent with his belief that the United States needed to equally oppose imperialism and colonialism by both its West European allies and the Soviet Union in its foreign policy. Likewise, he had earlier opposed the continued French control of Indochina, which included Vietnam.[30] JFK believed that the United States would be hypocritical and less effective in preventing the spread of Communism in the Third World if it implicitly accepted West European colonialism.[31]

Worried about this controversial reaction to his speech on Algeria, JFK consulted his father. JPK replied, "You lucky mush. You don't know it and neither does anyone else, but within a few months everyone is going to know just how right you were on Algeria."[32] JPK's words were prophetic. JFK's statements on Algeria did not cause any lasting political damage to his relationship to his constituents in Massachusetts or his national reputation.

In an apparent response to those who criticized him for denouncing French imperialism instead of Soviet imperialism, JFK delivered a Senate speech regarding Poland and other Communist countries in eastern and central Europe on August 21, 1957.[33] He urged changes in American foreign aid and trade policies toward countries behind the Iron Curtain so that they could become more economically independent of the Soviet Union. In submitting a bill to make these policy changes, JFK concluded, "Recent dispatches from Warsaw have made it all too clear that the brave people of Poland are still, even under present conditions, in a prison—however more tolerable their jailers may have become."[34]

On that same day, JFK submitted a bill to amend the Immigration and Nationality Act of 1952, commonly known as the McCarran-Walter Act. In general, he wanted to make it easier for immigrants from southern, central, and eastern Europe to enter the United States, especially for the purposes of family reunification and political refuge from Communist governments.[35] This bill had a broader purpose than JFK's earlier bill. Submitted on June 27, 1957, JFK's previous immigration bill proposed to allow the admission of an additional 50,000 aliens during the next two years for various emergency reasons.[36]

JFK's emphasis on liberalizing American immigration laws, especially to favor immigrants from southern and eastern Europe, politically benefited him in Massachusetts. During the 1950s, Massachusetts had a higher percentage of residents who were either immigrants or the children of immigrants compared to any other state.[37] A televised campaign film for JFK's 1958 reelection to the Senate featured a family in Massachusetts expressing its gratitude for JFK's efforts to secure the immigration of a relative from Italy.[39]

JFK summarized and articulated his foreign policy ideas in an article entitled, "A Democrat Looks at Foreign Policy" that was published in the October 1957 issue of *Foreign Affairs*. In it, he cited the two major problems of current American foreign policy as "a failure to appreciate how the forces of nationalism are rewriting the geopolitical map of the world" and "a lack of decision and conviction in our leadership."[40] He contended that American foreign policy should adopt his proposals on foreign aid, trade, and national self-determination in order to more successfully fight the Cold War, especially in the Third World, by assuring these countries of the sincerity and effectiveness of American protection and promotion of freedom and democracy. JFK concluded that "there is an opportunity for the idealistic initiative of our people and the self-interest of the nation to intersect."[41]

In preparing for his 1958 reelection campaign and future presidential campaign, JFK also realized the importance of attracting more political support from Jews by communicating his foreign policy ideas, especially concerning Israel and the Middle East because of the recent Suez crisis. In a 1966 interview, Laurence J. Fuchs recalled that JFK consulted him in order to prepare several speeches for Jewish audiences. Fuchs was a political science professor at Brandeis University and had recently published his research on Jewish political behavior and the voting behavior of Irish Americans in Boston in the 1956 presidential election. Fuchs was also close to Eleanor Roosevelt, a trustee of Brandeis University, and JFK hoped to improve his political relationship with Eleanor Roosevelt through Fuchs.[42]

On November 19, 1957, JFK delivered a speech at Temple Emmanuel in New York City. After analyzing how the recent Soviet launching of the *Sputnik* satellite was already creating new challenges for American foreign policy, he stated that "as the Suez episode and the events surrounding it illustrated, there is important impact in the dissolution of the old European empires."[43] Two weeks later on December 3, 1957, JFK addressed the National Conference of Christians and Jews in Chicago. He expressed concern about the growing Soviet threat to the Middle East and what *Sputnik* revealed about how the United States was lagging behind the Soviet Union in science, technology, and education. However, he concluded this speech with an optimistic emphasis on "the principles of our Judaic-Christian heritage. It is a heritage which teaches us self-discipline—which will enable us to sacrifice economic convenience—and physical comfort to a degree sufficient to offset the sacrifice of human values and liberties which has been extracted from the Russian people."[44]

During the 85th Congress, JFK used his seat on the Senate Foreign Relations Committee to engage in rhetoric and legislative behavior that expressed his belief that the United States could and should synthesize idealism and realism in fighting the Cold War more successfully, especially in the Third World and eastern Europe.[45] Some of his foreign policy statements and proposals, especially regarding Algeria, attracted rebukes from the Eisenhower administration, Republicans in Congress, and Dean Acheson, a Democrat and former secretary of state.[46] However, they mostly benefited his political image in Massachusetts and throughout the United States. They portrayed JFK as an innovative, thoughtful statesman who was willing to attract criticism and controversy in order to develop and propose new ideas, methods, and perspectives for American foreign policy.

Civil rights, by contrast, was an issue that was fraught with peril for JFK's political career. JFK's voting record as a congressman and as a senator from 1953 to 1956 was similar to those of other northern Democrats in Congress. Unlike other northern Democrat senators, such as Hubert H. Humphrey and Paul Douglas, JFK, however, did not distinguish himself as a leading advocate of stronger federal civil rights policies for African Americans.

From the perspective of JFK's political interests, ambitions, and advancement, there were several factors that contributed to his passivity and obscurity on civil rights compared to other issues. African Americans comprised a very small percentage of the voters in Massachusetts and were usually not a crucial factor in determining the outcome of congressional and senatorial elections. Republican candidates in Massachusetts tended to be just as liberal on civil rights, if not more so, than their Democratic opponents. Thus, JFK made the reform of immigration laws a higher priority than civil rights since Italian Americans represented a much larger voting bloc than African Americans in his state.

Furthermore, the fact that JFK was not an outspoken, aggressive advocate of civil rights legislation helped him to receive favorable treatment from Senate Majority Leader Lyndon B. Johnson and the southern-dominated Democratic Steering Committee regarding his recent committee assignments. This fact also made JFK, unlike Humphrey, acceptable to many southern delegates for their party's vice presidential nomination at the Democratic national convention of 1956. The Democratic senator from Massachusetts was reluctant to sacrifice southern delegate support for a future presidential candidacy.

By 1957, civil rights became a more prominent, demanding, and urgent political and legislative issue. In the 1956 presidential election, Dwight D. Eisenhower received almost 40 percent of the black vote, a higher percentage than he had received in 1952.[47] White liberal activists within the Democratic Party, particularly ADA members, believed that the cautious, moderate wording and tone of the 1956 Democratic national platform and Adlai Stevenson's speeches on civil rights led African Americans to conclude that there was no meaningful difference on civil rights between the two major parties and their presidential nominees. In addition, the "Southern Manifesto" of 1956 and staunch opposition to the *Brown* decision on school desegregation by elected officials in the South convinced liberals and civil rights activists that Congress and the president must enact a law authorizing federal protection of voting rights for African Americans in the South during the 85th Congress.[48]

Compared to African Americans in Massachusetts, pro-civil rights white liberals, especially among ADA members and academics, were more influential in that state's politics. They were already skeptical and, in some cases, cynical and dismissive, about the sincerity and efficacy of JFK's liberalism.[49] JFK's liberal critics cited his failure to either vote to censure or publicly denounce Senator Joseph R. McCarthy of Wisconsin, some of his conservative statements and votes on legislation, the presumed influence of his conservative, controversial father, JFK's refusal to join the ADA and other liberal organizations, and the hostility of Eleanor Roosevelt to JFK.[50]

Consequently, unless JFK became more vocal and liberal on civil rights legislation during the 85th Congress, there were several ways in which liberal activists in Massachusetts could harm him politically. They could prevent the landslide reelection margin that he sought in 1958 by refusing to vote for him or by supporting a Republican opponent who was an outspoken liberal on civil rights. They could also embarrass him by saturating the newspapers of Massachusetts with letters to the editor and advertisements criticizing his record on civil rights and eliciting publicized anti-JFK statements from the NAACP.[51] Such political activities within Massachusetts could then spread nationally and make it more difficult for JFK to attract enough northern and western delegate support at the 1960 Democratic national convention, especially if he competed against a more liberal rival like Hubert H. Humphrey for their party's presidential nomination.[52]

For Senate Majority Leader Lyndon B. Johnson, civil rights was an issue that posed risks and dangers in his efforts to simultaneously maintain cooperative legislative relationships with both his southern and non-southern Democratic colleagues and retain his Senate seat from Texas. As a congressman and then a senator from Texas, Johnson had quietly yet consistently opposed previous civil rights proposals and policies, such as the creation of a permanent Fair Employment Practices Committee (FEPC), federal legislation against lynching and poll taxes, and the Truman administration's civil rights bills. Toward the end of the 1956 session of Congress, Johnson made sure that the Eisenhower administration's civil rights bill was sent to the Senate Judiciary Committee. This committee was chaired by Senator James Eastland of Mississippi, an unyielding segregationist, where it died. As recently as January 1957, Johnson worked closely with Senator Richard B. Russell of Georgia to prevent a change in filibuster rules that would have made it easier for pro-civil rights senators to stop or prevent filibusters by southern senators.[53]

As long as Johnson thwarted the passage of civil rights legislation, his political career, like that of Russell, his mentor, would be limited to the Senate. In 1956, Johnson seriously considered running for president or vice president.[54] If Johnson wanted to have a reasonable chance of being nominated for either position in 1960, then he needed to not only support but also lead the passage of a civil rights bill in the Senate. According to journalists Rowland Evans and Robert Novak, this accomplishment "would move him into the mainstream of the Democratic party for the first time since his early days as a young New Deal Congressman."[55]

In addition to its impact on the political careers and presidential aspirations of JFK and Johnson, civil rights legislation had the potential to make major coalitional changes within and between the two major parties. In his journal entry for March 30–31, 1957, historian Arthur M. Schlesinger, Jr., described a recent meeting with the Senate majority leader. Johnson told Schlesinger that he feared that non-southern Democrats in the Senate might create their own pro-civil rights liberal party because of their growing frustration with their southern colleagues on this issue.[56] Also, Dwight D. Eisenhower's relatively impressive electoral performance among African Americans was linked to the *Brown* decision and his attorney general's submission of a civil rights bill to Congress in 1956.[57] Adam Clayton Powell, Jr., a Democratic representative from New York and the most nationally prominent African American in Congress, endorsed Eisenhower instead of Stevenson in the 1956 presidential election.[58]

Shortly before the 85th Congress began, Attorney General Herbert Brownell submitted a civil rights bill to Congress. Brownell's 1957 civil rights bill was almost identical to his 1956 bill. While Brownell's civil rights bill focused almost entirely on voting rights, it included a provision known as Section III. Section III authorized the attorney general to directly enforce federal court orders to desegregate public schools and to enter state criminal cases, such as the recent murder of Emmett Till, in which the attorney general believed that the 14th amendment was violated. Other provisions of this bill included the creation of a civil rights commission, a separate civil rights division within the U.S. Department of Justice, and an enforcement process to guarantee the right to vote in federal elections, especially in the South where African Americans were systematically denied the right to vote by state laws and practices.[59]

On June 18, 1957, the U.S. House of Representatives passed the Eisenhower administration's civil rights bill by a vote of 286 to 126.[60] The bipartisan coalition in the Senate that supported this bill was led by Democratic Senator Paul Douglas of Illinois and Republican Senator William Knowland of California, the Senate minority leader. This bipartisan Senate majority succeeded in having Brownell's civil rights bill bypass the Senate Judiciary Committee. Senator Richard B. Russell then realized that southern reliance on filibusters could not prevent passage of this bill. Therefore, Russell decided to focus his efforts on weakening the content and effectiveness of the Brownell bill.

Russell and other southern senators insisted that Section III be eliminated from this bill and that the right to a trial by jury be added to criminal contempt cases regarding violations of voting rights. In a July 2, 1957 Senate speech, Russell denounced Section III and warned that it would empower the federal government to use military force not only to desegregate public schools but also to desegregate all aspects of public life in the South.[61] The influence of Russell's argument against Section III was apparent when Eisenhower expressed uncertainty and ambivalence about Brownell's civil rights bill, especially Section III.[62]

JFK joined Johnson, Russell and other southern senators in their unsuccessful effort to refer Brownell's bill to the Senate Judiciary Committee, but he also voted with the Douglas-Knowland coalition to retain Section III.[63] A majority of senators, however, agreed with

Russell to virtually eliminate Section III by a vote of 52 to 38.[64] After carefully consulting law professors about the right to a trial by jury, JFK voted with Russell, Johnson, and other southern senators to add a jury trial provision to Section IV of Brownell's bill. On August 1, 1957, the Senate voted 51 to 42 to adopt the jury trial amendment.[65] Liberal critics of this amendment argued that all-white juries in the South would never convict anyone of violating an African American's right to vote.[66]

The Senate passed its amended version of Brownell's civil rights bill on August 7, 1957, by a vote of 72 to 18 and a compromise bill drafted in the House of Representatives on August 29, 1957, by a vote of 60 to 15. Eisenhower signed the bill into law on September 9, 1957.[67] Five days later, Eisenhower conferred with Governor Orval Faubus of Arkansas regarding the governor's obstruction of the court-ordered desegregation of Central High School in Little Rock. The president later sent U.S. Army troops to enforce the court order.[68]

The emergence of the school desegregation crisis and controversy in Little Rock so soon after Eisenhower signed the Civil Rights Act of 1957 further inflamed tensions and conflicts between southern and non-southern Democrats. Even before the Senate passed the significantly weakened civil rights bill, JFK had to defend his vote against bypassing the Senate Judiciary Committee with its anti-civil rights chairman. In a letter to a liberal critic, JFK defensively wrote, "No Senator can claim a more consistent record than I in supporting civil rights measures."[69] Likewise, in a letter to NAACP lobbyist Clarence Mitchell, JFK wrote that bypassing the Senate Judiciary Committee would have been a "dangerous precedent" and added, "This is a precedent, after all, which can be used against our causes and other liberal issues in the future."[70]

JFK was an assertive, persistent advocate of retaining Section III with its increased powers for the attorney general to enforce federal court orders in school desegregation cases. His liberal critics, however, focused on his support of the jury trial amendment during the remainder of his Senate career and presidential campaign. From their perspective, JFK's vote for the jury trial amendment was a calculated, cynical decision to appease southern Democrats in his quest for southern support for his future presidential candidacy and remain loyal to Johnson's leadership of the Senate.[71]

Among non-southern Democratic senators, JFK was not the only one who voted for the jury trial amendment. Both of his Democratic colleagues from New England, Senators Theodore F. Green and John O. Pastore of Rhode Island, voted for it and so did almost all western Democratic senators, including Michael J. Mansfield of Montana and Frank Church of Idaho.[72] In a 1981 interview, Church contended that the adoption of the jury trial amendment was essential for the Senate's passage of the Civil Rights Act of 1957.[73]

While Senate Majority Leader Lyndon B. Johnson received much of the credit for Senate passage of the Civil Rights Act of 1957, JFK needed to explain and justify his vote on this law, especially to African Americans and white liberal activists in Massachusetts as he prepared for his reelection campaign. He also had to explain his position on school desegregation during his frequent speaking engagements in the South. Shortly after the desegregation controversy in Little Rock began and southern whites became increasingly angry about the possibility of the federal government's widespread use of military force to desegregate public schools in the South, JFK spoke to a meeting of Young Democrats in Jackson, Mississippi. Republican state chairman Wirt Yerger, Jr., publicly challenged JFK to state his position on school desegregation. As quoted in an October 8, 1957 press release from his Senate office, JFK told the Mississippi Democrats, "I have no hesitancy in telling him the same thing I have said in my own city of Boston—that I have accepted the Supreme Court's decision on desegregation as the law of the land. I know we do not all agree on that issue—but I think most of us do agree on the necessity to uphold law and order in every part of the land. I now invite Republican Chairman Yerger to tell us his views on President Eisenhower and Mr. Nixon."[74]

In its article about JFK's speech in Mississippi and the reaction of the white audience to it, *Time* magazine noted that JFK received warm, friendly applause. "The crowd came to its feet, alive, roaring and stomping its approval: Jack Kennedy had won it by his own display of courage and by turning all good Democrats against the odious

Republicans."[75] *Time* quoted James P. Coleman, the segregationist Democratic governor of Mississippi, as saying about JFK, "I think he is our best presidential prospect for 1960, and I am all for him."[76]

The potential of civil rights issues for dividing and weakening the Democratic Party in the 1958 elections was overshadowed by the 1957–1958 recession. The unemployment rate increased from 4.3 percent in 1957 to 6.8 percent in 1958.[77] Also, during this same period, wholesale prices for corn, wheat, milk, and cotton textiles declined.[78] In his analysis of the 1957–1958 recession, economist Harold G. Vatter wrote that "it is significant that the major culprit was the commodity-producing industries, wherein the total of such disbursements fell from $103.4 billion in June, 1957 to $95.0 billion in April, 1958."[79] Economist Alvin H. Hansen characterized the 1957–1958 recession as both an "inventory recession" and a "fixed capital recession." He noted that, unlike previous post-World War II recessions, the 1957–1958 recession included a modest increase in inflation.[80]

The economic suffering and losses caused or aggravated by the 1957–1958 recession were especially severe in the Midwest because of that region's dependence on corn, wheat, and dairy farming and on such heavy industries as automobiles and steel. This recession also worsened the already depressed conditions of coal mining in Appalachia and textile and shoe mills in New England. In a letter to White House press secretary James Hagerty, a woman from North Adams, a small city in western Massachusetts highly dependent on the textile industry for jobs, wrote, "Wouldn't President Eisenhower listen to me for five minutes so I could light my little candle and try to get the help we need so badly?"[81]

The Eisenhower administration was divided on how to respond to the recession. William McChesney Martin, chairman of the Federal Reserve Board (FRB), believed that inflation posed a greater long-term threat to the economy. Consequently, under his leadership, the FRB raised the discount rate, maintained a tight money supply, and pursued restrictive credit policies.[82] Raymond Saulnier, the chairman of the Council of Economic Advisers (CEA), generally opposed the FRB's policies and advocated a moderate stimulus program to end the recession.[83] Arthur Burns, Saulnier's predecessor as CEA chairman, publicly urged an immediate tax cut to stimulate the economy.[84] Meanwhile, Secretary of the Treasury Robert B. Anderson opposed increases in deficit spending or the enactment of tax cuts and emphasized the need to reduce federal spending in order to balance the budget.

During most of the 1957–1958 recession, Eisenhower generally sided with his more conservative economic advisers. He often perceived Democratic proposals to increase both domestic and defense spending to end the recession as fiscally irresponsible, inflationary, and politically motivated to benefit Democratic candidates in the 1958 elections.[85] In his September 3, 1957 press conference, Eisenhower firmly stated that, despite current economic problems, he would continue his "adherence to conservative principles in the finances of the Government."[86] In his February 12, 1958 statement on the economy, Eisenhower seemed more moderate and flexible in his position on the recession. After asserting his "conviction that the underlying forces of growth remain strong and undiminished," the president optimistically stated that the FRB's change toward a less restrictive credit policy and recent increases in domestic and defense spending were expediting an end of the recession.[87]

For JFK and other Democrats, the Eisenhower administration's response to the recession was too little and too late. On March 12, 1958, JFK addressed the AFL-CIO's conference on unemployment in Washington, DC. While expressing the need for more federal spending on public schools, hospitals, highways, dams, and other public works, he prioritized the urgent need to improve and expand the federal-state system of unemployment compensation through a bill that he and other senators recently sponsored.[88] Two weeks later, JFK delivered a speech in the Senate criticizing Eisenhower's proposal on unemployment compensation as inadequate. JFK stated, "I think the program is most unfortunately conceived. I think it will do little, in view of the seriousness of the problem."[89]

On March 22, 1958, JFK addressed a Jefferson-Jackson Day dinner in Des Moines, Iowa. After citing dismal economic statistics and examples, he contrasted the cautious, ineffective response of the Eisenhower administration to the current recession to Franklin D.

Roosevelt's dynamic, innovative leadership during the Great Depression. JFK was certainly aware that his narrow defeat for the 1956 Democratic vice presidential nomination was mostly attributed to his controversial, earlier support for the Eisenhower administration's unpopular flexible price support policy for agriculture. Therefore, he also used this speech to emphasize the fact that his voting record and ideas on agriculture had become more similar to those of Senator Hubert H. Humphrey of Minnesota. JFK specified that he voted for Humphrey's 1956 substitute bill to provide 90 percent parity for needy small farms "because I think farm prosperity is not just a local need—it is a national need." He then underscored the economic interdependence and integration of the Midwest and New England. He stated, "I want the people in Massachusetts and New England to realize that we can sell tools and fish and textiles in Iowa only when you have the farm income to pay for them."[90]

In speeches like these, JFK was developing a theme that pervaded his speeches throughout the United States from late 1957 to 1960. The content and tone of JFK's speeches were usually consistent with the policy statements of the DAC and the DNC's publicity division.[91] In an October 20, 1957 press release on the economy, the DAC blamed the recession and inflation on "the half-time, half-hearted, reluctant and uncertain administration which we now have."[92] On February 1, 1958, the DAC issued a press release that stated, "The United States is threatened with a serious deterioration of its military power, upon which not only its survival but the survival of civilization depends."[93]

Senator Stuart Symington of Missouri served as secretary of the air force in the Truman administration. He was an outspoken, persistent advocate of substantially expanding and modernizing the air force. He claimed that the United States suffered a "bomber gap" compared to the Soviet Union, and, by 1959, also charged that, with the Soviet launching of *Sputnik*, a "missile gap" also existed.[94] Compared to JFK, Symington became a better known, more knowledgeable critic of Eisenhower's budgetary policies concerning national defense and the space program. After his landslide reelection to the Senate in 1958, Symington was increasingly perceived as a dark horse, compromise candidate for president or vice president at the 1960 Democratic national convention.[95]

Meanwhile, Senator Hubert H. Humphrey of Minnesota was widely recognized among midwestern Democrats as an expert on agricultural issues, a harsh critic of the Eisenhower administration's agricultural policies, and a nationally recognized champion of a return to fixed price supports at 90 percent parity, especially for struggling small farmers.[96] Like Symington, Humphrey was also a possible candidate for the Democratic presidential or vice presidential nomination in 1960. In his Des Moines speech, JFK sought to ingratiate himself with his midwestern audience by revealing that he had begun regularly voting in the same way as Humphrey on fixed price supports, implicitly hoping that they and other farm state Democrats would forgive and forget his earlier support for "Bensonism."

JFK could not expect to equal or surpass Symington and Humphrey in their respective areas of policy specialization. On the issue of the proper role of the federal government in education, especially in the wake of *Sputnik*, JFK, like other senators during the 1950s, often expected the House of Representatives and the president to take the initiative. Consequently, he voted for passage of the National Defense Education Act of 1958. However, he did not fulfill an active, leading role in shaping the Senate version of this legislation and reconciling it with the House version and Eisenhower's original proposal.[97]

The issue of education provided JFK with an opportunity to develop a rhetorical strategy as an attractive national speaker for the Democratic Party in the 1958 midterm elections and for his future presidential campaign. On October 9, 1957, he addressed a teachers' convention in Swampscott, Massachusetts. He contended that the federal government needed to undertake a larger and more effective role in improving American education, especially in science and mathematics, so that the United States could successfully meet such current and future challenges as competing against the Soviet Union in missile and space technology and economic productivity. These challenges increased the responsibilities of not only the federal government but also Americans in general, especially teachers. He asserted, "In short, our position in the world and our hopes for survival ten, twenty or thirty years from now depend in large measure upon the kind of education which you in the teaching profession are able to offer your pupils today."[98]

On the following day, JFK addressed a teachers' convention in Baltimore, Maryland. The content and theme of JFK's Baltimore speech were quite similar to those of his Swampscott speech. In his Baltimore speech, though, JFK more explicitly and completely detailed the relationship between education and national security in the Cold War than he had in his Swampscott speech. He concluded his Baltimore speech by stating, "Teachers of America, we who hope for the future peace and security of our nation, and for the wisdom and courage of our leaders, ask once again that you bring us candles to illuminate the way."[99]

JFK's emphasis on the issue of education in his forgoing and future speeches enabled him to synthesize two major ideas in a coherent, eloquent theme that pervaded his speeches from 1958 to 1960. First, the president needed to provide bolder, more active, and more innovative leadership in making the federal government more effective in enabling the American economy, armed forces, educational institutions, and research and development facilities to increase economic growth and productivity, successfully compete against the Soviet Union militarily, economically, scientifically, and ideologically, and impress newly emerging Third World countries with the virtues and advantages of the American political and economic system.[100] Second, Americans should not expect to be merely passive recipients of more government spending and new programs. They should be willing and able to more actively and effectively serve their nation, assume more responsibilities, and meet new challenges as they cooperated with their fellow citizens in helping to achieve such policy goals as reducing poverty and unemployment, fighting the Cold War, and winning the space race. Improving educational quality and academic performance would be both a means to attain the above policy purposes and an end in itself.[101] By the time of JFK's presidential campaign, this evolving, education-driven theme was simplified and characterized for American voters as "getting this country moving again."[102]

Before JFK could conduct an extensive speaking tour on behalf of Democratic candidates throughout the nation and then concentrate on his own reelection, he needed to accomplish as much as he could on labor reform legislation during the remainder of Congress's 1958 legislative session. In March, 1958, the McClellan committee issued its interim report on labor reform.[103] On March 11, 1958, JFK, in his capacity as chairman of the subcommittee on labor legislation, delivered a Senate speech in which he introduced a bill based on the interim report of the McClellan committee. JFK's bill intended "to safeguard union finances and to curb certain improper and undemocratic practices" including "the abuse of trusteeships."[104] JFK added that the first, underlying principle of his bill was the following. "A strong, honest, and responsible trade union movement is an essential part of American economic life; and its orderly progress and overwhelmingly honest leadership should not be undermined by either unnecessarily restrictive legislation or the uncurbed malpractices of a few wrongdoers."[105]

In this and future speeches, JFK was careful to assert that the content and purpose of his bill intended to impartially serve the public interest, not the private interests of either labor union officials or business managers. The Teamsters (IBT), United Mine Workers (UMW), and a few other labor unions vociferously opposed JFK's bill. However, major, national labor leaders, such as George Meany and Walter Reuther, reluctantly and ambivalently accepted it. Journalists Rowland Evans and Robert Novak described JFK's labor reform bill as "a relatively mild labor reform bill that attempted to crack down on racketeering and thievery inside the unions without coming to grips with union power."[106]

In addition to his bill's moderate tone, content, and purposes, JFK hoped that it would attract broad bipartisan support in the Senate by sponsoring it with Senator Irving Ives of New York. Ives was a moderate Republican who was not seeking reelection in 1958. Ives also opposed Republican efforts to promote the adoption of right-to-work legislation in several states as part of the Republican campaign strategy in the 1958 midterm elections.

JFK was determined to prove that he was more than a speech making "show horse" and was equally effective as a legislative "work horse." He consulted experts on labor law and made compromises with both Democratic and Republican colleagues.[107] On June 10, 1958, JFK's subcommittee reported the Kennedy-Ives bill, formally named the Labor-Management Reporting and Disclosure Act of 1958, to the Senate. In a June 12th speech on the Senate floor, JFK not only explained the detailed provisions of this bill, now numbered S.3974. He also implicitly defended his bill against recent criticism of it by Secretary of Labor James Mitchell. JFK assured his listeners that, while S.3974 exempted small labor unions from its reporting provisions, it still empowered the Secretary of Labor to "revoke exemption whenever he considers it to be in the public interest to do so."[108]

Earlier in 1958, Mitchell had recommended labor reform legislation shortly before Eisenhower sent a special message to Congress on labor-management relations. In his January 23rd message, Eisenhower stated, "The Secretary of Labor has recommended to me a comprehensive program of legislation which, if enacted, will, I believe, give that reassurance to the American public."[109] After detailing Mitchell's recommendations, the president concluded, "These legislative recommendations are designed to benefit and protect the welfare of American workers and the general public, to curb abuses, and to provide greater harmony and stability in labor-management relations."[110] In his conclusion, Eisenhower also referred to "an effective right to organize and bargain collectively" as "an essential part of this Nation's free and democratic society."[111]

To the general public, the Kennedy-Ives bill and Mitchell's Eisenhower-endorsed recommendations might appear to be very similar. Mitchell criticized the Kennedy-Ives bill for being weak and inadequate, especially concerning the participatory rights of rank-and-file union members, its powers of investigation and administration, and its failure to tighten the ban on secondary boycotts and prohibit organizational picketing. On June 9, 1958, Mitchell issued a press release which argued that the Kennedy-Ives bill, if enacted, "would delude the workers of this country, and the American public into believing they had protections they did not in fact have."[112]

Mitchell's press release surprised and angered JFK, and the Senate began debate on the Kennedy-Ives bill on June 12. In an apparent retort to Mitchell and other fellow Republicans, Ives delivered a speech emphasizing the bipartisan nature and purpose of the labor reform bill that JFK crafted.[113] With the help of Senate Majority Leader Lyndon B. Johnson, JFK led the defeat of twenty proposed amendments to his bill. The only amendment that the Senate added to JFK's bill that he could not defeat was a requirement that both union officials and employers submit affidavits swearing that they were not Communists.[114]

In general, though, the Senate debate on the Kennedy-Ives bill went smoothly. Johnson allowed JFK to be the floor manager of the bill. On June 17, 1958, the Senate passed it by a vote of 88 to 1. Senator George Malone of Nevada, a Republican and an unyielding critic of labor unions, voted against it.[115] Even Senator Barry Goldwater of Arizona, the ranking Republican member of JFK's subcommittee and a champion of state right-to-work legislation, voted for it.[116]

While the Senate passed the Kennedy-Ives bill almost unanimously after only five days of debate, this bill experienced a very different political and legislative environment in the House of Representatives. Ever since Eisenhower submitted his special message to Congress on labor reform legislation in January, House Republicans led by Representative Robert Griffin of Michigan developed a bill based on the president's recommendations. Griffin, a member of the House Education and Labor Committee and its subcommittee on labor, faced staunch Democratic opposition to his bill. Griffin's subcommittee did not begin hearings on his bill until May 28, 1958.[117]

Meanwhile, Speaker of the House Sam Rayburn wanted to delay both further action on Griffin's bill and a vote on the Kennedy-Ives bill until legislation that became the Welfare and Pension Plans Disclosure Act of 1958 was in conference. Rayburn waited until July 29 to have the Kennedy-Ives bill sent to the House Education and Labor Committee. Secretary of Labor James Mitchell later quipped that Rayburn stalled House action on the Kennedy-Ives bill for "forty days and forty nights."[118]

Regardless of the sincerity or wisdom of Rayburn's decision for this delay, this long period of time gave interest groups that opposed the Kennedy-Ives bill more time to lobby against it.[119] The National Association of Manufacturers (NAM) and the U.S. Chamber of Commerce focused their efforts on House Republicans and southern Democrats while the Teamsters, United Mine Workers (UMW), and steel workers' union concentrated theirs on moderate and liberal non-southern Democrats.[120] Although the national leadership of the AFL-CIO publicly endorsed the Kennedy-Ives bill, it did not send AFL-CIO lobbyists to the House of Representatives to encourage its passage.[121]

With Congress scheduled to adjourn on August 24, 1958, several non-southern Democratic representatives, including George McGovern of South Dakota and Stewart Udall of Arizona, circulated a letter among their colleagues on August 16.[122] Their letter endorsed the Kennedy-Ives bill and proposed that the House of Representatives vote to suspend committee hearings and vote on the bill before adjournment. House rules required the votes of at least two thirds of the representatives to accomplish this.[123]

On August 18, 1958, the House of Representatives rejected this motion favoring the Kennedy-Ives bill by a vote of 198 to 190. Of the 198 representatives who voted against this motion, 137 were Republicans, and 61 were Democrats. Of the 190 voting for it, 149 were Democrats, and 41 were Republicans. Twenty-seven representatives, consisting of thirteen Democrats and fourteen Republicans, voted present. Sam Rayburn was one of the Democrats who voted present.[124]

Except for the representatives who voted present, 71 percent of the Democrats and 23 percent of the Republicans voted for the motion. Citing the small minority of House Republicans who voted for the Kennedy-Ives bill, Rayburn blamed them for its defeat. In his statement to the press, JFK specifically blamed Secretary of Labor James Mitchell for the defeat of the Kennedy-Ives bill in the House of Representatives.[125] In listing several reasons for the defeat of the Kennedy-Ives bill, journalist John Van Camp wrote, "Senator Kennedy's name on the bill had a baneful effect on the House Republicans."[126] House Republicans were especially determined to defeat a Senate bill on a major, prominent issue that bore the name of an ambitious young Democratic senator who was a popular campaign speaker for Democratic candidates and a possible presidential or vice presidential candidate in 1960.

On August 20, 1958, Eisenhower publicly expressed his disappointment that Congress failed to pass labor reform legislation that included all of the principles and objectives that he specified in his January 23 special message to Congress. He stated, "The bill passed by the Senate in June, the so-called Kennedy-Ives bill, fell far short of these recommendations."[127] The president concluded, "I still hope that before adjournment the Congress will pass a labor bill which will effectively protect the working men and women of our country."[128]

After the 85th Congress adjourned on August 24, JFK had to wait until 1959 and the first session of the 86th Congress to introduce a new labor reform bill with a new cosponsor.[129] Like Sam Rayburn and other fellow Democrats, JFK blamed House Republicans and Secretary of Labor James Mitchell for the death of his bill in 1958. In his 1958 campaign speeches in Massachusetts and other states, JFK asserted the need for a labor reform law whose specific provisions were fair and effective in being applied equally to labor union officials and employers while serving the public interest.[130]

After Congress adjourned, JFK's more active, regular speechmaking schedule served two purposes. First, JFK needed to implement a reelection strategy that sought a record-breaking, landslide reelection margin in November. JFK was endorsed for renomination and reelection by acclamation at the Democratic state convention in Boston a few days after the Senate voted 88 to 1 for the Kennedy-Ives bill. The Massachusetts Democratic primary would not be held until September 8, 1958. The fact that JFK faced no opposition for renomination and a weak, obscure Republican opponent for reelection meant that he could rely on surrogates, such as Democratic Representative Torbert Macdonald, a Harvard roommate of JFK, and family members to campaign on his behalf in Massachusetts until October.[131]

Second, from late August until early October, JFK traveled to several states in preparation of his future presidential campaign. JFK was determined to unite all of New England's delegates for the 1960 Democratic national convention behind his presidential candidacy.

Thus, he spoke at fund-raising dinners, campaign rallies, state conventions and other Democratic events in other New England states, especially in Connecticut, New Hampshire, and Maine. JFK's appearances in Connecticut provided him with opportunities to meet and confer with Governor Abraham Ribicoff and Democratic state chairman John M. Bailey. JFK would mostly rely on Ribicoff and Bailey to organize New England delegates from outside of Massachusetts for his future presidential candidacy. JFK's trips to Connecticut during the 1958 campaign season also helped him to harmonize and unite Connecticut Democrats behind him. The Ribicoff-Bailey dominance of the Democratic Party in that state was challenged by Thomas J. Dodd, a former congressman who was running for the Senate.[132] JFK hoped to make himself as popular with the Dodd Democrats as he was with the Ribicoff-Bailey Democrats.[133]

While the Democratic Party in Connecticut was well-organized and electorally successful, the Democratic Party in New Hampshire struggled to make itself a viable, competitive alternative in a state dominated by the Republican Party. No Democrat in New Hampshire had been elected as governor since 1922, as a U.S. representative since 1934, or as a U.S. senator since 1932. Republicans had controlled the state legislature since the Civil War.

New Hampshire Democrats, however, were optimistic about their chances to win the governorship in 1958. Because of the recession and higher unemployment, New Hampshire residents were expected to vote more Democratic than usual. New Hampshire Democrats contended that Lane Dwinell, the current Republican governor, did not join governors from other states in urging Eisenhower to sign Democratic-sponsored legislation extending unemployment compensation because of pressure from Sherman Adams, White House chief of staff and a former governor of New Hampshire.[134] Adams was being investigated by Congress for allegedly accepting gifts from Bernard Goldfine, a Boston businessman, for intervening with the Federal Trade Commission (FTC) and Securities and Exchange Commission (SEC) on behalf of Goldfine.

Furthermore, Dwinell had decided not to seek reelection, and New Hampshire Republicans became embroiled in a bitter, divisive contest for their party's gubernatorial nomination. Wesley Powell won the Republican gubernatorial primary by a margin of 29 votes.[135] As Maine Democrats did in 1954, New Hampshire Democrats hoped to exploit an internecine Republican conflict and a national Democratic trend in a midterm election in order to win their state's governorship. Like Maine Democrats, New Hampshire Democrats could then use a Democratic governorship as the basis for developing a competitive two-party system in a once overwhelmingly Republican state.

Unlike the Republicans, New Hampshire Democrats united behind their gubernatorial candidate, Bernard L. Boutin. Boutin was the mayor of Laconia and close to JFK. Boutin had first met JFK in Washington, DC, in 1956. He was New Hampshire's Democratic national committeeman and attended the 1956 Democratic national convention as an alternate. Boutin chaired the campaign of Senator Estes Kefauver in New Hampshire's Democratic presidential primary in 1956.[136] Of New Hampshire's eight delegate votes at the 1956 Democratic national convention, Kefauver received 7½ votes to JFK's ½ vote on the first ballot for the vice presidential nomination and all eight delegate votes on the second ballot.[137] On both ballots for his vice presidential candidacy, JFK's performance with New Hampshire's delegates was his weakest among the delegates of all six New England states.

New Hampshire Democrats were eager to feature JFK as a campaign speaker in order to energize their base and attract the votes of independents and Republicans alienated by their party's recent factionalism and the ethical controversy linked to Sherman Adams. JFK was motivated to ingratiate himself with New Hampshire voters in preparation for their state's "first in the nation" Democratic presidential primary in 1960. On June 7, 1958, only a few days before the Senate floor debate on the Kennedy-Ives bill, JFK addressed a Jefferson-Jackson Day dinner in Manchester, New Hampshire. He confidently stated that "1958 represents New Hampshire's best opportunity to cast off permanently the confining shackles of one-party rule."[138] He criticized the Eisenhower administration and Republicans in Congress for being unable or unwilling to provide effective, constructive leadership on such issues as the recession, distressed areas, namely, New England cities and towns dependent on declining textile and shoe factories, school construction, and the inadequacy of current policies on Social Security, minimum wages, and unemployment compensation. He added, "Here in New England, the oldest section of the country, we are particularly affected by this drift and lack of leadership."[139] The Massachusetts Democrat suggested that the Eisenhower administration and Republicans in Congress neglected the policy needs of New Hampshire because they perceived it as a predictably Republican, one-party state.

Nearly three weeks later, JFK delivered a speech at the Democratic state convention in Hartford, Connecticut, on June 27, 1958. He praised Governor Abraham Ribicoff as "one of the most outstanding state executives in the country" and that the Democratic senatorial nominee from Connecticut, who had not yet been chosen, would be elected in November.[140] In general, though, the content of JFK's Connecticut speech was similar to that of his New Hampshire speech. Besides criticizing Republicans for neglecting New England's policy needs, JFK also castigated them for failing to provide the leadership and policies needed to effectively compete against the Soviet Union and improve the national security of the United States and its allies. Toward the end of this speech, JFK dramatically stated, "We travel today along a knife-edged path which requires leadership better equipped than any since Lincoln's day to make clear to our people the vast spectrum of our challenges."[141]

In contrast to New Hampshire and Connecticut, JFK did not deliver any major campaign speeches in Maine in 1958. Democratic Governor Edmund S. Muskie of Maine was easily reelected to another two-year term in 1956, despite the Eisenhower landslide.[142] Also in 1956, Democratic congressional nominee James C. Oliver lost by only 29 votes while Democratic congressional nominee Frank Coffin won with 53.4 percent of the votes.[143] With bitter factionalism continuing to divide and weaken Maine's Republican Party, Muskie ran for the Senate against Frederick Payne, the vulnerable Republican incumbent, in 1958.[144]

With Muskie likely to win the Senate election and Democrats favored to win two of Maine's three congressional seats and the governorship, Maine Democrats did not need campaign visits from JFK in order to suceed in the 1958 elections.[145] Instead, JFK could wait until Muskie became a fellow senator to cooperate with him on shared regional policy issues, such as railroad freight rates in New England, distressed areas legislation, and high fuel oil prices, and to seek his help in uniting Maine's Democratic delegates behind his presidential candidacy in 1960. Muskie did not attend the 1956 Democratic national convention, and JFK received 7½ of Maine's 14 delegate votes for his vice presidential candidacy on the first ballot at that convention.[146]

Maine held its federal and state elections on Monday, September 8, 1958. Muskie was elected to the Senate with 60.8 percent of the votes.[147] His fellow Democrats won two of Maine's three congressional seats and retained the governorship. James Hagerty, Eisenhower's press secretary, informed the press that the president acknowledged that Maine's election results represented a major defeat for the Republican Party.[148] Donald E. Nicoll served as executive secretary to Maine's Democratic state committee and administrative assistant to U.S. Representative Frank Coffin. He later served as Muskie's secretary. In a 2002 interview, Nicoll partially attributed the rapid and impressive electoral success of Maine's Democratic Party from 1954 to 1958 to the fact that Muskie and Coffin "were not ideologues. They were pragmatic problem solvers in public policy."[149]

Of the three states of northern New England, Vermont seemed to be the least likely to experience a Democratic revolution in voting behavior and party strength during the 1950s.[150] Compared to Maine and New Hampshire, Vermont's population consisted of the smallest percentages of Catholics, labor union members, and urban residents.[151] The Democrats in Maine and New Hampshire had won a few gubernatorial and congressional elections during the 1930s, but no Democrat in Vermont had won a gubernatorial or congressional election since the nineteenth century.

However, there were actually more similarities than differences between Vermont and Maine in Democratic electoral prospects during the 1950s. In both states, Republican Party cohesion and electoral appeal were weakened by the competition between Eisenhower and

Senator Robert A. Taft of Ohio for the 1952 Republican presidential nomination, disagreements about whether to seek the political support of labor unions, and McCarthyism.[152] In each state, a Republican governor's reputation for honesty and efficiency was tainted by bureaucratic scandals.[153]

According to political scientist Douglas I. Hodgkin, Vermont and Maine, respectively, experienced "breakthrough" gubernatorial elections in 1952 and 1954. Hodgkin wrote, "A breakthrough election or series of elections is one in which the minority party in a state makes rather large gains which are sufficiently durable so that party competition is carried on at a more intense level."[154] The Democrats in Vermont lost that state's 1952 gubernatorial election. However, the Democratic percentage of votes cast in Vermont's gubernatorial elections sharply increased from 25.5 percent in 1950 to 39.8 percent in 1952. The Democratic percentages in Vermont's gubernatorial elections further increased to 47.7 percent in 1954 and then decreased slightly to 42.5 percent in 1956.[155]

Vermont Democrats were confident that the national Democratic trend of 1958 and speaking tours in Vermont by JFK and Muskie would help them to win their state's gubernatorial election and statewide congressional election. Republican Representative Winston Prouty was vacating Vermont's at-large congressional seat in order to run for the Senate. In 1958, six candidates ran in the Republican congressional primary to succeed Prouty.[156] Harold J. Arthur won the Republican congressional primary with only 30 percent of the votes.[157]

JFK visited Vermont in late September, and Senator-elect Muskie arrived in October to campaign for that state's Democratic ticket.[158] On September 26, 1958, JFK delivered a speech to a regional conference of the National Rural Electric Cooperative Association in Burlington, Vermont. In this speech's introductory paragraph, he referred to himself as "a citizen of New England, interested in the prosperity and development of all of New England; and, perhaps more importantly, I am a United States Senator concerned about the progress of all programs enacted by Congress for the benefit of the American people."[159] He proceeded to praise the positive effects of the Rural Electrification Administration (REA) in Vermont and rural western Massachusetts. In order to further reduce the cost of electricity in Vermont and Massachusetts, nuclear power plants needed to be established in New England. He concluded by saying, "That is why atomic energy holds such promise for the future development of this region and that is why I wish you every success, and I pledge you every cooperation, in your efforts to develop atomic energy generating plants for this and other regions."[160]

JFK's speech in Burlington tried to accomplish two political purposes. First, he wanted to assure his audience that, despite his growing prominence on national and international issues, he was still the "Senator from New England" who understood, addressed, and strived to satisfy the policy needs of New England.[161] Second, he was trying to mitigate or prevent a future political liability to his presidential candidacy that might be caused by his previous Senate votes against increasing funding and loan authorization for the REA.[162] Therefore, just as JFK's speech in Des Moines, Iowa, was an implied atonement for his earlier endorsement of flexible farm price supports, his speech in Burlington hoped to at least obscure his earlier votes against the REA.

Of the three states of northern New England, Vermont was the only one whose delegates cast their votes readily and unanimously for JFK's vice presidential candidacy on both ballots at the 1956 Democratic national convention. Vermont's delegation at this convention was chaired by E. Frank Branon. Branon was a dairy farmer, state senator, and Democratic state chairman. He was the Democratic nominee for governor in 1954 and 1956.[163] He lost both elections, but polled impressively for a Democrat. Branon's narrow defeat in 1954 was partially attributed to his advocacy of public funds for parochial schools. Branon was a Catholic with a large family that included a son who was a priest.[164]

While JFK relied on Edmund S. Muskie in Maine and Bernard L. Boutin in New Hampshire as his chief contacts with the Democratic parties of those states, he relied on E. Frank Branon in Vermont.[165] Branon helped to organize JFK's campaign appearances in Burlington and Rutland and introduced the senator from Massachusetts to

Bernard Leddy, Frederick Fayette, and William A. Meyer, Vermont's respective Democratic nominees for governor, U.S. senator, and U.S. representative.[166] Of the three Democratic nominees, Meyer seemed to have the best chance of being elected because of the highly divisive Republican congressional primary that chose his opponent and Meyer's folksy, non-partisan rhetoric and campaign style combined with his experience and expertise in farming and forestry.[167]

If Vermont was the most Republican of the six New England states, then Rhode Island was the most Democratic. It had the highest percentages of Catholics and urban residents in its population. It was the only New England state with two Democratic senators, and Democrats won control of both houses of the state legislature in Rhode Island long before they accomplished this partisan objective in Massachusetts and Connecticut.[168]

On federal policy issues that affected New England, JFK regularly collaborated with Senators Theodore F. Green and John O. Pastore of Rhode Island.[169] At the 1956 Democratic national convention, JFK received 15½ of Rhode Island's 16 delegate votes on both ballots.[170] In a September 7, 1956 letter to Pastore, JFK wrote, "The major reason for the close run that was made for the Vice Presidential nomination was the support given by you and the entire Rhode Island delegation during the days preceding the voting."[171]

Rhode Island's delegation to the 1956 Democratic national convention was chaired by Governor Dennis J. Roberts. JFK had learned that governors were more likely to control their state's delegates than senators. Roberts's governorship and the fact that he had joined Ribicoff and Bailey in promoting JFK for vice president and lobbying delegates from other states at the 1956 convention led JFK to depend primarily on Roberts instead of Pastore or Green to organize Rhode Island's future Democratic national convention delegates for him.[172]

Since 1950, Roberts had been elected to four successive two-year terms. With his incumbency, the strongly Democratic orientation of his state's voters, and the national Democratic tide, it initially seemed likely to most observers outside of Rhode Island that Roberts would be reelected in 1958. His political stature outside of Rhode Island was enhanced by his keynote address delivered on June 21, 1958, at the

Massachusetts Democratic state convention in Boston. In his speech, Roberts predicted a landslide reelection for JFK. This would launch JFK's presidential candidacy so that, as Roberts stated, "this son of Massachusetts will receive our support and will be called upon to assume the highest honor of our party—to restore in the Presidency the leadership it now lacks."[173]

However, the controversial circumstances of his reelection in 1956 and an aggressive challenge to his renomination in the September Democratic primary in Rhode Island made Roberts vulnerable to defeat in 1958. Roberts was opposed in the Democratic primary by Armand Cote, his lieutenant governor. Roberts defeated Cote by fewer than 8,000 votes in what one newspaper called, "one of the most bitterly contested primaries in the state's history."[174]

With Roberts's electoral appeal already weakened by a divisive primary, he confronted a more formidable opponent in the general election. Christopher Del Sesto was the Republican gubernatorial nominee in both 1956 and 1958. The initial results of the 1956 gubernatorial election indicated that Del Sesto defeated Roberts. After Roberts legally challenged these results, the state supreme court invalidated approximately 5,954 votes and ruled that Roberts had been reelected by a margin of 711 votes.[175] The way in which Roberts gained a fourth term as governor aroused suspicion and resentment among Rhode Island's numerous voters of Italian ancestry who became determined to elect Del Sesto in 1958.

Despite his unusually difficult chance of being reelected, Roberts did not ask JFK to campaign for him in Rhode Island. JFK was probably relieved that Roberts did not request this favor because he needed to be especially sensitive, responsive, and solicitous toward voters of Italian ancestry in both the Massachusetts Democratic primary on September 9 and the general election on November 4. JFK steadily improved his relationship with Governor Foster Furcolo and campaigned with Furcolo in 1956.[176] Nevertheless, there were still some Furcolo supporters who attributed Furcolo's narrow defeat in the 1954 Senate election to JFK's refusal to specifically and effectively endorse Furcolo.[177] JFK's campaign heard rumors that Furcolo wanted to embarrass JFK by telling voters of Italian ancestry to vote for Furcolo but not for JFK in the Democratic primary so that the governor would receive more votes than the senator.[178] Regardless of the reasons, Furcolo outpolled JFK in the state Democratic primary. Furcolo received 396,654 votes to JFK's 389,921 votes.[179] Furcolo's electoral superiority was particularly evident in Boston where he received 94,303 votes to JFK's 87,231 votes. The governor also received more votes than JFK in eighteen of Boston's twenty-two wards.[180]

JFK's determination to maximize his appeal to voters of Italian ancestry was further complicated by the fact that Vincent J. Celeste, his Republican opponent, had an Italian surname. Celeste was an East Boston attorney who had been JFK's Republican opponent in his 1950 congressional race. At the Republican state convention in Worcester, delegates were originally expected to endorse John S. Ames, Jr., the chairman of the state Republican Party's finance committee, for the Republican senatorial nomination. Celeste, however, won the endorsement after delivering an impassioned speech criticizing JFK's record as a senator.[181] With no Republican opponent, Celeste received 190,524 votes in the primary and was unanimously nominated for the Senate.[182]

Especially after Celeste became the presumptive Republican nominee in June, JFK's campaign distributed leaflets and issued press releases documenting the senator's legislative activities on such issues as the liberalization of immigration laws to benefit Italian immigrants and their families in Massachusetts and American foreign policy toward Italy.[183] His campaign literature also reminded voters of his status as an honorary citizen of Rome and Trieste, and his televised campaign film, *The U.S. Senator John F. Kennedy Story*, highlighted his efforts to unite an Italian immigrant with his family in Massachusetts.[184] On September 25, 1958, JFK issued a press release denouncing the use of the word "Mafia" in referring to organized crime as a slur against Americans of Italian ancestry. It stated, "Senator Kennedy deplored the misleading and unfair connotations arising from its use and stated he sympathizes and understands the resentment of citizens of Italian origin, being mindful of their contributions to the State and Nation."[185]

The above press release was suggested to JFK by Philip Cordero. Cordero was a journalist for an Italian-language newspaper and was hired by the Kennedy campaign as an adviser on Italian issues. He assisted Robert E. Thompson, the Kennedy campaign's press secretary, in communicating JFK's positions and accomplishments on these issues and his close, cooperative legislative relationship with Senator John O. Pastore of Rhode Island. Pastore was the first United States senator of Italian ancestry.[186]

JFK's meticulous cultivation of voters of Italian ancestry intensified by the middle of October. On October 13, he marched in a Columbus Day parade in East Boston, a mostly Italian neighborhood where Celeste lived. On October 18, he appeared in Boston with Rocco "Rocky" Marciano, a nationally famous boxer and a native of Massachusetts, when he accepted a Man of the Year award from the Sons of Italy.[187]

Because of complaints from several leaders of the Italian American community in Massachusetts, the Kennedy campaign changed its campaign slogan. As detailed previously, EMK, as JFK's campaign manager, and others changed JFK's campaign slogan to "Kennedy. He has served Massachusetts with distinction." It was acceptable to these Italian American leaders and became the new campaign slogan.[188]

Although EMK was the official campaign manager, he had no experience in running a Senate campaign. EMK relied on Stephen Smith, a Kennedy brother-in-law, for implementing the details of the campaign. Lawrence F. O'Brien revived the network of Kennedy "secretaries" and volunteers throughout Massachusetts. Kenneth P. O'Donnell spent less time in Massachusetts because of his job with the McClellan committee, but he helped O'Brien to organize JFK's speaking and campaign schedule in Massachusetts and accompanied O'Brien and JFK.[189] Senate aides Theodore C. Sorensen and Myer Feldman made sure that the campaign's publicity and speeches accurately and persuasively communicated JFK's legislative record and issue positions.[190]

According to Sorensen, JFK began preparing for his 1958 reelection campaign on the day after he was elected to the Senate in 1952. JFK told Sorensen that, because of the narrow margin of his victory in 1952, "anybody in the state can come into this office and claim credit for my winning."[191] For the next six years, JFK practiced five principles in preparing for his 1958 campaign. They included maintaining a personal organization based on his 1952 network of "secretaries" that did not conflict with the apparatus of the state Democratic Party; regularly mailing newsletters informing his constituents of how his legislative behavior and accomplishments were fulfilling his 1952 campaign promise to do more for Massachusetts; frequently providing interviews for the newspapers of Massachusetts, which were mostly Republican owned; and delivering speeches to interest groups, charities, schools, and civic and ethnic organizations.[192] JFK was also careful to always respond to critics of his legislative behavior and policy positions and try to persuade them that his decisions were reasonable. Among Republicans and independents in Massachusetts, JFK reminded them of how often he and Republican Senator Leverett Saltonstall of Massachusetts voted together and cosponsored legislation intended to benefit Massachusetts.[193]

JFK wanted to achieve a record-breaking landslide victory; he did not want the media, his critics, or anyone else to attribute his winning margin of votes to his family's wealth or the coattails of Governor Foster Furcolo, especially after Furcolo outpolled JFK in the primary. JFK wanted to conduct a frugal campaign in 1958 that spent far less than his 1952 campaign in order to convincingly refute criticism that he "bought" a landslide reelection margin and save money for his future presidential campaign.[194] Consequently, JFK's 1958 campaign intentionally limited spending on advertising, especially for television commercials and billboards. Instead, it emphasized door-to-door canvassing, mass mail operations by volunteers, and personal appearances by JFK, his wife Jacqueline, EMK, and other family members.

John J. McNally, Jr., was a real estate appraiser in Webster, a town in south central Massachusetts. He directed JFK's campaign in that area and coordinated his efforts with Paul Glennon, a Worcester attorney who directed JFK's campaign in all of central Massachusetts.[195] McNally wrote in his autobiography, "The biggest challenge in Senator Kennedy's campaign was to overcome complacency, the feeling that the Senator really had no contest for re-election, the real effort was to get out the vote, to get people to the polls."[196] In order to keep its volunteers enthusiastic and motivated, the Kennedy campaign's goal was to have its volunteers distribute 1,230,000 copies of its campaign newspaper so that the home of every voter in Massachusetts would receive a copy.[197]

JFK's determination to run an independent, highly personalized, and low-budget campaign conflicted with the campaign strategy of Governor Foster Furcolo. Furcolo wanted to conduct a joint campaign with JFK in which they often appeared together and spent large sums of money on billboards and other advertising that showed photographs of them together.[198] JFK was especially irritated and embarrassed to be associated with Furcolo's campaign events.[199]

Representative Thomas P. "Tip" O'Neill, Jr., considered running for governor in 1958 before Furcolo announced his candidacy for reelection. O'Neill then became Furcolo's campaign manager and liaison between the Kennedy and Furcolo campaigns.[200] He recalled that Stephen Smith often gave him JFK's campaign itinerary ten days in advance so that JFK and Furcolo would be campaigning in different areas of Massachusetts on the same days.[201] Nevertheless, shortly before election day, JFK joined Furcolo, House Majority Leader John W. McCormack, and Democratic state chairman John M. "Pat" Lynch in a television broadcast urging viewers to vote Democratic.[202]

The Kennedy campaign was careful not to publicly say anything that might inflate the expectations of the local and national media about JFK's electoral performance.[203] Privately and internally, however, the goal of the Kennedy campaign was for JFK to receive at least 70 percent of the votes.[204] Ever since the first popular election of a senator in Massachusetts in 1916, Leverett Saltonstall had received the highest percentage of votes in a Senate election in Massachusetts. Saltonstall won 64.3 percent of the votes in a 1944 special election.[205]

JFK was determined to break this record. Striving toward this goal would energize his campaign's volunteers and staff by assuring them that achieving this goal would enable JFK to run for president in 1960.[206] Paul Donelan, a Kennedy campaign worker, later recalled that, because of this motivation, "The campaign was run just as hard and vigorously as it possibly could."[207]

Jacqueline Kennedy proved to be a major asset for JFK in his reelection campaign. In a 1964 interview, she stated, "Somehow that seems to me the hardest campaign . . . that Senate campaign."[208] Her fluency in French and Italian endeared her to older voters of French-Canadian and Italian ancestry.[209] Kennedy campaign aides Kenneth P. O'Donnell and David F. Powers later recalled, "When Jackie was traveling with us, the size of the crowd at every stop was twice as big as it would have been if Jack was alone."[210]

Her more memorable campaign efforts included appearances in Webster, Worcester, and Chicopee, sometimes with her husband and sometimes without him. In Webster, she addressed a meeting of Women on Wheels, a Democratic women's organization, while JFK attended the ribbon-cutting ceremony of his local campaign headquarters.[211] In Worcester, she accompanied JFK in his appearances at a business college, an insurance company, and the opening of the state Democratic headquarters.[212] In Chicopee, Jacqueline Kennedy talked to a Catholic priest in French about his antique collection. Meanwhile, Kennedy campaign aides hastily recruited an audience from a nearby Catholic women's college for her reception at a parish hall.[213]

While the Kennedy campaign wanted to maximize voter turnout and JFK's victory margin by connecting JFK's 1958 senate campaign to his 1960 presidential campaign, it also wanted to attract more female voters by implying that voting for JFK in 1958 would eventually enable Jacqueline Kennedy to become First Lady. When she greeted working-class women at receptions, it was not uncommon for them to ask the poised, elegant senator's wife, "O Missus Kennedy, and when will we see you in the White House?"[214] According to Betty Taymor, a Kennedy "secretary" in Newton, "Some women would almost curtsey to Jacqueline Kennedy as she offered her white-gloved hand."[215]

In his speeches and statements to the press, JFK did not mention the name of his Republican opponent, Vincent J. Celeste. During his seventeen days of campaigning in Massachusetts, JFK's speeches and public statements mostly explained his policy record in benefiting Massachusetts and the need to enact future legislation in such policy areas as education, hospital construction, unemployment compensation, and economically distressed areas.[216] Most of his campaign appearances consisted of meeting and greeting constituents while exchanging social pleasantries.

The most significant policy speech that JFK gave during his 1958 reelection campaign was a speech that he delivered to a convention of the Massachusetts Federation of Labor in Boston on October 25, 1958. This organization, the state chapter of the AFL-CIO, granted JFK the Samuel Gompers Award for his work on the McClellan committee and sponsorship of the Kennedy-Ives bill. In his speech, JFK specified a five-point legislative agenda on labor issues for the 86th Congress.[217] It included an increase in the minimum wage and an expansion of its coverage, an extension and reform of the unemployment compensation system, and policies focused on the needs of the Massachusetts economy through more federal contracts for local factories, modernizing the port of Boston, and developing nuclear power plants. The most memorable words of JFK's speech were devoted to the need for the enactment of a labor reform bill, like the Kennedy-Ives bill, that would be both fair and effective in prohibiting and punishing criminal behavior and abuses of power by labor union officials. JFK stated, "I think it is important that we remind the nation that the labor movement itself has gone further than any other group in this country to clean its own house, regardless of cost."[218]

During the last two months of his Senate reelection campaign, JFK found the time to make major policy speeches outside of New England. In Miami Beach, Florida, he delivered a speech to the U.S. Mayors' Conference on September 11, 1958. JFK called for an "Urban Magna Carta" that included reapportionment so that major cities and their policy needs would be adequately represented in Congress and state legislatures, federal aid sent directly to local governments, and a more ambitious urban renewal program by the federal government.[219] In Omaha, Nebraska, on September 12, and in San Francisco on September 13, JFK delivered speeches criticizing Eisenhower's foreign and defense policies. In Omaha, JFK and former president Harry S. Truman were guest speakers at a regional Democratic conference. The Democratic senator from Massachusetts criticized Eisenhower's recent speech on Quemoy and Matsu, two islands threatened by the Communist government of China. He argued that the United States should not risk a war with China over two islands that were not vital to the defense of Taiwan.[220]

In San Francisco, JFK was the featured speaker at a Democratic fund-raising dinner for Representative Clair Engle, California's Democratic nominee for senator. In this speech, JFK broadened his attack on Eisenhower's foreign and defense policies to include Eisenhower's decision in July to send U.S. Marines to Lebanon. He stated, "The American people have no clear and consistent understanding of why we are in Lebanon; why we are committed to the defense of Matsu, if indeed we are; what we are going to do in either area, of what we hope to accomplish."[221] JFK concluded that, in general, the United States should only commit itself to the security of other nations if it was politically and militarily willing and able to do so.

Seven months after delivering a major speech on agricultural policies in Des Moines, Iowa, JFK delivered another speech on agriculture in Cedar Rapids, Iowa, on October 17, 1958. Cedar Rapids was hosting the National Corn Picking contest, and JFK and Eisenhower were guest speakers at this event. JFK addressed the audience before Eisenhower did. In his speech, JFK avoided explicit criticism of Eisenhower. He argued that those who believe that most farmers will vote Republican in 1958 because of recent increases in agricultural commodity prices incorrectly assume that "farmers are concerned only with farm problems—and that they know nothing about the issues of war and peace, inflation or recession, public power, transportation, and all the rest."[222] JFK directed his criticism at Secretary of Agriculture Ezra Taft Benson. The Massachusetts Democrat accused Benson of promoting "disunity and division—setting city against country, east against west, neighbor against neighbor."[223]

Earlier in the campaign season, JFK delivered a speech in West Virginia on June 11, 1958, one day before the Senate began its debate on the Kennedy-Ives bill. Because of the need to hold a special election due to the death of Senator Matthew Neely, in addition to a regular Senate election, West Virginia elected two Democratic senators, Jennings Randolph and Robert Byrd, in 1958. Since West

Virginia would be one of the few states to hold a Democratic presidential primary in 1960, Randolph later recalled that JFK frequently asked him about his chances of winning the West Virginia Democratic presidential primary of 1960 if he decided to enter it.[224]

On June 11, 1958, JFK delivered the keynote address at the Jefferson-Jackson Day dinner in Morgantown, West Virginia. He contended that West Virginia voters could benefit themselves and all of their fellow Americans by electing both Randolph and Byrd to the Senate. With Randolph and Byrd elected, the Democratic majority in that chamber could be increased beyond its current two-seat margin and provide more effective leadership for the nation in order to compensate for the lack of effective leadership from the Eisenhower administration.[225] JFK stated, "Today, we need leadership which is better equipped than any since Lincoln's day to make clear to the people the vast spectrum of our challenge."[226] Because of the large, enthusiastic crowd that greeted JFK, organizers broadcast it by radio.[227] Less than two weeks later, JFK returned to West Virginia to address a tobacco growers' convention in White Sulphur Springs on June 23, 1958. Although he had less than four weeks remaining to campaign in Massachusetts, JFK gave a speech in Parkersburg, West Virginia on October 9, 1958. In his Parkersburg speech, JFK accused the Republicans of being completely devoid of good ideas, and of pursuing policies which either worsened or neglected the nation's economic problems.[228]

New York Times columnist James Reston connected the frequency of JFK's trips to West Virginia and other states, despite his reelection campaign, to his presumed presidential candidacy in 1960. Reston wrote, "Though the voters are not even showing much interest as yet in the 1958 election, the handsome young New Englander was here today helping the West Virginia Democratic candidates in the hope that they will in turn help him two years from now."[229] Reston added, "Every trip he makes gets him in the papers, and on television locally. Every Senator or Congressman he helps get elected in 1958 is a potential Kennedy delegate at the 1960 convention."[230]

Vincent J. Celeste, JFK's Republican opponent, occasionally criticized JFK's frequent speaking engagements in other states to promote a future presidential candidacy. However, he concentrated his rhetorical attacks on the alleged use of the Kennedy family's wealth to buy a landslide victory in order to make JFK the front-runner for the 1960 Democratic presidential nomination. In a 1977 interview, Celeste, like some of JFK's campaign operatives, claimed that JFK wanted his Republican opponent to be a better known, better financed, upper-class Yankee Protestant so that a landslide victory would be more impressive to national Democratic politicians and the media.[231] Charles Gibbons, a former Republican speaker of the state house of representatives, ended his Senate candidacy in order to run for governor. John S. Ames, Jr., ended his Senate bid after failing to win the Republican state convention's endorsement.

Therefore, Celeste unexpectedly became JFK's Republican opponent. Celeste referred to JFK as "that millionaire Jack Kennedy" and JFK's political activities financed by his father's wealth as "immoral financial steam rolling tactics."[232] He contended that JFK voted for the St. Lawrence Seaway in order to benefit his father's business interests in Chicago.[233]

Celeste also tried to attract disaffected Democratic blue-collar voters by contrasting his working-class background and neighborhood with JFK's upper-class income and lifestyle. For voting purposes, JFK's official residence in Massachusetts was an apartment in Boston; yet he rarely lived there. While JFK and EMK were staying there during the campaign, they discovered that Celeste was holding a rally in the parking lot across the street from the apartment and charging that JFK's usually empty apartment proved that he was a "phony."[234]

JFK refused to publicly mention Celeste's name.[235] According to Celeste, JFK accepted his challenge to debate him. A debate sponsored by the League of Women Voters was scheduled in Winthrop, Massachusetts. JFK, however, did not appear at the debate. He sent Theodore C. Sorensen as his surrogate to debate Celeste. Celeste refused to debate Sorensen.[235]

Almost twenty years after his 1958 Senate race, Celeste revealed why he persisted in his obscure, poorly financed, underdog campaign against JFK. "And, frankly, I just made up my mind that I would keep fighting until the last gong, and I think I did. At least history had recorded that there was a fight in '58, and there was somebody named Celeste making some objections."[237]

In one of his more substantive speeches attacking JFK's policy record, Celeste told a Republican audience in Hyannis on Cape Cod that the Kennedy-Ives bill was "a phony bill, which doesn't remedy one percent of the wrongs."[238] Shortly after Celeste's Hyannis speech, the *Barnstable Patriot*, a newspaper on Cape Cod, published an editorial criticizing the Kennedy-Ives bill as weak and ineffective. While ignoring Celeste's speech, JFK replied to the editorial in a letter to the editor. In his letter to the editor of the *Barnstable Patriot*, JFK sternly wrote, "With respect to the merits of the bill itself, I can only conclude that you have not had an opportunity to examine the text of the bill."[239]

Celeste, like most Republican nominees for major offices, was also burdened by the growing Democratic national tide in the 1958 elections. This was caused by several factors. First, the lingering effects of the 1957-1958 recession made American voters more attracted to economic liberalism, especially Democratic proposals on unemployment compensation, rigid price supports for farmers, a higher minimum wage with broader coverage, urban renewal, and aid to distressed areas.[240] Second, Eisenhower's public approval rating declined from 60 percent in early January 1958 to 52 percent in early November 1958.[241]

Third, the ethical image of the Eisenhower administration and Republican Party was damaged by the highly publicized, extensive congressional investigation of Sherman Adams, who resigned on September 22, 1958. He returned to live in New Hampshire shortly after his resignation. Suspected of improperly accepting gifts from a businessman seeking favorable treatment by federal agencies, Adams was already perceived as an excessively powerful White House chief of staff.[242] The fact that Adams was a former governor of New Hampshire who had been instrumental in helping Eisenhower to win the 1952 Republican presidential primary in New Hampshire and eventually the GOP's presidential nomination made New Hampshire Democrats optimistic that the controversy surrounding Adams would help them to win their state's gubernatorial election.[243]

Fourth, JFK and other Democratic candidates were able to rhetorically exploit a growing fear and uneasiness among Americans about their nation's ability to successfully compete against the Soviet Union militarily, economically, and educationally. In a Gallup poll released on October 27, 1958, 49 percent of the Americans surveyed agreed that the Soviet Union was ahead of the United States in developing missiles while only 32 percent disagreed.[244] An earlier Gallup poll released on December 13, 1957, reported that the Americans surveyed were more likely to blame the Eisenhower administration or Republicans in general for the alleged missile gap than any other individual cause.[245]

Even before Eisenhower began regularly campaigning for Republican candidates in the middle of October, Republicans throughout the nation advised him, his staff, and Meade Alcorn, the Republican national chairman, on how to win the midterm elections or at least how to limit expected Republican losses. In an October 5, 1958 letter to Eisenhower, Stephen N. Weld, a Republican from Milton, Massachusetts, urged the president to emphasize economic conservatism in order to distinguish the two parties.[246] In an October 26, 1958 follow-up letter to White House aide Howard Pyle, Weld recommended the complete elimination of agricultural price supports and the federal highway program in order to balance the budget.[247] Weld concluded, "The Republican State Committee in Massachusetts is making a valiant effort to show that the Republican Party is really different from the Democrats . . . But the record of the Administration cited above does not make it easy to prove that these statements of principle are what the party really does stand for."[248]

While Weld and other grassroots party regulars encouraged Eisenhower to emphasize conservative principles and policy behavior, Meade Alcorn recommended a less ideological, more pragmatic approach. In a letter to White House press secretary James Hagerty, Alcorn suggested that the president specifically and repeatedly remind voters of Republican policy success in cutting taxes and stimulating economic growth during peace time. He also needed to warn them of the dire consequences of the election of a more liberal Democratic Congress in 1958. Alcorn wrote, "Nationalization, socialization of industry would inevitably follow. All of us would become pawns of a super state."[249]

Eisenhower seemed to adopt and express the suggestions of Weld and Alcorn in several of his campaign speeches.[250] In a speech broadcast from Los Angeles, Eisenhower repeatedly referred to liberal Democrats in Congress as "radicals." After citing the accomplishments of his administration regarding peace and prosperity, he warned his audience that the policy proposals of Democratic "radicals" threatened "the destruction of the economic machinery that provides jobs."[251] In a similar speech broadcast from Chicago, Eisenhower stated, "The most deceptive notion taught by self-styled liberals is that when the economy starts to slow up, only a vast outpouring of your tax dollars will pump us out of trouble. That means trying to live on new debts."[252]

Two days after Eisenhower delivered this speech in Chicago, Vincent J. Celeste met the president in the White House on October 24, 1958. Celeste told the press that Eisenhower "graciously gave me 15 minutes of his most valuable time this morning and I had an opportunity to give him a complete report of my campaign against the Kennedy millions."[253] Unfortunately for Celeste, Eisenhower did not schedule a campaign appearance with him in Massachusetts or ask Alcorn to channel a substantial amount of Republican campaign funds into Celeste's campaign.

Despite Eisenhower's confident campaign speeches and Alcorn's efforts to generate enthusiasm and optimism among Republican campaign workers and candidates, Republicans in New England were especially discouraged by the results of the federal and gubernatorial elections held in Maine on Monday, September 8, 1958. The Democrats scored landmark, historic victories in the senatorial and gubernatorial elections and in two of the three congressional elections. The candidacy of Senator Frederick Payne, the incumbent Republican seeking reelection, was damaged by his acceptance of gifts from Bernard Goldfine, the Boston businessman implicated in the Sherman Adams scandal. Since early 1958, Republicans from Maine and New Hampshire had written to the White House and warned Eisenhower and his staff that high unemployment in Maine and the inadequacy of the current system of unemployment compensation would contribute to major Republican defeats in September.[254] Nevertheless, shortly after the Maine elections, White House aide Howard Pyle wrote to a Republican couple in Maine, "We have the feeling that internal problems in our own party in Maine contributed about as much to the defeats we suffered there as any other one thing."[255]

Just as a connection to Bernard Goldfine may have contributed to the defeat of Senator Frederick Payne in Maine's September elections, Democrats in New Hampshire hoped that the ethical controversy surrounding Bernard Goldfine and Sherman Adams would help them to win their state's gubernatorial election. Adams returned to his home in New Hampshire and refused to grant media interviews or issue public statements about his resignation. Meanwhile, Wesley Powell, the Republican nominee for governor, publicly admitted that he had accepted gifts from Goldfine.[256]

In his campaign against Powell, Bernard L. Boutin, the Democratic gubernatorial nominee and JFK's top liaison with New Hampshire Democrats, emphasized the need to improve public education, recreational areas, and industrial development in order to improve New Hampshire's future. To pre-empt Republican charges and perceptions that Democratic officials raise taxes, Boutin also stressed his opposition to a state sales tax.[257] In a 1964 interview, Boutin recalled that JFK had encouraged him to run for governor. Boutin stated, "We knew that we had to have control with decent, strong people in the Democratic Party organization in New Hampshire if we were going to do a meaningful job in 1960."[258]

William L. Dunfey was a New Hampshire businessman who worked closely with Boutin and Democratic national chairman Paul M. Butler in trying to improve Democratic electoral strength in this state. In a 1971 interview, Dunfey recalled that JFK helped to finance Boutin's 1958 gubernatorial campaign. JFK recognized the potential for a Democrat to be elected governor of New Hampshire after a Democratic congressional nominee in that state lost by a few votes in a recount in 1954. Dunfey added, "So '58 was just a rebounding again, almost again in Vermont and New Hampshire, with Maine winning again. We were just on the edge of it."[259]

Despite the national Democratic landslide, the encouragement of JFK, and state factors weakening and dividing New Hampshire's Republican Party, Boutin lost the 1958 gubernatorial election with 48.3 percent of the votes to Wesley Powell's 51.7 percent.[260] Powell defeated Boutin by a margin of 6,835 votes.[261] It was the closest gubernatorial election in New Hampshire since 1940. Meanwhile, the Republicans easily won both of New Hampshire's U.S. House seats.

The Democrats in Vermont found their state's election results in 1958 to be more indicative of future success. Like Boutin, Democratic gubernatorial nominee Bernard Leddy also lost, but by an even narrower margin. He received 49.7 percent of the votes compared to Republican gubernatorial nominee Robert T. Stafford's 50.3 percent and lost by a margin of only 719 votes.[262] Democratic senatorial nominee Frederick J. Fayette lost, but William H. Meyer became the first Democrat from Vermont to be elected to the U.S. House since 1850.[263] Meyer's victory with 51.5 percent of the votes was mostly attributed to divisions within Vermont's Republican Party, the fact that his Republican opponent was unpopular among Republican voters, the help of pro-Democratic political activists, and campaign spending by labor unions concerned about a right-to-work proposal.[264]

While the Democrats in New Hampshire and Vermont struggled to win major offices and end one-party Republican rule, the Democrats in Connecticut enjoyed an impressive electoral resurgence in that competitive, two-party state. In 1954, Abraham Ribicoff, a Democrat, was elected governor with 49.5 percent of the votes and a margin of approximately 3,000 votes. In 1958, he was reelected with 62.3 percent of the votes and a margin of nearly 250,000 votes.[265]

In 1956, the Republicans won all six of Connecticut's U.S. House seats.[266] In 1958, the Democrats won all of these U.S. House seats and majorities in both houses of the Connecticut state legislature. They had not won a majority of seats in the state house of representatives since 1876.[267]

Ribicoff's capable and innovative executive leadership and sophisticated media skills made him an unusually popular Democratic governor among Republican and independent voters. His Republican opponent was Fred Zeller, the state controller, who proved to be a dull campaigner. Because of his landslide reelection margin and the fact that his party now controlled the state legislature, Ribicoff would have more freedom and an enhanced political status in serving as JFK's surrogate to unite all of New England's Democratic delegates in 1960 and lobby Democratic governors from other states about JFK's presidential candidacy.

With Ribicoff's landslide reelection a foregone conclusion for the media and the general public, Connecticut's 1958 Senate election generated greater interest. Thomas J. Dodd, a former Democratic congressman who ran unsuccessfully for the Senate in 1956, opposed the Republican incumbent, Senator William A. Purtell.[268] Like other Democratic senatorial nominees running against Republican incumbents, Dodd criticized his opponent and the Eisenhower administration for their policy behavior regarding unemployment, distressed areas, education, hospital construction, and Social Security.[269] With a congressional voting record and reputation as an anti-Communist zealot, Dodd also emphasized the need to build at least one hundred nuclear submarines and ensure that American foreign aid and trade policies did not unintentionally benefit Communist governments.[270] Dodd was elected to the Senate with 57.5 percent of the votes.[271]

In addition to Ribicoff, the other New England governor who had been a major asset in lobbying for delegates for JFK at the 1956 Democratic national convention was Governor Dennis J. Roberts of Rhode Island. Unfortunately for JFK, Roberts was defeated for reelection in 1958 by a margin of 6,230 votes.[272] Since Rhode Island was the most Democratic state in New England and Senator John O. Pastore was reelected with 64.5 percent of the votes in 1958, Roberts's narrow loss to Christopher Del Sesto, his Republican opponent and a former Democrat of Italian ancestry, was commonly attributed to ethnic, rather than partisan, reasons.[273] Many voters of Italian ancestry were determined to elect Del Sesto governor in 1958 because they resented how Roberts, an Irish Catholic, had defeated Del Sesto in the 1956 election through a controversial recount and court decision.[274] Although Roberts was no longer a public official, he remained JFK's main contact in Rhode Island in preparation for the 1960 presidential campaign.

The 1958 election results in Massachusetts were similar to those of Connecticut. Governor Foster Furcolo was reelected with 56.2 percent of the votes, and the Democrats won control of both houses of the state legislature for the first time in history.[275] Compared to the 1956 congressional elections in Massachusetts, the Democrats made a net gain of one seat in the 1958 congressional elections so that they would control eight of the state's fourteen U.S. House seats during the 86th Congress.[276] "Democrats today held almost total control of the political destiny of Massachusetts for the first time in history," concluded a newspaper in western Massachusetts.[277]

As impressive and comprehensive as the electoral success of the Democratic ticket was in Massachusetts in 1958, it was superseded by the enormity and national significance of JFK's record-breaking, history-making reelection to the Senate. JFK received 73.2 percent of the votes and a winning margin of 874,608 votes.[278] Using the pseudonym "The Bay Stater," a columnist for the *Worcester Telegram*, a Republican-owned newspaper, noticed that, whenever anyone criticized JFK's reelection campaign as the foundation for his 1960 presidential campaign, voters seemed to become more likely to vote for JFK. One month before the election, "The Bay Stater" wrote, "The thought of having Massachusetts represented on a national ticket in 1960 doubtless is a glamorous and appealing notion to thousands of Bay State voters."[279]

Initially, JFK and his campaign workers had hoped that he would exceed former Democratic Governor Paul Dever's margin of approximately 250,000 votes in the 1950 gubernatorial election.[280] As they became more confident of a wider victory margin, they hoped to beat Senator Leverett Saltonstall's record of receiving 64.3 percent of the votes and a margin of 561,668 votes in a 1944 special Senate election.[281] By surpassing the electoral performances of Dever in 1950 and Saltonstall in 1944, JFK received the highest percentage of popular votes received by any Senate nominee in the history of Massachusetts. The last gubernatorial nominee in Massachusetts who received more than 73 percent of the votes was Alexander Bullock in 1866.[282]

JFK carried all of the fourteen counties in Massachusetts. Among the state's largest cities, JFK's percentages of the two-party vote ranged from 70.74 percent in Springfield to 88 percent in Fall River. His percentage in Boston was 84.77 percent.[283]

The most striking changes in JFK's electoral performance in 1958 compared to 1952 occurred in staunchly Republican small towns in western and southeastern Massachusetts. In western Massachusetts, JFK received 16 percent of the votes in Hancock and 17.64 percent of the votes in Mount Washington in the 1952 Senate election. In 1958, he received 52.14 percent of the votes in Hancock and 55.55 percent of the votes in Mount Washington. In southeastern Massachusetts, JFK received 29.24 percent of the votes in Nantucket and 26.88 percent of the votes in Edgartown in 1952. In 1958, he respectively received 57.6 percent and 51.24 percent in these two island towns.[284]

Nationally, the Democrats accomplished net gains of forty-eight U.S. House seats, fifteen Senate seats, and eight governorships.[285] In addition to the recession, unemployment, falling farm income, Eisenhower's declining popularity, and an uneasy feeling that the United States was falling behind the Soviet Union, Democratic candidates benefited from a Republican effort to promote right-to-work legislation in several states as a way to mobilize conservative voters. The Republican right-to-work campaign backfired as labor unions succeeded in mobilizing a larger number of voters to oppose this legislation and elect pro-union Democratic candidates.[286] Among Republican nominees for major offices, the few noteworthy victories included Nelson Rockefeller's election as governor of New York and the reelection of Senator Barry Goldwater of Arizona, an outspoken advocate of right-to-work legislation.[287]

While the record-breaking magnitude of JFK's reelection statistics attracted mostly favorable attention from the national media, the election results of 1958 also yielded new, possible complications for JFK's presidential candidacy. Senator Stuart Symington of Missouri, who was often mentioned as a likely Democratic presidential candidate for 1960, was reelected with approximately two-thirds of the votes. In contrast to JFK's rhetorical and legislative record on McCarthyism, liberal activists remembered and admired Symington's outspoken, persistent opposition to McCarthyism. Also, if a Protestant became the Democratic presidential nominee of 1960 and chose a Catholic running mate, he now had several choices besides JFK. In the 1958 elections, Catholic Democrats were elected as senators in Minnesota, Maine, and Connecticut, and reelected as senators in Montana, Rhode Island, and New Mexico. Catholic Democrats were also elected governors of California, Ohio, and Pennsylvania.[288]

As the first Catholic to be elected governor of Pennsylvania, David L. Lawrence would prove to be an obstacle to JFK's presidential candidacy. Because of his memories of Al Smith's 1928 presidential candidacy, Lawrence believed that a Democratic presidential or vice presidential nominee who was Catholic would be more of a liability than an asset in attracting votes and winning a presidential election and in affecting voting behavior in congressional, state, and local elections. As governor, he would control even more delegates at the 1960 Democratic national convention than he had as the mayor of Pittsburgh at the 1956 Democratic national convention.[289]

The 1958 election results also changed the political environment for Dwight D. Eisenhower, Richard M. Nixon, and Lyndon B. Johnson. At his first press conference after the election, Eisenhower expressed his assumption that the Democrats in the 86th Congress would propose excessive, reckless amounts of federal spending and his determination to reject such spending and achieve balanced budgets.[290] Vice President Nixon, as the presumptive Republican presidential nominee of 1960, privately advised Eisenhower to be less fiscally conservative and more cooperative with Democratic spending proposals in order to make the Republican Party more attractive to voters in the 1960 elections.[291] Regardless of whether his leadership title was Senate minority leader or majority leader during the first six years of Eisenhower's presidency, Johnson was able to exercise an unusual degree of legislative and political power as the leader of the Senate Democrats because the majority party of the Senate, regardless of whether it was Republican or Democratic, held a margin of only one or two seats. Since the Democratic majority in the Senate now had a thirty-seat margin for the upcoming 86th Congress, Johnson would be less powerful and his fellow Democrats less compliant with his leadership.[292]

Two days after the 1958 elections, JFK announced that he would leave for Alaska on Sunday, November 9, 1958, to campaign for Democratic nominees there. Alaska would become a state on January 3, 1959, so Alaskans held their federal and gubernatorial elections on November 25, 1958. Nixon had already campaigned there.[293]

JFK arrived in Alaska to campaign for that state's Democratic nominees for its two Senate seats, at-large U.S. House seat, and governorship. He made appearances in Fairbanks, Ketchikan, Anchorage, and Juneau.[294] John Harris, a reporter for the *Boston Globe*, accompanied JFK on his trip to Alaska. Despite harsh weather, Harris was impressed at how large and enthusiastic the crowds that greeted JFK were in Ketchikan. In a 1964 interview, Harris recalled, "I don't think there were five or six empty seats. Jack was introduced as the next president of the United States."[295]

On November 10, 1958, JFK delivered a speech in Juneau to endorse Ernest Gruening and Edward L. "Bob" Bartlett for the U.S. Senate and Ralph Rivers for the U.S. House of Representatives. Addressing an audience of approximately 700 people in the Gross 20th Century Theatre, JFK humorously stated, "I came to Alaska to pay a debt of gratitude. If I had been successful in receiving all the votes of the Alaska delegation at the last Democratic convention, I might have been nominated for Vice President of the United States and my political career would now be over. So I've come here to express my thanks for your not supporting me."[296] The Alaskans warmly applauded JFK's speech and elected Democrats to all three federal offices and the governorship on November 25.

While JFK was in Alaska, he learned that James Michael Curley had died. Theodore C. Sorensen wrote a draft of a press statement for JFK regarding Curley's death. As the senator revised Sorensen's draft, he said to journalist John Harris, "The Kennedys and Curleys haven't always gotten along too well. He hadn't been too kind to the Kennedys."[297]

During the last two years of his life, Curley had been a minor obstacle to the advancement of JFK's political career and an occasional irritant. As the Democratic national committeeman from Massachusetts, Curley and Democratic national committeewoman

Margaret O'Riordan supported Representative John W. McCormack and William "Onions" Burke in JFK's struggle to remove Burke as Democratic state chairman and control the state's delegation to the 1956 Democratic national convention. JFK then wanted Curley to resign as Democratic national committeeman so that he could give this position to Burke as a consolation. Curley refused and defiantly stated, "He hasn't got enough money to buy me."[298] Some of JFK's campaign operatives attributed JFK's relatively disappointing performance in several Boston wards in the 1958 Democratic primary in Massachusetts to pro-Curley, anti-JFK voters.[299]

Because of Curley's death, JFK was able to determine the selection of the next Democratic national committeeman from Massachusetts. This was an important position in helping to contact DNC members from other states for JFK's 1960 presidential campaign. JFK chose John B. Hynes, the mayor of Boston who had become a political enemy of Curley.[300]

JFK, of course, did not reveal to *Boston Globe* reporter John Harris that an agreement between Curley and JFK's father had been essential to the beginning of JFK's political career. Heavily in debt and facing the legal costs of a second federal indictment for mail fraud, Curley accepted JPK's offer of financial assistance in exchange for vacating his congressional seat and running for mayor of Boston in 1945.[301] Curley's decision enabled JFK to be elected from an open congressional seat in 1946. Peter Cloherty, a Curley ally and assistant city greeter, later recalled that, while James Michael Curley was publicly neutral in the competitive 1946 Democratic primary for his congressional seat, George Curley, one of his sons, worked in JFK's primary campaign.[302]

Curley's agreement with JPK enabled JFK to enter politics, but JFK became a very different type of Irish-Catholic Boston politician than Curley. From 1953 to 1957, JFK compiled a moderately liberal legislative record with some conservative votes, especially on agriculture, water and dam projects, and rural electrification. During this time, he tended to vote the same as Senator Leverett Saltonstall of Massachusetts and other Republican senators from New England on economic issues unique or particularly important to their region, such as textiles, railroad freight rates, and the fishing industry. As a founder and chairman of the New England Senators' Conference, JFK sought to convince most of his constituents, regardless of their differences in party affiliation, that he was a diligent and effective advocate of the policy needs of their state and region.

However, after the narrow defeat of his vice presidential candidacy at the 1956 Democratic national convention, JFK's legislative behavior, rhetoric, and speaking engagements reflected those of a more partisan, national political figure instead of a non-partisan advocate of New England policy interests. During the 1957 and 1958 sessions of Congress, he developed and pursued a more conventionally and consistently liberal legislative record. JFK began to pattern his voting record on agricultural issues on that of Senator Hubert H. Humphrey of Minnesota. He crafted and promoted a labor reform bill that was acceptable to George Meany, Walter Reuther, and most other major labor leaders.

During the 1958 campaigns season, JFK was the most popular guest speaker at Democratic state conventions, fund-raising dinners, and other partisan events. By the end of 1958, he was the front-runner for the Democratic presidential nomination of 1960. His next challenge was to develop and implement a strategy for winning his party's presidential nomination based on a regional foundation of united Democratic delegates from New England.

6

JFK and the Politics of 1959

IN THE FALL OF 1959, JOSEPH P. KENNEDY (JPK) bluntly told journalist Ed Plaut that his son JFK was "the greatest attraction in the country today" and compared him to movie stars Cary Grant and James Stewart. He confidently predicted that the Democratic Party would nominate JFK for president because party leaders knew that JFK was the only Democrat who could be elected president in 1960. JPK concluded his analysis for Plaut by saying, "The nomination is a cinch. I'm not a bit worried about the nomination."[1]

JFK and his closest advisers and aides were optimistic that a well-organized, well-financed, professionally conducted, full-time campaign could secure the Democratic presidential nomination of 1960. They lacked, however, JPK's certitude. Compared to JPK, they were more familiar with the uncertainty and volatility of public opinion, voting behavior, and promises of delegate support. For example, Dwight D. Eisenhower's declining popularity had contributed to Republican losses in the 1958 midterm elections. In a Gallup poll released on November 7, 1958, Eisenhower's job approval rating was 52 percent. But it increased substantially to 64 percent in a Gallup poll released on May 29, 1959.[2]

Gallup polls that surveyed Democratic voters in 1958 and 1959 about their preferences for their party's presidential nominee in 1960 revealed similar fluctuations for JFK. A Gallup poll released on February 7, 1958, revealed that 56 percent of the interviewees favored JFK as their party's 1960 presidential nominee.[3] A December 3, 1958 poll showed JFK and Adlai Stevenson tied at 42 percent each for the 1960

Democratic presidential nomination. A Gallup poll released on June 10, 1959, disclosed that the Democrats surveyed preferred Stevenson to JFK 29 percent to 26 percent.[4] One of the first presidential campaign decisions that JFK made a few weeks after the 1958 elections was to hire his own pollster, Louis Harris.[5]

JFK did not publicly and formally announce his presidential candidacy until January 2, 1960. Nonetheless, during and after his 1958 reelection campaign, JFK made his presidential ambition more obvious to his supporters in Massachusetts. Shortly after the 1958 elections, JFK held a meeting of his campaign workers at the Algonquin Club in Boston. He told them, "With only about four hours of work and a handful of supporters, I came within thirty three and a half votes of winning the Vice Presidential nomination in 1956. If we all work hard, we ought to be able to pick up all the marbles."[6] JFK previously and privately conveyed the same message to campaign aide David F. Powers a few weeks after the 1956 presidential election.[7]

Indeed, a major reason why JFK won almost 75 percent of the votes in his reelection to the Senate was that his campaign workers and political allies urged the voters of Massachusetts to vote for him in 1958 as a way to encourage and strengthen his 1960 presidential campaign. This electoral appeal based on home state pride in promoting the first election of a Massachusetts senator to the presidency since 1824 was especially directed at Republican and independent voters. These voters were less likely to support JFK's reelection to the Senate if the Kennedy campaign emphasized JFK's party affiliation and increasingly liberal rhetoric and voting record.[8]

Therefore, one of the foundations of JFK's campaign for the Democratic presidential nomination was an emphasis on such nonpartisan personal qualities as his televised appearance, style of public speaking, and attractive personality instead of his Senate voting record and policy proposals. Regardless of whether they identified themselves as Democrats, Republicans, or independents, respondents in a 1959 Gallup poll used such words as "deep thinking," "nice looking," and "from good background" to describe JFK.[9] JPK, of course, had always been a key strategist in developing and promoting an attractive media image for his son. A major challenge for the Kennedy campaign was to maximize the private use of JPK's business, political, and media connections and shrewd judgment to benefit JFK's presidential candidacy while minimizing public awareness of JPK's influence.

This challenge became especially difficult after Eleanor Roosevelt appeared on a televised discussion program. During a broadcast of the television program *College News Conference* from Washington, DC, on December 7, 1958, Roosevelt stated that she supported Senator Hubert H. Humphrey of Minnesota for the 1960 Democratic presidential nomination, partially because it was unlikely that Adlai Stevenson would run for president again. She spoke dismissively of JFK as a charming young man who apparently knew how to write a book about political courage but was unable to exercise it, especially on the issue of McCarthyism.[10] Her most severe criticism was directed at JPK. She accused JPK of spending "oodles of money all over the country" to promote JFK's presidential candidacy and probably having "paid representatives in every state by now."[11]

JFK felt compelled to directly rebut her charges. In a December 11, 1958 letter to the former First Lady, the senator challenged her to provide him with proof of her accusations. In her December 18 letter to JFK, Roosevelt refused to retract her televised statements. She wrote, "I was told your father said openly he would spend any money to make his son the first Catholic President of this country . . . This seems commonly accepted as fact."[12]

In his December 29 letter replying to Eleanor Roosevelt, JFK again challenged her to prove her statements with specific evidence, instead of repeating gossip and rumors. He wrote that, if she could not provide evidence of paid representatives, then he expected her to "correct the record in a fair and gracious manner."[13] The former First Lady still did not issue a public retraction.

Fortunately for JFK, Eleanor Roosevelt firmly and clearly stated that JFK's Catholicism was not a liability for his presumed presidential candidacy during her December 7 television appearance and on other occasions.[14] Nevertheless, in her December 18 letter to JFK, she specified JFK's religion by writing that JPK wanted his son to become the first Catholic president of the United States of America. JFK's

Catholicism had been a national political issue since the release of the Bailey Memorandum and his narrow defeat for the Democratic vice presidential nomination in 1956. However, JFK had not yet developed an effective, consistent rhetorical strategy for addressing concerns and questions about the possibility of a Catholic becoming president in the near future. When asked by journalists, he often dismissed questions about a presidential candidate's Catholicism as irrelevant in influencing current American voting behavior.[15]

JFK, however, unintentionally inflamed the religious issue in an interview given to *Look* magazine in February, 1959.[16] In it, JFK emphasized his devotion to the constitutional separation of church and state. He also specified that several of his votes in the Senate differed from the policy positions and interests of the Catholic church, such as his opposition to federal aid to parochial schools.[17]

JFK was soon criticized by two Catholic publications, *Commonweal* and *America*.[18] *Commonweal* criticized the Democratic senator from Massachusetts for failing to clarify that there was no so-called "Catholic position" on current policy issues and that the Constitution could be interpreted differently in order to allow federal aid to parochial schools. *America*, a Jesuit journal, censured JFK more harshly. An editorial in *America* accused JFK of trying to appease anti-Catholic bigots and refuted his statement that a public official's oath of office supersedes his religious beliefs.[19] It also criticized *Look* for, in effect, submitting JFK, as a Catholic, to a religious test prohibited by the Constitution and JFK for taking this test.[20] *Ave Maria*, a magazine published by the Fathers of the Holy Cross at the University of Notre Dame, and Catholic diocesan newspapers throughout the nation printed similar criticisms of JFK's statements in *Look*.

The *Catholic Free Press*, a publication of the Catholic diocese of Worcester, Massachusetts, was one of the few diocesan newspapers that defended JFK's statements. The bishop of this diocese was the Most Reverend John J. Wright. JPK had a friendly relationship with Wright, and the bishop was grateful for JPK's donations to Catholic institutions in his diocese, especially after a tornado devastated the Worcester area in 1953.[21] JPK enlisted Bishop Wright to privately advise JFK on how to explain the relationship between his faith and the prospect of a Catholic being elected president in 1960 in order to satisfy both Catholic and Protestant critics of JFK.[22]

By the early spring of 1959, the Kennedys had not yet developed effective responses to questions about JPK's influence on JFK's political career and the religious issue. They did, however, begin to develop a campaign organization and strategy in early April. A meeting was held at JPK's estate in Palm Beach, Florida, on April 1 and 2, 1959. Participants included JFK, RFK, Lawrence F. O'Brien, Kenneth P. O'Donnell, Louis Harris, and Stephen Smith. Smith was a brother-in-law of JFK and managed the Kennedy family's finances. He had already opened an unofficial campaign office for JFK in Washington, DC. In his autobiography, O'Brien wrote, "Our main conclusion was that America is one hell of a big country and no set of rules applied to all of its states."[23] Few major, definitive decisions about JFK's presidential campaign were made at this time. No campaign manager was appointed because RFK was still busy working as the chief counsel for the McClellan committee.

It was already understood that JFK needed to win impressive victories in a few contested presidential primaries in 1960, especially in Wisconsin. Wisconsin was important to JFK's campaign for the 1960 Democratic presidential nomination for several reasons. Historically, it was the first state to establish presidential primaries for each major party. Strongly influenced by Progressive Era reforms in politics and government, Wisconsin included many ADA members and other liberal activists in its state Democratic Party. While Milwaukee, Green Bay, and other industrial cities held concentrations of mostly Democratic labor union members and central and eastern European Catholics, especially Polish Americans, rural areas were populated by mostly Protestant farmers and German Catholics who tended to vote Republican. Since Wisconsin's 1960 Democratic presidential primary would be an open primary, Republicans and independents could vote in it.[24]

Most importantly, if Senator Hubert H. Humphrey of Minnesota ran for president in 1960, then JFK needed to decisively defeat Humphrey in the Wisconsin primary. Humphrey was widely respected among Wisconsin farmers as their state's "third senator" on agricultural issues. Although JFK had campaigned for Senator William Proxmire of Wisconsin in a 1957 special election, it was assumed that Proxmire would actively support Humphrey's presidential candidacy in the primary.[25]

Consequently, JFK began a three-day speaking tour on April 9, 1959, one week after the end of the Palm Beach meeting. JFK arrived in Milwaukee on a Thursday night to address a press club dinner. During his subsequent press conference, he refused to state whether he planned to run for president in 1960 and distanced himself from Proxmire's outspoken criticism of Senate Majority Leader Lyndon B. Johnson. JFK also stated that it was reasonable for voters and the media to ask political candidates about their beliefs regarding the separation of church and state.[26]

JFK's speaking trip in Wisconsin included six other cities. The newspaper coverage of JFK's April visit to Wisconsin generally found the public's reception to the Massachusetts senator to be friendly and enthusiastic. JFK's most serious and extensive policy speech concerned the five principles which the senator specified as the basis for improving the nation's agricultural policies.[27] He was not forced to explain and defend his earlier Senate votes in favor of the Eisenhower administration's flexible price support program, which was especially unpopular among dairy and grain farmers in the Midwest.

Ironically, but perhaps not coincidentally, JFK ended his Wisconsin itinerary in Appleton. Following his death in Bethesda, Maryland, Senator Joseph R. McCarthy was buried in Appleton on May 7, 1957. RFK was one of the few nationally prominent political figures to fly from Washington, DC, to Appleton in order to attend McCarthy's burial service.[28] Earlier, when JFK and Jacqueline Kennedy visited Madison, a newspaper publisher mistakenly introduced them as Mr. and Mrs. McCarthy.[29]

Despite the generally positive newspaper articles and commentaries from the Wisconsin press, Joseph Alsop, a nationally syndicated columnist, traveled to Wisconsin to cover JFK's trip. Alsop expected a brutal primary fight between JFK and Humphrey in 1960. In his column published on April 13, 1959, Alsop wrote, "Kennedy wonders whether he needs to risk his massive support in other states in a messy Wisconsin primary."[30]

JFK, of course, knew that planning a successful primary campaign meant more than developing a reputation as an attractive and popular public speaker in Wisconsin. When Kennedy campaigned for Proxmire in 1957, he met Jerry Bruno. The senator from Massachusetts admired the advance work that Bruno did for Proxmire. After he returned to Washington, DC, JFK contacted Bruno, who was a staff aide to Proxmire, and hired him to work on his still unannounced presidential campaign.[31] In late June 1959, Proxmire announced to the press that Bruno was leaving his staff in order to work for the Kennedy for President Committee of Wisconsin, chaired by Ivan Nestingen, the mayor of Madison. Proxmire added that he might run in his state's Democratic presidential primary at the request of Governor Gaylord Nelson in order to discourage intraparty conflicts resulting from an expected battle between JFK and Humphrey.[32]

In addition to his recruitment of Bruno, JFK strengthened his vote-getting ability in Wisconsin by attracting the active backing of Clement Zablocki, a Democratic congressman whose district include large Polish American neighborhoods in Milwaukee. Even before JFK's April trip to Wisconsin, Zablocki had invited Kennedy to deliver a speech in Milwaukee on Pulaski Day.[33] Zablocki served as the honorary chairman of the Wisconsin Kennedy for President Club, and his congressional district served as the electoral base for JFK's primary campaign.[34]

By late April of 1959, JFK was busy trying to save the Kennedy-Ervin labor reform bill from amendments favored by a bipartisan coalition of southern Democrats and Republicans and opposed by AFL-CIO and UAW leaders. On April 22, 1959, the Senate added a "bill of rights" amendment by a vote of 47 to 46. This amendment was sponsored by Senator John McClellan of Arkansas and opposed by JFK. With the Senate divided by a vote of 45 to 45 on a motion to reconsider the McClellan amendment, Vice President Richard M. Nixon cast the tie-breaking vote in favor of the "bill of rights" amendment for union members.[35]

From late August until early September, JFK chaired a conference committee that reconciled differences between the House and Senate versions of what was now known as the Landrum-Griffin bill on labor reform. The Senate passed the conference committee's report on September 3 by a vote of 95 to 2, and the House of Representatives passed it on September 4 by a vote of 353 to 52. Satisfied that this bill had most of the provisions that he wanted, Eisenhower signed the Landrum-Griffin bill into law as the Labor-Management Reporting and Disclosure Act of 1959 on September 14, 1959.[36]

Shortly before and after Eisenhower's enactment of this legislation, the content and tone of JFK's public statements conveyed his reluctance and equivocation in supporting a bill that included some provisions that he regarded as unfair to the legitimate interests and rights of labor unions and authorizing excessive federal regulation of union affairs.[37] Privately, JFK was concerned that labor leaders would blame him for the Landrum-Griffin Act and be less likely to back his presidential candidacy. The Massachusetts senator was relieved when he was greeted with rousing applause and cheers at the annual meeting of the AFL-CIO's building and construction trade unions in San Francisco on September 11, 1959. JFK devoted much of his speech to denouncing right-to-work laws and corruption in the Teamsters union.[38]

A harbinger of JFK's friendly reception in San Francisco was a three-day speaking tour of Oregon in early August which included speeches in Portland at a Democratic dinner and in Seaside at a state AFL-CIO convention.[39] In July, Senator Wayne Morse of Oregon filed an affidavit in Salem, the state capital, stating that he did not intend to be a presidential candidate in 1960. This legal action made it unlikely at this time that Morse would compete in Oregon's presidential primary, one of the primaries that JFK planned to enter.[40]

Morse later decided to run against JFK in Oregon and several other presidential primaries. His July affidavit, however, motivated Representative Edith Green, a Democratic congresswoman from Oregon, to endorse JFK for president and participate in his August visit to her state. In his speech to the labor union audience in Seaside, JFK said that, without the changes that he advocated in the current labor reform bill, there was the possibility that a "Republican–southern Democratic coalition in the House of Representatives will substitute for a responsible committee bill, an anti-labor, unworkable, punitive measure."[41]

In a 1974 interview, Edith Green recalled that she suspected that Senator Wayne Morse had pressured the leaders and delegates at the state AFL-CIO convention in Seaside to give JFK a cool reception. Nevertheless, the audience was so impressed by JFK's speech on labor reform that it spontaneously gave him an effusive, standing ovation.[42] Later, Morse was one of two senators to vote against the conference report on the Landrum-Griffin bill. He frequently criticized JFK for hurting the interests and rights of labor unions by making too many concessions to Republicans and conservative southern Democrats.[43] By the end of 1959, Morse formally entered Oregon's Democratic presidential primary.[44]

With JFK visiting Wisconsin and Oregon as possible primary states for his presidential candidacy, Lawrence F. O'Brien went to Indiana on April 10, 1959. As a Kennedy campaign aide and adviser since JFK's 1952 Senate race, O'Brien specialized in the creation and management of campaign organizations. During his visit to Indiana, O'Brien found a few local Democratic officials who had heard of JFK and were willing to support him in a presidential primary.[45] Compared to the Democrats in Wisconsin, the Democrats in Indiana tended to be more conservative and less competitive against the state's Republican Party. Only a few cities in Indiana had significant concentrations of Catholics, African Americans, and labor union members.[46]

Furthermore, Indiana's Democratic Party included socially conservative, rural Protestants in southern Indiana. During the 1920s, Indiana experienced widespread political activities by the Ku Klux Klan, which stridently denounced the presence of African Americans, Catholics, Jews, and immigrants. O'Brien was wary of having JFK enter a presidential primary in Indiana, especially if it became a hotly contested race against Senator Stuart Symington of Missouri.[47]

Nevertheless, JFK flew to Indiana for a two-day speaking tour immediately after his Wisconsin trip.[48] On April 12, 1959, he addressed a national convention of the United Negro College Fund in Indianapolis. In his speech, Kennedy linked the importance of higher education to the global responsibilities of the United States, especially toward the Third World. He also connected the struggles of African Americans against segregation and discrimination to the struggles of newly independent Third World countries against the legacy of colonialism. The Massachusetts senator stated, "It is my hope, therefore, that at least some of our Negro colleges and universities, perhaps because the crisis for them is greater and sharper than that facing American education generally, will adapt their curriculum with this in mind. The new curriculum would be designed to fit Americans for the rigors facing them in the new frontiers of the world."[49]

Experimenting with the concept of the New Frontier as a campaign theme, JFK addressed students at Purdue University in West Lafayette on the following day and spoke about the need for American college students to prepare for the global challenges of the 1960s. JFK delivered a less esoteric, more partisan speech at a Jefferson-Jackson Day dinner for Adams County Democrats in Decatur. Kennedy stated that he and his fellow Democrats in Congress "are challenged by problems which were never even foreseen by Franklin Roosevelt." He also accused the Republicans of having "no new ideas, no bold action" to respond to foreign and domestic policy problems.[50] JFK ended his Indiana trip with a luncheon in Indianapolis with several prominent Democrats, including a former governor and a former DNC chairman.

Undeterred by O'Brien's skeptical analysis of Indiana's political environment, JFK conducted a more highly publicized and extensive three-day speaking tour of Indiana in early October. By this time, RFK had resigned as chief counsel to the McClellan committee. Pierre Salinger, who had worked with RFK on this committee, now served as JFK's press secretary. Salinger arranged to have televised news coverage of JFK's press conference in Indianapolis on October 2, 1959.[51] JFK's October visit to Indiana also included speeches at Democratic fundraisers, rallies, and county committee meetings in several cities and towns.[52] JFK's speech in Indianapolis commented on Soviet premier Nikita Khrushchev's recent visit to the United States.[53]

During JFK's October tour of Indiana, he was accompanied by Senator Vance Hartke of Indiana.[54] Hartke had not endorsed JFK for president, but his escorting of JFK in Indiana conveyed a misleading image of endorsement.[55] Furthermore, Hartke privately urged Senator Lyndon B. Johnson in December 1959, to announce his presidential candidacy so that Hartke could organize Johnson's campaign for Indiana's Democratic presidential primary.[56]

Regardless of whether JFK could defeat Johnson, Humphrey, or Symington in a fiercely contested presidential primary in Indiana, the Kennedy campaign hoped that media and public perceptions of JFK's April and October visits to Indiana would create and communicate the impression of widespread and enthusiastic electoral support in this state, thereby discouraging the other potential presidential candidates from entering the Indiana primary.[57] Thus, the Kennedy campaign did not discourage Indiana Democrats from creating their own pro-JFK campaign organizations in order to encourage JFK to run for president.[58] JFK also had O'Brien privately contact them about coordinating their efforts with JFK's expected entry into the Indiana primary.[59]

While the Kennedy campaign made tentative plans to enter the Wisconsin, Oregon, and Indiana primaries, it was jolted by a poll published by the *Chicago Daily News* in April 1959. This poll surveyed all of the delegates from New England who attended the 1956 Democratic national convention. Approximately 70 percent expected to be delegates at the 1960 Democratic national convention. The overwhelming majority of delegates from the three states of southern New England indicated that they would vote to nominate JFK at the 1960 convention.

However, only a small minority of the 1956 delegates from the three states of northern New England stated that they would vote for JFK at the 1960 convention. JFK received only one and one-half of Maine's fourteen delegate votes and four of New Hampshire's eight delegate votes. JFK did not receive any of Vermont's six delegate votes in this poll.[60]

With the six New England states allocated a total of 114 delegate votes for the 1960 Democratic national convention, the Kennedy campaign wanted to secure and publicize unanimous support from all of New England's delegates long before the 1960 convention began in Los Angeles. Since the early 1950s, JFK made frequent fundraising and speaking trips to New Hampshire and Maine in order to promote the development of more competitive Democratic parties in these Republican-dominated states and eventually benefit from this political change.[61] Even if New Hampshire's 1960 Democratic presidential primary was contested, JFK needed to attract a high voter turnout and an overwhelming percentage of votes, similar to his 1958 electoral performance in Massachusetts, in order to establish himself nationally as the frontrunner for his party's presidential nomination.

As the New Hampshire's Democratic Party expanded, however, it experienced more factional conflicts which threatened to prevent the selection of a unanimously pro-Kennedy delegation to the 1960 Democratic national convention.[62] JFK sent his brother Edward M. Kennedy (EMK) to speak on his behalf at New Hampshire's 1959 Jefferson-Jackson Day dinner. Bernard L. Boutin, JFK's top Democratic contact in New Hampshire, later wrote to EMK and assured him that his speech at this dinner "will help us a great deal in trying to secure the highest vote in the history of the State for your brother, Jack, in the Democratic Primary next March."[63]

Despite these encouraging words from Boutin, the Kennedy campaign was concerned that Senator Stuart Symington seemed to have a surprising degree of political strength in New Hampshire and, even more so, in Maine.[64] In New Hampshire, some state and local Democratic officials wanted to keep their party weak and divided in order to receive patronage appointments and other favors from Republican governors and senators.[65] In Maine, the Democrats gained much in the 1958 elections. They won the gubernatorial, senatorial, and two of the three congressional elections. They won these elections partially because they had expanded and diversified Maine's Democratic Party beyond its small Catholic base to include a growing number of disaffected Protestant voters among Republicans and independents.[66]

Therefore, some Maine Democrats feared that if JFK, as a Catholic, were nominated for president in 1960, then his presence at the top of Maine's ballot would contribute to Democratic losses in

Maine's gubernatorial, senatorial, congressional, and state legislative elections.[67] Among all of the New England states, the Ku Klux Klan was especially powerful in Maine during the 1920s with an emphasis on anti-Catholicism.[68] A divided Maine delegation at the 1960 Democratic national convention could also be politically detrimental to Senator Edmund S. Muskie, especially after he became the first senator to publicly endorse JFK for president.[69]

JFK arrived in Augusta, Maine, on November 15, 1959, in order to address a Democratic issues conference. During the previous two days, JFK spoke at Democratic events in Milwaukee and Oklahoma City.[70] In all three cities, JFK claimed that, during the Eisenhower administration, the United States had fallen behind the Soviet Union in economic growth, scientific advancement, and world prestige. In Augusta, he stated, "Every time we fail . . . and demonstrate that we are not number one . . . we not only let down our country, but we let down the world."[71]

Before JFK arrived in Maine, his private plane stopped in Hartford to pick up Governor Abraham Ribicoff of Connecticut so that Ribicoff could join him and Muskie at a press conference in Augusta.[72] While JFK and Ribicoff met privately with Muskie, Governor Clinton Clauson, and other Maine Democrats in the governor's mansion, they discussed whether the Democratic state committee of Maine should endorse JFK for president then or wait until JFK announced his candidacy in 1960. In a 1964 interview, Frank M. Coffin, who was a Democratic congressman from Maine in 1959, recalled that JFK would definitely "have no opposition in securing the Maine endorsement. The issue was solely that of proper timing that would be of the greatest help to Senator Kennedy and to the Democratic ticket in Maine."[73]

The Maine Democrats were eager to announce united support for JFK's presidential candidacy partially because they were attracted to the Massachusetts senator's earlier emphasis on using new federal policies to promote economic development and cooperation in New England as a distinct region. Governor Clinton Clauson told John E. Byrne, his press secretary, "He's a New England man. We're naturally all going to go for him." Likewise, Muskie told Byrne that "this is a chance for the whole region to get behind somebody who can do something for this whole region."[74]

On January 4, 1960, two days after JFK officially announced his presidential candidacy, he received the endorsements of Muskie, Maine's two Democratic congressmen, and the late Governor Clauson, who died on December 30, 1959.[75] Clauson was buried on the same day as JFK's announcement, and RFK attended the funeral.[76] This early endorsement from Maine's top Democratic politicians made it more likely that Maine's Democratic delegates would be united behind JFK by the time of the Democratic national convention in Los Angeles.

The fact that Ribicoff went with JFK to the Democratic issues convention was not unusual. Ever since Ribicoff delivered a nominating speech for JFK's vice presidential candidacy at the 1956 Democratic national convention in Chicago, he had been JFK's chief liaison with Democratic governors. Often accompanied by John M. Bailey, the Democratic state chairman of Connecticut, Ribicoff promoted JFK's presidential candidacy among his fellow Democratic governors in order to accomplish two objectives for JFK's still unannounced presidential campaign.[77] First, Ribicoff and Bailey wanted to learn how many delegate votes a Democratic governor could deliver to JFK on the first ballot at the 1960 Democratic national convention. Second, they wanted to discourage as many favorite son presidential candidacies among Democratic governors as they could. As early as the summer of 1959, the Kennedy campaign wanted to generate the appearance of a growing bandwagon effect among Democratic delegates throughout the nation in order to create the fact of a bandwagon by the summer of 1960 for securing the Democratic presidential nomination on the first ballot at the national convention.[78]

The most prominent example of Ribicoff's efforts on behalf of JFK among Democratic governors in 1959 was his lobbying of them at the Governors' Conference held in San Juan, Puerto Rico, in early August. In his statements to the press, Ribicoff asserted that Democratic governors should not become favorite son presidential candidates because no Democratic governor could be a serious, nationally competitive presidential candidate in the 1960 general election. Furthermore, according to Ribicoff, the Democratic presidential nomination should not be determined by a brokered, "smoke-filled room" process at the Democratic national convention. Ribicoff also stated that Adlai Stevenson could not be nominated for president in 1960.[79]

One week after the Governors' Conference ended, Bailey sent JFK a report on the results of his and Ribicoff's experiences there. Bailey's private report was as confident as Ribicoff's public statements. According to Bailey, there was no significant support for Governors Robert Meyner of New Jersey and G. Mennen "Soapy" Williams of Michigan for president. Bailey also perceived Minnesota Governor Orville Freeman's lobbying activities for Senator Hubert H. Humphrey's anticipated presidential candidacy to be weak and ineffective compared to those of Ribicoff for JFK.[80]

Most of the Democratic governors whom Ribicoff consulted were either neutral or favorable toward JFK's prospective presidential candidacy. Bailey's report provided its most extensive analysis for Governor Edmund G. "Pat" Brown of California. The Kennedy campaign was concerned that if Brown decided to run for president in 1960 he could prevent JFK from winning the Democratic presidential nomination. Like JFK, Brown was Catholic. The 1960 Democratic national convention would be held in Los Angeles. If Brown was an active presidential candidate, he could not only control most of California's delegates but would also be attractive to delegates from other states as a Catholic running mate for a Protestant presidential nominee. JFK had already met privately with Brown in the spring of 1959 but could not elicit a definite answer from Brown about whether or not he would run for president.[81]

In his report, Bailey assured JFK that if Brown became a presidential candidate he would have little delegate strength outside of California. Bailey wrote, "One thing that I think affects the California situation is that in our talks with the other western Governors there was no great enthusiasm for Brown to be a candidate."[82] Bailey concluded that Brown's political advisers were urging him to encourage media speculation about a possible presidential candidacy in order to attract favorable media coverage of his governorship in general, thereby improving his poll ratings in California.[83]

Despite Bailey's optimism that Brown would not be a serious threat to JFK's presidential candidacy, JFK arrived in Oakland, California, on October 30, 1959, to begin a four-day speaking tour of that state.[84] In his speeches and interviews in California, JFK mostly emphasized his foreign policy views, such as his support for a conditional, bilateral ban on nuclear bomb tests by the United States and Soviet Union and his opposition to diplomatic recognition of Communist China. After reporters repeatedly asked him about his and Brown's prospective presidential candidacies, JFK stated that he probably would not enter California's 1960 Democratic presidential primary. JFK's statement was interpreted as an apparent concession that Brown would lead California's delegates as a favorite son presidential candidate at the Democratic national convention.[85]

Two days before JFK arrived in Oakland, the Kennedy campaign held its second organizational meeting on October 28, 1959, at RFK's home in Hyannis Port, Massachusetts. JFK conducted the meeting. He and the other participants reviewed what they had learned and accomplished since the Palm Beach meeting in April. JFK did most of the talking and demonstrated to his campaign aides his shrewd, detailed knowledge about the delegate situation in every state.[86] RFK would be the campaign manager, and John M. Bailey would continue his efforts to ensure that all of New England's Democratic delegates would be committed to JFK on the first ballot at the Democratic national convention and to seek delegates from upstate and western New York. Hyman Raskin, an attorney from Chicago, would seek delegates from Iowa and western states while EMK focused his delegate hunting on the Rocky Mountain states.[87] Louis Harris would conduct polls for JFK in key states, and campaign films would be produced for the primary states.

Regarding the sixteen states that would hold presidential primaries, the Hyannis Port meeting did not determine most of JFK's choices. He would definitely run in New Hampshire as the "first in the nation" presidential primary and as a stimulus for uniting New England's Democratic delegates behind him. Other primaries, especially Wisconsin's, were still being debated among the Hyannis Port meeting's participants.[88] Eventually, JFK entered seven presidential primaries.[89]

The Kennedy campaign realized, of course, that only a small minority of the 761 Democratic delegates needed to nominate a presidential candidate would be chosen through primaries. Moreover, most delegates from several primary states were not required to vote for a presidential candidate at a Democratic national convention according to the electoral results of their primaries because these primaries, such as West Virginia's, were non-binding advisory primaries. Likewise, several states, such as Connecticut and Indiana, practiced the unit rule. According to the unit rule, all of a state's delegates were required to vote for a presidential candidate if a majority of those delegates, however narrow, supported him.[90]

Consequently, either JFK or one of his surrogates, especially JPK, EMK, RFK, Bailey, Ribicoff, and O'Brien, privately met with Democratic politicians throughout the nation who could influence delegates. By the end of 1959, the Kennedy campaign at least wanted to know if these political figures supported JFK, another prospective presidential candidate, or wanted to be neutral during the nomination process. On November 19, 1959, a few days after his appearance at a Democratic issues conference in Maine, JFK arrived in Kansas City, Missouri. He visited former president Harry S. Truman at his presidential library in Independence and later addressed a Democratic dinner in Kansas City.[91]

Other than photo opportunities of JFK with Truman, nothing beneficial for JFK's still unannounced presidential candidacy resulted from this meeting.[92] JFK did not expect Truman to endorse him. He assumed that Truman, like most Missouri Democrats, backed Senator Stuart Symington as a favorite son presidential candidate. JFK hoped but failed to discern the strength and effectiveness of Truman's commitment to Symington in terms of Truman's ability and willingness to seek delegates for Symington outside of Missouri.[93] JFK was also unable to determine the extent to which Truman would do whatever he could to prevent JFK's nomination at the 1960 convention. Truman was known for his long-held animosity toward JPK and his belief that JPK was trying to buy the presidency for his son.[94]

On the same day that JFK met Truman, RFK conferred with Senator Lyndon B. Johnson at his ranch in Texas.[95] RFK had recently delivered a lecture on his work for the McClellan committee at the

University of Texas in Austin.[96] The conclusions that RFK made from his meeting with Johnson were the following: Johnson was not running for president because of his health, i.e., the lingering effects of his heart attack, and the fact that it was still politically impossible for a southerner to win the Democratic presidential nomination. The Texan would neither support nor oppose JFK's candidacy for the Democratic presidential nomination. Johnson was definite and firm about his opposition to a third presidential nomination for Adlai Stevenson.[97]

The credibility and reliability of Johnson's denial of his presidential candidacy, however, were limited for the Kennedy campaign. RFK's suspicious, hostile perception of Johnson made him unlikely to believe anything that the Senate majority leader said regarding his own political ambition.[98] The Texas state legislature and governor made a law in 1959 that allowed candidates to run for two offices on the same ballot.[99] This law enabled Johnson to run for either president or vice president in November 1960, while also running for reelection to the Senate.

This new Texas law, promoted by Texas Democrats who urged Johnson to run for president, revealed and confirmed a characteristic of Johnson's political behavior. He never wanted to risk losing his current public office by running for and failing to be elected to a higher office. As a U.S. representative, Johnson decided to run for a Senate seat in 1941, partially because it was a special election with an open seat. He could still run for reelection to the U.S. House of Representatives in 1942 if he lost the 1941 Democratic senatorial primary.[100] After narrowly losing his 1941 Senate race, Johnson gradually adopted more conservative rhetoric and policy behavior, especially on civil rights, labor, and oil and gas issues. In 1948, Johnson ran for an open Senate seat against Coke Stevenson, a former governor of Texas, in the Democratic primary. Johnson ran a vigorous, well-financed campaign which emphasized his conservative policy positions. Nevertheless, Johnson defeated Stevenson in the runoff primary by a margin of only 87 votes that was confirmed by a controversial court decision.[101] Investigations revealed ballot fraud by both campaigns.

Johnson's Senate aides and political associates disagreed about the reasons why he refused to announce his presidential candidacy until July 5, 1960, while allowing campaign activities on his behalf. George Reedy, who served as staff director of the Senate Policy Committee, suggested that Johnson was indecisive about running for president because of a midlife crisis.[102] Bobby Baker, secretary to the Senate majority leader, wrote, "I think the problem was LBJ's fear of being defeated."[103] In particular, Johnson feared that primary losses to JFK and the other Democratic presidential candidates would weaken his power in the Senate and his political base in Texas. As the manager of Johnson's presidential campaign at the 1960 Democratic national convention, John B. Connally described Johnson's presidential campaign as "halfhearted" and wrote that it "started too late, did too little, and did it the wrong way."[104]

Despite Johnson's replies to RFK's questions at his ranch, the Kennedy campaign made decisions on the assumption that Johnson was a presidential candidate but was employing a different strategy than JFK. Kenneth P. O'Donnell suspected that Johnson wanted to weaken JFK's presidential candidacy and increase the chances of a deadlocked convention that would nominate the Texan for president as a compromise candidate by funneling money and political talent into Senator Hubert H. Humphrey's presidential campaign in the primaries.[105] In short, O'Donnell suspected that Humphrey was a "stalking horse" for Johnson.[106]

By late 1959, there were two other elements in Lyndon B. Johnson's tentative, exploratory presidential campaign. First, in the search for Democratic delegates from outside of the South, he became more solicitous of Democratic senators from western states. In particular, he was more likely to grant them legislative favors, especially on water and power projects. Second, Johnson became more likely to accept speaking engagements at Democratic functions in northern states. He was especially pleased and surprised by the warm, enthusiastic reception of his speech at a Democratic fund-raising dinner in Harrisburg, Pennsylvania.[107]

The possibility that Johnson might receive even a minority of Pennsylvania's 81 delegate votes at the Democratic national convention concerned the Kennedy campaign. Political relations between the Kennedys and Governor David L. Lawrence had been cool and distant ever since Lawrence supported Estes Kefauver instead of JFK for vice president at the 1956 Democratic national convention. Lawrence's backing of Kefauver against JFK in 1956 and his apparent reluctance to endorse JFK for president were often attributed to Lawrence's belief that JFK's Catholicism would cost Democratic candidates in Pennsylvania Protestant votes in the 1960 elections and make it unlikely that he would be elected president. As a Catholic, Lawrence assumed that Al Smith's Catholicism contributed to his landslide defeat in the 1928 presidential election.[108]

In his correspondence, however, Lawrence firmly denied that JFK's religion affected the governor's political perception and treatment of the Massachusetts senator.[109] After learning that RFK told an audience in Pittsburgh in the fall of 1959 that he opposed JFK's 1956 vice presidential candidacy for religious reasons, Lawrence sent RFK a stern letter. He wrote, "This statement is entirely wrong and there is no foundation for it."[110] Two weeks later, RFK sent Lawrence an equally assertive, unequivocal reply.[111] He stated that Lawrence's expressed concern about JFK's Catholicism as an electoral liability was confirmed by several Catholic priests and James Finnegan, a Pennsylvania Democrat and Adlai Stevenson's campaign manager in 1956.[112] RFK further wrote, "Certainly, my brother is not assured of obtaining the nomination, but I think it would be most unfortunate if he was turned down on the grounds that he is a Catholic—by non-Catholics who are bigots or by Catholics who have a fear of 'rocking the boat.'"[113]

Another factor that prevented Lawrence from actively promoting JFK's presidential candidacy was his hope that Adlai Stevenson would be nominated for president again.[114] In a nationally televised interview broadcast on August 16, 1959, Lawrence stated that Stevenson was the best qualified person in either party to be president and should be considered as a presidential candidate in 1960.[115] Since Pennsylvania's 1960 Democratic presidential primary was non-binding and advisory, Lawrence could deliver most of Pennsylvania's delegate votes to Stevenson at the Democratic national convention even if JFK won the primary.

By early December, JFK realized that he needed to communicate with Lawrence more cautiously and tactfully than RFK had.

He accepted an invitation to address a Democratic luncheon in Pittsburgh as a pretext for privately meeting with Lawrence.[116] On December 10, 1959, JFK met Lawrence at the Penn Sheraton Hotel in Pittsburgh. He told the governor that if he won several contested primaries but was still denied the presidential nomination at the Democratic national convention because of his religion, then such a denial would reduce Democratic electoral strength in the November elections.[117] Lawrence remained aloof toward JFK's prospective presidential candidacy.

On December 17, one week after JFK's meeting with Lawrence and other Pennsylvania Democrats in Pittsburgh, United Press International (UPI) obtained a letter from the Kennedy campaign stating that JFK would formally announce his presidential candidacy on January 2, 1960. In a form letter dated December 28, 1959, and later sent to thousands of Democrats, JFK expressed his confidence that he would win the Democratic presidential nomination and the presidential election.[118] JFK wrote, "1960 will mark a turning point for our country. The people who assemble at the convention in Los Angeles will be the vital force which will determine the Democratic principles and leadership needed to guide this nation through the critical years again. Yours will be an important role, and I welcome your support."[119]

7

From New England to the Nation: 1960

Returning from a vacation in Jamaica, JFK announced his presidential candidacy in the caucus room of the Senate office building on January 2, 1960. His statement to the press was relatively brief for the announcement of a presidential candidacy. JFK cited the need for effective presidential leadership during the 1960s in order to address such important issues as Cold War competition with the Soviet Union, education, science, urban blight, unemployment, and agricultural decline. Regarding his qualifications for the presidency, JFK referred to his military service in World War II, fourteen years in Congress, and extensive international travel. He concluded, "From all of this, I have developed an image of America as fulfilling a noble and historic role as the defender of freedom in a time of maximum peril—and of the American people as confident, courageous and persevering."[1]

On January 14, 1960, JFK delivered a speech at the National Press Club in Washington, DC. In it, he explained the nature and purpose of the modern American presidency, and the need for presidential activism during the 1960s. By contrast, he implicitly criticized Eisenhower's presidency for being passive and ineffective in responding to current and future policy issues. JFK stated, "Whatever the political affiliation of our next President, whatever his views may be on all the issues and problems that rush in upon us, he must above all be the Chief Executive in every sense of the word."[2]

JFK's January 14 speech established a rhetorical foundation for many of his speeches during the Democratic presidential nomination process and in his general election campaign against Vice President Richard M. Nixon. Regardless of whether JFK addressed issues as different as education, the "missile gap" with the Soviet Union, the spread of Communism in the Third World, farm income, or urban renewal, he emphasized the need to elect a president in 1960 who would have the leadership ability to meet these and other challenges and crises during a new decade.[3] In his campaign speeches, JFK made historical references to activist presidents of the past as his role models. He was careful to equally balance Democratic presidents like Woodrow Wilson and Franklin D. Roosevelt with Republican presidents like Abraham Lincoln and Theodore Roosevelt. In order to highlight his supposedly non-partisan belief in presidential activism, he increasingly referred to Lincoln as the year 1960 progressed.[4]

On January 23, 1960, JFK attended a DNC fund-raising dinner in Washington, DC. Except for Adlai Stevenson, all of the announced and prospective Democratic presidential candidates attended this event. More dramatically and aggressively than in his recent speeches, JFK accused the Eisenhower administration of setting "a collision course toward war," substituting "pageants for policy in world affairs," and giving the nation "eight years of inaction and reaction."[5] In his analysis of the speeches delivered at this dinner, columnist James Reston criticized JFK's speech for its increasingly predictable, tiresome denunciation of Eisenhower's presidency. He expressed more positive perceptions of the speeches delivered by Senators Hubert H. Humphrey and Stuart Symington. Reston especially admired Symington's use of subtle wit in trying to elicit a public endorsement for his still unannounced presidential candidacy from Harry S. Truman, the dinner's featured guest.[6]

On the following evening, JFK appeared at the annual Jefferson-Jackson Day dinner of the Massachusetts Democratic Party in Boston.[7] JFK listened as Governor Foster Furcolo, Democratic state treasurer Edward P. Gilgun, and other speakers praised his presidential candidacy. The dinner raised approximately $174,000, and Gilgun gave JFK a $50,000 check for his presidential campaign.[8] Most of the speakers emphasized that JFK was the favorite son of not only Massachusetts but all of New England. Democratic officials from the other five New England states attended this dinner. They publicly pledged all of their delegate votes to JFK at the Democratic national convention in Los Angeles.

What was more beneficial to the national credibility of JFK's presidential candidacy than this public expression of regional unity of delegate support from New England Democrats was an earlier announcement that all sixty-four of Ohio's delegate votes were pledged to JFK through Governor Michael V. DiSalle's favorite son presidential candidacy.[9] DiSalle further explained in his January 5 announcement that he, not JFK, would run in Ohio's May 3 Democratic presidential primary. In his autobiography, Lawrence F. O'Brien referred to DiSalle's announcement as "a major breakthrough" which fueled optimism within the Kennedy campaign that JFK would be nominated on the first ballot at the 1960 Democratic national convention.[10]

While DiSalle's early, delegate-rich endorsement of JFK seemed surprising to the public, the Kennedy campaign expected it. DiSalle was a recently elected Catholic governor of a mostly Protestant state that was highly competitive between the two major parties. Unlike Governor David L. Lawrence of Pennsylvania, DiSalle did not exert strong control of his state's Democratic Party. In his study of Ohio's Democratic Party during the 1950s and 1960s, political scientist John H. Fenton wrote, "There was, in fact, no statewide Democratic party in Ohio."[11] Frank J. Lausche, Ohio's senior Democratic senator and a maverick conservative, refused to join DiSalle's endorsement of JFK. Conversely, Ray Miller, the Democratic county chairman in Cleveland, was an early backer of JFK's presidential candidacy and, like Lausche, a political rival of DiSalle.

After DiSalle met separately and privately with RFK and JFK, the Kennedys showed the governor polls indicating that JFK could decisively defeat DiSalle in Ohio's Democratic presidential primary. With the help of Miller and other pro-Kennedy factional leaders in Ohio, JFK could conduct a well-financed, highly publicized, victorious primary campaign that could not only win control of most of Ohio's delegate votes but also endanger DiSalle's political status in his home state. In particular, a humiliating loss to JFK in the primary could make it more difficult for DiSalle to attract enough Democratic votes in the state legislature for his policy agenda or even to be renominated by his party for governor in 1962.[12]

The Kennedy campaign understood that DiSalle's commitment of Ohio's large bloc of delegate votes to JFK in early January would be more impressive to Democratic politicians from other states that controlled large blocs of delegate votes than a victory in the New Hampshire primary. Scheduled for March 8, New Hampshire's Democratic presidential primary chose twenty-two delegates who shared eleven votes at the 1960 Democratic national convention.[13] There was a possibility in 1959 that Stevenson or Symington might receive a few delegate votes from New Hampshire because of factional disputes.[14] JFK was now assured of receiving all of New Hampshire's delegate votes and a landslide majority of the popular votes.[15]

However, the national significance of a victory in the New Hampshire primary would be undermined if JFK ran unopposed and received fewer votes than Estes Kefauver in that state's 1956 Democratic presidential primary because of low voter turnout. Fortunately for JFK, there was one other candidate listed on the ballot of this state's 1960 Democratic presidential primary. Paul C. Fisher, a ballpoint pen manufacturer from Illinois, received enough valid signatures to qualify for the ballot. Fisher's major policy proposal was to abolish federal income taxes on incomes below $10,000 per year.[16]

Through press releases and newspaper ads, Fisher repeatedly challenged JFK to a debate. In particular, he wanted the Massachusetts senator to explain to the voters of New Hampshire how he would achieve balanced budgets, lower interest payments on the national debt, and tax cuts if he were elected president. JFK simply ignored Fisher's challenge and blandly replied in a written statement that his positions on fiscal issues were a matter of public record because of his nearly fourteen years of service in Congress.[17]

JFK officially began campaigning in New Hampshire on January 25 when he visited the city hall in Nashua and his campaign headquarters in Manchester. Kennedy, though, did relatively little campaigning in New Hampshire until March 5. From late January until then, he relied on his campaign staff and volunteers, the state's

Democratic politicians, and widespread advertising to mobilize the largest possible voter turnout for his candidacy in the New Hampshire primary.[18]

Before he began a three-day political tour of New Hampshire on March 5, JFK delivered speeches in other states where he emphasized the importance of contested presidential primaries in each party's nomination process. On February 6, JFK told a Democratic audience in Jamestown, North Dakota, that Democratic presidential candidates needed to compete in primaries so that their party's nominee would be experienced enough to run a victorious presidential campaign against Nixon in the general election.[19] On February 7, JFK addressed a rally in Albuquerque, New Mexico, that immediately followed the conclusion of the Western States Democratic Conference. He bluntly stated, "If the people don't love them in May, they won't in November. If I am beaten in the primaries, I'm out."[20]

JFK's prepared speeches in New Hampshire were few and similar in content to recent speeches delivered throughout the nation. They criticized the Eisenhower administration's record on foreign, defense, and domestic policy issues while urging the election of a president in 1960 who could lead the nation in making progress in these policy areas. In general, JFK spent the three days before the primary traveling throughout New Hampshire to meet and greet state residents.[21]

The only unexpected, controversial incident was Wesley Powell's televised accusation that JFK was soft on Communism. Powell was the Republican governor of New Hampshire and Nixon's campaign manager in the state's Republican presidential primary. Immediately after Powell's televised speech against JFK, Bernard L. Boutin delivered a televised speech refuting Powell's charges. The Kennedy campaign paid $75,000 for fifteen minutes of air time for Boutin's rebuttal.[22]

Nixon promptly and publicly repudiated Powell's accusations and defended JFK's record on Communism. Powell then sent a telegram to Nixon criticizing him for defending JFK. Powell told Nixon that "if you and the Republican Party expect to win, you had better be on the attack."[23] At a press conference held at the University of New Hampshire in Durham, JFK dismissed Powell's charges as "an unwarranted attack."[24]

For the Kennedy campaign, what was most important was how the national media would interpret and communicate the voting statistics of both the Democratic and Republican presidential primaries in New Hampshire. In particular, the Kennedy campaign hoped that JFK would receive enough votes so that he would greatly exceed the number of votes that Estes Kefauver received in New Hampshire's 1956 Democratic presidential primary. Moreover, New Hampshire was a mostly Republican state, and twice as many of its residents voted in the Republican presidential primary than in the Democratic presidential primary in 1956.[25] The Kennedy campaign wanted JFK to attract enough votes so that he would reduce this disparity in his favor compared to the number of votes that Nixon received.

In New Hampshire's Democratic primary of 1960, JFK received 43,372 votes and 85.2 percent of the votes. In 1956, Estes Kefauver received 21,701 votes and 84.6 percent. JFK also received 2,196 write-in votes in the Republican presidential primary. Vice President Richard M. Nixon received 65,204 votes and 89.3 percent of the votes in the 1960 Republican presidential primary. Eisenhower received 56,464 votes and 98.9 percent of the votes in New Hampshire's 1956 Republican presidential primary.[26] Nixon received almost 9,000 more votes than Eisenhower. Eisenhower, though, received more than twice as many votes as Kefauver in 1956, while Nixon's proportional advantage over JFK was much narrower, three to two.

Journalists and columnists throughout the United States generally concluded that the results of New Hampshire's presidential primaries were more beneficial to JFK than to Nixon. *New York Times* reporter William H. Lawrence wrote, "Some Democrats and Republicans thought his record-breaking showing in a traditionally Republican state had helped move him toward the Democratic Presidential nomination on an early ballot at the Los Angeles convention, which opens July 11."[27] A United Press International (UPI) article stated that JFK's "presidential stock skyrocketed to new highs today as a result of his recent record-toppling performance in the New Hampshire primary."[28] In an Associated Press (AP) article published in a Wisconsin newspaper, however, journalist Jack Bell minimized the national significance of JFK's victory in New Hampshire. He wrote,

"The suspicion is growing among some politicians that Wisconsin may furnish some surprises that what happened in New Hampshire may not necessarily betoken the trend hailed in both the Nixon and Kennedy camps."[29]

Even before all of the votes in New Hampshire were counted, JFK was campaigning in Wisconsin. JFK periodically visited and spoke in Wisconsin since September 1958.[30] JFK, however, had delayed filing his candidacy in Wisconsin because of an internal debate within his campaign organization about whether he should compete against Humphrey in Wisconsin. In particular, RFK opposed JFK running in Wisconsin because of his belief that Humphrey had too many advantages in that state.[31]

JFK eventually decided to run in Wisconsin. The Ohio primary was no longer an option for JFK to demonstrate his vote getting ability outside of New England after his agreement with Ohio governor Michael V. DiSalle. Also, Wisconsin's Democratic presidential primary was scheduled for April 5, 1960. This date was early enough in the year and the nomination process so that a decisive Kennedy victory in Wisconsin might force Senator Hubert H. Humphrey to end his presidential campaign. Furthermore, Louis Harris provided JFK with a poll indicating that he had a surprising degree of popularity in Wisconsin compared to Humphrey.[32]

Nevertheless, JFK still confronted challenges in running against Humphrey in Wisconsin. Humphrey was known as Wisconsin's "third senator." Humphrey was more knowledgeable about agricultural issues than JFK, and his Senate voting record on agriculture was much more acceptable to Wisconsin farmers than JFK's. Humphrey could also prove to be more attractive to African Americans and white liberals because of his more liberal voting record and rhetoric on civil rights.[33] Moreover, there was some hostility toward JFK and RFK among local union officials because of RFK's investigative work on the McClellan committee and JFK's introduction and promotion of a labor reform bill that was the basis for the Landrum-Griffin Act of 1959.[34] After campaigning with her husband in the Wisconsin primary, Jacqueline Kennedy later commented, "In Wisconsin, those people would stare at you like [sic] sort of animals . . . and they're so suspicious."[35]

Benefiting from a private plane, a large staff, and the active participation of relatives and political allies from Massachusetts, JFK was able to visit more communities in Wisconsin and meet more prospective voters than Humphrey. JFK wanted to counteract Humphrey's more liberal record on domestic policy issues and promote his recently more liberal record on these same issues. Consequently, JFK delivered speeches in Wisconsin that detailed his policy positions on civil rights, labor reform, agriculture, unemployment, and medical care for the elderly.[36]

The greatest contrast in campaign rhetoric in Wisconsin between JFK and Humphrey was evident in JFK's speeches on Cold War foreign and defense policies. JFK often sounded more hawkish than Humphrey. In a March 24, 1960 speech in Milwaukee, JFK stated that, if the United States did not rapidly and substantially improve its conventional armed forces to protect West Berlin, then it "would be showing the entire world that we lacked the will and the strength and the courage to come to the defense of threatened freedom."[37] In a speech to a state convention of Young Democrats in Racine, he said that the greatest challenge facing the next president will be "strengthening the undeveloped world against the instabilities that lead to either Communism or war."[38]

JFK's hawkish rhetoric may have been influenced by the fact that Wisconsin had the only open Democratic presidential primary in 1960. This meant that Republicans and independents could vote in Wisconsin's Democratic presidential primary. Wisconsin Democrats who worked in JFK's primary campaign later estimated that many of the Republicans who were campaign volunteers and voters for JFK were Catholics.[39]

JFK wanted to avoid specifically and extensively addressing the religious issue in his speeches and at his press conferences. However, there was evidence that anti-Catholic literature was being distributed in Wisconsin. Reporters who interviewed likely voters often asked them to identify their church affiliations.[40] As primary day approached and JFK's supporters became confident of a major victory, the Kennedy campaign realized that the frequent newspaper and magazine photos of JFK with Catholic priests, nuns, and uniformed parochial school students could become a liability in influencing how JFK's victory in Wisconsin would be perceived and analyzed by the media and Democratic politicians from other states.[41]

In his autobiography, Hubert H. Humphrey complained that it was impossible for him to successfully compete against JFK in Wisconsin. JFK had so many advantages in terms of money, publicity, advance work, and an extended family to serve as surrogate speakers and campaigners. Humphrey wrote that the Kennedy campaign had "an element of ruthlessness and toughness that I had trouble either accepting or forgetting."[42] In an earlier interview, Humphrey stated that he was particularly offended by the insinuation that he and voters backing him were anti-Catholic.[43]

Ideally, the Kennedy campaign wanted the media to portray JFK as the underdog candidate who was struggling to defeat the better-known Humphrey in an uphill battle despite anti-Catholic prejudice, less name recognition, and unfair, inaccurate criticism of his policy record.[44] Unfortunately for JFK, newspapers increasingly predicted that JFK would win the Wisconsin primary by a wide margin and suggested that his Catholicism was an asset rather than a liability among Wisconsin voters. Four days before the primary, a lengthy article in the *New York Times* emphasized that Wisconsin's population was 32 percent Catholic, much higher than the national average, and that 40 percent of the votes in the Democratic presidential primary would be cast in southeastern Wisconsin, the most Catholic area of the state.[45] The article mentioned that JFK's candidacy would benefit from the votes of Catholic Republicans who intended to vote for JFK partially because of his religion. A UPI article published in newspapers throughout the nation stated, "Returns Tuesday will be analyzed in large part on the basis of Kennedy's showing in various counties in relation to the religious complexion of those counties."[46] Nationally syndicated columnist Joseph Alsop wrote, "His Catholicism has unquestionably helped Kennedy very greatly in eastern Wisconsin; but it has not handicapped him in the Protestant western districts."[47]

At first glance, the results of Wisconsin's Democratic presidential primary of April 5 seemed impressive for JFK. He received 56.5 percent of the votes, and approximately 110,000 more votes than Humphrey.[48] JFK also received nearly 40,000 more votes than Eisenhower received in Wisconsin's uncontested 1956 Republican presidential primary.[49] The Massachusetts senator carried six of Wisconsin's ten congressional districts. Because this was a binding primary, two-thirds of Wisconsin's delegates were committed to JFK on the first ballot at the Democratic national convention.[50]

Unfortunately for JFK, he lost the expectations game in Wisconsin.[51] More reporters heard that the Kennedy campaign expected a landslide victory. Edwin Bayley, a Kennedy backer and secretary to Governor Gaylord Nelson, publicly predicted that JFK would carry all ten congressional districts.[52] Influenced by optimistic polls and other political information, JFK invested a disproportionate amount of time in the final days of his Wisconsin campaign visiting the mostly Protestant and rural ninth and tenth congressional districts.[53]

JFK lost the ninth and tenth congressional districts by wide margins. He also lost the second district based in Madison. The state chairman of JFK's Wisconsin campaign was Ivan Nestingen, the mayor of Madison.[54] Humphrey later told Pierre Salinger that if JFK had carried seven instead of six congressional districts he would have ended his presidential campaign then.[55] Instead, the fact that Humphrey carried four districts and almost carried a fifth district influenced his decision to continue his presidential campaign.[56]

Before JFK competed against Humphrey in West Virginia's May 10 primary, presidential primaries were held in six states and the District of Columbia. JFK did not enter his name in the Illinois, Massachusetts, and Pennsylvania primaries; but he easily won all three as a write-in candidate. The New Jersey and Ohio primaries were entirely uncontested. All of the Democratic delegates in New Jersey were unpledged yet unofficially controlled by Governor Robert Meyner as a favorite son candidate. All of the Democratic delegates in Ohio were pledged to Governor Michael V. DiSalle who had endorsed JFK in January. JFK carefully stayed out of the District of Columbia's primary where Humphrey defeated Senator Wayne Morse of Oregon.[57]

JFK originally hoped that if he entered Indiana's Democratic presidential primary then Senator Stuart Symington of Missouri would feel compelled to formally announce his presidential candidacy and compete against JFK in Indiana in order to prove his vote-getting ability.[58] Although Symington formally announced his presidential candidacy on March 24, 1960, he did not enter the Indiana primary.[59] Except for JFK, the only other candidates who were listed on the ballot of Indiana's Democratic presidential primary were Lar Daly and John H. Latham. Daly was an isolationist "America First" candidate from Chicago who often campaigned wearing an Uncle Sam costume. Latham was a retired pipe fitter from Rockville, Indiana.[60]

JFK was disappointed that he was not opposed in the Indiana primary by Humphrey, Symington, or Johnson. At the very least, JFK hoped that a victory in Indiana would boost his national campaign by proving that he could receive a record number of primary votes in a conservative midwestern farm state that had fewer Catholics and presumably more anti-Catholic prejudice than Wisconsin.[61] Indeed, after JFK arrived in Indianapolis to file his candidacy for the primary, he was confronted by Protestant demonstrators who insisted that he debate them on the religious issue.[62] JFK refused to debate them and did not devote any major speeches in Indiana to the religious issue.

After all of the votes were counted in Indiana's May 3 Democratic presidential primary, JFK won 353,832 votes and 81 percent of all votes cast.[63] Since this was a binding primary and the state Democratic Party used the unit rule, all thirty-four of Indiana's delegate votes were committed to JFK on the first ballot at the Democratic national convention. He received more than three times as many votes as Estes Kefauver in Indiana's 1956 Democratic presidential primary. JFK also received nearly 3,000 more votes than Eisenhower did in Indiana's 1956 Republican presidential primary.[64]

Although JFK's victory in Indiana committed more delegate votes to him, the media's analysis of the primary results did little to strengthen the national status of his presidential candidacy. Newspaper accounts of the results emphasized that two eccentric, fringe candidates succeeded in winning approximately 82,000 votes and 18 percent of the votes against JFK in the Indiana primary. Meanwhile, Vice President Richard M. Nixon, unlike JFK, did no personal campaigning in Indiana. Nonetheless, Nixon received approximately

55,000 more votes than JFK in the Republican presidential primary.[65] Since the Democrats in Indiana had been so successful in the 1958 midterm elections and 1959 mayoral elections, some journalists currently perceived Indiana as a competitive two-party state rather than as a Republican-dominated state. In an article for the *New York Times*, Damon Stetson wrote, "There was no doubt, however, that the vote for Vice President Nixon in a popularity contest with Senator John F. Kennedy carried the greatest political impact nationally."[66]

Nebraska held its presidential primaries on the same day as West Virginia, May 10. JFK was the only candidate listed on the ballot of Nebraska's Democratic presidential primary. He received 88.7 percent of the votes, 80,408 votes, and approximately 6,000 more votes than Nixon.[67] Although it was an advisory, non-binding primary, twenty of the thirty-two Democratic delegates elected voluntarily endorsed JFK. All of the other votes cast in Nebraska's Democratic presidential primary went to write-in candidates, including Humphrey, Symington, Stevenson, and Johnson.[68] However, because no other candidate's name was listed on the ballot in Nebraska's Democratic presidential primary and most of the nation's attention focused on the West Virginia primary, JFK's victory in Nebraska was not generally perceived as significant for his national presidential campaign, except for the increase in the number of delegates committed to him.[69]

In Wisconsin, JFK tried to ignore and dismiss the religious issue in his public statements. In West Virginia, though, the Kennedy campaign highlighted the religious issue. It was estimated that West Virginia's population was 95 percent Protestant and 3.9 percent Catholic.[70] A poll conducted by Louis Harris before the Wisconsin primary showed JFK defeating Humphrey in West Virginia 70 percent to 30 percent. However, a Harris poll taken shortly after the Wisconsin primary, when JFK's Catholicism became a nationally prominent issue, showed Humphrey defeating JFK in West Virginia 60 percent to 40 percent.[71] Regularly reminding reporters of these polling statistics, the Kennedy campaign made a more persuasive argument in West Virginia than Wisconsin that JFK was the underdog candidate. Also, if JFK directly confronted the religious issue in West Virginia and won the primary decisively, then he hoped to dispel the religious issue for the remainder of his presidential campaign.[72]

Both JFK and Humphrey took a brief hiatus from their campaigning in West Virginia and returned to Washington, DC, in late April. While there, they spoke to a conference of the American Society of Newspaper Editors and addressed the religious issue on April 21. JFK bluntly stated, "I am not the Catholic candidate for President." He then chastised journalists and editors for exaggerating the religious issue and neglecting more important issues. He added that the "press, while not creating the issue, will largely determine whether or not the issue becomes dominant."[73] Humphrey mostly spoke about the future of nuclear arms control with the Soviet Union but briefly reaffirmed JFK's statement about the religious issue. The Minnesota senator told the editors that "religious labeling in news is as undesirable as racial labeling."[74]

Most of JFK's speeches in West Virginia focused on economic issues instead of the religious issue. With West Virginia suffering from widespread poverty, hunger, and high unemployment, JFK frequently criticized the Eisenhower administration's failure or refusal to solve these problems while making favorable, contrasting references to Franklin D. Roosevelt and recent Democratic bills on food stamps and distressed areas rejected by the Republicans.[75] In order to further underscore the Kennedy campaign's strategy of associating JFK with FDR in the minds of West Virginia voters, Joseph P. Kennedy (JPK) recruited former New York congressman Franklin D. Roosevelt, Jr., to campaign for JFK in West Virginia.[76]

In addition to FDR, Jr., associating JFK with FDR and New Deal policies that benefited West Virginia, the Kennedy campaign used him to help the Catholic senator address the religious issue. In Logan, FDR, Jr., told an audience, "As a Protestant, I urge all my fellow Protestants not to make a religious issue in the West Virginia campaign."[77] JFK also referred to his military service in World War II to address the religious issue. He contended that since the navy did not reject him for religious reasons then neither should voters.

In this context, FDR, Jr., made a controversial remark about Humphrey's lack of military service in an April 27 speech. Four days before the primary, he implicitly accused Humphrey of being a draft dodger during World War II.[78] JFK either failed or refused to require Roosevelt to publicly retract his insinuation of draft dodging.

Humphrey later wrote that this was the only aspect of the West Virginia campaign which he could not forgive because the Kennedys knew that he had been rejected for military service for medical reasons.[79]

Despite the controversy over FDR, Jr.'s smearing of Humphrey, the Kennedy campaign's contention that religion should not play a role in any American's qualifications for either the military or the presidency resonated with the people of West Virginia. It was a state that was proud of its tradition of military service, and its residents suffered disproportionately high rates of casualties in World War II and the Korean War.[80] West Virginians were regularly reminded of JFK's highly decorated combat heroism and war-related injuries through television broadcasts, newspaper ads, and reprints of the *Reader's Digest* article about PT-109.

In addition to using television to remind voters of his distinguished military service, JFK's skillful use of television directly answered any lingering religious questions that Protestants might have about voting for a Catholic presidential candidate. Two days before the primary, FDR, Jr., interviewed JFK in a televised program about the separation of church and state and whether the Catholic hierarchy would influence his use of presidential powers.[81] JFK used another television broadcast to replicate a president-elect taking the oath of office with one hand on the Bible. He told viewers that if a president violated his oath to the Constitution, which includes the separation of church and state, then he would be committing "a crime against the Constitution" and "a sin against God."[82]

One estimate is that JFK spent at least $250,000 while Humphrey spent at most $30,000 in the West Virginia primary.[83] Much of JFK's spending went to newspaper, radio, and television advertising and campaign contributions to local Democratic Party organizations. Despite rumors and accusations that JFK "bought" his primary victory in West Virginia through bribery and JPK's influence with gangsters, later investigations by local journalists, West Virginia's attorney general, the FBI, and private detectives hired by the Nixon campaign concluded that JFK did not illegally "buy" the West Virginia primary.[84] The Kennedy campaign had much more money to spend legally than the Humphrey campaign and spent it more effectively on such legitimate expenses as hiring cars and drivers to drive West Virginia voters to and from their voting precincts. JFK spent more on advance work and canvassing so that audiences for his speeches tended to be much larger than those for Humphrey's speeches.[85]

JFK also spent more money on slating and spent it more effectively compared to Humphrey. Slating was a legal and customary practice of paying county Democratic organizations to print and distribute cards recommending candidates in the Democratic primaries to voters. Undecided voters especially found slating to be helpful because of the confusing complexity of primary ballots. In a mostly Democratic state like West Virginia, there were often several candidates competing for the Democratic nomination to the same office.[86]

Besides having more money for slating, JFK was more knowledgeable about the practice than Humphrey. JFK first met Robert McDonough, his campaign manager in West Virginia, at the 1956 Democratic national convention. McDonough, a printing company owner in Parkersburg, helped the Massachusetts senator to understand which Democratic factional leaders to embrace and which ones to avoid in seeking endorsements and voter mobilization efforts through slating.[87] Since 1958, JFK had also been periodically consulting Senator Jennings Randolph of West Virginia about the intricacies of his state's Democratic presidential primary.[88]

In West Virginia's May 10 Democratic presidential primary, JFK received 60.8 percent of the votes to Humphrey's 39.2 percent.[89] JFK carried forty-eight of the state's fifty-five counties.[90] Unlike his performance in Wisconsin, JFK's electoral support in West Virginia was widespread both geographically and demographically. Senator Robert C. Byrd, a former Ku Klux Klan leader, urged West Virginians to vote for Humphrey as a way to help Senator Lyndon B. Johnson become the Democratic presidential nominee. Reacting against Byrd's efforts, 75 percent of West Virginia's African-American voters in the primary supported JFK.[91] Among white Protestant voters, electoral support for JFK was broadly distributed, despite differences among them in terms of location, occupation, income, and education.[92]

Because West Virginia's presidential primaries were advisory and non-binding, JFK was not guaranteed any of West Virginia's 25 delegate votes at the Democratic national convention. The national political impact of his victory in West Virginia, however, was exactly what JFK wanted. Newspaper and magazine articles, columnists, and editorials characterized JFK's primary victory as an upset by an underdog that vanquished the religious issue as a major liability of his presidential candidacy and proved his vote getting ability among Protestants.[93]

JFK's victory in West Virginia prompted Humphrey to announce the end of his presidential candidacy. It also facilitated JFK's victories in the Maryland and Oregon primaries. In Oregon's Democratic presidential primary held on May 20, JFK defeated Senator Wayne Morse in his home state 51 percent to 31.9 percent.[94] Since this was a binding primary, all seventeen of Oregon's delegate votes were pledged to JFK. It was estimated that JFK now had 317½ of the 761 delegate votes needed to win the Democratic presidential nomination.[95]

On May 27, 1960, a Gallup poll that asked Democratic voters about their preferences for their party's presidential nomination was released. JFK was ranked first with 41 percent of the respondents choosing him. Adlai Stevenson, who repeatedly denied that he was a presidential candidate, ranked second at 21 percent. Senator Lyndon B. Johnson ranked a distant third at 11 percent.[96]

While Stevenson had clearly stated that he was not running for president in 1960, the Kennedy campaign and others interpreted his words to mean that he was willing to be drafted for a third presidential nomination at the Democratic national convention in Los Angeles. Since 1959, a Draft Stevenson movement had opened campaign offices throughout the nation. Four days after the West Virginia primary, JFK told Arthur M. Schlesinger, Jr., that Stevenson's endorsement of his presidential candidacy was necessary so that he could be nominated on the first ballot.[97]

Shortly after the Oregon primary, JFK flew to Libertyville, Illinois, to meet Stevenson at his home. On the day after this meeting, JFK telephoned Schlesinger. According to JFK, Stevenson insisted that he would remain neutral in the competition for the Democratic presidential nomination and remained inscrutable about whether he would accept a draft. At the conclusion of his phone call, JFK told Schlesinger, "I guess there's nothing I can do except go out and collect as many votes as possible and hope that Stevenson will decide to come along."[98]

Key members of the Kennedy campaign, especially RFK, assumed that Stevenson's purported neutrality was part of the so-called Stop Kennedy movement to prevent a first ballot victory for JFK that would eventually benefit Symington or Johnson at a deadlocked convention.[99] Realizing that Stevenson was especially popular among delegates from California and Pennsylvania, the Kennedy campaign continued to seek delegates from other states. New York had 114 delegate votes, as many as all six of the New England states combined. Representative Adam Clayton Powell, Jr., of New York, the most powerful African American in Congress, had endorsed Johnson in 1959. Carmine DeSapio, the leader of Tammany Hall in Manhattan, was a divisive, controversial figure whose candidates lost several races to anti-Tammany reform Democrats in the June 7 primary. Michael Prendergast, the Democratic state chairman, was an ally of DeSapio and did not exert strong control over New York's Democratic Party.[100]

With JPK and John M. Bailey as his major surrogates, JFK began seeking delegate commitments from New York as early as 1959. Carefully avoiding the bitter, seemingly irreconcilable intraparty conflicts in Manhattan, the Kennedy campaign contacted Democratic Congressmen Charles Buckley from the Bronx and Eugene Keogh from Brooklyn as well as Peter Crotty, the Democratic county chairman in Buffalo, and Daniel O'Connell, Albany's Democratic machine boss, for their assistance in securing delegate votes for JFK. In late June, a poll of New York's delegates to the Democratic national convention indicated that JFK would receive 87 of their 114 votes.[101]

Supporters of Senator Lyndon B. Johnson's still unofficial presidential candidacy portrayed Johnson as a westerner instead of a southerner in order to increase his appeal among delegates from western states.[102] Johnson was confident of receiving most of the delegate votes from the Rocky Mountain and southwestern states because of endorsements from their Democratic senators.[103] By the end of June, the Kennedy campaign succeeded in significantly reducing Johnson's delegate support in these states, especially Montana, Arizona, Colorado, and Wyoming.[104]

JFK assigned EMK the task of attracting and organizing delegates from several western states. In his autobiography, EMK recalled how he began delegate hunting in the West in September, 1959.[105] EMK quickly learned that Teno Roncalio, the Democratic state chairman, would be more influential with Wyoming's delegates than Senator Gale McGee, who backed Johnson for president. EMK's prolonged, vigorous lobbying of Wyoming's delegates proved to be essential to JFK's nomination for president. By early June, JFK was expected to receive at least ten of Wyoming's fifteen delegate votes at the Democratic national convention.[106] At the convention in Los Angeles, EMK persuaded Tracy McCraken, the chairman of this state's delegation, to declare all of Wyoming's delegate votes for JFK. Wyoming thereby provided JFK with enough delegate votes to win the Democratic presidential nomination.[107]

Despite the growing evidence that Johnson's power in the Senate did not extend to controlling delegates at the 1960 Democratic national convention, Johnson and Speaker of the House Sam Rayburn decided to recess, instead of adjourn, Congress so that it would resume its session after the Democratic and Republican national conventions in August.[108] The public explanation of Johnson and Rayburn for this decision was that Congress needed to resume its session in August in order to vote on important legislation, including Cuba's sugar quota, a medical care bill for the elderly, and a twelve-nation treaty regarding scientific research in Antarctica.[109] However, Johnson's critics, including some Kennedy backers, perceived his call for a "rump session" to be a blatant attempt to pressure undecided or neutral Democratic senators to support his expected presidential candidacy at the convention in Los Angeles.

This suspicion was sharpened by the fact that, a few days after Johnson and Rayburn called for a "rump session," Johnson formally announced his presidential candidacy on July 5, 1960 at a press conference in Washington, DC. The Texas senator emphasized that the next president must be a mature, experienced leader. He predicted that he would receive 500 votes on the first ballot at the Democratic national convention and eventually be nominated for president.[110]

Johnson's declaration of his presidential candidacy occurred three days after former president Harry S. Truman announced that he had resigned as a delegate from Missouri because the Democratic national convention seemed to be "a prearranged affair."[111] Truman accused his party's national convention of already being rigged in favor of JFK's nomination for president and questioned JFK's qualifications for the presidency. While endorsing Senator Stuart Symington for president, Truman expressed confidence in Johnson's qualifications for the presidency.

In addition to these announcements by Johnson and Truman, Adlai Stevenson's comments after arriving in Los Angeles for the opening of the Democratic national convention increased the suspicions of the Kennedy campaign that Stevenson had become a more active leader of the Stop Kennedy movement. Stevenson was greeted in Los Angeles on July 9 by a large, well-organized, and enthusiastic crowd. He stated that he was not running for president but would "willingly accept" the Democratic presidential nomination.[112] In a nationally televised interview on July 10, Stevenson stated that, while he was not seeking his party's presidential nomination, "if called upon, of course, I will serve."[113]

Fortunately for JFK, he had already learned from Mayor Richard J. Daley of Chicago that he would receive 59½ of Illinois's 69 delegate votes and Stevenson would receive only two delegate votes.[114] After the Democratic national convention opened on July 11, the Kennedy campaign was still concerned about the efforts of the Draft Stevenson movement on other big state delegations, especially those of California and Pennsylvania. Richard K. Donahue was an attorney from Lowell, Massachusetts, who assisted RFK in organizing delegates at the convention. Donahue later recalled that Governor David L. Lawrence "was trying to raise ruptures in the Pennsylvania delegation. He was always a Stevenson man."[115] Garrett H. Byrne, a delegate from Massachusetts, believed that his position as the district attorney of Boston's Suffolk County helped him to lobby delegates from other states who were also district attorneys.[116] Thomas P. Costin, another delegate from Massachusetts and the mayor of Lynn, found that his office as mayor helped him to influence other mayors who were delegates.[117]

By far, the most helpful Massachusetts delegate for JFK at the Democratic national convention was Representative John W.

McCormack, the House majority leader and chairman of the Massachusetts delegation. As the House majority leader and a close ally of Sam Rayburn, McCormack was especially instrumental in later attracting delegate support from northern liberal delegates for JFK's choice of Senator Lyndon B. Johnson as his running mate.[118] In a 1968 interview, McCormack stated that as early as 1958 he believed that Johnson would be the best running mate for JFK.[119] The House majority leader also helped to make the most liberal planks of the 1960 Democratic national convention more acceptable to southern conservative delegates.[120]

Of the Democratic delegates from other New England states, John M. Bailey and Governor Abraham Ribicoff from Connecticut were busy contacting delegates from other states. In particular, Bailey and Ribicoff wanted to ensure that New Jersey, whose delegates were entirely committed to Governor Robert Meyner as a favorite son on the first ballot, would deliver all 41 of its delegate votes to JFK if a second ballot was taken to determine the Democratic presidential nomination.[121] Although Senator Thomas J. Dodd gave a speech seconding Johnson's nomination for president, he was required to vote for JFK's nomination with all of Connecticut's other delegates because of the unit rule.[122] Bailey and Ribicoff were confident that all 114 of New England's delegate votes would go to JFK on the first ballot.

Bailey's delegate hunting efforts at the Democratic national convention were most fruitful with the Pennsylvania delegation. Regardless of Governor Lawrence's persistent pleas, Adlai Stevenson refused to declare himself to be a presidential candidate. Lawrence's frustration and dismay with Stevenson's refusal led him to allow a poll of his state's delegates in a closed caucus and suspend the unit rule so that Pennsylvania's delegates could vote individually for presidential candidates at the convention. Bailey joined Matthew McCloskey, the DNC's treasurer and a Philadelphia contractor, and other pro-Kennedy Democrats to lobby Pennsylvania's delegates for JFK.[123] Pennsylvania's delegates gave 68 of their 81 votes to JFK on the first and only ballot to determine the Democratic presidential nomination. Stevenson received only 7½ delegate votes from Pennsylvania.[124]

By the end of the first and only ballot for the presidential nomination at the 1960 Democratic national convention, JFK received 806 delegate votes, more than enough to be nominated for president.[125] Except for the initial opposition of RFK and Kenneth P. O'Donnell to JFK's selection of Senator Lyndon B. Johnson as his running mate, the other top officials of the Kennedy campaign acknowledged that JFK needed Johnson to carry Texas and several other southern states in the Electoral College.[126] JFK wanted to avoid a roll call vote on Johnson's nomination for vice president that might result in protests from delegates, especially those from Michigan.

At JFK's request, McCormack arranged with Governor LeRoy Collins of Florida, the chairman of the convention, to make a motion to suspend the rules and nominate Johnson by acclamation. Ribicoff prepared to be recognized by Collins for the same purposes. Collins recognized McCormack and interpreted the collective oral response of the delegates in general so that he suspended the rules and announced that Johnson had been nominated for vice president by acclamation.[127] Thus, John W. McCormack, with whom JFK occasionally experienced a difficult relationship in Massachusetts, proved to be essential in helping JFK to avoid a potentially divisive and embarrassing balloting process for Johnson's nomination for vice president.

Some of the New Englanders who attended the Democratic national convention as delegates, alternates, or campaign workers traveled throughout the United States for the Kennedy-Johnson campaign.[128] Most of them, however, returned to their home states. Some of them were candidates running for election or reelection.[129] Like the Kennedy campaign officials, they assumed that JFK would easily carry the three states of southern New England in the Electoral College while losing the three states of northern New England. In particular, Maine Democrats assumed that the religious issue and more straight-ticket voting by Republicans in their state would generate enough Republican votes to defeat not only JFK in Maine but also their nominees for governor, senator, and all three congressional seats. They were correct.[130]

William L. Dunfey was a New Hampshire Democrat who served as JFK's campaign coordinator for New Hampshire, Maine, and Vermont. Dunfey communicated with Lawrence F. O'Brien and Timothy "Ted" Reardon, a Senate aide to JFK, about having JFK campaign in all three states of northern New England.[131] Because of scheduling constraints and JFK's need to spend more time campaigning in other states and conducting press conferences in Washington, DC, JFK delayed his campaign swing in northern New England until early September. He limited his visits to New Hampshire and Maine on September 2, 1960.[132]

After JFK arrived in Manchester, New Hampshire, on September 2, 1960, he revived his earlier policy emphasis of changing the economic policies of the federal government in order to alleviate the regional economic problems of New England. He said, "I do not accept the idea at all that New England is finished. I think it is possible both in the State of New Hampshire and in the Nation, to set a governmental climate which will permit us to prosper."[133] As he did in his 1953 Senate speeches on the economic problems of New England, JFK specifically mentioned protecting New England's chronically ailing textile and shoe industries from unfair foreign competition. In Manchester, JFK also linked the economic needs of New England with those of the nation in general. He concluded, "This is a program for New England—and New England's program for America."[134]

On that same day, JFK traveled to Maine and spoke in Presque Isle, Bangor, and Portland. Dunfey organized JFK's speaking tour with Senator Edmund S. Muskie and Representative Frank M. Coffin. In Presque Isle, JFK linked the location of this potato growing, rural area of northeastern Maine to the national security needs of the United States in the Cold War. In Bangor, JFK urged the Republican voters of Maine to engage in split-ticket voting in order to elect the best candidates. He stated, "We believe in securing the best of our country because nothing but the best will do, because we believe this is the best country, and because we realize it isn't the President of the United States that is in trouble, it isn't the Republican party that is in trouble, it is the country that is in trouble and it is we who are in trouble."[135] In a speech at Portland Stadium, he said that Mainers, like other New Englanders, want to elect a president "who understands this section and its needs, but they also want someone who will speak for the country in a difficult and trying period."[136]

Covering JFK's one-day trip to New Hampshire and Maine, *New York Times* reporter William H. Lawrence wrote that JFK "hoped to set up a counter-irritant to manifestations favorable to Vice President Nixon in sections of the usually Democratic South."[137] He also noted that, according to local journalists, the audience that listened to JFK in Maine was larger and more enthusiastic than Nixon's during the vice president's August 13 speech at the same stadium. Nixon's visit to Maine was especially notable for a press conference in Portland in which he distanced himself from the Eisenhower administration's agricultural policies.[138]

While JFK was campaigning in California, Senator Lyndon B. Johnson spoke in Boston at Symphony Hall on September 8, 1960. Governor Foster Furcolo and Representative John W. McCormack accompanied the Texas senator in a motorcade from Boston's Logan International Airport to a press conference at the Sheraton Plaza Hotel. The press estimated the crowds that lined Johnson's motorcade route at 100,000 people. At Symphony Hall, Johnson said, "The real issue of this campaign is the deterioration of this nation's position in the world."[139]

Johnson's campaign trip to Boston was intended to accomplish two purposes. First, Johnson's visit to Boston personified the intra-party and multiregional harmony and cooperation of the Kennedy-Johnson ticket's celebrated "Boston-Austin axis." Second, Johnson's appearance in Boston was part of a personal effort of JFK and his campaign staff to fulfill Johnson's requests that he be allowed to campaign more in the Northeast.[140] Kenneth P. O'Donnell, who planned and organized Johnson's campaign schedule, later revealed that Johnson's campaign visit to Boston was mostly intended to improve the Texan's morale. According to O'Donnell, JFK put him "in charge of the care and feeding of Lyndon Johnson."[141]

While Johnson was in Boston, Henry Cabot Lodge, Jr., was campaigning in Boston, Worcester, and Lowell. JFK defeated Lodge in his 1952 Senate race. Since 1953, Lodge had served as the U.S. Ambassador to the United Nations. Vice President Richard M. Nixon was impressed by Lodge's televised speeches and interviews at the UN and believed that his campaign needed to emphasize experienced, effective leadership and articulate, sound judgment in Cold War foreign policy in order to win the presidential election.[142] Also, ever since his rapprochement with Governor Nelson A. Rockefeller of New York regarding the Republican national platform, Nixon chose Lodge in order to increase his voter appeal among moderate and liberal Republicans in the Northeast. Nevertheless, Lodge later wrote, "Never having thought of myself presidentially or vice-presidentially, I tried to figure out why I had been chosen."[143]

Nixon knew that Lodge could not help him carry Massachusetts against JFK. Lodge did not highlight domestic policy issues peculiar to New England or partisan attacks on the Kennedy-Johnson ticket in his home state. Instead, Lodge's speeches in Massachusetts were consistent with those that he delivered in other states by emphasizing foreign policy. In Worcester, Lodge told an audience, "You are saying that you approve of the course which the United States has followed in the United Nations."[144] In Lowell, he stated, "We of the United States must live up to our ideals. Enthusiasm for a bad ideal is no more dangerous than a lack of enthusiasm for a good one."[145]

By contrast, Johnson used a September 9 speech in Hartford, Connecticut, to stridently attack the credibility of the Republican presidential campaign and the policy record of the Eisenhower administration. He said, "Republicans are preaching fiscal fear, fiscal doubt and fiscal hesitation."[146] While in Hartford, the Texan bluntly addressed the religious issue. Johnson said, "If it develops that people do apply the religious test as a qualification for office, then we tear up the Bill of Rights and throw our Constitution into the waste basket."[147] This statement preceded JFK's September 12 speech in Houston elaborating on the religious issue.

After JFK's four nationally televised debates with Nixon, he concentrated his personal campaigning on highly competitive battleground states in the Northeast and industrial Midwest as well as on California. He did not return to New England for regular campaigning until November 6, two days before the presidential election. During those two days, JFK visited all six of the New England states. In Springfield, Vermont, JFK said that Richard M. Nixon was incapable of being president because of his "failure to tell the truth to the American people or perhaps his failure to understand the truth."[148]

Before a crowd of approximately 7,000 people in Burlington, Vermont, the Massachusetts senator repeated this charge against Nixon.

Covering JFK's New England campaign swing for the *New York Times*, John H. Fenton wrote, "Democrats throughout the region are still pinning their hopes on last minute visits by Senator Kennedy tomorrow before he comes to Boston to wind up his campaign."[149] Democratic nominees for major offices throughout New England associated their names with JFK in newspaper ads and campaign literature.[150] Of the six New England states, Connecticut had the most equally competitive and volatile two-party system, especially in congressional elections.[151] In 1956, the Republicans won control of all six of Connecticut's U.S. House seats. In 1958, the Democrats won all six seats.[152]

Representative John S. Monagan was a Democratic congressman from Connecticut who was first elected to the U.S. House of Representatives in 1958. He was eager to have JFK campaign in Waterbury, a city in his district.[153] Monagan joined Governor Abraham Ribicoff and Senator Thomas J. Dodd in accompanying JFK to a street rally in Waterbury. In a 1978 interview, Monagan recalled that the crowds which waited for JFK were "in a sort of frenzy" and "had no sense of what they were doing" in their unruly enthusiasm.[154]

In the early morning of November 6, JFK told his audience in Waterbury, "Anyway, New England has not had a Democratic President since Franklin Pierce, 104 years ago, and I think it is about time."[155] A few hours later, JFK told an audience in New Haven that Connecticut was the first state in the roll call of balloting to support his candidacies for vice president and president at the 1956 and 1960 Democratic national conventions.[156] After trips to five other states, JFK returned to Connecticut on November 7 to address an audience in Hartford. In the conclusion of his Hartford speech, JFK stated, "I ask your help in a race between the comfortable and the concerned, between those who are satisfied and those who want to move ahead."[157]

On November 7, JFK was in Manchester, New Hampshire, in order to address a campaign rally and conduct a nationally televised broadcast. In a speech in Manchester, JFK connected the well-being of New England to that of the entire nation. He said, "I believe that New England, the oldest section of our country, also can be the first section in the future."[158] On the previous day, JFK stated in Lewiston, Maine, "The needs of Maine and the needs of Massachusetts are very much the same, and the needs of the United States are very much the same."[159]

Privately, Democratic politicians in Maine feared that JFK's coattail effects would be detrimental, rather than beneficial, to their state's Democratic nominees for major offices, partially because of the religious issue.[160] Likewise, Democrats in Vermont concluded that Nixon's coattail effects in Vermont made it unlikely that their nominees would win their state's gubernatorial and congressional elections. In his analysis of Vermont politics during the 1950s and 1960s, political scientist Harris E. Thurber wrote, "Though a New Englander himself, John F. Kennedy did not receive any great outpouring of votes from 'friends and neighbors' in Vermont since Richard Nixon ran even more strongly than the state candidates, defeating Kennedy by about 29,000 votes."[161]

The Democrats in New Hampshire, however, were more optimistic about the expected effects of JFK's presidential candidacy on Bernard L. Boutin, their state's 1960 Democratic nominee for governor. Boutin had been the Democratic nominee for governor in 1958 and lost that election by fewer than 7,000 votes. More than any other Democratic politician in northern New England, he was closely identified with JFK's presidential candidacy. New Hampshire was also the most urban, industrial, and Catholic state in northern New England. Many New Hampshire voters were still proud of JFK's overwhelming victory in their state's Democratic presidential primary. In it, he received twice as many votes as Estes Kefauver in 1956.[162]

In the three heavily Catholic, more Democratic states of southern New England, it was initially assumed that JFK's presidential nomination would benefit their Democratic nominees for major, statewide offices. Since 1959, Dennis J. Roberts, a former governor of Rhode Island, had been busy with Governor Abraham Ribicoff and

John M. Bailey in seeking delegates for JFK throughout the United States.[163] Rhode Island experienced an especially bitter, divisive Democratic senatorial primary in late September of 1960. After Senator Theodore F. Green announced his retirement, Roberts, J. Howard McGrath, and Claiborne Pell competed in the Democratic primary for his Senate seat. McGrath was a former governor and senator who had also served as DNC chairman and attorney general during the Truman administration. Pell was a former Foreign Service officer and served as chief delegation tally clerk at the Democratic national convention in Los Angeles.[164]

McGrath concentrated his rhetorical attacks on Roberts and received a taped endorsement from Harry S. Truman that was broadcast on television and radio.[165] The conflict between Roberts and McGrath was widely perceived as a grudge match. McGrath supported an opposing candidate in the Democratic gubernatorial primary when Roberts ran for renomination as governor in 1958. Roberts believed that this divisive primary caused his defeat in the 1958 gubernatorial election.[166]

With Roberts endorsed by the Democratic state committee, Pell campaigned as a "good government" grassroots candidate who opposed machine politics and whose extensive international travel as a diplomat and multilingual fluency qualified him for the Senate. Just as Franklin D. Roosevelt, Jr., campaigned for JFK in the West Virginia primary, he campaigned for Pell in Rhode Island's Democratic senatorial primary.[167] Pell was 41-years-old and portrayed himself as being more similar to JFK in terms of age, ideas, and orientation toward the future compared to his much older opponents. Pell won the primary with 61 percent of the votes.[168]

John A. Notte, the Democratic nominee for governor, was now eager to closely associate himself with Pell as he sought to defeat a Republican governor running for reelection.[169] For nearly three weeks, Pell and other Rhode Island Democrats were busy organizing a November 7 rally for JFK in front of the city hall in Providence.[170] They hoped to maximize the size of the crowds and media coverage for JFK in order to unite their factionalized party and encourage straight-ticket voting by Democrats and Democratic-leaning independents.[171]

Accompanied by Pell, Green, and other Rhode Island Democrats, JFK addressed a crowd of approximately 25,000 people in Providence on November 7, 1960. Most of JFK's speech focused on the significance of the 1960 presidential election in the context of the Cold War struggle with the Soviet Union. In his conclusion, he stated, "I can assure you that if we are successful, all of us in this State who seek office under the banner of the Democratic Party, I can assure you that our party in 1961 will meet its responsibilities, not only to the people of this country, but to all those around the world who look to us with confidence and hope."[172] On the following day, JFK received 63.6 percent of the popular votes in Rhode Island, his highest percentage in the nation, and the state's Democratic gubernatorial and senatorial nominees were elected.[173]

By contrast, the Democrats in Massachusetts were less fortunate. Like those in Rhode Island, they experienced bitter, divisive primaries for governor and senator. Joseph Ward and Thomas O'Connor, the respective Democratic nominees for governor and senator, avidly associated themselves with JFK in their speeches and advertising.[174] By late September, however, there was a growing trend in newspaper editorials to encourage the voters of Massachusetts to split their tickets by supporting JFK for president and John Volpe, a Republican, for governor. Bipartisan electoral support for Volpe was developing because of allegations of corruption in the Furcolo administration and Ward's ineffective, evasive responses to them.[175] Meanwhile, O'Connor, the mayor of Springfield, faced an uphill battle in his campaign to defeat Senator Leverett Saltonstall. Saltonstall enjoyed bipartisan popularity in Massachusetts and a mostly cooperative, mutually beneficial relationship with JFK regarding the policy interests of their state.[176]

JFK ended his New England campaign swing in Boston on the evening of November 7. Lawrence F. O'Brien recalled that, when JFK arrived at Boston Garden, "there was an explosion of total, deafening, shouting, stomping, unrestrained enthusiasm—I've never experienced anything like it, before or since."[177] Addressing an audience of approximately 22,000 people in Boston Garden, JFK continued his current rhetorical theme of the Cold War struggle and the need for effective presidential leadership to meet the challenges of the 1960s. Toward the end of this speech, he said, "I have spent many days in nearly every State, and I come back to Boston, Mass., with a stronger feeling of confidence, of hope, of knowledge of the vitality and energy of this society and our people than I could have ever had before."[178]

In his speech at Faneuil Hall in Boston, JFK noted that, in this same meeting place, James Otis and Samuel Adams delivered speeches which inspired the American Revolution. He said, "All of the past tells us something about the future. I've traveled all over the United States—been to 50 states in the last month—and I must say I come back to this old city with the strongest possible confidence in the future of the United States, in the ability of its people to meet its responsibilities, to bear our burdens, to strengthen our cause, to identify ourselves and others with the cause of freedom around the world."[179] JFK concluded this speech by expressing his confidence that "in 1960, November 8, this country will once again choose to go forward, this country will once again choose to go to work to build a strong society here and to build a peaceful and productive world."[180]

On the morning of November 8, 1960, JFK and Jacqueline Kennedy voted in Boston and then flew to Hyannis. After being driven to the Kennedy compound in Hyannis Port, they joined family, friends, campaign staff, and volunteers to await the election returns at RFK's house.[181] In a 1964 interview, Jacqueline Kennedy remarked that JFK was calm as he waited to hear about the first election results. He had an extensive conversation with author Cornelius Ryan about his best-selling book, *The Longest Day: June 6, 1944*.[182]

The first presidential election results from New England were mixed. As expected, tiny hamlets in northern New Hampshire like Dixville Notch voted almost unanimously for Nixon.[183] In Connecticut, JFK's winning margins in the cities of Bridgeport and Danbury were narrower than expected as Nixon easily carried affluent suburbs and mostly Protestant small towns. Eventually, JFK carried Connecticut by a margin of nearly 92,000 votes. Approximately 78,000 of these votes came from the cities of Hartford, New Haven, and Waterbury.[184] In his study of political parties in southern New England, political scientist John K. White noted that Nixon carried three of

Connecticut's eight counties in 1960.[185] Also, the Republicans gained two of Connecticut's six congressional seats.

In his home state of Massachusetts, JFK received 60.2 percent of the popular votes, his third highest percentage among the states after Rhode Island and Georgia.[186] Historically Republican counties, like Dukes, Barnstable, and Nantucket, that had voted mostly for JFK in his 1958 Senate race by narrow margins, gave Nixon larger majorities of their votes.[187] The frenzied excitement of Bay Staters for JFK's presidential candidacy did not transfer to the Democratic campaigns for governor and senator. The Republicans easily won these two elections.

By the early morning of November 9, it was apparent that JFK had eked out a narrow victory in the 1960 presidential election. JFK was surprised that Vice President Richard M. Nixon publicly conceded the election so soon.[188] The media had established a communications center at the national guard armory in Hyannis. JFK appeared there to issue a public statement accepting Nixon's concession and Eisenhower's message of congratulations. Toward the end of his speech, JFK said, "The election may have been a close one, but I think there is general agreement by all of our citizens that a supreme national effort will be needed in the years ahead to move this country safely through the 1960s."[189]

By the end of his victorious presidential campaign, JFK was truly a national political figure. For the president-elect, the entire nation, instead of one state or a particular region, was now his constituency. As his presidential candidacy developed in the late 1950s, JFK spoke less about the policy interests and needs either unique to or especially pronounced in Massachusetts and New England and more about those common to the entire nation. When JFK campaigned in New England during the last few days before the 1960 presidential election, he only made brief references to his home state and region. Whenever he did, he usually made them subordinate to or integrated with the national interest.[190]

In the last chapter of *Profiles in Courage*, JFK explained that when a senator is confronted by conflicting partisan, regional, and national loyalties and responsibilities political courage becomes most important regarding the national interest. He wrote, "In regional disputes, his regional responsibilities will likely guide his course. It is on national issues, on matters of conscience which challenge party and regional loyalties, that the test of courage is presented."[191]

Epilogue

After John F. Kennedy became president, he continued his relationship with New England in general and Massachusetts in particular. He regularly traveled to the Kennedy compound in Hyannis Port for family visits and vacations. JFK occasionally, yet reluctantly, involved himself in Massachusetts politics. This was especially true after John W. McCormack became Speaker of the House and Edward M. Kennedy ran for the Senate in 1962.

As president, JFK needed to focus on national and international policy issues. Nonetheless, he did not neglect the policy interests of Massachusetts and New England. It was personally satisfying for him to sign legislation that established the Cape Cod National Seashore. As he did during his 1952 Senate campaign, service in the Senate, and presidential campaign, JFK emphasized a complementary relationship between the policy interests of New England and those of the nation while he was president. On July 16, 1963, JFK announced the results of a feasibility study of how the tides of Passamaquoddy Bay in Maine could be used to generate electricity. The president stated that, while the completion of this hydroelectric power project would benefit the economy of Maine and consumers of electricity throughout New England, it "now meets the national interest test."[1] He concluded, "I think it will mean a good deal to New England and a good deal to the country."[2]

On October 19, 1963, approximately one month before he died, JFK traveled to Boston to attend a dinner in his honor entitled, "New England's Salute to the President." Guests at this dinner included Senator Edward M. Kennedy, Speaker of the House John W. McCormack, and the Democratic governors of Massachusetts, Connecticut, New Hampshire, and Vermont. In his speech, JFK summarized and praised the recent legislative accomplishments of Congress. He cited this progress in policy making to justify his optimism about the future of New England, the United States of America, and the free world in the Cold War. The president concluded, "This is the night in which I hope we can commit this state and area to the future."[3]

After JFK's death, the voting behavior of all six New England states generally and eventually became more Democratic, especially in presidential elections. The presidential election of 1984 was the last presidential election in which the Republican presidential nominee carried all of the New England states. In 2004, 2008, and 2012, Democratic presidential nominees carried all of the New England states. Furthermore, New England became the most cohesively liberal region of the nation on such issues as abortion rights, same-sex marriage, and environmental protection. This political change was a sharp contrast to the Massachusetts Democratic Party's opposition to the legalization of contraceptive information in 1948, JFK's stridently anti-Communist rhetoric in his 1952 Senate campaign, and his later enthusiasm for the development of nuclear power plants in New England.

John F. Kennedy's use of his Senate seat to promote and serve the policy interests of New England helped him to develop a bipartisan following in New England on these issues. It also helped him to develop a partisan following and Democratic alliances in New England for the purpose of winning his party's presidential nomination and the presidential election of 1960. As a senator and a presidential candidate, JFK tried to symbiotically and successfully combine his service to his state, region, and nation with his political ambition. In the last chapter of *Profiles in Courage*, JFK wrote, "It may take courage to battle one's President, one's party, or the overwhelming sentiment of one's nation; but these do not compare, it seems to me, to the courage required of the Senator defying the angry power of the very constituents who control his future."[4]

Notes

Chapter 1

1. JFK POF, Box 34, JFK's address to Massachusetts state legislature, January 9, 1961, JFKL.

2. Ibid.

3. Ibid.

4. Theodore C. Sorensen, *Kennedy* (New York: Harper and Row, 1965): 234.

5. Ibid.

6. Theodore H. White, *The Making of the President 1960* (New York: New American Library, 1961): 116.

7. Arthur M. Schlesinger, Jr., *A Thousand Days: John F. Kennedy in The White House* (Boston: Houghton Mifflin, 1965): 31–32.

8. Perry Miller, *The New England Mind: From Colony to Province* (Boston: Beacon Press, 1953): 4.

9. John Harris, "Massachusetts: Cauldron Bubble," in *States in Crisis: Politics in Ten American States*, ed. by A. James Reichley (Chapel Hill: University of North Carolina Press, 1964): 162.

10. Edgar Litt, *The Political Cultures of Massachusetts* (Cambridge, MA: MIT Press, 1965): 17–19.

11. Edward C. Banfield and James Q. Wilson, *City Politics* (New York: Vintage, 1958): 41–43.

12. James MacGregor Burns, *John Kennedy: A Political Profile* (New York: Avon Book Division, 1960): 102–103; and Edward C. Banfield and James Q. Wilson, "Ethnic Membership and Urban Voting," in *Racial and Ethnic Relations*, ed. by Bernard E. Segal (New York: Crowell, 1966): 168–177.

NOTES TO CHAPTER I

13. Banfield and Wilson, "Ethnic Membership and Urban Voting," in Segal, 173.

14. David Hackett Fischer, *Albion's Seed: Four British Folkways in America* (New York: Oxford University Press, 1989): 873.

15. Gabriel A. Almond, "Comparative Political Systems," *Journal of Politics* 18 (August 1956): 391–409.

16. Gabriel A. Almond and Sidney Verba, *The Civic Culture: Political Attitudes and Democracy in Five Nations* (Boston: Little, Brown and Company, 1963).

17. Robert A. Dahl, *Who Governs? Democracy and Power in An American City* (New Haven, CT: Yale University Press, 1961).

18. Daniel J. Elazar, *American Federalism: A View from the States* (New York: Thomas Y. Crowell, 1966).

19. Ibid., 96–112; and Neal R. Peirce, *The New England States* (New York: Norton, 1976): 62–67.

20. Litt, 7–25.

21. Ronald P. Formisano, "The Concept of Political Culture," *Journal of Interdisciplinary History* 31 (Winter 2001): 393–426.

22. Banfield and Wilson, *City Politics*, 58.

23. Louis M. Lyons, "Boston: Study in Inertia," in *Our Fair City*, ed. by Robert S. Allen (New York: Vanguard, 1947): 16–36.

24. William V. Shannon, "Massachusetts: Prisoner of the Past," in *Our Sovereign State*, ed. by Robert S. Allen (New York: Vanguard, 1949): 53.

25. Jack Lait and Lee Mortimer, *U.S.A. Confidential* (New York: Crown, 1952): 86, 88.

26. John Gunther, *Inside U.S.A.* (New York: Harper and Row, 1947): 460.

27. Jack Beatty, *The Rascal King: The Life and Times of James Michael Curley, 1874–1958* (New York: Addison-Wesley, 1992): 475.

28. Ibid., 456–457; Ronald Kessler, *The Sins of the Father: Joseph P. Kennedy and the Dynasty He Founded* (New York: Warner Books, 1996): 291; and Nigel Hamilton, *JFK: Reckless Youth* (New York: Random House, 1992): 677–678, 704.

29. Edward M. Kennedy, *True Compass: A Memoir* (New York: Twelve Books, 2009): 89. Subsequently cited as EMK, *True Compass*.

30. JPK Papers, Box 220, speech by John F. Fitzgerald, July 7, 1942, JFKL.

31. Richard J. Whalen, *The Founding Father: The Story of Joseph P. Kennedy* (New York: New American Library, 1964): 364–365.

32. David E. Koskoff, *Joseph P. Kennedy: A Life and Times* (Englewood Cliffs, NJ: Prentice-Hall, 1974): 319–321; and JPK Papers, Box 225, letter, Joe Kane to JPK, December 28, 1942, JFKL.

33. Ibid., letter, JPK to Joseph L. Kane, March 9, 1944, JFKL.

34. Ibid., letters, Kane to JPK, January 25, 1943, and, Box 215, John Burns to JPK, December 29, 1944, JFKL.

35. Joseph F. Dinneen, *The Kennedy Family* (Boston: Little, Brown and Company, 1959): 118; Herbert S. Parmet, *Jack: The Struggles of John F. Kennedy* (New York: Dial Press, 1980): 125; Thomas C. Reeves, *A Question of Character: A Life of John F. Kennedy* (New York: Free Press, 1991): 76–79; and Joe McCarthy, *The Remarkable Kennedys* (New York: Popular Library, 1960): 89.

36. Richard J. Whalen, 390.

37. JPK Papers, Box 272, letters, JPK to Daniel Bloomfield, February 2, 1946, and JPK to D. S. Kaplinger, October 6, 1945; and Box 263, speech by JPK, "Farm and Factory in Massachusetts," January 9, 1946, JFKL.

38. OH, Torbert Macdonald, August 11, 1965, 16, JFKL.

39. Thomas P. O'Neill, Jr., *Man of the House: The Life and Political Memoirs of Speaker Tip O'Neill* (New York: St. Martin's Press, 1987): 82–83; and John A. Farrell, *Tip O'Neill and the Democratic Century* (Boston: Little, Brown and Company, 2001): 92–93.

40. JPK Papers, Box 225, letter, Joseph L. Kane to JPK, March 7, 1946, JFKL.

41. Ibid., January 29, 1946, JFKL.

42. Ibid., January 15 and February 25, 1946, JFKL.

43. Deidre Henderson (ed.), *Prelude to Leadership: The European Diary of John F. Kennedy, Summer 1945* (New York: Regnery, 1995): ix–xlv; and Barbara Leaming, *Jack Kennedy: The Education of a Statesman* (New York: Norton, 2006): 71–72.

44. Peter Collier and David Horowitz, *The Kennedys: An American Drama* (New York: Summit Books, 1984): 148–151.

45. Amanda Smith (ed.), *Hostage to Fortune: The Letters of Joseph P. Kennedy* (New York: Viking Press, 2001): 625–626.

46. JPK Papers, Box 225, press release from Carroll L. Meins, April 30, 1945, and Box 272, letter, W. H. Weinger to JPK, September 19, 1945, JFKL; and David I. Walsh Papers, letter, Henry Harris to Walsh, October 30, 1946, CHC.

47. Ibid., Walsh to Michael J. Neville, September 12, 1946, CHC; Shannon, 53; and JPK Papers, Box 225, letter, Joseph L. Kane to JPK, February 25, 1946, JFKL.

48. Geoffrey Perret, *Jack: A Life Like No Other* (New York: Random House, 2001): 133.
49. Kenneth P. O'Donnell and David F. Powers, *"Johnny We Hardly Knew Ye": Memories of John F. Kennedy* (New York: Pocket Books, 1973): 54.
50. John Henry Cutler, *"Honey Fitz": Three Steps to the White House* (New York: Bobbs-Merrill, 1962): 304–309.
51. Dinneen, *The Kennedy Family*, 123.
52. O'Neill, 86.
53. O'Donnell and Powers, 52.
54. OH, David F. Powers, April 13, 1969, 2–3, JFKL.
55. JFK PPP, Box 98, copy of JFK's 1946 platform, JFKL.
56. OH, Joseph A. DeGuglielmo, May 3, 1969, 6, JFKL.
57. OH, Mark Dalton, August 4, 1964, 11, JFKL.
58. Francis Russell, *The President Makers: From Mark Hanna to Joseph P. Kennedy* (Boston: Little, Brown and Company, 2001): 370.
59. Ralph G. Martin and Ed Plaut, *Front Runner, Dark Horse* (Garden City, NY: Doubleday, 1960): 133–134.
60. O'Neill, 88.
61. Parmet, *Jack*, 162.
62. *Congressional Quarterly, Guide to U.S. Elections* (Washington, DC: CQ Press, 1975): 809. Subsequently cited as *CQ, Guide*.
63. Harold W. Stanley and Richard G. Niemi, *Vital Statistics on American Politics* (Washington, DC: CQ Press, 1994): 205.
64. O'Donnell and Powers, 85–86.
65. "A Kennedy Runs for Congress: The Boston-Bred Scion of a Former Ambassador is a Fighting Conservative," *Look* 10 (June 11, 1946): 32–36.
66. Christopher J. Matthews, *Kennedy and Nixon: The Rivalry That Shaped Postwar America* (New York: Simon and Schuster, 1996): 49–50.
67. John K. White, *Still Seeing Red: How the Cold War Shapes the New American Politics* (Boulder, CO: Westview Press, 1997): 52–53.
68. JFK PPP, Box 95, JFK's speech in Salem, Massachusetts, January 30, 1949, JFKL.
69. Ibid., Box 94, letters, Salvatore Solimine to JFK, April 12, 1951, and Rosalynn Henning to JFK, April 17, 1951, JFKL: and Lance Morrow, *The Best Year of Their Lives: Kennedy, Johnson, and Nixon in 1948* (New York: Basic Books, 2005): 7–8.
70. *CQ, Guide*, 812, 817.
71. OH, Herbert Tucker, March 9, 1967, 2–3, JFKL; and Richard J. Whalen, 405–406.

72. Quoted in Burns, 100.

73. James M. Curley Collection, telegram from Archbishop Richard Cushing to Curley, June 12, 1947, CHC; Ibid., undated 1947 letter, John W. McCormack to Edward J. McCormack, CHC; and Parmet, *Jack*, 182–183.

74. Robert Dallek, *An Unfinished Life: John F. Kennedy, 1917–1963* (Boston: Little, Brown and Company, 2003): 156–157.

75. Schlesinger, *A Thousand Days*, 91.

76. Martin and Plaut, 162.

77. CQ, *Guide*, 413–414.

78. Shannon in Allen, 23–68.

79. Robert Bradford Papers, Box 17, letter, Ernest J. Goulston to Bradford, October 29, 1947, MHS.

80. Paul A. Dever Papers, Box 1, biography of Dever, MSL.

81. CQ, *Guide*, 414; and Stanley and Niemi, 205.

82. Sean J. Savage, *Truman and the Democratic Party* (Lexington: University Press of Kentucky, 1997): 138–139.

83. O'Neill, 61–72.

84. Thomas J. Whalen, *Kennedy versus Lodge: The 1952 Massachusetts Senate Race* (Boston: Northeastern University Press, 2000): 31–32.

85. CQ, *Guide*, 494.

86. Leverett Saltonstall Papers, Box 13, letter, Roy Williams to Saltonstall, March 11, 1946, MHS.

87. Leverett Saltonstall, *Salty: Recollections of a Yankee in Politics* (Boston: Boston Globe, 1976): 63.

88. Doris Kearns Goodwin, *The Fitzgeralds and the Kennedys: An American Saga* (New York: Simon and Schuster, 1987): 756.

89. Alden Hatch, *The Lodges of Massachusetts* (New York: Hawthorn Books, 1973): 122–141.

90. Victor Lasky, *J.F.K.: The Man and the Myth* (New York: Macmillan, 1963): 151.

91. David I. Walsh Papers, letter, Walsh to Burton K. Wheeler, November 9, 1946, CHC.

92. William J. Miller, *Henry Cabot Lodge: A Biography* (New York: James H. Heineman, Inc., 1967): 180–186; and Duane Lockard, *New England State Politics* (Princeton, NJ: Princeton University Press, 1959): 143–144.

93. Henry Cabot Lodge II Papers, reel 8, clipping, *Boston Post*, February 5, 1951, MHS.

94. *Worcester Telegram*, August 7, 1951.

95. Martin and Plaut, 148.

96. John F. Kennedy, *John Fitzgerald Kennedy: A Compendium of Speeches, Statements, and Remarks Delivered During His Service in the Congress of the United States* (Washington, DC: GPO, 1964): 978–982. Subsequently cited as Kennedy, *Compendium*.

97. Ibid., 73.

98. Burns, 88–92.

99. OH, Hirsh Freed, June 5, 1964, 22–23, JFKL.

100. Reeves, 119.

101. JPK Papers, Box 230, letter, JPK to John W. McCormack, August 8, 1951, JFKL.

102. Richard J. Whalen, 415.

103. OH, Edward J. McCormack, Jr., September 25, 1967, 8, JFKL.

104. http://www.bing.com/videos/watch/video/john-f-kennedy-december-2-1951/17wsi4gn4?q=Congressman+John+F+Kennedy+AND+19.

105. JPK Papers, Box 214, letter, Leland Bickford to JPK, February 7, 1952, JFKL.

106. Ibid., Box 288, letter, JPK to David F. Powers, February 14, 1952, JFKL.

107. Ibid., letter, JPK to Mark J. Dalton, February 14, 1952, JFKL.

108. Ibid., letter, February 26, 1952, JFKL.

109. Ibid.

110. O'Donnell and Powers, 92; and OH, Edward J. McCormack, 4–5, JFKL.

111. http://www.jfklibrary.org/Research/Research-Aids/Ready-Reference/JFK-Fast-Facts/Statement-of-Candidacy-1952.aspx.

112. Burns, 111.

113. OH, Mark J. Dalton, August 4, 1964, 27–28, JFKL.

114. Richard J. Whalen, 409–410.

115. Helen O'Donnell, *A Common Good: The Friendship of Robert F. Kennedy and Kenneth P. O'Donnell* (New York: William Morrow and Company, 1998): 77.

116. O'Brien, *No Final Victories*, 11–18.

117. Ibid., 30–31.

118. OH, Edward J. McCormack, Jr., 3–4, JFKL.

119. Lasky, 144–145.

120. Thomas J. Whalen, 112.

121. JPK Papers, Box 288, memo, Ralph Coghlan to James Landis, August 8, 1952, 9–10, JFKL.

122. Thomas J. Whalen, 67–69.

123. JPK Papers, Box 288, letter, Walter French to JFK, April 9, 1952, JFKL

124. *Springfield Daily News*, July 16, 1952; Robert W. Eisenmerger, *The Dynamics of Growth in New England's Economy, 1870–1964* (Middletown, CT: Wesleyan University, 1967): 9–10; and C. Girard Davidson Papers, Box 22, Davidson's speech delivered to Textile Workers Union of America on May 14, 1949 in Worcester, Massachusetts, HSTL.

125. *Berkshire Eagle*, September 8, 1952.

126. *Worcester Telegram*, October 24, 1952.

127. *New Bedford Times*, October 31, 1952; and Thomas J. Whalen, 104–107.

128. David F. Powers Papers, Box 30, JFK press release, October 6, 1952, JFKL.

129. Henry Cabot Lodge II Papers, reel 18, Lodge press release, "Of Interest to Massachusetts," 1952, MHS.

130. Ibid., "Absent and Not Recorded," 1952, MHS.

131. Ibid., clipping, *Boston Herald*, September 2, 1952, MHS.

132. Ibid., clipping, *North Adams Transcript*, August 29, 1952, MHS.

133. John F. Kennedy, *A Nation of Immigrants* (New York: Harper and Row, 1964): 77–83.

134. *Worcester Telegram*, October 4, 1952.

135. http://www.archive.org/details/longines-jfk.

136. Ibid.

137. JPK Papers, Box 288, undated, unsigned 1952 memo about meeting with Richard Russell, JFKL.

138. Ibid., letter, R. Sargent Shriver to Betsy Walsh, September 8, 1952, JFKL.

139. David W. Reinhard, *The Republican Right Since 1945* (Lexington: University Press of Kentucky, 1983): 79–90; and JPK Papers, Box 289, campaign ad, "American Firsters vs. Senator Lodge," 1952, JFKL.

140. JPK Papers, Box 290, copy of JFK's speech, October 5, 1952, 4, JFKL.

141. *New Bedford Standard Times*, October 24, 1952.

142. Thomas J. Whalen, 130–132; and JPK Papers, Box 288, letter, Betsy Walsh to Mrs. George Connelly, September 30, 1952, JFKL.

143. Richard J. Whalen, 419–420.

144. Henry Cabot Lodge II Papers, reel 18, memo, "Analysis of Poll," September 5, 1952, MHS; *Worcester Telegram*, October 27, 1952; and

Leverett Saltonstall Papers, Box 94, report, "Massachusetts Political Survey, August, 1952," submitted on September 22, 1952 by Opinion Research Corporation, MHS.

145. JPK Papers, Box 292, letter, Edward J. Dunn to RFK, September 30, 1952, JFKL.

146. Thomas C. Reeves, *The Life and Times of Joe McCarthy: A Biography* (New York: Stein and Day, 1982): 442–443.

147. JPK Papers, Box 288, letter, Arthur M. Schlesinger, Jr., to James Landis, July 10, 1952, JFKL; and John P. Mallan, "Massachusetts: Liberal and Corrupt," *New Republic* 127 (October 13, 1952): 10–12.

148. Richard J. Whalen, 416–417.

149. Thomas J. Whalen, 138–145.

150. *New Bedford Standard Times*, October 27, 1952; *Worcester Telegram*, October 21, 1952; *Lowell Sun*, October 16, 1952; and *Springfield Daily News*, October 22, 1952.

151. Leverett Saltonstall Papers, Box 94, poll, September 22, 1952, 1–3, MHS.

152. Henry Cabot Lodge II Papers, reel 18, "Lodge Release," November 1, 1952, MHS; and Thomas J. Whalen, 151.

153. CQ, Guide, 292, 494.

154. Ibid., 414.

155. *Worcester Telegram*, November 6, 1952; and Joseph W. Martin, Jr., Papers, clipping, *Fall River Herald News*, November 6, 1952, SC.

156. *New Bedford Standard Times*, November 2, 1952.

157. John T. Woolley and Gerhard Peters, *The American Presidency Project* (online). 2013. Santa Barbara, CA. http://presidency.ucsb.edu/ws/?pid=html as 9829. Subsequently cited as Woolley and Peters with pid number as html.

158. Lasky, 168–169.

159. Ibid., 165.

160. Theodore C. Sorensen Papers, Box 14, memo, March 5, JFKL; and JFK PPP, Box 896, speech by JFK, "New England's Economic Prospects," October 19, 1956, JFKL.

161. Theodore C. Sorensen, *Counselor: A Life at the Edge of History* (New York: Harper Collins, 2008): 99.

162. Vito N. Silvestri, *Becoming JFK: A Profile in Communication* (Westport, CT: Praeger, 2000): 51–53; and Theodore C. Sorensen Papers, Box 3, draft of article for *Harvard Business Review*, 1954, JFKL.

163. Theodore C. Sorensen Papers, Box 11, joint press release from

JFK and Saltonstall, September 5, 1954, JFKL; and author's interview with John J. McNally, Jr., in Webster, Massachusetts, September 15, 2011.

164. OH, Leverett Saltonstall, November 19, 1964, 6, JFKL.

165. Saltonstall, 187.

166. Lyn Ragsdale, *Vital Statistics on the Presidency: Washington to Clinton* (Washington, DC: Congressional Quarterly, Inc., 1996): 371.

167. Foster Furcolo Papers, Box 1, Furcolo campaign brochure, 1954, MSL.

168. Litt, 45–46.

169. OH, Foster Furcolo, June 9, 1964, 6, JFKL.

170. Harris in Reichley, 153–154; Schlesinger, *A Thousand Days*, 31; Sorensen, *Kennedy*, 73–74; and O'Donnell and Powers, 96–97.

171. O'Brien, *No Final Victories*, 11–24.

172. OH, Leverett Saltonstall, November 19, 1964, 15, JFKL.

173. Leverett Saltonstall Papers, Box 314, press release, September 16, 1954, MHS.

174. Ibid., report from John Jackson, October 25, 1954; report from Mrs. Marion R. T. Hollingsworth, October 25, 1954; undated report from David Graham on Worcester County; and Box 301, undated 1954 poll of Senate race, A-27, MHS.

175. O'Brien, *No Final Victories*, 45.

176. Ibid., 44–46.

177. Harvey Rachlin, *The Kennedys: A Chronological History, 1823–Present* (New York: World Almanac Books, 1986): 132.

178. Ibid.

179. Ibid.

180. CQ, *Guide*, 494.

181. Ibid., 414.

182. Alec Barbrook, *God Save the Commonwealth: An Electoral History of Massachusetts* (Amherst: University of Massachusetts Press, 1973): 99, 181.

183. *Boston Globe*, November 3, 1954.

184. Ibid.

185. *Springfield Daily News*, November 4, 1954.

186. Kenneth P. O'Donnell Papers, Box 14, clipping, *Boston Post*, August 22, 1954, JFKL.

187. John W. McCormack Papers, Box 14, letter, Francis E. Kelly to McCormack, November 23, 1954, BU.

188. Lockard, 127.

NOTES TO CHAPTER 1

189. Harris in Reichley, 154–155.
190. OH, Garrett H. Byrne September 28, 1967, 14, JFKL.
191. Ibid., 20.
192. Sean J. Savage, "JFK and the DNC," *White House Studies* 2 (Summer 2002): 143–144.
193. JFK PPP, Box 896, memos, JFK to Kenneth P. O'Donnell, March 8, 1955, and Lawrence F. O'Brien to JFK, undated 1955, JFKL.
194. Rachlin, 140.
195. John W. McCormack Papers, Box 47, letter, John E. Powers to McCormack, January 5, 1956, BU.
196. Lawrence H. Fuchs, "Presidential Politics in Boston: The Irish Response to Stevenson," *New England Quarterly* v. 30, n. 4 (December 1957): 435–447.
197. CQ, *Guide*, 336.
198. Harris in Reichley, 155; and O'Donnell and Powers, 130–132.
199. Charles A. H. Thomson and Frances M. Shattuck, *The 1956 Presidential Campaign* (Washington, DC: Brookings Institution, 1960): 157–163; and Parmet, *Jack*, 378–383.
200. CQ, *Guide*, 167.
201. OH, Jackson J. Holtz, May 7, 1964, 8, JFKL.
202. Barbrook, 116.
203. *Boston Globe*, November 4, 1956.
204. Ibid.
205. Ibid., October 19, 1956.
206. CQ, *Guide*, 295; Fuchs, "Presidential Politics in Boston: The Irish Response to Stevenson," 442; and Lawrence H. Fuchs, *The Political Behavior of American Jews* (Glencoe, IL: Free Press, 1956): 113–118.
207. CQ, *Guide*, 414.
208. *Boston Globe*, November 7, 1956.
209. Ibid., November 8, 1956.
210. JFK PPP, Box 505, Robert X. Tivnan to JFK, November 13, 1956, JFKL.
211. Foster Furcolo Collection, copy of article by Foster Furcolo, "What the Limited Sales Tax Means to You," *The Lens* (April 1957), BPL.
212. John P. Mallan and George Blackwood, "The Tax that Beat a Governor: The Ordeal of Massachusetts," in *The Uses of Power*, ed. by Alan F. Westin (New York: Harcourt, Brace, and World, 1962); 318.
213. Ibid., 320–321.

214. Foster Furcolo Papers, Box 1, message from Governor Furcolo, March 1, 1959, MSL.

215. Foster Furcolo, *Ballots Anyone?* (Cambridge, MA: Schenkman, 1982): 87–88.

216. Foster Furcolo Papers, Box 1, JFK and Furcolo campaign materials, 1958, MSL.

217. Kenneth P. O'Donnell Papers, Box 5, interview of John H. Treanor, Jr., November 26, 1973, 11, JFKL.

218. EMK, *True Compass*, 124.

219. Ibid., 123–124.

220. Ibid., 124.

221. Theodore C. Sorensen Papers, letter, JFK to Mrs. W.G. Dwight, July 10, 1957; and letter, JFK to Clarence Mitchell, July 10, 1957, JFKL.

222. Parmet, *Jack*, 454.

223. Mark Stern, *Calculating Visions: Kennedy, Johnson, and Civil Rights* (New Brunswick, NJ: Rutgers University Press, 1992): 21.

224. Theodore C. Sorensen Papers, Box 19, press release, September 25, 1958; and JPK Papers. Box 29, campaign memo, "Why Republicans Should Vote to Re-elect Senator Kennedy," 1958, JFKL.

225. JFK PPP, Box 901, JFK's speech in Lawrence, Massachusetts, May 15, 1958, JFKL.

226. Ibid., JFK's speech at Boston College, May 15, 1958, JFKL.

227. Theodore C. Sorensen Papers, Box 19, letter, Robert E. Thompson to Leland Bickford, June 24, 1958, JFKL.

228. Helen O'Donnell, 157; and O'Brien, *No Final Victories*, 57.

229. JFK PPP, Box 906, JFK's speeches, June 7, 1958 in Manchester, New Hampshire, and Box 901, June 27, 1958 in Hartford, Connecticut, JFKL.

230. Theodore C. Sorensen Papers, Box 19, clipping, *Youngstown Vindicator*, August 21, 1958, JFKL.

231. *Worcester Telegram*, October 5, 1958.

232. JPK Papers, Box 218, letter, Rev. Armand H. Desautels to JPK, February 26, 1954, JFKL.

233. Ibid., Box 213, letter, Desautels to JPK, October 3, 1958, JFKL.

234. Ibid.

235. Ibid., Box 239, letter, Rev. John J. Wright to JPK, September 26, 1958, JFKL.

236. Parmet, *Jack*, 456–457.

237. O'Brien, *No Final Victories*, 54–56; and O'Donnell and Powers, 160–161.
238. Helen O'Donnell, 162–163.
239. OH, Edward J. McCormack, Jr., September 25, 1967, 23, JFKL.
240. Ibid., 24.
241. Kenneth P. O'Donnell Papers, Box 5, Treanor interview, 32, JFKL.
242. Leverett Saltonstall Papers, Box 84, RNC press release, April 8, 1958, MHS.
243. Barbrook, 103–104.
244. *New Bedford Times Standard*, October 29, 1958.
245. Ibid.
246. CQ, *Guide*, 494.
247. Ibid., 414.
248. "National Affairs," *Time* v. 72, n. 19 (November 10, 1958): 25–29.
249. Cornelius Dalton and James J. Dobbins, *Leading the Way: A History of the Massachusetts General Court, 1629–1980* (Boston: Commonwealth of Massachusetts, 1984): 314.
250. *New Bedford Standard Times*, November 5, 1958.
251. *Worcester Telegram*, November 5, 1958.
252. *Springfield Daily News*, November 5, 1958.
253. Ibid.
254. RFK Papers, Political Files, April 1959 poll of Wisconsin for 1960 primary, JFKL; and OH, John E. Powers, March 9, 1967, 22, JFKL.
255. Bryant Danner, *Campaign Decision-Makers* (Cambridge, MA: Harvard University Press, 1960): 6–7.
256. John Henry Cutler, *Cardinal Cushing of Boston* (New York: Hawthorn Books, 1970): 176–177; and OH, Byrne, 29, JFKL.
257. Murray B. Levin, *The Alienated Voter: Politics in Boston* (New York: Holt, Rinehart and Winston, Inc., 1960): 12.
258. Ibid., 20.
259. Thomas H. O'Connor, *Building a New Boston: Politics and Urban Renewal, 1950 to 1970* (Boston: Northeastern University Press, 1993): 156.
260. Ibid., 156–157; and Russell B. Adams, Jr., *The Boston Money Tree* (New York: Thomas Y. Crowell, 1977): 307.
261. O'Connor, 158–159.
262. Levin, *The Alienated Voter*, 24.

263. O'Connor, 159.

264. Edward C. Banfield and Martha Derthick, *A Report on the Politics of Boston* (Cambridge, MA: Joint Center for Urban Studies, 1960): part IV, 13–14.

265. Dalton and Dobbins, 279–280; and Barbrook, 127–133.

266. OH, Edward J. McCormack, Jr., 3, JFKL.

267. Abraham Ribicoff Papers, Box 11, letter, Theodore C. Sorensen to Ribicoff, July 28, 1959, LOC; OH, John S. Monagan, August 3, 1966, 3, JFKL; and OH, John M. Bailey, April 10, 1964, 15–16, JFKL.

268. Democratic National Committee (DNC), *Official Report of the Proceedings of the Democratic National Convention, 1952* (Washington, DC: DNC, 1952): 185.

269. Barbrook, 130–131.

270. Foster Furcolo Papers, Box 1, clipping, *Boston Globe*, July 25, 1960, MSL; and OH, Peter Cloherty, September 29, 1967, 41, JFKL.

271. Dalton and Dobbins, 280–283.

272. Murray B. Levin and George Blackwood, *The Compleat Politician: Political Strategy in Massachusetts* (Indianapolis: Bobbs-Merrill, 1962): 36; and Lockard, 125–126.

273. Levin and Blackwood, 77–103; and Kevin H. White (ed.), *Election Statistics: The Commonwealth of Massachusetts, 1960* (Boston: Commonwealth of Massachusetts, 1961): 157.

274. Barbrook, 130–132.

275. Kevin H. White (ed.), 153.

276. http://www.thecrimson.com/article/1960/10/27/mediocrity-in-massachusetts-pmassachusetts-politics-often/.

277. CQ, *Guide*, 298, 414, and 495.

278. Elliot Richardson, "Poisoned Politics: The Real Tragedy in Massachusetts," *Atlantic Monthly*, v. 208, n. 4 (October 1961): 77–82; Edward R.F. Sheehan, "Massachusetts: Rogues and Reformers in a State on Trial," *Saturday Evening Post* 238 (June 5, 1965); 25–32; and Barbrook, 138.

279. Massachusetts Crime Commission, *Comprehensive Report*, No. 5 (Boston: George Dean, 1965): 2.

280. Levin and Blackwood, 70.

281. JFK POF, Box 34, JFK's address to Massachusetts state legislature, January 9, 1961, JFKL.

282. Harris in Reichley, 160–161.

283. Sheehan, 27.

284. Savage, "JFK and the DNC."

Chapter 2

1. JPK Papers, Box 288, letter, Ralph Coghlan to James Landis, August 8, 1952, JFKL.
2. Ibid., Box 218, undated, unsigned 1945 memo, 3, JFKL.
3. Shannon in Allen, 67–68.
4. John K. Galbraith Papers, Box 104, speech by Galbraith, June 13, 1952, 3, JFKL.
5. Seymour E. Harris, *The Economics of New England* (Cambridge, MA: Harvard University Press, 1952): 304.
6. Ibid.
7. Lynn Elaine Brown and Steven Sass, "The Transition from a Mill-Based to a Knowledge-Based Economy: New England, 1940–2000," in *Engines of Enterprise: An Economic History of New England*, ed. by Peter Temin (Cambridge, MA: Harvard University Press, 2000): 201–202.
8. Leverett Saltonstall Papers, Box 85, memo, JFK to Saltonstall, December, 1954, MHS.
9. William J. Miller, 258–259; and Sinclair Weeks Papers, Box 1, letter, Helen B. Patterson to Weeks, November 29, 1950, DTC.
10. Sherman Adams, *First-Hand Report: The Story of the Eisenhower Administration* (New York: Harper and Brothers, 1961): 50.
11. Sherman Adams Papers, Box 30, Bert Georges to Adams, July 1, 1955, DDEL.
12. Gary W. Reichard, *The Reaffirmation of Republicanism: Eisenhower and the Eighty-Third Congress* (Knoxville: University of Tennessee Press, 1975): 174–175.
13. DDE Papers, Administration Series, Box 26, letter, DDE to Joseph W. Martin, Jr., December 31, 1953, DDEL.
14. Sherman Adams Papers, Scrapbook 18, clipping, *Manchester Union Leader*, March 26, 1949, DTC.
15. Ibid., Box 8, speech by Adams to New York Inter-Agency Committee, September 6, 1951, 3, DTC.
16. OH, Sherman Adams, April 10, 1967, 25, DDEL.
17. Margaret Chase Smith Papers, 1954 Election File, letter, James D. Ewing to JFK, June 18, 1953, MCSL.
18. U.S. Bureau of the Census, *Statistical Abstract of the United States: 1960* (Washington, DC: GPO, 1960): 205; and Browne and Sass, 202.
19. Eisenmerger, 9–10.
20. Council of Economic Advisers, *The New England Economy: A Report to the President* (Washington, DC: GPO, 1951): 8.

21. Kennedy, *Compendium*, 138.
22. Ibid., 157–180.
23. Ibid., 189.
24. Ibid., 197–220.
25. Ibid., 249.
26. John F. Kennedy, "What's the Matter with New England?" *New York Times Magazine* (November 8, 1953): 32.
27. John F. Kennedy, "New England and the South," *Atlantic Monthly* 193 (January 1954): 36.
28. Parmet, *Jack*, 266.
29. Theodore C. Sorensen Papers, Box 14, memo, "Pending Bills of Special Interest to New England," March 5, 1954, JFKL.
30. http://www.findingcamelot.net/remarks-of-senator-john-f-kennedy-on-the-boston-army-pier-to-the-senate-may-11-1954/; Leverett Saltonstall Papers, Box 301, press release, July 9, 1954; and Ibid., Box 186, letter, JFK to Saltonstall, July 6, 1953, MHS.
31. Sorensen, *Kennedy*, 58.
32. Leverett Saltonstall Papers, Box 314, press release, September 5, 1954, MHS.
33. Theodore C. Sorensen Papers, Box 11, copy of agenda, New England Senators' Conference, February 6, 1957, JFKL.
34. Sorensen, *Counselor*, 127–128; and Margaret Chase Smith Papers, Election 1954 File, letters, Rev. George Bullens to Smith, May 8, 1954, and Mrs. Edward Godfrey to Smith, February 17, 1954, MCSL.
35. Margaret Chase Smith Papers, St. Lawrence Seaway File, clipping, *Portland Press Herald*, August 29, 1954, MCSL; and DDE Diary Series, Box 4, White House staff memo, February 9, 1953, DDEL.
36. WHCF, OF 124, report on Lawrence, Massachusetts, Roy Williams to DDE, March 3, 1954; Ibid., letter, Bayard Ewing to Sherman Adams, February 23, 1954, DDEL.
37. DDE Papers, Administration Series, Box 24, letter, Henry Cabot Lodge, Jr., to DDE, February 16, 1954, DDEL.
38. Theodore C. Sorensen Papers, Box 14, JFK's speech on ICC, July 16, 1954, JFKL.
39. Margaret Chase Smith Papers, New England Governors' Conference File, letter, Donald W. Campbell to Dennis J. Roberts, May 9, 1956, MCSL.
40. Committee of New England of the National Planning Association. *The Economic State of New England* (New Haven, CT: Yale University Press, 1954).

41. Ibid., 449–621.
42. Ibid., 225–419.
43. Ibid., 721.
44. Theodore F. Green Papers, Box 838, speech by Alfred C. Neal, December 15, 1954, LOC.
45. Ibid., 5.
46. Ibid., 11.
47. Committee of New England, 599.
48. *Worcester Gazette*, August 6, 1954.
49. Theodore C. Sorensen Papers, Box 6, letter, JFK to Ayton F. Smith, August 13, 1954, 2, JFKL.
50. Leverett Saltonstall Papers, Box 314, unsigned memo, "Massachusetts and New England," September 20, 1954, MHS; and DDE Diary Series, Box 4, staff memo, December 13, 1954, DDEL.
51. Lasky, 168–170; Herbert S. Parmet, *Eisenhower and the American Crusades* (New York: Macmillan, 1972): 320–325; and Chester J. Pach, Jr., and Elmo Richardson, *The Presidency of Dwight D. Eisenhower* (Lawrence: University Press of Kansas, 1991): 72–73.
52. Dwight D. Eisenhower, *The White House Years: Mandate for Change, 1953–1956* (New York: Doubleday, 1963): 552–553.
53. WHCF, OF 138, Massachusetts (2) folder, letter, H.G. Barth to DDE, October 28, 1956, DDEL.
54. William E. Leuchtenburg, "Power in New England," *The Survey* 85 (September 1949): 460–464; and William E. Leuchtenburg, *Flood Control Politics: The Connecticut River Valley Problem, 1927–1950* (Cambridge, MA: Harvard University Press, 1953): 244–257.
55. WHCF, OF 155-B, Flood Control (1) folder, letter, Wilton B. Persons to Margaret Chase Smith, May 4, 1953, DDEL.
56. Prescott Bush Papers, Box 2, form letter from Bush, July 21, 1956, UCT; and WHCF, Box 23, memo, "Damage Bulletin," August 22, 1955, DDEL.
57. Prescott Bush Papers, Box 6, letter, New England Senators' Conference to Clarence Cannon, March 19, 1956, 2, UCT.
58. WHCF, OF 155-B, resolution from the New England Governors' Conference to the President of the United States, September 23, 1955, DDEL.
59. OH, Prescott Bush, July 7, 1966, 87–88, DDEL.
60. http://www.jfklibrary.org/Research/Research-Aids/JFK-Speeches/Springfield-MA-Rotary-Club_19561019.aspx.

61. Ibid.

62. Mark Rose, *Interstate: Express Politics, 1941–1956* (Lawrence: University Press of Kansas, 1979): 79–85.

63. Theodore C. Sorensen Papers, Box 11, letter, John W. McCormack to JFK, May 11, 1956, JFKL.

64. Ibid.

65. Ibid., memo, New England Senators' Conference Report, 1956, JFKL.

66. Sherman Adams, 264–265.

67. Eisenhower, *Mandate*, 555–556; and JFK PPP, Box 896, press release, October 19, 1956, 8, JFKL.

68. Theodore C. Sorensen Papers, Box 14, letter, George Aiken and Margaret Chase Smith to JFK, January 24, 1957, JFKL.

69. Ibid., Box 11, agenda for New England Senators' Conference, February 6, 1957, JFKL.

70. Margaret Chase Smith Papers, Statements and Speeches Collection, v. 14, Smith's statement to the O'Mahoney Committee, February 21, 1957, 2, MCSL.

71. Ibid., 6.

72. Ibid., clipping, *Waterville Sentinel*, May 17, 1957, MCSL.

73. Norris Cotton, *In the Senate: Amidst the Conflict and the Turmoil* (New York: Dodd, Mead, and Company, 1978): 149.

74. Theodore C. Sorensen Papers, Box 14, agenda for New England Senators' Conference, January 30, 1958, JFKL.

75. Sherman Adams, 394.

76. U.S. Bureau of the Census, 718–719.

77. Rowland Evans and Robert Novak, *Lyndon B. Johnson: The Exercise of Power* (New York: New American Library, 1966): 166.

78. Robert A. Caro, *The Years of Lyndon Johnson: Master of the Senate* (New York: Alfred A. Knopf, 2002): 859.

79. Theodore C. Sorensen Papers, Box 14, agenda of New England Senators' Conference, January 30, 1958, JFKL.

80. U.S. Bureau of the Census, 205.

81. Eisenhower, *Mandate*, 552–553.

82. Kennedy, *Compendium*, 138.

83. Ibid., 221–222; and R. Alton Lee, "Federal Assistance to Depressed Areas in the Postwar Recessions," *Western Economic Journal* 2 (September 1963): 1–5.

84. Kennedy, *Compendium*, 229–230; Paul H. Douglas, *In the Fullness of Time: The Memoir of Paul H. Douglas* (New York: Harcourt Brace

Jovanovich, Inc., 1971): 512–515; and Roger Biles, *Crusading Liberal: Paul H. Douglas of Illinois* (DeKalb: Northern Illinois University Press, 2002): 134.

85. Theodore C. Sorensen Papers, Box 11, memo, "New England Senators Conference: Report of Secretary on Activities during the 84th Congress, 1955–1956," released on August 6, 1956; and Box 14, press release, July 1, 1958, JFKL; and Lasky, 167–168.

86. Douglas, 513.

87. Evans and Novak, 113–114.

88. Douglas, 513.

89. WHCF, OF 124-A-1, report on Lawrence, Massachusetts, Roy Williams to DDE, March 3, 1954, 4, DDEL.

90. Ibid., letter, Robert H. Ryan to Gabriel Hauge, July 29, 1955, 2, DDEL.

91. OH, William L. Batt, October 26, 1966, 1–3, JFKL.

92. Robert H. Ferrell (ed.), *The Eisenhower Diaries* (New York: W. W. Norton and Company, 1981): 277–278; and Sherman Adams, 361–362.

93. OH, Batt, 1–5, JFKL.

94. Douglas, 516.

95. Sar A. Levitan, *Federal Aid to Depressed Areas: An Evaluation of the Area Redevelopment Administration* (Baltimore: The Johns Hopkins University Press, 1964): 5–6.

96. Douglas, 516.

97. Theo Lippman, Jr., and Donald C. Hansen, *Muskie* (New York: W.W. Norton and Company, 1971): 96–97.

98. James L. Sundquist, *Politics and Policy: The Eisenhower, Kennedy, and Johnson Years* (Washington, DC: Brookings Institution, 1968): 62–65.

99. R. Alton Lee, *Eisenhower and Landrum-Griffin: A Study in Labor-Management Politics* (Lexington: University Press of Kentucky, 1990): 82–83.

100. OH, Batt, 13, JFKL.

101. Lee, "Federal Assistance to Distressed Areas in the Postwar Recessions," 20; and Sundquist, 68–70.

102. Raymond J. Saulnier, *Constructive Years: The U.S. Economy under Eisenhower* (Lanham, MD: University Press of America, 1991): 183.

103. Woolley and Peters, 11127.

104. Eisenhower, *Mandate*, 553.

105. Biles, 147; and Sundquist, 63.

106. Woolley and Peters, 11781.

107. Levitan, 30.

108. Eisenhower, *Mandate*, 553; and Parmet, *Jack*, 270–271.

109. Irving Bernstein, *Promises Kept: John F. Kennedy's New Frontier* (New York: Oxford University Press, 1991): 168–171.

110. Kennedy, *Compendium*, 637.

111. Mark I. Gelfand, *A Nation of Cities: The Federal Government and Urban America, 1933–1965* (New York: Oxford University Press, 1975): 194.

112. Theodore C. Sorensen Papers, Box 14, agenda for New England Senators' Conference, January 30, 1958, JFKL; and DDE Diary Series, Box 4, staff memo, December 13, 1954, DDEL.

113. Michael P. Weber, *Don't Call Me Boss: David L. Lawrence, Pittsburgh's Renaissance Mayor* (Pittsburgh: University of Pittsburgh Press, 1988): 228; and David Kruh, *Always Something Doing: A History of Boston's Scollay Square* (Boston: Faber and Faber, 1990): 127.

114. Richard O. Davies, *Housing Reform During the Truman Administration* (Columbia: University of Missouri Press, 1966): 113–114.

115. O'Connor, 75–80.

116. Mark I. Gelfand, *Trustee for a City: Ralph Lowell of Boston* (Boston: Northeastern University Press, 1998): 260–261.

117. O'Connor, 106: and John H. Mollenkopf, *The Contested City* (Princeton, NJ: Princeton University Press, 1983): 150.

118. Gelfand, *Trustee for a City*, 272.

119. OH, Edward J. Logue, January 23, 1976, 1–2, JFKL.

120. Robert Dahl, "Urban Renewal in New Haven," in *Urban Renewal: People, Politics, and Planning*, ed. by Jewel Bellush and Murray Hausknecht (New York: Doubleday, 1967): 225–238.

121. David Rusk, *Inside Game/Outside Game: Winning Strategies for Saving Urban America* (Washington, DC: Brookings Institution, 1999): 90; Peter Wagner, *The Scope and Financing of Urban Renewal and Development* (Washington, DC: National Planning Association, 1963): 9–11; and Dennis R. Judd and Todd Swanstrom, *City Politics: Private Power and Public Policy* (New York: Harper Collins, 1994): 141–142.

122. Gelfand, *A Nation of Cities*, 292–293.

123. John K. Galbraith Papers, Box 75, letter, Raymond S. Rubinow to JFK, October 14, 1960, JFKL.

124. Bernstein, 30–34, 51–52.

125. Sean J. Savage, *JFK, LBJ, and the Democratic Party* (Albany: State University of New York Press, 2004): 101–102.

126. John W. Sloan, *Eisenhower and the Management of Prosperity* (Lawrence: University Press of Kansas, 1991): 157.

127. *Congressional Quarterly, Politics in America, 1945–1964* (Washington, DC: Congressional Quarterly Service, 1965): 30–32; and Pach and Richardson, 167–169.

128. Gelfand, *A Nation of Cities*, 193–194, 293–294.

129. http://www.findingcamelot.net/speeches/1960/remarks-of-senator-john-f-kennedy-at-urban-affairs-conference-pittsburgh-pennsylvania-october-10-1960/.

130. Richard M. Flanagan, "The Housing Act of 1954: The Sea Change in National Urban Policy," *Urban Affairs Review* v. 33, n. 2 (November 1997): 265.

131. Dahl, *Who Governs?*, 115–140.

132. Davies, 125–136.

133. Flanagan, 271–284; and D. Bradford Hunt, "How Did Public Housing Survive the 1950s?" *Journal of Policy History* v. 17, n. 2 (Spring 2005): 196–212.

134. Gelfand, *A Nation of Cities*, 191.

135. Kennedy, *Compendium*, 189–193.

136. Ibid., 189.

137. Dwight D. Eisenhower, *The White House Years: Waging Peace, 1956–1961* (New York: Doubleday, 1965): 376.

138. Richard T. Mahoney, *Sons and Brothers: The Days of Jack and Bobby Kennedy* (New York: Arcade Publishing, 1999): 23–27.

139. Joseph C. Goulden, *Meany: The Unchallenged Strong Man of Labor* (New York: Atheneum, 1972): 247–254.

140. Kevin Boyle, *The UAW and the Heyday of American Liberalism, 1945–1968* (Ithaca, NY: Cornell University Press, 1995): 132–133; and Arthur A. Sloane, *Hoffa* (Cambridge, MA: MIT Press, 1991): 50.

141. http://www.findingcamelot.net/speeches/remarks-of-senator-john-f-kennedy-at-the-associated-industries-of-massachusetts-annual-meeting--in-boston-massachusetts-october-24-1957/.

142. Ibid.

143. Savage, *JFK, LBJ, and the Democratic Party*, 40.

144. Theodore C. Sorensen Papers, Box 19, undated 1958 memo, "Why Republicans Should Vote to Re-Elect Senator Kennedy," JFKL.

145. Lee, *Eisenhower and Landrum-Griffin*, 81–82.

146. Robert F. Kennedy, *The Enemy Within* (New York: Popular Library, 1960): 304–307.

147. Lee, *Eisenhower and Landrum-Griffin*, 102–111.

148. Ibid., 130–132.

149. RFK, *The Enemy Within*, 306.

150. George H. Gallup, *The Gallup Poll: Public Opinion, 1935–1971*, v. 3 (New York: Random House, 1972): 1642–1643.

151. Saltonstall, 184.

152. OH, Bernard L. Boutin, June 3, 1964, 1–4, JFKL; and OH, Peter Kyros, Jr., June 4, 1999, 11, BTC.

153. JFK PPP, Box 906, JFK's speech in Manchester, NH, June 7, 1958, 5, JFKL.

154. Lippman and Hansen, 103.

155. OH, Donald E. Nicoll, November 14, 2002, 3–17, BTC.

156. Patricia Ward Wallace, *Politics of Conscience: A Biography of Margaret Chase Smith* (Westport, CT: Praeger, 1995): 151–152: and Margaret Chase Smith Papers, Election 1960 File, letter, Smith to Thomas J. Lloyd and Patrick Gorman, April 14, 1961, MCSL.

157. Charles H. W. Foster, *The Cape Cod National Seashore: A Landmark Alliance* (Hanover, NH: University Press of New England, 1985): vii.

158. Thad L. Beyle, "The Cape Cod National Sea Shore: A Study in Conflict," PhD diss., University of Illinois, 1963: 29–32.

159. Ibid., 1–2.

160. Ibid., 104–105, 129–131.

161. Francis P. Burling, *The Birth of the Cape Cod National Seashore* (Plymouth, MA: Leyden Press, 1979): 66.

162. Kennedy, *Compendium*, 901.

163. Leo Damore, *The Cape Cod Years of John Fitzgerald Kennedy* (New York: Four Walls Eight Windows Press, 1993): 112.

164. Ibid., 169.

165. Beyle, 147–150.

166. U.S. Senate, *Cape Cod National Seashore Park*, Hearing before the Subcommittee on Public Lands of the Committee on Interior and Insular Affairs, U.S. Senate, 87th Cong., 1st session, on S. 857, March 9, 1961 (Washington, DC: GPO, 1961): 58.

167. Ibid., 124.

168. Woolley and Peters, 8273.

169. Burling, 54.

Chapter 3

1. Kennedy, *Compendium*, 173.

2. Bertha R. Brown, "The Economic Background of Vermont's Republican Opposition to the New Deal in 1936," MA thesis, Claremont College, 1944: 55–68; Frank M. Bryan, *Yankee Politics in Rural Vermont*

(Hanover, NH: University Press of New England, 1974): 202–203; and Leuchtenburg, *Flood Control Politics*, 84–85.

3. James Wright, "Growing Up Progressive," in *The Political Legacy of George D. Aiken: Wise Old Owl of the U.S. Senate*, ed. by Michael Sherman (Woodstock, VT: Countryman Press, 1995): 32–33.

4. Charles F. O'Brien, "George Aiken and Canada," in Sherman, 117–122.

5. Leverett Saltonstall Papers, Box 134, press release, February 23, 1948, MHS.

6. William R. Willoughby, *The St. Lawrence Seaway: A Study in Politics and Diplomacy* (Madison: University of Wisconsin Press, 1961): 196.

7. Carleton Mabee, *The Seaway Story* (New York: Macmillan, 1961): 140.

8. George D. Aiken Papers, Box 46, Aiken's speech to Boston City Club, November 14, 1945, 4–7, UVM.

9. Ibid., 24.

10. Mabee, 150–151; Erwin L. Levine, *Theodore Francis Green: The Washington Years, 1937–1960* (Providence, RI: Brown University Press, 1971): 36–37; and OF 24, letter, HST to Joseph W. Martin, Jr., January 26, 1948, HSTL.

11. Mabee, 57.

12. Willoughby, *The St. Lawrence Seaway*, 145.

13. Ibid., 92.

14. Woolley and Peters, 23433.

15. Ibid., 14857.

16. Ibid., 14829.

17. Mabee, 103.

18. Woolley and Peters, 16124.

19. U.S. Department of Commerce, *The St. Lawrence Survey, Part IV: The Effect of the St. Lawrence Seaway Upon Existing Harbors* (Washington, DC: GPO, 1941): 44–45.

20. Ibid., 49.

21. Freeman Lincoln, "Battle of the St. Lawrence," *U.S. News and World Report* 46 (June 1, 1959): 50–54.

22. William R. Willoughby, "Canadian-American Defense Co-Operation," *Journal of Politics* v. 13, n. 4 (November 1951): 675–696.

23. Woolley and Peters, 12337.

24. OF 24, letter, HST to Joseph W. Martin, Jr., January 26, 1948, 2, HSTL.

25. Willoughby, *The St. Lawrence Seaway*, 205.

26. U.S. Senate, *St. Lawrence Seaway Project*, hearings before a subcommittee of the Committee on Foreign Relations, U.S. Senate, 80th Cong., 1st session, on S.J. Res. 111 (Washington, DC: GPO, 1947): 168–184.

27. Ibid., 169–170.

28. Ibid., 182–184.

29. Ibid., 235.

30. Ibid., 271.

31. Association of American Railroads, *The Great Delusion: Facts You Should Know about the Proposal to Build a St. Lawrence "Seaway"* (Washington, DC: Association of American Railroads, 1947): 9–11.

32. Ibid., 20.

33. Willoughby, *The St. Lawrence Seaway*, 207.

34. Ibid.

35. Leverett Saltonstall Papers, Box 134, letter, Saltonstall to Robert A. Taft, January 13, 1948, MHS.

36. Ibid., press release, February 23, 1948, 1–3, MHS.

37. Ibid., 4.

38. Mabee, 146.

39. William R. Willoughby, "Power Along the St. Lawrence," *Current History* (May 1958): 287.

40. Woolley and Peters, 13045.

41. Sherman Adams Papers, Scrapbook 13, clipping, *Manchester Union Leader*, November 18, 1948, DTC.

42. Willoughby, *The St. Lawrence Seaway*, 208.

43. Woolley and Peters, 13293.

44. Willoughby, *The St. Lawrence Seaway*, 226.

45. http://www.thecrimson.com/article/1949/11/18/brass-tacks-pif-currentpredictions-come/.

46. Claire Puccia Parham, *The St. Lawrence Seaway and Power Project: An Oral History of the Greatest Construction Show on Earth* (Syracuse, NY: Syracuse University Press, 2009): 16–19.

47. L. J. Rogers, "The St. Lawrence Seaway Project Is Vital to Canada's Progress," *Saturday Night* 64 (September 27, 1942): 30, 34; and H. C. Cochrane, "Could We Build the Seaway Alone?" *Canadian Business* (December 1950): 32–41.

48. Lionel Chevrier, *The St. Lawrence Seaway* (New York: St. Martin's Press, 1959): 42–43.

49. William R. Willoughby, "The St. Lawrence Waterway Understandings," *International Journal* v. 10, n. 3 (Summer 1955): 247.

50. Mabee, 157–158.

51. Woolley and Peters, 14228.

52. Willoughby, "The St. Lawrence Waterway Understandings," 238–239.

53. Freeman Lincoln, 189.

54. Great Lakes–St. Lawrence Association, *The Heartland: The Story of the Great Lakes–St. Lawrence Valley* (Washington, DC: Great Lakes–St. Lawrence Association, 1951); 19.

55. Iwan W. Morgan, *Eisenhower versus "The Spenders": The Eisenhower Administration, The Democrats, and the Budget, 1953–1960* (New York: St. Martin's Press, 1990): 15–17.

56. Aaron Wildavsky, *Dixon-Yates: A Study in Power Politics* (New Haven, CT: Yale University Press, 1962): 17.

57. Nathaniel R. Howard (ed.), *The Basic Papers of George M. Humphrey as Secretary of the Treasury, 1953–1957* (Cleveland: Western Reserve Society, 1965): 18–23.

58. DDE Diary Series, Box 4, staff memo, February 9, 1953, DDEL.

59. Mabee, 161–162.

60. Woolley and Peters, 9656.

61. Ibid., 9734.

62. Ibid.

63. Sherman Adams, 5; Sinclair Weeks Papers, Box 21, letter, Henry Cabot Lodge, Jr., to Weeks, December 3, 1952, DTC; and Herbert Brownell, *Advising Ike: The Memoirs of Attorney General Herbert Brownell* (Lawrence: University Press of Kansas, 1993): 135.

64. DDE Papers, Administration Series, Box 32, memo, March 30, 1953, DDEL.

65. Joe Martin, *My First Fifty Years in Politics* (New York: McGraw-Hill, 1960): 234.

66. James T. Patterson, *Mr. Republican: A Biography of Robert A. Taft* (Boston: Houghton Mifflin, 1972): 193.

67. Reichard, *The Reaffirmation of Republicanism*, 168; and Willoughby, *The St. Lawrence Seaway*, 287.

68. Woolley and Peters, 9825.

69. Willoughby, *The St. Lawrence Seaway*, 251.

NOTES TO CHAPTER 3

70. Leverett Saltonstall Papers, Box 134, letter, Christian A. Herter to John J. Holloran, April 14, 1953, MHS.
71. Ibid., press release from Paul T. Rothwell, December 20, 1952, 9, MHS.
72. TPO Papers, Box 291, letter, TPO to T.G. Sugrue, April 27, 1953, BC.
73. Ibid., telegram, Paul T. Rothwell to TPO, June 20, 1953, BC.
74. Ibid., letter, Maurice O'Connor to TPO, March 10, 1953, BC.
75. Ibid., letter, N. R. Danielian to TPO, January 29, 1953, BC.
76. Ibid., Box 125, letter, James Luchini to TPO, March 19, 1954, BC.
77. Ibid., letter, John W. Edelman to TPO, March 3, 1954, BC.
78. Ibid., undated 1954 speech draft by TPO, BC.
79. http://www.govtrack.us/congress/vote.xpd?vote=h1954-92.
80. Ibid.
81. Mabee, 288.
82. Parmet, *Jack*, 266–267.
83. Sorensen, *Kennedy*, 58–59.
84. http://www.jfklibrary.org/Asset-Viewer/Archives/JFKPP-039-005.aspx.
85. Ibid.
86. Committee of New England of the National Planning Association, 510–511.
87. Harris, *The Economics of New England*, 250.
88. Committee of New England of the National Planning Association, 540.
89. Sorensen, *Kennedy*, 59.
90. Kennedy, *Compendium*, 271.
91. Ibid., 276.
92. Willoughby, *The St. Lawrence Seaway*, 256.
93. Margaret Chase Smith papers, Scrapbooks, v. 144, 65, clipping, *Lewiston Sun*, January 21, 1954, MCSL.
94. Ibid.
95. Ibid.
96. Wallace, 103–121.
97. Quoted in Mabee, 288.
98. OH, George D. Aiken, April 25, 1964, 3–4, JFKL.
99. Saltonstall, 184.
100. O'Neill, 103.

NOTES TO CHAPTER 3

101. JFK PPP, Box 649, letter, John H. Alexander to JFK, January 16, 1954, JFKL.

102. Ibid., letter, Robert J. Mullins to JFK, January 15, 1954, JFKL; and Sorensen, *Kennedy*, 59.

103. Ibid., letters, Thomas F. Balfrey to JFK, January 15, 1954, and Arthur R. Garvey to JFK, January 16, 1954, JFKL.

104. TPO Papers, Box 125, letter, John W. Edelman to TPO, March 3, 1954, BC.

105. Quoted in Rachlin, 128.

106. http://www.findingcamelot.net/speeches/remarks-by-senator-john-f-kennedy-at-the-introduction-of-governor-g-mennen-williams-of-michigan-to-the-massachusetts-democratic-party-at-the-jefferson-jackson-day-dinner-boston-january-23-1954/.

107. Ibid.

108. John Buchan, *Pilgrim's Way: An Essay in Recollection* (Cambridge, MA: Houghton Mifflin, 1940): 231.

109. Leaming, 34–37.

110. John F. Kennedy, *Why England Slept* (New York: Doubleday, 1961): 17.

111. Ibid., 185.

112. http://www.findingcamelot.net/speeches/remarks-of-senator-john-f-kennedy-for-the-northeastern-university-convocation-symphony-hall-boston-massachusetts-december-2-1953/.

113. Ibid.

114. Ibid.; and Stanley Ayling, *Edmund Burke: His Life and Opinions* (New York: St. Martin's Press, 1988): 98–99.

115. OH, Herbert S. Parmet, August 9, 1983, 26–28, JFKL; Sorensen, *Counselor*, 147–149; and Christopher J. Matthews, *Jack Kennedy: Elusive Hero* (New York: Simon and Schuster, 2011): 190–191.

116. John F. Kennedy, *Profiles in Courage* (New York: Harper and Row, 1964): xvi.

117. Jacqueline Kennedy, *Historic Conversations on Life with John F. Kennedy: Interviews with Arthur M. Schlesinger, Jr., 1964* (New York: Hyperion, 2011): 59–62.

118. Sorensen, *Counselor*, 260.

119. Kennedy, *Profiles in Courage*, 43.

120. Parmet, *Jack*, 320–333.

121. OH, Parmet, 26, JFKL.

122. Parmet. *Jack*, 323.
123. Ibid., 333.
124. Ronald Kessler, *The Sins of the Father: Joseph P. Kennedy and the Dynasty He Founded* (New York: Warner Books, 1996): 350–351.
125. Robert Dallek, *An Unfinished Journey: John F. Kennedy, 1917–1963* (Boston: Little, Brown and Company, 2003): 123.
126. Arthur M. Schlesinger, Jr., *Journals: 1952–2000* (New York: Penguin Books, 2007): 57.
127. Arthur Krock, *Memoirs: Sixty Years on the Firing Line* (New York: Funk and Wagnalls, 1968): 376.
128. http://www.govtrack.us/congress/votes/83-1954/s95.
129. Margaret Chase Smith Papers, letter, Rev. George Bullens to Smith, May 8, 1954, MCSL.
130. Ibid., Scrapbooks, v. 136, 66, clipping, *Boston Sunday Herald*, March 21, 1954, MCSL.
131. Matthews, *Elusive Hero*, 170–171.
132. Kennedy, *Compendium*. 271–276.
133. Ibid., 138–139.

Chapter 4

1. Rachlin, 132–133.
2. http://www.findingcamelot.net/speeches/remarks-of-senator-john-f-kennedy-commencement-address-assumption-college-worcester-massachusetts-june-3-1955/.
3. JPK Papers, Box 231, letter, Frank Morrissey to JPK, June 28, 1955, JFKL.
4. Quoted in Damore, 145.
5. Ibid.
6. http://www.govtrack.us/congress/votes/84-1955/s40.
7. http://www.findingcamelot.net/speeches/remarks-of-senator-john-f-kennedy-before-the-annual-alumni-association-banquet-of-boston-college-business-administration-in-boston-october-29-1955/.
8. Ibid.
9. Ragsdale, 195.
10. Samuel Lubell, *Revolt of the Moderates* (New York: Harper and Brothers, 1956): 84.

11. CQ, *Politics in America, 1945–1964*, 20.
12. JPK Papers, Box 235, letter, George Smathers to JPK, November 9, 1954, JFKL.
13. Sinclair Weeks Papers, Basil Brewer folder, letter, Weeks to Brewer, December 14, 1954, DTC.
14. Clare Booth Luce Papers, Box 619, letter, Luce to JFK, November 12, 1955, LOC.
15. Rachlin, 136.
16. Eisenhower, *Mandate*, 535; and David A. Nichols, *Eisenhower 1956: The President's Year of Crisis, Suez and the Brink of War* (New York: Simon and Schuster, 2011): 20–23.
17. Ferrell, 304; and Stephen E. Ambrose, *Nixon: The Education of a Politician, 1913–1962* (New York: Simon and Schuster, 1987): 396–397.
18. Woolley and Peters, 10742.
19. Earl Mazo and Stephen Hess, *Nixon: A Political Portrait* (New York: Harper and Row, 1968): 144; and Jean Edward Smith, *Eisenhower in War and Peace* (New York: Random House, 2012): 84–85.
20. Mazo and Hess, 146.
21. Sherman Adams, 21.
22. Ibid., 239.
23. Mazo and Hess, 155.
24. Richard M. Nixon, *Six Crises* (New York: Doubleday, 1962): 167.
25. Martin and Plaut, 18–19.
26. Robert Dallek, *Lone Star Rising: Lyndon Johnson and His Times, 1908–1960* (New York: Oxford University Press, 1991): 489–490.
27. Ibid., 490–491.
28. David McKean, *Tommy the Cork: Washington's Ultimate Insider from Roosevelt to Reagan* (South Royalton, VT: Steerforth Press, 2004): 231.
29. Dallek, *Lone Star Rising*, 489.
30. *NYT*, November 16, 1955.
31. Ibid., December 4, 1955.
32. John Bartlow Martin, *Adlai Stevenson and the World* (New York: Doubleday, 1977): 236.
33. OH, Fletcher Knebel, August 1, 1977, 4, JFKL.
34. Dallek, *An Unfinished Life*, 204.
35. *NYT*, February 5, 1956.
36. Rachlin, 139.

37. OH, Maurice Donahue, April 27, 1976, 12, JFKL.

38. Ibid.

39. Thomson and Shattuck, 32.

40. Rudy Abramson, *Spanning the Century: The Life of W. Averell Harriman, 1891–1986* (New York: Morrow, 1992): 532–538.

41. Parmet, *Jack*, 338.

42. Sean J. Savage, *Roosevelt: The Party Leader, 1932–1945* (Lexington: University Press of Kentucky, 1991): 127; and Savage, *Truman and the Democratic Party*, 202.

43. John Bartlow Martin, 208.

44. Fuchs, "Presidential Politics in Boston: The Irish Response to Stevenson," 435–444.

45. *NYT*, December 17, 1955.

46. Russell Baker, *The Good Times* (New York: William Morrow and Company, 1989): 302.

47. CQ, *Guide*, 334.

48. Adam Cohen and Elizabeth Taylor, *American Pharaoh: Mayor Richard J. Daley, His Battle for Chicago and the Nation* (Boston: Little, Brown and Company, 2000): 194–195; and David Halberstam, *The Fifties* (New York: Villard Books, 1993): 190–194.

49. *NYT*, December 17, 1955.

50. Caro, *Master of the Senate*, 785–786.

51. Jeff Broadwater, *Adlai Stevenson and American Politics: The Odyssey of a Cold War Liberal* (New York: Twayne, 1994): 156–157.

52. Rachlin, 140.

53. CQ, *Guide*, 336.

54. Charles A. H. Thomson and Frances M. Shattuck, *The 1956 Presidential Campaign* (Washington, DC: Brookings Institution, 1960): 38.

55. Hubert H. Humphrey, *The Education of a Public Man: My Life and Politics* (New York; Doubleday, 1976): 136.

56. CQ, *Guide*, 336.

57. *NYT*, March 22, 1956.

58. Thomson and Shattuck, 41–42.

59. John Bartlow Martin, 268.

60. Burns, 170–171.

61. CQ, *Guide*, 336.

62. *NYT*, April 26, 1956.

63. O'Donnell and Powers, 129–133.

64. Sorensen, *Counselor*, 170.
65. Lasky, 590.
66. Scott Stossel, *Sarge: The Life and Times of Sargent Shriver* (Washington, DC: Smithsonian Books, 2004): 132.
67. Martin and Plaut, 23.
68. Amanda Smith, 671.
69. *NYT*, May 31, 1956.
70. http://www.jfklibrary.org/Asset-Viewer/4VOsnH5ay0SrXm3fyVkgqw.aspx.
71. *NYT*, June 10, 1956.
72. Ibid., June 26, 1956.
73. Amanda Smith, 672.
74. Thomson and Shattuck, 63–64.
75. Ibid., 62–63.
76. Abramson, 532–538.
77. *NYT*, August 1, 1956.
78. Charles L. Fontenay, *Estes Kefauver: A Biography* (Knoxville: University of Tennessee Press, 1980): 264.
79. Rachlin, 144.
80. John Bartlow Martin, 343.
81. *NYT*, July 20, 1956.
82. Humphrey, 136.
83. Ibid., 137.
84. Kennedy, *Compendium*, 455.
85. Rachlin, 144.
86. Ronald Brownstein, *The Power and the Glitter: The Hollywood-Washington Connection* (New York: Pantheon Books, 1990): 146.
87. McCarthy, 121; and Democratic National Committee (DNC), *Official Report of the Proceedings of the Democratic National Convention, 1956* (Washington, DC: Democratic National Committee, 1956): 36. Subsequently cited as DNC, *1956 Proceedings*.
88. John Bartlow Martin, 344.
89. Sorensen, *Kennedy*, 84.
90. Ibid.
91. http://www.jfklibrary.org/Asset-Viewer/Archives/JFKPOF-135-016.aspx.
92. *NYT*, August 9, 1956.
93. Ibid., August 10, 1956.

94. Ibid.
95. Rachlin, 144.
96. O'Donnell and Powers, 135.
97. O'Brien, *No Final Victories*, 51.
98. Amanda Smith, 676.
99. Ibid.
100. *NYT*, August 9, 1956.
101. Ibid., August 13, 1956.
102. Ibid., August 12, 1956.
103. Robert Sherrill and Harry W. Ernst, *The Drugstore Liberal: Hubert Humphrey in Politics* (New York: Grossman, 1968): 150; and DNC, *1956 Proceedings*, 201–203.
104. *Worcester Telegram*, August 13, 1956.
105. *NYT*, August 12, 1956.
106. Dinneen, *The Kennedy Family*, 191.
107. *Worcester Telegram*, August 13, 1956.
108. Ibid., August 14, 1956.
109. Ibid., August 15, 1956.
110. Dinneen, *The Kennedy Family*, 194.
111. Rachlin, 144; and OH, Edmund S. Muskie, January 4, 1966, 14, JFKL.
112. Eleanor Roosevelt, *On My Own* (New York: Harper and Brothers, 1958): 162–163.
113. Broadwater, 161.
114. Sorensen, *Kennedy*, 86.
115. Ibid., 87.
116. DNC, *1956 Proceedings*, 345.
117. Ibid., 405–406.
118. Ibid., 411.
119. CQ, *Guide*, 45.
120. DNC, *1956 Proceedings*, 420.
121. Ibid.
122. Martin and Plaut, 17–19.
123. Fontenay, 264.
124. Weber, 338; and Ralph G. Martin, *Ballots and Bandwagons* (New York: Rand McNally, 1964): 383.
125. Roosevelt, *On My Own*, 164.
126. O'Donnell and Powers, 135–136.

127. C. David Heymann, *RFK: A Candid Biography of Robert F. Kennedy* (New York: Dutton, 1998): 109–111; and Mahoney, 23.
128. Kessler, 361.
129. Stossel, 133.
130. Cohen and Taylor, 194–195.
131. DNC, *1956 Proceedings*, 438.
132. Ibid., 439.
133. Thomson and Shattuck, 158.
134. Lasky, 183–184.
135. OH, Camille F. Gravel, May 23, 1967, 6–10, JFKL.
136. Ibid., 14.
137. DNC, *1956 Proceedings*, 465.
138. OH, William C. Battle, March 2, 1970, 3–5, JFKL; and OH, Luther H. Hodges, March 19, 1964, 1–2, JFKL.
139. DNC, *1956 Proceedings*, 471, 473.
140. Ibid., 473.
141. Caro, *Master of the Senate*, 826–827.
142. OH, Albert A. Gore, Sr., August 13 and 21, 1964, 4–6, JFKL.
143. Martin, *Ballots and Bandwagons*, 442; and Fontenay, 277.
144. Thomson and Shattuck, 161.
145. DNC, *1956 Proceedings*, 481.
146. Thomson and Shattuck, 161.
147. DNC, *1956 Proceedings*, 482.
148. Amanda Smith, 677.
149. OH, Charles Bartlett, January 6, 1965, 33–34, JFKL.
150. Sorensen, *Kennedy*, 100.
151. Wildavsky, 235–236; and John Bartlow Martin, 365–367.
152. Adlai E. Stevenson, *The New America* (London: Rupert Hart-Davis, 1957): 49.
153. Ralph Toledano, *R.F.K.: The Man Who Would Be President* (New York: Dell Books, 1967): 147.
154. http://www.findingcamelot.net/speeches/1956/remarks-of-senator-john-f-kennedy-at-the-los-angeles-world-affairs-council-luncheon-at-the-biltmore-hotel-on-september-21-1956/.
155. Ibid.
156. http://www.findingcamelot.net/speeches/1956/remarks-of-senator-john-f-kennedy-at-the-annual-convention-banquet-of-young-democrats-of-north-carolina-in-winston-salem-nc-october-5-1956/.

157. http://www.findingcamelot.net/speeches/1956/remarks-of-senator-john-f-kennedy-at-the-junior-chamber-of-commerce-dinner-in-richmond-virginia-october-15-1956/.

158. Robert E. Thompson and Hortense Myers, *Robert F. Kennedy: The Brother Within* (New York: Dell Books, 1962): 184–185.

159. JFK PPP, New Hampshire folder, letter, Henry P. Sullivan to Sorensen, September 27, 1956, JFKL.

160. Ibid., Maine folder, letter, Donald E. Nicoll to Sorensen, October 10, 1956, JFKL.

161. Ibid.

162. Lockard, 100–103.

163. OH, Donald E. Nicoll, November 14, 2002, 21–23, BTC.

164. DNC, *1956 Proceedings*, 464, 480.

165. OH, Peter Kyros, Jr., June 4, 1999, 3–11, BTC; and Edmund S. Muskie Papers, Series 10, Box 88, letter, Dennis Roberts to Muskie, August 27, 1956, BTC.

166. OH, Furcolo, 6–7, JFKL.

167. OH, Richard K. Donahue, November 1, 1966, 42–43, JFKL.

168. Ibid., 44.

169. JFK POF, Box 136, letters, J. Lincoln Ritchie to JFK, September 20, 1956, H. Clinton Leef to JFK, October 29, 1956, and Louise Pickering to JFK, October 29, 1956, JFKL.

170. JFK POF, Box 135, letter, JFK to Chattie Slayton, October 16, 1956, JFKL.

171. Lasky, 195.

172. OH, Richard K. Donahue, 43–45, JFKL.

173. Arthur M. Schlesinger, Jr., *Robert Kennedy and His Times* (New York: Ballantine Books, 1978): 144–146.

174. Heymann, 116.

175. Stevenson, 274–278.

176. Ibid., 278.

177. JFK POF, Box 135, clipping, *Berkshire Eagle*, October 15, 1956, JFKL.

178. Woolley and Peters, 10655.

179. Ibid., 10681.

180. Stephen E. Ambrose, *Eisenhower: Soldier and President* (New York: Simon and Schuster, 1990): 423–440.

181. Woolley and Peters, 10685.

182. CQ, *Guide*, 256, 295.
183. CQ, *Politics in America, 1945–1964*, 23.
184. Ibid., 26.
185. Angus Campbell, Philip E. Converse, Warren E. Miller, and Donald E. Stokes, *The American Voter: An Abridgement* (New York: Werbel and Peck, 1964): 16–28.
186. CQ, *Guide*, 295.
187. Ibid., 832.
188. Ibid., 414.
189. *Springfield Daily News*, November 7, 1956.
190. *Worcester Telegram*, November 8, 1956.
191. Ibid.
192. Ibid.
193. JFK PPP, Box 896, copy, remarks of Senator John F. Kennedy, Tavern Club, November 8, 1956, JFKL.
194. Ibid., 3.
195. Ibid., 5–6.
196. Ibid., 15.
197. James Q. Wilson, *The Amateur Democrat: Club Politics in Three Cities* (Chicago: University of Chicago Press, 1962): 53–55.
198. JFK POF, Box 136, letter, Russell F. Taylor to JFK, October 30, 1956, JFKL.
199. *Worcester Telegram*, August 18, 1956.
200. Ibid., November 7, 1956.
201. *Boston Globe*, November 7, 1956.
202. JFK POF, Box 136, letter, J. Lincoln Ritchie to JFK, September 20, 1956, JFKL.
203. JFK PPP, Box 505, letter, Robert X. Tivnan to JFK, November 13, 1956, JFKL.
204. JFK POF, Box 135, telegram, W.E. Dupre to JFK, August 14, 1956, JFKL.

Chapter 5

1. DDE Papers, Administration Series, Box 1, unsigned, undated RNC memo to DDE, 1956, DDEL.
2. Ibid., 2.

3. George C. Roberts, *Paul M. Butler: Hoosier Politician and National Political Leader* (Lanham, MD: University Press of America, 1987): 105–106.

4. Theodore C. Sorensen Papers, Box 11, letter, JFK to Paul M. Butler, February 7, 1957, JFKL; and Sidney Hyman, "The Collective Leadership of Paul M. Butler," *The Reporter* 21 (December 24, 1959): 11.

5. D. B. Hardeman and Donald C. Bacon, *Rayburn: A Biography* (New York: Madison Books, 1987): 407.

6. Philip A. Klinkner, *The Losing Parties: Out-Party National Committees, 1956–1993* (New Haven, CT: Yale University Press, 1994): 23–24; and Roberts, 91–100.

7. Savage, *Truman and the Democratic Party*, 202; and Robert H. Ferrell (ed.), *Off the Record: The Private Papers of Harry S. Truman* (New York: Penguin Books, 1982); 381–383.

8. *NYT*, December 7, 1956.

9. Ibid., January 9, 1957.

10. Caro, *Master of the Senate*, 858–860.

11. LBJA, Congressional Files, Box 55, letter, Estes Kefauver to LBJ, January 9, 1957, LBJL.

12. Ibid., letter, LBJ to Kefauver, January 10, 1957, LBJL.

13. Robert F. Kennedy, *The Enemy Within*, 15–16.

14. Pierre Salinger, *With Kennedy* (New York: Avon Books, 1966): 41–42.

15. Sloane, 95–96.

16. Dallek, *Lone Star Rising*, 555.

17. Sorensen, *Kennedy*, 51.

18. Russell Turner, "Senator Kennedy: The Perfect Politician," *American Mercury* 84 (March 1957): 33.

19. McCarthy, 132.

20. Boyle, 140.

21. OH, Barry M. Goldwater, January 24, 1965, 1–3, JFKL.

22. http://www.jfklibrary.org/Asset-Viewer/ixCZibQPOai_yWm-HAGXag.aspx.

23. http://www.jfklibrary.org/Asset-Viewer/PoMHdkbcxE-SvBkTX-Wdqg.aspx.

24. http://www.jfklibrary.org/Asset-Viewer/X4LGdOg9UEOvvOM-4mThPKQ.aspx.

25. Kennedy, *Compendium*, 530.

26. Ibid., 532.

27. Woolley and Peters, 10828.

28. *NYT*, July 8, 1957.

29. Alistair Horne, *A Savage War of Peace: Algeria, 1954–1962* (New York: Penguin Books, 1977): 247.

30. Sorensen, *Kennedy*, 65.

31. Ronald J. Nurse, "Critic of Colonialism: JFK and Algerian Independence," *Historian* 39 (February 1977): 307–326.

32. Burns, 187.

33. Kennedy, *Compendium*, 549.

34. Ibid., 564.

35. Ibid., 548–549.

36. Ibid., 506–511.

37. John F. Kennedy, *A Nation of Immigrants* (New York: Harper and Row, 1964): x.

38. Joshua L. Rosenbloom, "The Challenges of Economic Maturity: New England, 1880–1940," in Temin, 173–174.

39. http://www.jfklibrary.org/Asset-Viewer/Archives/JFKPPP-64.aspx.

40. John F. Kennedy, "A Democrat Looks at Foreign Policy," *Foreign Affairs* 36 (October 1957): 44.

41. Ibid., 59.

42. OH, Lawrence H. Fuchs, November 28, 1966, 1–8, JFKL.

43. http://www.jfklibrary.org/Asset-Viewer/ZkLppoxhHEySBMYcAQ-M5A.aspx.

44. Ibid.

45. Nurse, 323–326.

46. Silvestri, 79.

47. Stanley and Niemi, 105.

48. Stern, 15–16; and Robert Mann, *The Walls of Jericho: Lyndon Johnson, Richard Russell, and the Struggle for Civil Rights* (New York: Harcourt Brace and Company, 1996): 154–166.

49. OH, Robert R. Nathan, June 9, 1967, 3–5, JFKL.

50. OH, Samuel H. Beer, November 7, 2002, 39–40, JFKL; Lasky, 134–136; Murray B. Levin, *Kennedy Campaigning* (Boston: Beacon Press, 1966): 39–40; and Allida M. Black, *Casting Her Own Shadow: Eleanor Roosevelt and the Shaping of Postwar Liberalism* (New York: Columbia University Press, 1996): 169–175.

51. OH, John L. Saltonstall, January 16, 1969, 10–11, JFKL.

52. OH, Joseph L. Rauh, Jr., December 23, 1965, 39–40, JFKL.

53. Stern, 120–128.
54. Caro, *Master of the Senate*, 811–813.
55. Evans and Novak, 137.
56. Schlesinger, *Journals: 1952–2000*, 52.
57. Brownell, 218–220.
58. Charles V. Hamilton. *Adam Clayton Powell, Jr.: The Political Biography of an American Dilemma* (New York: Collier Books, 1991): 266–281.
59. Brownell, 218–219.
60. Mann, 184.
61. Biles, 120–121.
62. Stern, 135–136.
63. Mann, 186.
64. Biles, 122.
65. Ibid., 124.
66. Evans and Novak, 146.
67. Biles, 124–125.
68. James C. Duram, *A Moderate among Extremists: Dwight D. Eisenhower and the School Desegregation Crisis* (Chicago: Nelson-Hall, 1981): 148–157.
69. Theodore C. Sorensen Papers, Box 19, letter, JFK to Mrs. W. G. Dwight, July 10, 1957, JFKL.
70. Ibid., letter, JFK to Clarence Mitchell, July 10, 1957, JFKL.
71. Stern, 17–19.
72. http://www.govtrack.us/congress/votes/85-1957/s73.
73. OH, Frank Church, November 5, 1981, 2–4, JFKL.
74. Theodore C. Sorensen Papers, Box 10, JFK press release, October 18, 1957, JFKL.
75. "Through the Roadblock," *Time* v. 70, n. 18 (October 28, 1957): 25.
76. Ibid.
77. U.S. Bureau of the Census, 205.
78. Ibid., 332–335.
79. Harold G. Vatter, *The U.S. Economy in the 1950s: An Economic History* (New York: W. W. Norton and Company, 1963): 116.
80. Alvin H. Hansen, *Economic Issues of the 1960s* (New York: McGraw-Hill, 1960): 142.
81. WHCF, GF 126-I-1, Box 965, letter, Mrs. Richard Jillson to James Hagerty, June 3, 1958, DDEL.

82. Sloan, 144; and Hugh S. Norton, *The Quest for Economic Stability: From Roosevelt to Bush* (Columbia: University of South Carolina Press, 1991): 124–125.

83. Raymond J. Saulnier, *Constructive Years: The U.S. Economy under Eisenhower* (Lanham, MD: University Press of America, 1991): 96–97.

84. Eisenhower, *Waging Peace*, 310.

85. Sloan, 150.

86. Woolley and Peters, 10877.

87. Ibid., 11262.

88. http://www.jfklibrary.org/Research/Research-Aids/JFK-Speeches/Remarks-of-Senator-John-F-Kennedy-at-the-Annual-Dinner-and-Reception-of-the-Democratic-Party-of-Cook.aspx.

89. Kennedy, *Compendium*, 590.

90. http://www.jfklibrary.org/Asset-Viewer/DX3cX8LT70u_UhskAlynPg.aspx.

91. Klinkner, 25–26; and Cornelius P. Cotter and Bernard C. Hennessy, *Politics Without Power: The National Party Committees* (New York: Atherton Press, 1964): 130–131.

92. Drexel A. Sprecher Papers, Box 7, DAC press release, October 20, 1957, 7, JFKL.

93. Ibid., February 1, 1958, 1, JFKL.

94. Theodore H. White, 49–56.

95. Edward P. Morgan, "The Missouri Compromise: Stuart Symington," in *Candidates 1960*, ed. by Eric Sevareid (New York: Basic Books, 1959): 245–279.

96. Carl Solberg, *Hubert Humphrey: A Biography* (New York: W. W. Norton and Company, 1984): 166–168.

97. Pach and Richardson, 178; and Eisenhower, *Waging Peace*, 243.

98. http://www.jfklibrary.org/Asset-Viewer/LsiFsGcdskuv9w46MYDuvg.aspx.

99. Ibid.

100. Fletcher Knebel, "Pulitzer Prize Entry: John F. Kennedy," in *Candidates 1960*, 187.

101. Silvestri, 94–95.

102. James N. Giglio, *The Presidency of John F. Kennedy* (Lawrence: University Press of Kansas, 1991): 17.

103. Lee, *Eisenhower and Landrum-Griffin*, 72–73.

104. Kennedy, *Compendium*, 585.

105. Ibid., 587.

106. Evans and Novak, 232.

107. OH, Ralph A. Dungan, December 9, 1967, 35–36; and Sorensen, *Kennedy*, 53–54.

108. Kennedy, *Compendium*, 669.

109. Woolley and Peters, 11163.

110. Ibid.

111. Ibid.

112. Quoted in Lee, *Eisenhower and Landrum Griffin*, 84.

113. Ibid.

114. Ralph K. Huitt, "Democratic Party Leadership in the Senate," *American Political Science Review* v. 55, n. 2 (June 1961): 340.

115. Parmet, *Jack*, 430.

116. Lee, *Eisenhower and Landrum-Griffin*, 34; and OH, Goldwater, 1–4, JFKL.

117. Lee, *Eisenhower and Landrum-Griffin*, 86.

118. John Van Camp, "What Happened to the Labor Reform Bill?" *The Reporter* 19 (October 2, 1958): 24.

119. OH, Andrew J. Biemiller, March 11, 1965, 4, JFKL.

120. "Done to Death," *Time* v. 72, n. 9 (September 1, 1958): 1.

121. Parmet, *Jack*, 431.

122. OH, George S. McGovern, April 24, 1964, 1–7, JFKL.

123. Lee, *Eisenhower and Landrum-Griffin*, 87.

124. Ibid, 88–89; and *NYT*, August 19, 1958.

125. Parmet, *Jack*, 431.

126. Van Camp, 28.

127. Woolley and Peters, 11181.

128. Ibid.

129. Burns, 211.

130. *Lowell Sun*, October 26, 1958.

131. JFK PPP, Box 901, JFK speech delivered by Torbert Macdonald in Fitchburg, Massachusetts on May 10, 1958, JFKL; and author's interview with John J. McNally, Jr., in Webster, Massachusetts on September 15, 2011.

132. James Boyd, *Above the Law: The Rise and Fall of Senator Thomas J. Dodd* (New York: New American Library, 1968): 18–23; and Joseph I. Lieberman, *The Power Broker: A Biography of John M. Bailey, Modern Political Boss* (Boston: Houghton Mifflin, 1966): 207.

133. Thomas J. Dodd Papers, Box 276, Dodd press release, May 28, 1958, UCT.

134. *Portsmouth Herald*, June 9, 1958.

135. Lockard, 52.

136. OH, Bernard L. Boutin, June 3, 1964, 1–3, JFKL.

137. DNC, *1956 Proceedings*, 465, 481.

138. JFK PPP, Box 901, JFK's speech in Manchester, New Hampshire, June 7, 1958, 5, JFKL.

139. Ibid., 17.

140. JFK PPP, Box 901, JFK's speech in Hartford, Connecticut, June 27, 1958, JFKL.

141. Ibid., 25.

142. CQ, *Guide*, 411.

143. Ibid., 832.

144. Lippman and Hansen, 92.

145. OH, John C. Donovan, June 19, 1978, 7, JFKL.

146. DNC, *1956 Proceedings*, 464.

147. CQ, *Guide*, 493.

148. *Biddeford Journal*, September 9, 1958.

149. OH, Nicoll, 2002, 11, BTC.

150. Lockard, 13.

151. Bryan,*Yankee Politics in Rural Vermont*, 94–96.

152. Samuel B. Hand and Paul M. Searls, "Transition Politics: Vermont, 1940–1952," *Vermont History* v. 62, n. 2 (April 1994): 15–17; Harris E. Thurber, "Vermont: The Stirrings of Change," in *Party Politics in New England States*, ed. by George Goodwin, Jr., and Victoria Schuck (Durham, NH: New England Center for Continuing Education, 1968): 71–78; and Wallace, 120–127.

153. Douglas I. Hodgkin, "Breakthrough Elections: Elements of Large and Durable Minority Party Gains in Selected States Since 1944," PhD diss., Duke University, 1966: 77–79; and OH, Donald E. Nicoll, February 27, 1992, 12–16, BTC.

154. Hodgkin, 11.

155. CQ, *Guide*, 434.

156. William Doyle, *The Vermont Political Tradition and Those Who Helped Make It* (Barre, VT: Northlight Studio Press, 1984): 200.

157. *Bennington Evening Banner*, September 29, 1958.

158. Ibid., September 25, 1958.

159. JFK PPP, Box 901, JFK's speech in Burlington, Vermont, September 26, 1958, 1, JFKL.

160. Ibid., 7.

NOTES TO CHAPTER 5

161. JFK PPP, Box 966, letter, Clyde T. Ellis to JFK, September 30, 1958, JFKL.
162. Lasky, 168–169.
163. *NYT*, May 27, 1956.
164. Samuel B. Hand, *The Star That Set: The Vermont Republican Party, 1854–1974* (New York: Rowman and Littlefield, 2003): 218.
165. JFK PPP, Box 966, letter, JFK to E. Frank Branon, June 17, 1958, JFKL.
166. Ibid., letters, JFK to Charles McDevitt and William A. Meyer, both November 3, 1958, JFKL.
167. *Bennington Evening Banner*, September 29, 1959.
168. Maureen Moakley and Elmer Cornwell, *Rhode Island Politics and Government* (Lincoln: University of Nebraska Press, 2001): 27; and Murray S. Stedman, "The Rise of the Democratic Party of Rhode Island," *New England Quarterly* v. 24, n. 3 (September 1951): 329–351.
169. Levine, 62; and John O. Pastore Papers, General Files, letters, JFK to Pastore, July 25, 1953 and January 30, 1958, PC.
170. DNC, *1956 Proceedings*, 465, 481.
171. Ibid., letter, JFK to Pastore, September 7, 1956, PC.
172. OH, John E. Fogarty, April 14, 1965, 4–5, JFKL; and OH, Dennis J. Roberts, December 1, 1966, 2–7, JFKL.
173. *Bridgeport Post*, June 22, 1958.
174. *North Adams Transcript*, September 18, 1958.
175. "Roberts' Rules of Order," *Time* v. 69, n. 2 (January 14, 1957): 25.
176. *Worcester Telegram*, November 5, 1956.
177. Lockard, 144.
178. O'Brien, *No Final Victories*, 54–55.
179. Joseph D. Ward (ed.), *Election Statistics: Commonwealth of Massachusetts, 1958* (Boston: Commonwealth of Massachusetts, 1959): 44, 50.
180. O'Donnell and Powers, 160.
181. *NYT*, October 19, 1958.
182. Ward (ed.), 152.
183. Theodore C. Sorensen Papers, Box 19, memo, "What Senator Kennedy Has Done for Italians," undated 1958, JFKL.
184. JFK POF, Box 136, letter, JFK to Adamo D'Ambrosia, October 23, 1958, JFKL.
185. Theodore C. Sorensen Papers, Box 19, JFK press release, September 25, 1958, JFKL.

186. Ibid., undated 1958 memo, Robert E. Thompson to Philip Cordaro, JFKL.
187. *Newport Daily News*, October 17, 1958.
188. EMK, *True Compass*, 123–124.
189. Helen O'Donnell, 154–165.
190. Evelyn Lincoln, *My Twelve Years with John F. Kennedy* (New York: David McKay, 1965): 115–116.
191. Sorensen, *Kennedy*, 74.
192. Ibid., 75.
193. Burns, 206.
194. OH, Richard K. Donahue, 49–50, JFKL; and McNally interview, September 23, 2011.
195. John J. McNally, Jr., *From the Little Green House to the White House and Beyond* (Anaheim, CA: Creative Continuum, 2008): 21; and OH, Paul W. Glennon, October 17, 1977, 5–6, JFKL.
196. McNally book, 22.
197. Ibid.
198. OH, Joseph A. Curnane, November 29, 1966, 46–47, and OH, John H. Treanor, Jr., September 28, 1977, 3, both JFKL.
199. Helen O'Donnell, 163.
200. Parmet, *Jack*, 457.
201. Farrell, 150.
202. OH, Thomas P. Costin, April 5, 1976, 9–10, JFKL.
203. OH, Samuel Bornstein, April 15, 1977, 1–2, JFKL.
204. McNally interview, September 23, 2011.
205. CQ, *Guide*, 494.
206. *Lowell Sun*, October 25, 1958.
207. OH, Paul G. Donelan, April 7, 1964, 6, JFKL.
208. Jacqueline Kennedy, 35.
209. OH, Francis X. Morrissey, June 9, 1964, 53, JFKL; and O'Brien, *No Final Victories*, 57.
210. O'Donnell and Powers, 162–163.
211. *Telegram Towns*, September 22, 2011.
212. Theodore C. Sorensen Papers, Box 19, clipping, *Boston Traveler*, October 6, 1958, JFKL.
213. O'Brien, *No Final Victories*, 57.
214. Burton Hersh, *Edward Kennedy: An Intimate Biography* (Berkeley, CA: Counterpoint Press, 2010): 98.

215. Betty Taymor, *Running Against the Wind: The Struggle of Women in Massachusetts* (Boston: Northeastern University Press, 2000): 41.
216. Theodore C. Sorensen Papers, Box 19, memo, JFK to staff, December, 1957, JFKL.
217. *Lowell Sun*, October 26, 1958.
218. Ibid.
219. *NYT*, September 12, 1958.
220. Ibid., September 13, 1958.
221. Ibid., September 14, 1958.
222. Ibid., October 18, 1958.
223. *Oelwein Daily Register*, October 17, 1958.
224. OH, Randolph, 2, JFKL.
225. *Charleston Daily Mail*, June 12, 1958.
226. *Morgantown Post*, June 12, 1958.
227. http://www.wvculture.org/history/1960presidentialcampaign/annotatedtimeline.html.
228. *Charleston Daily Mail*, October 10, 1958.
229. *NYT*, October 10, 1958.
230. Ibid.
231. OH, Vincent J. Celeste, October 3, 1977, 33–34, JFKL.
232. *Lowell Sun*, October 25, 1958.
233. *NYT*, October 19, 1958.
234. EMK, *True Compass*, 125.
235. *Worcester Telegram*, October 5, 1958.
236. OH, Celeste, 48–49, JFKL
237. Ibid., 51–52.
238. Damore, 159.
239. Ibid., 159.
240. GF 126-I-1, Box 264, letter, W. Rea Long to Maxwell Rabb, March 12, 1958, DDEL.
241. Ragsdale, 196.
242. Pach and Richardson, 180–182.
243. *Portsmouth Herald*, October 27, 1958.
244. Gallup, v. 2, 1521.
245. Ibid., 1528.
246. WHCF, General File, Box 505, letter, Stephen N. Weld to DDE, October 26, 1958, DDEL.
247. Ibid., letter, Weld to Howard Pyle, October 26, 1958, DDEL.

248. Ibid.
249. DDE Papers, Administration Series, Box 1, Meade Alcorn to James Hagerty, October 2, 1958, 2–3, DDEL.
250. Ibid., letter, Alcorn to DDE, September 29, 1958, DDEL.
251. Woolley and Peters, 11265.
252. Ibid., 11269.
253. *Lowell Sun*, October 25, 1958.
254. WHCF, Box 964, GF 126-I-1, letters, William Loeb to DDE, February 20, 1958, and Box 965, GF 126-I-1, Michael Schoonjans to DDE, March 12, 1958, DDEL.
255. WHCF, Box 504, GF 109-A-2, Maine (2) folder, letter, Howard Pyle to Mr. and Mrs. Harry Seymour Parker, September 18, 1958, DDEL.
256. *Portsmouth Herald*, October 27, 1958.
257. Ibid., October 23, 1958.
258. OH, Boutin, 2, JFKL.
259. OH, William L. Dunfey, December 15, 1971, 6, JFKL.
260. CQ, *Guide*, 421.
261. Ibid.
262. Ibid., 434.
263. Ibid., 839, 592.
264. Ibid., 839; *Portsmouth Herald*, November 5, 1958; and *Bennington Evening Banner*, November 5, 1958.
265. CQ, *Guide*, 402.
266. Ibid., 831, 836.
267. Lockard, 269.
268. Thomas J. Dodd Papers, Box 269, letter, Dodd to George Sokolsky, September 24, 1958, UCT.
269. Ibid., Box 267, undated memo, "Voting Record of Senator William A. Purtell (R.Conn.)," UCT.
270. Ibid., Box 276, Dodd press release, September 1, 1958, and Box 269, letter, Jim Boyd to Ella Grasso, September 26, 1958, UCT.
271. CQ, *Guide*, 488.
272. Ibid., 428.
273. Ibid., 504.
274. John K. White, *The Fractured Electorate: Political Parties and Social Change in Southern New England* (Hanover, NH: University Press of New England, 1983): 15; and Moakley, 92.
275. CQ, *Guide*, 414; and *Berkshire Eagle*, November 6, 1958.
276. CQ, *Guide*, 837.

277. *North Adams Transcript*, November 6, 1958.
278. CQ, Guide, 494.
279. *Worcester Telegram*, October 5, 1958.
280. Burton Hersh, *The Education of Edward Kennedy: A Family Biography* (New York: William Morrow and Company, 1972): 111.
281. CQ, Guide, 494.
282. Ibid., 412.
283. Ward (ed.), 236–241.
284. Edward J. Cronin (ed.), *Election Statistics: The Commonwealth of Massachusetts, 1952* (Boston: Commonwealth of Massachusetts, 1953): 352–356; and Ward (ed.), 236–241.
285. CQ, *Politics in America, 1945–1964*, 29.
286. "Cause and Effect," *Time*, v. 72, n. 20 (November 17, 1958): 19–22.
287. "Political Chaos Coming?" *U.S. News and World Report* v. 45, n. 20 (November 14, 1958): 36.
288. Ibid., 54–55.
289. Weber, 338, 359–364.
290. Woolley and Peters, 11286.
291. Ambrose, *Nixon*, 495–510.
292. Caro, *Master of the Senate*, 1015–1018.
293. *North Adams Transcript*, November 7, 1958.
294. *Fairbanks Daily News Miner*, November 8, 1958; and *Daily Sitka Sentinel*, November 12, 1958.
295. OH, Andrew Dazzi and John Harris, April 22, 1964, 4, JFKL.
296. http://www.eed.state.ak.us/news/releases/2007/ak_digital_archives-JFK.pdf.
297. OH, Dazzi and Harris, 7, JFKL.
298. Beatty, 520.
299. O'Donnell and Powers, 161.
300. OH, Garrett H. Byrne, September 28, 1967, 39–40, JFKL.
301. Nigel Hamilton, 674; and Beatty, 456.
302. OH, Peter J. Cloherty, September 29, 1967, 13–16, JFKL.

Chapter 6

1. Seymour M. Hersh, *The Dark Side of Camelot* (Boston: Little, Brown and Company, 1997): 89.

2. Ragsdale, 196.
3. Gallup, v.2, 1539.
4. Ibid., 1613.
5. Sorensen, *Kennedy*, 106–107.
6. Quoted in McNally's book, 24.
7. O'Donnell and Powers, 146.
8. OH, Celeste, 38–41, JFKL.
9. Gallup, v. 3, 1623.
10. *Yuma Daily Sun*, December 11, 1958.
11. *NYT*, December 8, 1958.
12. Amanda Smith, 681.
13. Ibid., 681–682.
14. *NYT*, December 8, 1958; and Fletcher Knebel, "Democratic Forecast: A Catholic in 1960," *Look* 23 (March 3, 1959): 17.
15. Sorensen, *Kennedy*, 108.
16. Kenebel, "Democratic Forecast," 16–17.
17. *NYT*, March 1, 1959.
18. OH, John Cogley, February 20, 1968, 1–2, JFKL.
19. *NYT*, March 1, 1959.
20. *Titusville Herald*, March 2, 1959.
21. Catholic Diocese of Worcester, letters, Bishop John J. Wright to JPK, July 3, 1953 and September 25, 1953.
22. David Nasaw, *The Patriarch: The Remarkable Life and Turbulent Times of Joseph P. Kennedy* (New York: Penguin Press, 2012): 713–714; and Shaun A. Casey, *The Making of a Catholic President: Kennedy vs. Nixon* (New York: Oxford University Press, 2009): 18–19.
23. O'Brien, *No Final Victories*, 59.
24. John H. Fenton, *Midwest Politics* (New York: Holt, Rinehart and Winston, 1966): 44–63; and OH, James B. Brennan, December 9, 1965, 14, JFKL.
25. OH, Clement J. Zablocki, October 29, 1965, 7, JFKL.
26. *Racine Journal-Times*, April 10, 1959.
27. *Appleton Post-Crescent*, April 13, 1959.
28. Toledano, 74.
29. *Appleton Post-Crescent*, April 13, 1959.
30. *Sheboygan Press*, April 13, 1959.
31. Helen O'Donnell, 166–167.
32. *Racine Journal-Times*, June 26, 1959.
33. OH, Zablocki, 11, JFKL.
34. Ibid., 27; and *Sheboygan Press*, June 25, 1959.

35. *NYT*, April 23, 1959; and Alan K. McAdams, *Power and Politics in Labor Legislation* (New York: Columbia University Press, 1964): 90–97.
36. Lee, *Eisenhower and Landrum-Griffin*, 156.
37. Burns, 214.
38. *NYT*, September 12, 1959.
39. *Racine Journal-Times*, August 1, 1959.
40. Mason Drukman, *Wayne Morse: A Political Biography* (Portland: Oregon Historical Society Press, 1997): 325.
41. *Victoria Advocate*, August 4, 1959.
42. OH, Edith S. Green, June 22, 1974, 11–12, JFKL.
43. Lee, *Eisenhower and Landrum-Griffin*, 158.
44. Drukman, 326.
45. O'Brien, *No Final Victories*, 60.
46. Fenton, 155–156.
47. Savage, *JFK, LBJ, and the Democratic Party*, 49.
48. *NYT*, April 13, 1959.
49. http://www.findingcamelot.net/speeches/remarks-at-the-convocation-of-the-united-negro-college-fund-indianapolis-indiana-april 12-1959/.
50. *Logansport Press*, April 14, 1959.
51. JFK PPP, Indiana folder 1959–60, letter, Pierre Salinger to Gilbert Forbes, September 28, 1959, JFKL.
52. *Valparaiso Vidette Messenger*, October 1, 1959.
53. *Logansport Press*, October 3, 1959.
54. JFK PPP, Indiana folder 1959–60, copy of JFK's itinerary, JFKL.
55. *Anderson Herald Bulletin*, October 2, 1959.
56. Evans and Novak, 264.
57. O'Brien, *No Final Victories*, 60–61.
58. JFK PPP, Indiana 1959–60 folder, press release from Marshall Kizer and Albert O. Deluse, December 7, 1959, JFKL.
59. Ibid., letter, Lawrence F. O'Brien to Albert O. Deluse, December 3, 1959, JFKL.
60. Martin and Plaut, 466.
61. William L. Dunfey Papers, Box 4, letter, Alfred Catalfo to Dunfey, May 1,1958, JFKL.
62. *Manchester Union Leader*, February 7, 1960.
63. Bernard L. Boutin Papers, Box 1, letter, Boutin to EMK, October 26, 1959, JFKL.
64. JFK PPP, New Hampshire 1959–60 folder, letter, Lawrence F. O'Brien to Bernard L. Boutin, September 25, 1959, JFKL; and Martin and Plaut, 466.

65. Lockard, 67–68; and Douglass Cater, "Senator Styles Bridges and His Far-flung Constituents," *The Reporter* v. 10, n. 13 (July 20, 1954): 21.

66. OH, Donald E. Nicoll and Frank M. Coffin, November 20, 1996, 4–12, BTC.

67. OH, Fred Nutter, March 5, 1999, 32, BTC.

68. Kenneth T. Palmer, G. Thomas Taylor, and Marcus A. LiBrizzi, *Maine Politics and Government* (Lincoln: University of Nebraska Press, 1992): 17.

69. *Lowell Sun*, January 4, 1960.

70. *Biddeford-Saco Journal*, November 16, 1959.

71. Ibid.

72. *Lowell Sun*, November 16, 1959.

73. OH, Frank M. Coffin, March 2–3, 1964, 3, JFKL.

74. OH, John E. Byrne, August 29, 1968, 18, JFKL.

75. *Berkshire Eagle*, January 5, 1960.

76. OH, John E. Byrne, 27–28, JFKL.

77. Abraham Ribicoff Papers, Box 11, letters, Ribicoff to JFK, March 5, 1959, and Theodore C. Sorensen to Ribicoff, July 28, 1959, LOC.

78. Savage, *JFK, LBJ, and Democratic Party*, 48.

79. *NYT*, August 3, 1959.

80. JFK PPP, Box 928, cover letter of John M. Bailey's report to JFK, August 14, 1959, JFKL.

81. O'Donnell and Powers, 117–118.

82. JFK PPP, Box 928, Bailey's report to JFK, 5, JFKL.

83. Ibid.

84. *Oakland Tribune*, October 31, 1959.

85. *NYT*, November 3, 1959.

86. Sorensen, *Kennedy*, 120–121.

87. Theodore H. White, 72.

88. Ibid., 70.

89. O'Brien, *No Final Victories*, 63.

90. *Naugatuck Daily News*, August 5, 1959.

91. JFK PPP, Missouri: Delegates, 1956–59 folder, unsigned memo, October 9, 1959, and letter, JFK to James Aylward, Jr., November 2, 1959, JFKL.

92. *Iola Register*, November 20, 1959.

93. Theodore H. White, 52.

94. Nasaw, 575–576.

95. *Big Spring Herald*, November 19, 1959.
96. *Paris News*, November 18, 1959.
97. Dallek, *Lone Star Rising*, 559.
98. Jeff Shesol, *Mutual Contempt: Lyndon Johnson, Robert Kennedy, and the Feud that Defined a Decade* (New York: Norton, 1997): 1–9.
99. O. Douglas Weeks, *Texas in the 1960 Presidential Election* (Austin: University of Texas Institute of Public Affairs, 1961): 11–18; and David Pietrusza, *1960: LBJ vs. JFK vs. Nixon, the Epic Campaign That Forged Three Presidencies* (New York: Union Square Press, 2008): 31.
100. Dallek, *Lone Star Rising*, 222–224.
101. Robert A. Caro, *The Years of Lyndon Johnson: Means of Ascent* (New York: Alfred A. Knopf, 1990): 395.
102. George Reedy, *Lyndon B. Johnson: A Memoir* (New York: Andrews and McMeel, 1982): 140–141.
103. Bobby Baker, *Wheeling and Dealing* (New York: Norton, 1978): 44.
104. John Connally, *In History's Shadow: An American Odyssey* (New York: Hyperion, 1993): 161.
105. OH, James H. Rowe, Jr., May 10, 1964, 2–3, JFKL.
106. OH, Kenneth P. O'Donnell, July 23, 1969, 7–9, LBJL.
107. Robert A. Caro, *The Years of Lyndon Johnson: The Passage of Power* (New York: Alfred A. Knopf, 2012): 56–59.
108. Weber, 338.
109. JFK PPP, Pennsylvania: Delegates-at-Large: D–L folder, letter, David L. Lawrence to Philip H. Goodman, August 31, 1959, JFKL.
110. Ibid., letter, David L. Lawrence to RFK, November 19, 1959, JFKL.
111. Ibid., letter, RFK to David L. Lawrence, December 4, 1959, JFKL.
112. Ibid.
113. Ibid., 2.
114. OH, David L. Lawrence, January 26, 1966, 4, JFKL.
115. *NYT*, August 17, 1959.
116. JFK PPP, Pennsylvania Delegates-at-Large folder, letter, JFK to Joseph M. Barr, December 14, 1959, JFKL.
117. Ibid., Pennsylvania, 9 October 1959–23 February 1960 folder, copy of JFK's December 10, 1959 schedule, JFKL.
118. *Lowell Sun*, December 18, 1959.
119. Ibid.

Chapter 7

1. JFK PPP, Speeches and Remarks by JFK, folder 2, JFK statement, January 2, 1960, JFKL.
2. *NYT*, January 15, 1960.
3. Sorensen, *Kennedy*, 177–188.
4. Silvestri, 133.
5. *Joplin Globe*, January 24, 1960.
6. *NYT*, January 25, 1960.
7. *Berkshire Eagle*, January 23, 1960.
8. *NYT*, January 25, 1960; and OH, Howard W. Fitzpatrick, September 29, 1967, 8, 15, JFKL.
9. *Lima News*, January 5, 1960; and OH, Michael V. DiSalle, November 24, 1964, 9–10, JFKL.
10. O'Brien, *No Final Victories*, 65.
11. Fenton, 137.
12. Lasky, 324–325.
13. *Fitchburg Sentinel*, March 9, 1960.
14. Sorensen, *Kennedy*, 121.
15. OH, Boutin, 2–8, JFKL.
16. Pietrusza, 82.
17. *Nashua Telegraph*, February 9, 1960.
18. Ibid., January 28, February 8, and March 4, 1960.
19. *Billings Gazette*, November 7, 1960.
20. *NYT*, February 8, 1960.
21. OH, Boutin, 5–7, JFKL.
22. O'Brien, *No Final Victories*, 65.
23. *Boston Globe*, March 8, 1960.
24. Ibid.
25. CQ, *Guide*, 336.
26. Ibid., 336, 338.
27. *NYT*, March 10, 1960.
28. *Berkshire Eagle*, March 9, 1960.
29. *Stevens Point Daily Journal*, March 10, 1960.
30. Salinger, 53.
31. O'Donnell and Powers, 174–175.
32. Sorensen, *Kennedy*, 134.
33. OH, Isaac Coggs, December 8, 1965, 2–6, JFKL.
34. OH, Patrick Lucey, January 6, 1972, 26–31, JFKL.

35. Jacqueline Kennedy, 67–68.
36. JFK PPP. Senate Speech File, JFK's speeches of March 23, March 20, March 9, March 18, and April 1, 1960, JFKL.
37. Ibid, JFK's speech at the University of Wisconsin in Milwaukee, March 24, 1960, JFKL.
38. Ibid., JFK's speech in Racine, March 19, 1960, JFKL.
39. OH, Peter Dugal, January 14, 1966, 13, JFKL; and OH, Brennan, 14–15, JFKL.
40. Sorensen, *Kennedy*, 136–137.
41. *Lowell Sun*, April 3, 1960; OH, Dugal, 5, 15, JFKL; OH, Richard K. Donahue, 56–58, JFKL; and Helen O'Donnell, 171–172.
42. Humphrey, 208.
43. OH, Hubert H. Humphrey, December 14, 1964, 90–91, JFKL.
44. O'Donnell and Powers, 175–176.
45. *NYT*, April 1, 1960.
46. *Huron Daily Plainsman*, April 4, 1960.
47. *Terre Haute Star*, April 4, 1960.
48. CQ, *Guide*, 338.
49. Ibid., 338.
50. Sorensen, *Kennedy*, 137.
51. OH, Brennan, 17, JFKL.
52. Pietrusza, 91.
53. Theodore H. White, 100–101; and OH, Richard K. Donahue, 58–65, JFKL.
54. *NYT*, April 7, 1960.
55. Salinger, 57.
56. Humphrey, 211.
57. CQ, *Guide*, 338.
58. O'Brien, *No Final Victories*, 60–61.
59. James C. Olson, *Stuart Symington: A Life* (Columbia: University of Missouri Press, 2003): 355.
60. *Logansport Pharos-Tribune*, May 4, 1960.
61. JFK PPP, Indiana Trips folder, letter, Thurman M. DeMoss to Larry O'Brien, March 22, 1960, JFKL.
62. *NYT*, March 22, 1960.
63. CQ, *Guide*, 338.
64. Ibid., 336.
65. Ibid., 338; and *Logansport Pharos-Tribune*, May 4, 1960.
66. *NYT*, May 5, 1960.

67. CQ, *Guide*, 339.
68. *NYT*, May 12, 1960.
69. *The Progress-Index*, May 12, 1960.
70. Pietrusza, 115: and Herbert S. Parmet, *JFK: The Presidency of John F. Kennedy* (New York: Dial Press, 1983): 38.
71. Sorensen, *Kennedy*, 139.
72. Salinger, 58.
73. *NYT*, April 22, 1960.
74. Ibid.
75. JFK PPP, Senate Speech File, JFK's speeches of April 11, April 18, and April 19, 1960, JFKL.
76. F. Keith Davis, *West Virginia Tough Boys: Vote Buying, Fist Fighting, and A President Named JFK* (Chapmanville, WV: Woodland Press, 2003): 169–170; and Schlesinger, *Robert Kennedy and His Times*, 213–215.
77. Quoted in Harry W. Ernst, *The Campaign That Made A President: West Virginia 1960* (New York: McGraw-Hill, 1962): 11.
78. Toledano, 157.
79. Humphrey, 475.
80. Ernst, 13.
81. Casey, 75.
82. O'Donnell and Powers, 192.
83. Ernst, 30.
84. Ibid., 31; Ted Schwarz, *Joseph P. Kennedy: The Mogul, The Mob, The Statesman, and The Making of An American Myth* (New York: John Wiley and Sons, Inc., 2003): 392–393, 411; and Davis, 171–172.
85. Jerry Bruno and Jeff Greenfield, *The Advance Man* (New York: William Morrow and Company, Inc., 1971): 43.
86. O'Brien, *No Final Victories*, 69–70.
87. Davis, 2; and OH, Claude Ellis, September 9, 1964, 8, JFKL.
88. OH, Jennings Randolph, July 5, 1965, 2–4, JFKL.
89. CQ, *Guide*, 339.
90. Parmet, *JFK*, 38.
91. Ernst, 28.
92. OH, David Fox, Jr., July 10, 1964, 2–5, JFKL; OH, Sidney L. Christie, July 16, 1964, 2–4, JFKL; and Sorensen, *Kennedy*, 146.
93. "West Virginia Aftermath," *The Reporter* v. 22, n. 11 (May 26, 1960): 2; *NYT*, May 12, 1960; and *Sheboygan Press*, May 11, 1960.

94. CQ, *Guide*, 339.
95. *NYT*, May 21, 1960.
96. Gallup, v.3, 1669.
97. Schlesinger, *Journals*, 66.
98. Ibid., 68.
99. McKeever, 449.
100. Edward N. Costikyan, *Behind Closed Doors: Politics in the Public Interest* (New York: Harcourt, Brace, and World, Inc., 1966): 27–28.
101. Theodore H. White, 163–164.
102. DNC Files, copy of press release from ADA, June 30, 1960, LBJL.
103. Evans and Novak, 271.
104. Theodore H. White, 166–168; and OH, Carl Hayden, October 28, 1968, 19–20, LBJL.
105. EMK, *True Compass*, 128.
106. *NYT*, June 4, 1960.
107. Democratic National Committee (DNC), *Official Report of the Proceedings of the Democratic National Convention and Committee, 1960* (Washington, DC: National Document Publishers, Inc., 1964): 168. Subsequently cited as DNC, *1960 Proceedings*.
108. *Farmington Daily Times*, July 3, 1960.
109. Dallek, *Lone Star Rising*, 570.
110. *NYT*, July 6, 1960.
111. Ibid., July 3, 1960.
112. Ibid., July 10, 1960.
113. Porter McKeever, *Adlai Stevenson: His Life and Legacy* (New York: Quill Books, 1989): 455.
114. Ibid.
115. OH, Richard K. Donahue, 76. JFKL.
116. OH, Garrett H. Byrne, September 28, 1967, 30–31, JFKL.
117. OH, Costin, 24–25, JFKL.
118. OH, John W. McCormack, March 30, 1977, 25–27, JFKL.
119. OH, John W. McCormack, September 23, 1968, 12, LBJL.
120. OH, Edward J. McCormack, Jr., 25, JFKL.
121. OH, Bailey, 40, JFKL.
122. Lieberman, 253.
123. Weber, 362–363.
124. DNC, *1960 Proceedings*, 168.
125. Ibid.

126. Edwin O. Guthman and Jeffrey Shulman (ed.), *Robert Kennedy: In His Own Words* (New York: Bantam Press, 1988): 19–22; OH, O'Donnell, 11, LBJL; and Sorensen, *Kennedy*, 165–166.

127. O'Brien, *No Final Victories*, 87–88.

128. OH, McNally, 13–17, JFKL.

129. OH, David F. Powers, 23, JFKL.

130. OH, Coffin, 7, JFKL.

131. William L. Dunfey Papers, Box 11, undated 1960 memo, Dunfey to Lawrence F. O'Brien, JFKL.

132. OH, Dunfey, 12–13, JFKL.

133. U.S. Senate, *Freedom of Communications: Final Report of the Committee on Commerce, United States Senate, Part I: The Speeches, Remarks, Press Conferences and Statements of Senator John F. Kennedy, August 1 Through November 7, 1960* (Washington, DC: GPO, 1961): 78.

134. Ibid., 80.

135. Ibid., 83.

136. Ibid., 93.

137. *NYT*, September 3, 1960.

138. *Lowell Sun*, August 14, 1960.

139. Ibid., September 9, 1960.

140. O'Brien, *No Final Victories*, 91; and Caro, *The Passage of Power*, 156.

141. OH, O'Donnell, 25, LBJL.

142. Richard M. Nixon, *RN: The Memoirs of Richard Nixon* (New York: Simon and Schuster, Inc., 1990): 216–217.

143. Henry Cabot Lodge, *The Storm Has Eyes: A Personal Narrative* (New York: W. W. Norton and Company, 1973): 183.

144. *Berkshire Eagle*, September 9, 1960.

145. *Lowell Sun*, September 9, 1960.

146. *Las Cruces Sun News*, September 11, 1960.

147. Quoted in Evans and Novak, 317.

148. *NYT*, November 8, 1960.

149. Ibid., November 7, 1960.

150. *Fitchburg Sentinel*, November 7, 1960; and William L. Dunfey Papers, Box 4, letter, Bernard L. Boutin to Dunfey, August 2, 1960, JFKL.

151. Lockard, 228–304.

152. CQ, *Guide*, 831, 836.

153. John S. Monagan Papers, Campaign—Political File, letter, Monagan to RFK, September 28, 1960, DTC.

154. Ibid., copy of May 27, 1978 oral history interview transcripts for Former Members of Congress, Inc., 25, DTC.
155. U.S. Senate, *Freedom of Communications*, 912.
156. Ibid., 913–914.
157. Ibid., 938.
158. Ibid., 940.
159. Ibid., 928.
160. OH, Muskie, 29, JFKL.
161. Harris E. Thurber, "Vermont: The Stirrings of Change," in Goodwin and Schuck, 73.
162. CQ, *Guide*, 336, 338.
163. Dennis Roberts Papers, Box 6, copy of memo on New Mexico trip, EMK to RFK, December 23, 1959, PC.
164. Claiborne Pell Papers, Box 2, DNC press release, July 11, 1960, URI.
165. *NYT*, September 25, 1960.
166. Claiborne Pell Papers, Box 7, copy of unsigned report, "Rhode Island Primary: 1960," March, 1961, 12–23, URI.
167. Ibid., 37–38.
168. *NYT*, September 29, 1960.
169. Claiborne Pell Papers, Box 4, memo, Paul Goulding to Ray Nelson, October 21, 1960, URI.
170. Ibid., memo, Ray Nelson to Claiborne Pell, November 2, 1960, URI.
171. *Newport Daily News*, September 30, 1960.
172. U.S. Senate, *Freedom of Communications*, 933.
173. CQ, *Guide*, 296.
174. *Worcester Telegram*, September 14, 1960.
175. *Fitchburg Sentinel*, November 7, 1960; and Levin and Blackwood, 104–130.
176. Leverett Saltonstall Papers, Box 109, letter, Albert L. McDermott to Harold Putnam, October 13, 1960, MHS.
177. O'Brien, *No Final Victories*, 96.
178. U.S. Senate, *Freedom of Communications*, 953.
179. Ibid., 958.
180. Ibid.
181. Parmet, *JFK*, 56–57.
182. Jacqueline Kennedy, 96–97.
183. Pietrusza, 392.

184. *NYT*, November 9, 1960.
185. John K. White, *The Fractured Electorate*, 52.
186. *CQ, Guide*, 296.
187. Barbrook, 185.
188. Theodore H. White, 36.
189. Quoted in Damore, 229.
190. U.S. Senate, *Freedom of Communications*, 911–959.
191. John F. Kennedy, *Profiles in Courage*, 213.

Epilogue

1. Woolley and Peters, 9344.
2. Ibid.
3. Ibid., 9484.
4. John F. Kennedy, *Profiles in Courage*, 213.

Selected Bibliography

Books

Abramson, Rudy. *Spanning the Century: The Life of W. Averell Harriman, 1891–1986.* New York: Morrow, 1992.

Adams, Russell B., Jr. *The Boston Money Tree.* New York: Thomas Y. Crowell, 1977.

Adams, Sherman. *First-Hand Report: The Story of the Eisenhower Administration.* New York: Harper and Brothers, 1961.

Allen, Robert S. (ed.). *Our Sovereign State.* New York: Vanguard Press, 1949.

Almond, Gabriel A., and Sidney Verba. *The Civic Culture: Political Attitudes and Democracy in Five Nations* (Boston: Little, Brown and Company, 1963.

Ambrose, Stephen E. *Eisenhower: Soldier and President.* New York: Simon and Schuster, 1990.

———. *Nixon: The Education of a Politician, 1913–1962.* New York: Simon and Schuster, 1987.

Baker, Bobby. *Wheeling and Dealing: Confessions of a Capitol Hill Operator.* New York: W. W. Norton, 1978.

Banfield, Edward C., and Martha Derthick. *A Report on the Politics of Boston.* Cambridge: Joint Center for Urban Studies, 1960.

———, and James Q. Wilson. *City Politics.* New York: Vintage, 1958.

Barbrook, Alec. *God Save the Commonwealth: An Electoral History of Massachusetts.* Amherst: University of Massachusetts Press, 1973.

Beatty, Jack. *The Rascal King: The Life and Times of James Michael Curley, 1874–1958.* New York: Addison-Wesley, 1992.

Bellush, Jewel, and Murray Hausknecht (ed.). *Urban Renewal: People, Politics, and Planning.* New York: Doubleday, 1967.

Bernstein, Irving. *Promises Kept: John F. Kennedy's New Frontier*. New York: Oxford University Press, 1991.

Biles, Roger. *Crusading Liberal: Paul H. Douglas of Illinois*. DeKalb: Northern Illinois University Press, 2002.

Binstock, Robert H. *A Report on Politics in Worcester, Massachusetts*. Cambridge: Joint Center for Urban Studies, 1960.

Black, Allida M. *Casting Her Own Shadow: Eleanor Roosevelt and the Shaping of Postwar Liberalism*. New York: Columbia University Press, 1996.

Boyd, James. *Above the Law: The Rise and Fall of Senator Thomas J. Dodd*. New York: New American Library, 1968.

Boyle, Kevin. *The UAW and the Heyday of American Liberalism, 1945–1968*. Ithaca, NY: Cornell University Press, 1995.

Broadwater, Jeff. *Adlai Stevenson and American Politics: The Odyssey of a Cold War Liberal*. New York: Twayne, 1994.

Brownell, Herbert. *Advising Ike: The Memoirs of Attorney General Herbert Brownell*. Lawrence: University Press of Kansas, 1993.

Brownstein, Ronald. *The Power and the Glitter: The Hollywood-Washington Connection*. New York: Pantheon Books, 1990.

Bryan, Frank M. *Yankee Politics in Rural Vermont*. Hanover, NH: University Press of New England, 1974.

Buchan, John. *Pilgrim's Way: An Essay in Recollection*. Cambridge: Houghton Mifflin, 1940.

Burling, Francis P. *The Birth of the Cape Cod National Seashore*. Plymouth, MA: Leyden Press, 1979.

Burns, James MacGregor. *John Kennedy: A Political Profile*. New York: Avon Book Division, 1960.

Campbell, Angus, Philip E. Converse, Warren E. Miller, and Donald E. Stokes. *The American Voter: An Abridgement*. New York: Werbel and Peck, 1964.

Caro, Robert A. *The Years of Lyndon Johnson: Master of the Senate*. New York: Alfred A. Knopf, 2002.

———. *The Years of Lyndon Johnson: Means of Ascent*. New York: Alfred A. Knopf, 1990.

———. *The Years of Lyndon Johnson: The Passage of Power*. New York: Alfred A. Knopf, 2012.

Casey, Shaun A. *The Making of a Catholic President: Kennedy vs. Nixon*. New York: Oxford University Press, 2009.

Chevrier, Lionel. *The St. Lawrence Seaway*. New York: St. Martin's Press, 1959.

Cohen, Adam, and Elizabeth Taylor. *American Pharaoh: Mayor Richard J. Daley, His Battle for Chicago and the Nation.* Boston: Little, Brown and Company, 2000.

Committee of New England of the National Planning Association. *The Economic State of New England.* New Haven: Yale University Press, 1954.

Congressional Quarterly. *Guide to U.S. Elections.* Washington, DC: CQ Press, 1975.

———. *Politics in America, 1945–1964.* Washington, DC: CQ Press, 1965.

Connally, John. *In History's Shadow: An American Odyssey.* New York: Hyperion, 1993.

Cotter, Cornelius P., and Bernard C. Hennessy. *Politics Without Power: The National Party Committees.* New York: Atherton Press, 1964.

Cotton, Norris. *In the Senate: Amidst the Conflict and the Turmoil.* New York: Dodd, Mead, and Company, 1978.

Council of Economic Advisers. *The New England Economy: A Report to the President.* Washington, DC: GPO, 1951.

Curley, James Michael. *I'd Do It Again!.* New York: Prentice-Hall, 1957.

Cutler, John Henry. *Cardinal Cushing of Boston.* New York: Hawthorn Books, 1970.

———. *"Honey Fitz": Three Steps to the White House.* New York: Bobbs-Merrill, 1962.

Dahl, Robert A. *Who Governs? Democracy and Power in An American City.* New Haven, CT: Yale University Press, 1961.

Dallek, Robert. *Lone Star Rising: Lyndon Johnson and His Times, 1908–1960.* New York: Oxford University Press, 1991.

———. *An Unfinished Life: John F. Kennedy, 1917–1963.* Boston: Little, Brown and Company, 2003.

Dalton, Cornelius and James J. Dobbins. *Leading the Way: A History of the Massachusetts General Court, 1629–1980.* Boston: Commonwealth of Massachusetts, 1984.

Damore, Leo. *The Cape Cod Years of John Fitzgerald Kennedy.* New York: Four Walls Eight Windows, 1993.

Davis, F. Keith. *West Virginia Tough Boys: Vote Buying, Fist Fighting, and A President Named JFK.* Chapmanville, WV: Woodland Press, 2003.

Dinneen, Joseph F. *The Kennedy Family.* Boston: Little, Brown and Company, 1959.

———. *The Purple Shamrock.* New York: W. W. Norton and Company, 1949.

Donovan, John C. *Congressional Campaign: Maine Elects a Democrat.* New York: Henry Holt, 1958.

Douglas, Paul H. *In the Fullness of Time: The Memoir of Paul H. Douglas.* New York; Harcourt Brace Jovanovich, Inc., 1971.

Doyle, William. *The Vermont Political Tradition: And Those Who Helped Make It.* Barre, VT: Northlight Studio Press, 1984.

Drukman, Mason. *Wayne Morse: A Political Biography.* Portland: Oregon Historical Society Press, 1997.

Eisenhower, Dwight D. *The White House Years: Mandate for Change, 1953–1956.* New York: Doubleday, 1963.

———. *The White House Years: Waging Peace, 1956–1961.* New York: Doubleday, 1965.

Eisenmenger, Robert W. *The Dynamics of Growth in New England's Economy, 1870–1964.* Middletown, CT: Wesleyan University Press, 1967.

Elazar, Daniel J. *American Federalism: A View from the States.* New York: Thomas Y. Crowell, 1966.

Ernst, Harry W. *The Campaign That Made A President: West Virginia 1960.* New York: McGraw-Hill, 1962.

Evans, Rowland and Robert Novak. *Lyndon B. Johnson: The Exercise of Power.* New York: New American Library, 1966.

Farrell, John A. *Tip O'Neill and the Democratic Century.* Boston: Little, Brown and Company, 2001.

Fenton, John H. *Midwest Politics.* New York: Holt, Rinehart and Winston, 1966.

Ferrell, Robert H. (ed.). *The Eisenhower Diaries.* New York: W. W. Norton and Company, 1981.

Fischer, David Hackett. *Albion's Seed: Four British Folkways in America.* New York: Oxford University Press, 1989.

Fontenay, Charles L. *Estes Kefauver: A Biography.* Knoxville: University of Tennessee Press, 1980.

Foster, Charles H.W. *The Cape Cod National Seashore: A Landmark Alliance.* Hanover, NH: University Press of New England, 1985.

Fuchs, Lawrence H. *The Political Behavior of American Jews.* Glencoe, IL: Free Press, 1956.

Furcolo, Foster. *Ballots Anyone?* Cambridge: Schenkman, 1982.

Gabriel, Richard A. *The Political Machine in Rhode Island.* Kingston, RI: University of Rhode Island, 1970.

Gallup, George H. *The Gallup Poll: Public Opinion, 1935–1971.* New York: Random House, 1972. Cited with volume number.

Gelfand, Mark I. *A Nation of Cities: The Federal Government and Urban America, 1933–1965.* New York: Oxford University Press, 1975.

———. *Trustee for a City: Ralph Lowell of Boston*. Boston: Northeastern University Press, 1998.

Giglio, James N. *The Presidency of John F. Kennedy*. Lawrence: University Press of Kansas, 1991.

Goodwin, George, Jr. and Victoria Schuck (ed.). *Party Politics in the New England States*. Durham, NH: New England Center for Continuing Education, 1968.

Great Lakes-St. Lawrence Association. *The Heartland: The Story of the Great Lakes-St. Lawrence Valley*. Washington, DC: Great Lakes–St. Lawrence Association, 1951.

Guthman, Edwin O. and Jeffrey Shulman (ed.). *Robert Kennedy: In His Own Words*. New York: Bantam Press, 1988.

Hamilton, Charles V. *Adam Clayton Powell, Jr.: The Political Biography of an American Dilemma*. New York: Collier Books, 1991.

Hamilton, Nigel. *JFK: Reckless Youth*. New York: Random House, 1992.

Hand, Samuel B. *The Star That Set: The Vermont Republican Party, 1854–1974*. New York: Rowman and Littlefield, 2003.

Hardeman, D. B. and Bacon, Donald C. *Rayburn: A Biography*. New York: Madison Books, 1987.

Harris, Seymour E. *The Economics of New England*. Cambridge: Harvard University Press, 1952.

Hatch, Alden. *The Lodges of Massachusetts*. New York: Hawthorn Books, 1973.

Henderson, Deirdre (ed.). *Prelude to Leadership: The European Diary of John F. Kennedy, Summer 1945*. New York: Regnery, 1995.

Hersh, Burton. *The Education of Edward Kennedy: A Family Biography*. New York: William Morrow and Company, 1972.

———. *Edward Kennedy: An Intimate Biography*. Berkeley, CA: Counterpoint Press, 2010.

Hersh, Seymour M. *The Dark Side of Camelot*. Boston: Little, Brown and Company, 1997.

Herskowitz, Mickey. *Duty, Honor, Country: The Life and Legacy of Prescott Bush*. Nashville, TN: Rutledge Hill Press, 2003.

Hogarty, Richard A. *Massachusetts Politics and Public Policy: Studies in Power and Leadership*. Amherst: University of Massachusetts Press, 2002.

Humphrey, Hubert H. *The Education of a Public Man: My Life and Politics*. New York: Doubleday, 1976.

Judd, Dennis R. and Todd Swanstrom. *City Politics: Private Power and Public Policy*. New York: Harper Collins, 1994.

Kennedy, Edward M. *True Compass: A Memoir*. New York: Twelve Books, 2009.

Kennedy, Jacqueline. *Historic Conversations on Life with John F. Kennedy: Interviews with Arthur M. Schlesinger, Jr., 1964*. New York: Hyperion, 2011.

Kennedy, John F. *John Fitzgerald Kennedy: A Compendium of Speeches, Statements, and Remarks Delivered During His Service in the Congress of the United States*. Washington, DC: GPO, 1964.

———. *A Nation of Immigrants*. New York: Harper and Row, 1964.

———. *Profiles in Courage*. New York: Harper and Row, 1964.

———. *Why England Slept*. New York: Doubleday, 1961.

Key, V. O., Jr. *Southern Politics in State and Nation*. Knoxville: University of Tennessee Press, 1984.

Klinkner, Philip A. *The Losing Parties: Out-Party National Committees, 1956–1993*. New Haven, CT: Yale University Press, 1994.

Lasky, Victor. *J.F.K.: The Man and the Myth*. New York: Macmillan, 1963.

Leaming, Barbara. *Jack Kennedy: The Education of a Statesman*. New York: Norton, 2006.

Lee, R. Alton. *Eisenhower and Landrum-Griffin: A Study in Labor-Management Politics*. Lexington: University Press of Kentucky, 1990.

Leuchtenburg, William E. *Flood Control Politics: The Connecticut River Valley Problem, 1927–1950*. Cambridge: Harvard University Press, 1953.

Levin, Murray B. *The Alienated Voter: Politics in Boston*. New York: Holt, Rinehart and Winston, 1960.

———. *Kennedy and Campaigning*. Boston: Beacon Press, 1966.

Levin, Murray B. and George Blackwood. *The Compleat Politician: Political Strategy in Massachusetts*. Indianapolis: Bobbs-Merrill, 1962.

Levitan, Sar A. *Federal Aid to Depressed Areas: An Evaluation of the Area Redevelopment Administration*. Baltimore: The Johns Hopkins University Press, 1964.

Lieberman, Joseph I. *The Power Broker: A Biography of John M. Bailey, Modern Political Boss*. Boston: Houghton Mifflin, 1966.

Lippman, Theo, Jr., and Donald C. Hansen. *Muskie*. New York: W. W. Norton and Company, 1971.

Litt, Edgar. *The Political Cultures of Massachusetts*. Cambridge: MIT Press, 1965.

Lockard, Duane. *New England State Politics*. Princeton: Princeton University Press, 1959.

Lodge, Henry Cabot. *The Storm Has Many Eyes: A Personal Narrative*. New York: W. W. Norton and Company, 1973.

Lombardo, Daniel. *Cape Cod National Seashore: The First 50 Years*. Chicago: Arcadia Publishing, 2010.
Lubell, Samuel. *Revolt of the Moderates*. New York: Harper and Brothers, 1956.
Mabee, Carleton. *The Seaway Story*. New York: Macmillan, 1961.
McAdams, Alan K. *Power and Politics in Labor Legislation*. New York: Columbia University Press, 1964.
McCarthy, Joe. *The Remarkable Kennedys*. New York: Popular Library, 1960.
McKeever, Porter. *Adlai Stevenson: His Life and Legacy*. New York: Quill Books, 1989.
McNally, John J., Jr. *From the Little Green House to the White House and Beyond*. Anaheim, CA: Creative Continuum, 2008.
Mann, Robert. *The Walls of Jericho: Lyndon Johnson, Richard Russell, and the Struggle for Civil Rights*. New York: Harcourt Brace and Company, 1996.
Martin, Joe. *My First Fifty Years in Politics*. New York: McGraw-Hill, 1960.
Martin, John Bartlow. *Adlai Stevenson and the World*. New York: Doubleday, 1977.
Martin, John F. *Civil Rights and the Crisis of Liberalism: The Democratic Party, 1945–1976*. Boulder, CO: Westview Press, 1979.
Martin, Ralph G. *Ballots and Bandwagons*. New York: Rand McNally, 1964.
Martin, Ralph G., and Ed Plaut. *Front Runner, Dark Horse*. New York: Doubleday, 1960.
Matthews, Christopher J. *Jack Kennedy: Elusive Hero*. New York: Simon and Schuster, 2011.
———. *Kennedy and Nixon: The Rivalry That Shaped Postwar America*. New York: Simon and Schuster, 1996.
Milburn, Josephine F. and William Doyle. *New England Political Parties*. Cambridge: Schenkman Publishing Company, Inc., 1983.
Miller, Perry. *The New England Mind: From Colony to Province*. Boston: Beacon Press, 1953.
Miller, William J. *Henry Cabot Lodge: A Biography*. New York: James H. Heineman, Inc., 1967.
Morgan, Iwan W. *Eisenhower versus "The Spenders": The Eisenhower Administration, the Democrats, and the Budget, 1953–60*. New York: St. Martin's Press, 1990.
Nasaw, David. *The Patriarch: The Remarkable and Turbulent Times of Joseph P. Kennedy*. New York: Penguin Press, 2012.
Nichols, David A. *Eisenhower 1956: The President's Year of Crisis, Suez and the Brink of War*. New York: Simon and Schuster, 2011.
Nixon, Richard M. *RN: The Memoirs of Richard Nixon*. New York: Simon and Schuster, 1990.

———. *Six Crises*. New York: Doubleday, 1962.
O'Brien, Lawrence F. *No Final Victories*. New York: Ballantine Books, 1974.
O'Brien, Michael. *John F. Kennedy: A Biography*. New York: Thomas Dunne Books, 2005.
O'Connor, Thomas H. *Building a New Boston: Politics and Urban Renewal, 1950 to 1970*. Boston: Northeastern University Press, 1993.
O'Donnell, Helen. *A Common Good: The Friendship of Robert F. Kennedy and Kenneth P. O'Donnell*. New York: William Morrow and Company, 1998.
O'Donnell, Kenneth P. and David F. Powers. *"Johnny We Hardly Knew Ye": Memories of John F. Kennedy*. New York: Pocket Books, 1973.
Olson, James C. *Stuart Symington: A Life*. Columbia: University of Missouri Press, 2003.
O'Neill, Thomas P., Jr. *Man of the House: The Life and Political Memoirs of Speaker Tip O'Neill*. New York: St. Martin's Press, 1987.
Pach, Chester J., Jr., and Elmo Richardson. *The Presidency of Dwight D. Eisenhower*. Lawrence: University Press of Kansas, 1991.
Parmet, Herbert S. *The Democrats: The Years after FDR*. New York: Oxford University Press, 1976.
———. *Eisenhower and the American Crusades*. New York: Macmillan, 1972.
———. *Jack: The Struggles of John F. Kennedy*. New York: Dial Press, 1980.
———. *JFK: The Presidency of John F. Kennedy*. New York: Dial Press, 1983.
Patterson, James T. *Mr. Republican: A Biography of Robert A. Taft*. Boston: Houghton Mifflin, 1972.
Pietrusza, David. *1960: LBJ vs. JFK vs. Nixon, The Epic Campaign That Forged Three Presidencies*. New York: Union Square, 2008.
Rachlin, Harvey. *The Kennedys: A Chronological History, 1823–Present*. New York: World Almanac Books, 1986.
Ragsdale, Lyn. *Vital Statistics on the Presidency: Washington to Clinton*. Washington, DC: CQ Press, 1996.
Reedy, George. *Lyndon B. Johnson: A Memoir*. New York: Andrews and McMeel, 1982.
Reeves, Thomas C. *The Life and Times of Joe McCarthy: A Biography*. New York: Stein and Day, 1982.
———. *A Question of Character: A Life of John F. Kennedy*. New York: Free Press, 1991.
Reichard, Gary W. *Politics as Usual: The Age of Truman and Eisenhower*. Arlington Heights, IL: Harlan Davidson, Inc., 1988.
———. *The Reaffirmation of Republicanism: Eisenhower and the Eighty-Third Congress*. Knoxville: University of Tennessee Press, 1975.

Reinhard, David W. *The Republican Right Since 1945*. Lexington: University Press of Kentucky, 1983.

Richardson, Elmo. *Dams, Parks, and Politics: Resource Development and Preservation in the Truman-Eisenhower Era*. Lexington: University Press of Kentucky, 1973.

Roberts, George C. *Paul M. Butler: Hoosier Politician and National Political Leader*. Lanham, MD: University Press of America, 1987.

Rolde, Neil. *Maine Democrats: A Brief History*. Augusta: Maine Democratic Party, 2000.

Roosevelt, Eleanor. *On My Own*. New York: Harper and Brothers, 1958.

Russell, Francis. *The President Makers: From Mark Hanna to Joseph P. Kennedy*. Boston: Little, Brown and Company, 2001.

Salinger, Pierre. *With Kennedy*. New York: Avon Books, 1966.

Saltonstall, Leverett. *Salty: Recollections of a Yankee in Politics*. Boston: Boston Globe, 1976.

Savage, Sean J. *JFK, LBJ, and the Democratic Party*. Albany: State University of New York Press, 2004.

———. *Roosevelt: The Party Leader, 1932–1945*. Lexington: University Press of Kentucky, 1991.

———. *Truman and the Democratic Party*. Lexington: University Press of Kentucky, 1997.

Schlesinger, Arthur M., Jr. *Journals: 1952–2000*. New York: Penguin Books, 2007.

———. *Robert Kennedy and His Times*. New York: Ballantine Books, 1978.

———. *A Thousand Days: John F. Kennedy in the White House*. Boston: Houghton Mifflin, 1965.

Sevareid, Eric (ed.). *Candidates 1960*. New York: Basic Books, 1959.

Shaw, John T. *JFK in the Senate: Pathway to the Presidency*. New York: Palgrave Macmillan, 2013.

Sherman, Michael (ed.). *The Political Legacy of George D. Aiken: Wise Old Owl of the U.S. Senate*. Woodstock, VT: Countryman Press, 1995.

Shesol, Jeff. *Mutual Contempt: Lyndon Johnson, Robert Kennedy, and the Feud that Defined a Decade*. New York: Norton, 1997.

Silvestri, Vito N. *Becoming JFK: A Profile in Communication*. Westport, CT: Praeger, 2000.

Sloan, John W. *Eisenhower and the Management of Prosperity*. Lawrence: University Press of Kansas, 1991.

Sloane, Arthur A. *Hoffa*. Cambridge: MIT Press, 1991.

Smith, Amanda (ed.). *Hostage to Fortune: The Letters of Joseph P. Kennedy.* New York: Viking Press, 2001.

Smith, Jean Edward. *Eisenhower in War and Peace.* New York: Random House, 2012.

Sorensen, Theodore C. *Counselor: A Life at the Edge of History.* New York: Harper Collins, 2008.

———. *Kennedy.* New York: Harper and Row, 1965.

Stanley, Harold W., and Richard G. Niemi. *Vital Statistics on American Politics.* Washington, DC: CQ Press, 1994.

Stern, Mark. *Calculating Visions: Kennedy, Johnson, and Civil Rights.* New Brunswick: Rutgers University Press, 1992.

Stoll, Ira. *JFK, Conservative.* New York: Houghton Mifflin Harcourt, 2013.

Stossel, Scott. *Sarge: The Life and Times of Sargent Shriver.* Washington, DC: Smithsonian Books, 2004.

Sundquist, James L. *Politics and Policy: The Eisenhower, Kennedy, and Johnson Years.* Washington, DC: Brookings Institution, 1968.

Taymor, Betty. *Running against the Wind: The Struggle of Women in Massachusetts.* Boston: Northeastern University Press, 2000.

Temin, Peter (ed.). *Engines of Enterprise: An Economic History of New England.* Cambridge: Harvard University Press, 2000.

Thomson, Charles A. H., and Frances M. Shattuck. *The 1956 Presidential Campaign.* Washington, DC: Brookings Institution, 1960.

Tillett, Paul (ed.). *Inside Politics: The National Conventions, 1960.* New York: Oceana Publications, Inc., 1962.

Toledano, Ralph. *R.F.K.: The Man Who Would Be President.* New York: New American Library, 1967.

U.S. Senate. *Freedom of Communications: Final Report of the Committee on Commerce, United States Senate, Part I: The Speeches, Remarks, Press Conferences and Statements of Senator John F. Kennedy, August 1 Through November 7, 1960.* Washington, DC: GPO, 1961.

Wallace, Patricia Ward. *Politics of Conscience: A Biography of Margaret Chase Smith.* Westport, CT: Praeger, 1995.

Weber, Michael P. *Don't Call Me Boss: David L. Lawrence, Pittsburgh's Renaissance Mayor.* Pittsburgh: University of Pittsburgh Press, 1988.

Whalen, Richard J. *The Founding Father: The Story of Joseph P. Kennedy.* New York: New American Library, 1964.

Whalen, Thomas J. *Kennedy versus Lodge: The 1952 Massachusetts Senate Race.* Boston: Northeastern University Press, 2000.

White, John K. *The Fractured Electorate: Political Parties and Social Change in Southern New England.* Hanover, NH: University Press of New England, 1983.

———. *Still Seeing Red: How the Cold War Shapes the New American Politics.* Boulder, CO: Westview Press, 1997.

White, Theodore H. *The Making of the President 1960.* New York: New American Library, 1961.

Willoughby, William R. *The St. Lawrence Seaway: A Study in Politics and Diplomacy.* Madison: University of Wisconsin Press, 1961.

Wilson, James Q. *The Amateur Democrat: Club Politics in Three Cities.* Chicago: University of Chicago Press, 1962.

Articles

Abrams, Richard M. "A Paradox of Progressivism: Massachusetts on the Eve of Insurgency." *Political Science Quarterly* v. 75, n. 3 (September 1960): 379–399.

Almond, Gabriel A. "Comparative Political Systems." *Journal of Politics* v. 18, n. 3 (August 1956): 391–409.

Anderson, Totton J. "The 1958 Election in California." *Western Political Quarterly* 12 (March 1959): 276–300.

Atlas, Benjamin J. "Battle of the St. Lawrence." *Nation* 161 (September 8, 1945): 224–226.

Baggaley, Andrew R. "Patterns of Voting Change in Wisconsin Counties, 1952–1957." *Western Political Quarterly* 12 (March 1959): 141–144.

Banfield, Edward C., and James Q. Wilson. "Ethnic Membership and Urban Voting," in Bernard E. Segal (ed.), *Racial and Ethnic Relations* (New York: Crowell, 1966): 168–177.

Blagden, Ralph. "Cabot Lodge's Toughest Fight." *The Reporter* v. 7, n. 7 (September 30, 1952): 10–13.

Borchard, Edwin. "The St. Lawrence Waterway and Power Project." *American Journal of International Law* v. 43, n. 3 (July 1949): 411–434.

Braestrup, Peter. "What the Press Has Done to Boston and Vice Versa." *Harper's* 221 (October 1960): 79–94.

Bruner, Jerome S., and Sheldon J. Korchin. "The Boss and the Vote: Case Study in City Politics." *Public Opinion Quarterly* 10 (Spring 1946): 1–23.

Buenker, John D. "The Politics of Resistance: The Rural-Based Yankee Republican Machines of Connecticut and Rhode Island." *New England Quarterly* v. 47, n. 2 (June 1974): 212–237.

Clark, Terry N. "The Irish Ethic and the Spirit of Patronage." *Ethnicity* 2 (December 1975): 305–359.

Coffin, Tris. "John Kennedy: Young Man in a Hurry." *The Progressive* 23 (December 1959): 10–18.

Coleman, John J. "The Decline and Resurgence of Congressional Party Conflict." *Journal of Politics* v. 59, n. 1 (February 1997): 165–184.

Cornwell, Elmer E., Jr. "Party Absorption of Ethnic Groups: The Case of Providence, Rhode Island." *Social Forces* 38 (March 1960): 205–210.

Cotter, Cornelius P. "Eisenhower as Party Leader." *Political Science Quarterly* v. 98, n. 2 (Summer 1983): 255–283.

Cover, Albert D. "Surge and Decline in Congressional Elections." *Western Political Quarterly* v. 38, n. 4 (December 1985): 606–619.

Czudnowski, Moshe M. "A Salience Dimension of Politics for the Study of Political Culture." *American Political Science Review* v. 62, n. 3 (September 1968): 878–888.

Driggs, Don W. "The 1958 Election in Nevada." *Western Political Quarterly* v. 12, n. 1 (March 1959): 317–321.

Eisinger, Peter K. "Ethnic Political Transition in Boston, 1884–1933: Some Lessons for Contemporary Cities." *Political Science Quarterly* v. 93, n. 2 (Summer 1978): 217–239.

Flanagan, Richard M. "The Housing Act of 1954: The Sea Change in National Urban Policy." *Urban Affairs Review* v. 33, n. 2 (November 1997): 265–286.

Formisano, Ronald P. "The Concept of Political Culture." *Journal of Interdisciplinary History* 31 (Winter 2001): 393–426.

Fuchs, Lawrence H. "American Jews and the Presidential Vote." *American Political Science Review* v. 49, n. 2 (June 1955): 385–401.

———. "Presidential Politics in Boston: The Irish Response to Stevenson." *New England Quarterly* v. 30, n. 4 (December 1957): 435–447.

Gable, Richard W. "The Politics and Economics of the 1957–1958 Recession." *Western Political Quarterly* v. 12, n. 2 (June 1959): 557–559.

Galvin, John T. "The Dark Ages of Boston City Politics." *Proceedings of the Massachusetts Historical Society* 89 (1977): 88–111.

Glaeser, Edward L,. and Andrei Shleifer. "The Curley Effect: The Economics of Shaping the Electorate." *Journal of Law, Economics, and Organization* v. 21, n. 1 (2005):1–19.

Greenstein, Fred I., and Raymond E. Wolfinger. "The Suburbs and Shifting Party Loyalties." *Public Opinion Quarterly* v. 22, n. 4 (Winter 1958–59): 473–482.
Hand, Samuel B., and Paul M. Searls. "Transition Politics: Vermont, 1940–1952." *Vermont History* v. 62, n. 2 (April 1994): 5–25.
Harris, John. "Massachusetts: Cauldron Bubble," in *States in Crisis: Politics in Ten American States*, ed. by A. James Reichley (Chapel Hill: University of North Carolina Press, 1964): 142–162.
Harris, Seymour E. "New England's Decline in the American Economy." *Harvard Business Review* 25 (Spring 1947): 359–361.
Hastings, Philip K. "The Independent Voter in 1952: A Study of Pittsfield, Massachusetts." *American Political Science Review* v. 47, n. 3 (September 1953): 805–810.
Huitt, Ralph K. "Democratic Party Leadership in the Senate." *American Political Science Review* v. 55, n. 2 (June 1961): 333–344.
Hunt, D. Bradford. "How Did Public Housing Survive the 1950s?." *Journal of Policy History* v. 17, n. 2 (2005): 193–216.
Jacobs, Lawrence R., and Robert Y. Shapiro. "Issues, Candidate Image, and Priming: The Use of Private Polls in Kennedy's 1960 Presidential Campaign." *American Political Science Review* v. 88, n. 3 (September 1994): 527–540.
Kennedy, John F. "A Democrat Looks at Foreign Policy." *Foreign Affairs* 36 (October 1957): 44–59.
———. "New England and the South." *Atlantic Monthly* 193 (January 1954): 32–36.
Knebel, Fletcher. "Can a Catholic Become Vice President?" *Look* 20 (June 12, 1956): 33–35.
———. "Democratic Forecast: A Catholic in 1960." *Look* 23 (March 3, 1959): 13–17.
Koistinen, David. "Public Policies for Countering Deindustrialization in Postwar Massachusetts." *Journal of Policy History* v. 18, n. 3 (2006): 326–361.
Lapomarda, Vincent A. "Maurice Joseph Tobin: The Decline of Bossism in Boston." *New England Quarterly* 43 (September 1970): 355–381.
Lee, R. Alton. "Federal Assistance to Depressed Areas in the Postwar Recessions." *Western Economic Journal* 2 (September 1963): 1–23.
Lubin, Isadore. "Reducing Unemployment in Depressed Areas." *American Economic Review* v. 50, n. 2 (May 1960): 162–170.

MacRae, Duncan, Jr. "The Relation between Roll Call Votes and Constituencies in the Massachusetts House of Representatives." *American Political Science Review* v. 46, n. 4 (December 1952): 1046–1055.

Mallan, John P. "Massachusetts: Liberal and Corrupt." *New Republic* 127 (October 13, 1952): 10–12.

———, and George Blackwood. "The Tax that Beat a Governor: The Ordeal of Massachusetts," in *The Uses of Power*, ed. by Alan F. Westin (New York: Harcourt, Brace, and World, 1962): 286–322.

Nurse, Ronald J. "Critic of Colonialism: JFK and Algerian Independence." *Historian* 39 (February 1977): 307–326.

O'Brien, Charles F. "George Aiken and Canada," in *The Political Legacy of George D. Aiken: Wise Old Owl of the U.S. Senate*, ed. by Michael Sherman (Woodstock, VT: Countryman Press, 1995): 117–122.

Parenti, Michael. "Ethnic Politics and the Persistence of Ethnic Identification." *American Political Science Review* v. 61, n. 3 (September 1967): 717–726.

Peabody, Robert L., Norman J. Ornstein, and David W. Rohde. "The United States Senate as a Presidential Incubator: Many Are Called but Few Are Chosen." *Political Science Quarterly* v. 91, n. 2 (Summer 1976): 237–258.

Pierson, George W. "The Obstinate Concept of New England: A Study in Denudation." *New England Quarterly* 28 (March 1955): 3–17.

Putnam, Robert D. "Political Attitudes and the Local Community." *American Political Science Review* 60 (September 1966): 640–654.

Richardson, Elliot. "Poisoned Politics, The Real Tragedy of Massachusetts." *Atlantic Monthly* v. 208, n. 4 (October 1961): 77–82.

Savage, Sean J. "JFK and the DNC." *White House Studies* 2 (Summer 2002): 139–153.

Sharkansky, Ira. "The Utility of Elazar's Political Culture." *Polity* 2 (Fall 1969): 66–83.

Turner, Russell. "Senator Kennedy: The Perfect Politician." *American Mercury* 84 (March 1957): 33–40.

White, John K. "Alfred E. Smith's Rhode Island Revolution: The Election of 1928." *Rhode Island History* 42 (1983): 57–66.

Willoughby, William R. "Canadian-American Defense Co-Operation." *Journal of Politics* v. 13, n. 4 (November 1951): 675–696.

———. "The St. Lawrence Waterway Understandings." *International Journal* v. 10, n. 3 (Summer 1955): 242–252.

Wilson, James Q. "The Economy of Patronage." *The Journal of Political Economy* 59 (August 1961): 369–380.

———. "Political Ethos Revisited." *American Political Science Review* 65 (December 1971): 1048–1062.

Wistrich, E. B. "Party Organization and Election Methods in Massachusetts, 1952." *Parliamentary Affairs* 8 (Spring 1954): 221–232.

Wolfinger, Raymond E. "The Development and Persistence of Ethnic Voting." *American Political Science Review* v. 59, n. 4 (December 1965): 896–908.

———. "Why Political Machines Have Not Withered Away and Other Revisionist Thoughts." *Journal of Politics* v. 34, n. 2 (May 1972): 365–398.

Photographic Credits

cover — Photo of John F. Kennedy courtesy of Getty Images (taken from the LIFE Images Collection). Photographer: Verner Reed.

Plate 1 — Joseph P. Kennedy leaving the White House in 1937. *Courtesy: Library of Congress*

Plate 2 — The Kennedy family in Hyannis Port, Massachusetts during the 1940s. *Courtesy: John F. Kennedy Presidential Library and Museum, Boston*

Plate 3 — JFK and Henry Cabot Lodge, Jr. in 1952. *Courtesy: John F. Kennedy Presidential Library and Museum, Boston*

Plate 4 — JFK and Bishop John J. Wright at a church festival in Bolton, Massachusetts in 1952. *Courtesy: Catholic Diocese of Worcester*

Plate 5 — Labor union supporters of JFK's Senate candidacy in 1952. *Courtesy: Department of Special Collections and University Archives, W.E.B. DuBois Library, University of Massachusetts, Amherst*

Plate 6 — Harry S. Truman and Adlai E. Stevenson in the White House in 1952. *Courtesy: National Park Service, Abbie Rowe, Harry S. Truman Presidential Library and Museum*

Plate 7 — JFK examining tornado damage in Worcester, Massachusetts in 1953. *Courtesy: Catholic Diocese of Worcester*

PHOTOGRAPHIC CREDITS

Plate 8   JFK at Saint Michael's College in Colchester, Vermont in 1954. *Courtesy: Saint Michael's College Archives, Saint Michael's College, Colchester, Vermont*

Plate 9   JFK at a bill signing ceremony in the White House in 1954. *Courtesy: National Park Service and Dwight D. Eisenhower Presidential Library and Museum*

Plate 10 JFK listening to Sr. M. Rose Isabel at Anna Maria College in Paxton, Massachusetts in 1955. *Courtesy: Anna Maria College*

Plate 11 Leverett Saltonstall. *Courtesy: U.S. Senate Historical Office*

Plate 12 Margaret Chase Smith. *Courtesy: U.S. Senate Historical Office*

Plate 13 Lyndon B. Johnson in 1955. *Courtesy: Library of Congress*

Plate 14 Joseph W. Martin, Jr. in 1956. *Courtesy: Stonehill College: Joseph W. Martin, Jr. Papers*

Plate 15 Dwight D. Eisenhower in the White House in 1956. *Courtesy: National Park Service and Dwight D. Eisenhower Presidential Library and Museum*

Plate 16 Edmund S. Muskie voting in Waterville, Maine in 1956. *Courtesy: Edmund S. Muskie Archives and Special Collections Library, Bates College*

Plate 17 Foster Furcolo. *Courtesy: Foster Furcolo, Jr.*

Plate 18 JFK at Assumption College in Worcester, Massachusetts in 1958. *Courtesy: Assumption College*

Plate 19 Grace Dodd, Thomas J. Dodd, and JFK in Hartford, Connecticut in 1958. *Courtesy: Archives and Special Collections, University of Connecticut Libraries*

Plate 20 JFK and Jacqueline Kennedy with Merrimack College students in Andover, Massachusetts in 1958. *Courtesy: Frank J. Leone, Jr./Merrimack College*

PHOTOGRAPHIC CREDITS 323

Plate 21 JFK and Bernard L. Boutin in Manchester, New Hampshire in 1958. *Courtesy: Fay Foto/Boston and New Hampshire Historical Society*

Plate 22 JFK and campaign supporters at the Democratic state convention in Boston in 1958. *Courtesy: Department of Special Collections and University Archives, W.E.B. DuBois Library, University of Massachusetts, Amherst*

Plate 23 JFK campaigning in Brockton, Massachusetts in 1958. *Courtesy: Stonehill College Archives and Historical Collections: Stanley A. Bauman Photograph Collection*

Plate 24 JFK and Jacqueline Kennedy campaigning in Worcester, Massachusetts in 1958. *Courtesy: George P. Cocaine Collection, Worcester Historical Museum*

Plate 25 Queen Elizabeth II and Dwight D. Eisenhower at the dedication of the St. Lawrence Seaway in 1959. *Courtesy: U.S. Navy and Dwight D. Eisenhower Presidential Library and Museum*

Plate 26 JFK and Harry S. Truman in Independence, Missouri in 1959. *Courtesy: Harry S. Truman Presidential Library and Museum*

Plate 27 Jacqueline Kennedy and JFK in Wisconsin in 1959, Image WHi—58661. *Courtesy: Wisconsin Historical Society*

Plate 28 Thomas P. "Tip" O'Neill, Jr. and John W. McCormack in 1960. *Courtesy: Thomas P. O'Neill, Jr. Congressional Papers, CA 2009.001, John J. Burns Library, Boston College*

Plate 29 Dwight D. Eisenhower and Richard M. Nixon in the White House in 1960. *Courtesy: National Park Service and Dwight D. Eisenhower Presidential Library and Museum*

Plate 30 Abraham Ribicoff in Waterbury, Connecticut in 1960. *Courtesy: Michael Salvatore Smith*

PHOTOGRAPHIC CREDITS

Plate 31 JFK, Abram L. Sachar, and Eleanor Roosevelt at Brandeis University in Waltham, Massachusetts in 1960. *Courtesy: Brandeis University*

Plate 32 JFK at Dartmouth College in Hanover, New Hampshire in 1960. *Courtesy: Dartmouth College Library*

Index

Acheson, Dean, 88, 139, 147
ADA. *See* Americans for Democratic Action
Adams, Sherman, 43–44, 49, 89, 164, 181, 184
AFL-CIO, 67–68, 143, 155, 199–200
agricultural issues, 104–105
Aiken, George D., 56, 76–77, 80, 95–96
Almond, Gabriel, 3
American Federalism: A View from the States, 4
American Mercury, 142
Americans for Democratic Action, 14, 121, 135, 148–149, 197
Area Redevelopment Act of 1961, 61–63
Area Redevelopment Administration, 62
Atlantic Monthly, 47

Bailey, John M., 114
  and JFK presidential nomination, 1960, 164, 206–209, 231, 234, 241
  and JFK vice presidential nomination, 1956, 116, 120, 126
Banfield, Edward C., 3–4
Barnstable Patriot, 181
Batt, William L., 60–61
Beck, David, 141
Ben-Gurion, David, 13
Benson, Ezra Taft, 104–105, 178
Berkshire Eagle, 133
Boston Globe, 2, 25, 29, 136, 191
Boston Herald, 19
Boston Post, 20, 25
Boston Redevelopment Authority, 64
Boutin, Bernard L., 165, 184–185, 240, *plate 21*
  and JFK, 169, 204, 219
BRA. *See* Boston Redevelopment Authority
Branon, E. Frank, 169
Brewer, Basil, 20, 106
Brown, Edmund G. "Pat," 207–208
Brownell, Herbert, 150
Bruno, Jerry, 199
Buchan, John, 97–98

Burke, Edmund, 97–98
Burke, William "Onions," 26–27, 114, 123, 191
Burns, James MacGregor, 3–4
Bush, Prescott, 48, 54
Bush-McCormack Act of 1956, 53–54
Butler, Paul M., 139–140
Byrne, Garrett H., 26

Cannon, Clarence, 53
Cape Cod National Seashore Park, 70–72
Carr, John, 26
Catholic vote, 109–111, 114, 119, 196–197, 212
Celeste, Vincent J., 30–33, 172, 176, 179–181
Chevrier, Lionel, 87
Churchill, Winston, 98
The Civic Culture: Political Attitudes and Democracy in Five Nations, 3
Civil Rights Act of 1957, 31, 152–153
Clark, Joseph, 63
Clauson, Clinton, 205–206
Coffin, Frank M., 131, 205, 236
Coghlan, Ralph, 41
Collins, John F., 64
Collins, LeRoy, 235
Connally, Thomas T., 86
Corcoran, Thomas G., 108–109
Cotton, Norris, 57
Council of Economic Advisors, 42, 45, 60, 154
Curley, James Michael, 5–6, 8, 10, 12, 97, 190

DAC. *See* Democratic National Committee: Democratic Advisory Council
Dalton, Mark J., 9, 15–16
DeGuglielmo, Joseph A., 9
Democratic National Committee, 139
  Democratic Advisory Council, 65, 139–140, 156
Dever, Paul, 9, 21, 23–24, 26–28, 122
  and JFK, 11–17, 123
Dewey, Thomas F., 84–85
DiSalle, Michael V., 217–218, 221, 224
disaster relief, 53–54
DNC. *See* Democratic National Committee
Dodd, Grace, *plate 19*
Dodd, Thomas J., 186, 239, *plate 19*
Douglas, Paul, 59–63, 151
Dulles, John Foster, 90, 107, 144
Dunfey, William L., 184, 235–236
Dunn, Edward J., 20

The Economic State of New England, 50–51, 94
The Economics of New England, 42, 94
Eisenhower, Dwight D., 15, 28–29, 105, 134, 139, *plates 15, 25, 29*
  elections, 1958, activity in, 182–183, 189
  health issues, 106–108, 121, 125, 133
  policies
    civil rights, 148, 150
    economic, 21, 43–44, 49, 52, 60, 62–63, 155

foreign, 144
urban renewal, 66–67
St. Lawrence Seaway, 89–90
Elazar, Daniel J., 4
Elizabeth II (queen), *plate 25*
The Enemy Within, 69
Ervin, Sam, 68

Fair Employment Practices Committee, 149
Federal Aid Highway Act of 1956, 55
Federal Power Commission, 84, 86, 91
Federal Reserve Bank of Boston, 42, 50
Federal Reserve Board, 154–155
Feldman, Myer, 173
Finnegan, James, 118
Fisher, Paul C., 218
Fitzgerald, John F. "Honey Fitz," 6, 8, 12–13
Flood, Daniel, 61
Fox, John J., 20, 114
Fuchs, Laurence J., 146–147
Fulbright, J. William, 47, 61
Furcolo, Foster, 16, 23, 134, 175, 187, *plate 17*
  Ballots Anyone?, 30
  and JFK presidential campaign, 216, 237
  rift with JFK, 25, 28–30, 32, 104, 132, 171–172

Galbraith, John Kenneth, 42
Gilgun, Edward P., 216
Goldwater, Barry, 143, 161, 188
Gore, Albert A., Sr., 115, 127–129
Grace, Edward P., 117–118
Gray, Gordon, 57
Great Lakes-St. Lawrence Association, 88, 92
Green, Edith, 200–201
Green, Theodore F., 48, 76–77, 140, 170, 242
"Green Brahmin," 2
Griffin, Robert, 161

Harriman, W. Averell, 110, 113, 117, 123–125
Harris, Louis, 197, 208
Harris, Seymour, 42, 94
Hartke, Vance, 203
Harvard Business Review, 41
Herter, Christian A., 21, 25, 91, 107–108
Hoover, Herbert, 78
House Education and Labor Committee, 161
Housing Act of 1949, 64
Housing Act of 1954, 65–66
Humphrey, George, 90
Humphrey, Hubert H., 113
  policies, agricultural, 157, 192
  presidential nomination, 1960, 195, 197–198, 211, 216, 221–225, 227–230
  vice presidential nomination, 1956, 118, 120, 122, 129
Hynes, John B., 64

Immigration and Nationality Act of 1952. *See* McCarran-Walter Act
International Brotherhood of Teamsters, 141

Interstate Commerce Commission, 56
interstate highways, funding of, 104
Ives, Irving, 68, 159

Jackson, John, 24
Johnson, Lyndon B., 52, 106, 139–140, 189, 232
    and JFK Senate career, 137, 141, 148
    and JFK vice presidential nomination, 1956, 128
    policies, civil rights, 149–150, 153
    presidential nomination, 1956, 108–109, 115, 125
    presidential nomination, 1960, 203, 209–211, 225, 229–231, 234
    vice presidential nomination, 1960, 235, 237–238, *plate 13*

Kane, Joe, 6–7
Kefauver, Estes, 140
    and Adlai Stevenson presidential nomination, 1956, 124, 126
    policies, civil rights, 112
    presidential nomination, 1956, 110–111, 113, 116–117, 220
    vice presidential nomination, 1956, 118, 122, 128–129, 131, 211
Keith, Hastings, 71–72
Kelley, Francis X., 25–26
Kennedy, Edward M., 5, 30, 129, 176, 204, 208–209, 232, *plate 2*
Kennedy, Jacqueline, 31, 176, 221, 242, *plate 20, plate 24, plate 27*

Kennedy, John F., *plates 2–4, 7–10, 18–24, 26–27, 31*
    Catholicism of, 103, 106, 116, 118–120, 195–198, 204–205, 207, 212–213, 222–223, 226–228, 235, 238
    Congressional career, 9, 39
    family influence on political career, 5–9, 12, 14–17, 41, 99, 108–110, 114–116, 121, 123, 126–127, 180, 191, 193–194, 196–197, 209, 222–223, 228
    health, 103, 121
    military service, 227–228
    policies
        agricultural, 116, 137, 156, 178, 192, 198, 221–222
        civil rights, 30–31, 100, 127, 137, 147–149, 151–154, 201–202, 222
        defense, 10, 13–15, 166, 178, 182, 222, 242
        economic, 42, 44–47, 51–52, 59, 63–65, 72, 95, 222, 227, 236
        educational, 157–158
        energy, 75–76
        environmental conservation, 70–72
        fiscal, 218
        foreign, 7, 10, 13–15, 17, 19–20, 103, 106, 144–147, 202, 208, 222
        immigration, 146
        labor, 18, 46–48, 55, 58–59, 61, 63, 66–68, 105, 142–143, 159–163, 177, 192, 199–201, 221–222

INDEX

political campaigns
  Congressional, 1946, 4–9, 11, 75
    Survival campaign brochure, 8
  Congressional, 1948, 10
  Congressional, 1950, 10
  presidential, 1960, 29, 34, 36–37, 44, 58, 65, 68–69, 136, 142, 158, 163, 167, 169, 171, 180, 186–187, 192–195, 197–199, 201, 203, 205–213, 215–243
  Senate, 1952, 10–21, 41–42, 72, 75, *plate 5*
  Senate, 1958, 30–34, 48, 65, 69, 142, 146, 163, 171–172, 174–182, 187–188, *plates 22–24*
  vice presidential nomination, 1956, 52, 110, 114–118, 120–124, 126–129, 135, 156, 192, 194, 206, 211–212
presidential activism, 215–216, 242
The Pursuit of Happiness, 119, 135–136
Senate career, 3, 22, 39, 73, 141–142, 192
Senate committees, 58, 140–141
speeches
  1948, 13
  1949, 10
  1951, 13
  1952, 17–18, 22, 41, 44
  1953, 45–46, 58–59, 66, 75–76, 98
  1954, 77, 95, 100–101
  1955, 103, 105
  1956, 28, 52, 54, 119, 129–130, 135
  1957, 67–68, 143–145, 147, 153, 156–158
  1958, 63, 69–70, 155–157, 159, 163–166, 168–169, 177–179
  1959, 156, 190, 198, 200–202, 205, 208
  1960, 65, 156, 215–216, 219, 222, 227, 239–240, 242–244
  1961, 1–2
  1963, 247–248
writings
  "A Democrat Looks at Foreign Policy," 146
  "New England and the South," 47
  Profiles in Courage, 26, 99–100, 244
  "What's the Matter with New England?," 46
  Why England Slept, 7, 98
Kennedy, Joseph P., 6–7, 20, 99, 129, 193–194, *plates 1–2*
  and JFK political career
    Congressional, 5, 8–9, 191
    presidential nomination, 1960, 195–197, 209, 227–228, 231
    Senate, 12, 14–16, 32, 41
    vice presidential nomination, 1956, 108–110, 115, 121
Kennedy, Robert F., 67, 69, 109, 129, 131, 133, 141–143, 202, 212, 217
  and JFK political career
    presidential nomination, 1960, 197, 209–211, 221, 235, *plate 2*
    Senate campaign, 1952, 16, 20, 24
    vice presidential nomination, 1956, 110

Kennedy, Rose, 8, *plate 2*
Kennedy-Ives bill, 160–163, 177–178, 181
Korean War, 88

Labor-Management Reporting and Disclosure Act of 1959, 199–200
Lait, Jack, 5
Landrum-Griffin Act of 1959, 61, 69, 221
Lawrence, David L., 189, 211–213, 217, 233–234
Lockard, Duane, 4
Lodge, Henry Cabot, Jr., 49, *plate 3*
  and presidential campaign, 1960, 237–238
  Senate career, 6, 12–13, 15, 17–20, 75, 82–83, 89
Logue, Edward, 64
Longines Chronoscope, 19
Look, 109, 196
Luce, Clare Booth, 106, 115
Lynch, John M. "Pat," 27, 175

Martin, Joseph W., Jr., 21, 43, 81, 89–90, *plate 14*
Massachusetts
  economy, 13, 15, 17–18, 21–22, 28–31, 41–73, 75–77, 82, 84, 86, 92–93, 101, 105
  energy prices, 56–58
  federal aid, 42–45, 48, 50, 52, 54–55, 58–61, 63–64
  unemployment, 45–46, 49, 63
Massachusetts Democratic Party, 7–8, 16, 26, 36–37, 39
McCarran-Walter Act of 1952, 106, 145

McCarran-Walter bill, 19
McCarthy, Joseph R., 20
McClellan, John, 67, 199
McCormack, Edward J., Jr., 32
McCormack, John W., 9–10, 14, 26–27, 54, 64, 175, 191, *plate 28*
  and JFK presidential nomination, 1960, 233–235, 237
  and presidential election, 1956, 123–125
McGrath, J. Howard, 241
McNally, John J., Jr., 174
Meany, George, 192
Meet the Press, 14, 132
Miller, Perry, 2
Miller, Ray, 217
Monagan, John S., 239
Morrissey, Francis X., 24
Morse, Wayne, 200–201, 224, 230
Mortimer, Lee, 5
Murphy, Robert, 24–25
Muskie, Edmund S., 131, 166–169, 205–206, 236, *plate 16*

National Association of Manufacturers, 162
National Defense Education Act of 1958, 157
National Planning Association, 42, 49–50
Neville, Michael, 8–9
New Bedford Standard Times, 20, 33, 106
New England Council, 49
New England Governors' Conference, 49, 54
The New England Mind: From Colony to Province, 2

New England Senators' Conference, 44, 46, 48–49, 52–58, 63, 69–70, 72–73, 76, 192
New England State Politics, 4
New York Times Magazine, 46
Nicoll, Donald E., 131, 167
Nixon, Richard M., 69, 189, 199, plate 29
　presidential nomination, 1960, 216, 219–220, 225–226, 237–240, 242, 244
　vice presidential nomination, 1956, 107–108, 125, 130
North Adams Transcript, 19
Notte, John A., 241

O'Brien, Lawrence F., 16, 23, 26–27, 121, 176, 197, 201–203, 209, 235, 242
O'Conor, Herbert, 88
ODM. *See* Office of Defense Mobilization
O'Donnell, Kenneth P., 8, 16, 26–27, 121, 126, 132, 176, 197, 211, 235, 237
Office of Defense Mobilization, 57
O'Neill, Thomas P. "Tip," Jr., 8–9, 12, 92–93, 96, 175, plate 28
"open convention," 125–127
O'Riordan, Margaret, 191

Pastore, John O., 48, 170
Patterson, Robert, 80
Payne, Frederick, 61
Pell, Claiborne, 241–242
Pilgrim's Way, 98
Powell, Adam Clayton, Jr., 150
Powell, Wesley, 219
Powers, David F., 8, 121, 176, 194

Powers, John E., 17, 123
presidential campaign, 1960, 243–244. *See also* names of individual politicians
　Democratic National Convention, 233–235
　primaries, 224, 226, 230
　　Indiana, 224–226
　　New Hampshire, 165, 218, 220–221
　　West Virginia, 179, 224, 226–230
　　Wisconsin, 221–224, 226
Purtell, William, 48
Putnam, George M., 85

Quigley, Andrew, 110

Rabb, Max, 43
Raskin, Hyman, 208
Rayburn, Sam, 139–140, 161
Reardon, Timothy "Ted," 235
recession, 1957–1958, 154–155
Reeves, Thomas L., 20
Republican National Committee, 139
Reston, James, 216
Reuther, Walter, 192
Ribicoff, Abraham, 166, 185–186, plate 30
　and JFK political career
　　presidential nomination, 1960, 164, 205–207, 209, 234–235, 239–240
　　vice presidential nomination, 1956, 115–116, 121, 123, 126–127
RNC. *See* Republican National Committee
Roberts, Dennis J., 49, 170–171, 186, 241

Rockefeller, Nelson A., 188, 238
Roosevelt, Eleanor, 100, 124, 126, 139, 146–147, 149, 195, *plate 31*
Roosevelt, Franklin D., Jr., 227–228
Royal, Kenneth, 81–82
Rural Electrification Administration, 169
Russell, Richard B., 47, 51, 150–151

Sachar, Abram L., *plate 31*
Saltonstall, Leverett, 25, 69, 72, 89, 175, 242, *plate 11*
  and JFK, 22–24, 31, 33, 43, 47–48, 52, 64, 71, 75, 191
  Senate career, 12
  St. Lawrence Seaway, 82–84, 96
Schlesinger, Arthur M., Jr., 2, 11, 99–100, 116, 118, 120, 150, 230
Senate Armed Services Committee, 23
Senate Foreign Relations Committee, 58, 81, 83–84, 88–89, 91, 106, 140, 144, 147
  African Affairs subcommittee, 140
  Internal Organization Affairs subcommittee, 140
Senate Judiciary Committee, 150–151
Senate Labor and Public Welfare Committee, 58–59, 63
  Select Committee on Improper Activities in the Labor Management Field, 141
Shannon, William V., 41
Shefferman, Nathan W., 141

Shriver, R. Sargent, 20, 114–115, 123, 127
Six Crises, 108
Smith, Benjamin A., 72
Smith, Margaret Chase, 43–44, 48, 53, 56–57, 70, 95–96, 101, *plate 12*
Smith, Stephen, 176, 197
Somervell, Brehon B., 80
Sorensen, Theodore C., 1, 22, 46, 48, 93–95, 99, 110, 114, 120, 124, 129, 131, 176, 180, 190
Sparkman, John, 61
Springfield Daily News, 25
St. Laurent, Louis, 87–88
St. Lawrence Deep Waterway Treaty, 78–79
St. Lawrence Seaway, 12, 48, 51, 64, 69, 73, 75–101
  defense, 77, 79–82, 86, 88, 93
  energy production, 78–80, 84–88, 91, 93
  financing, 80, 82–83
  The Great Delusion, 83
  navigation, 76–78, 80, 83–85, 87
St. Lawrence Seaway Authority (Canadian), 87
The St. Lawrence Seaway, 87
Stevenson, Adlai E., 233, *plate 6*
  policy, civil rights, 148
  presidential nomination, 1952, 21
  presidential nomination, 1956, 27–29, 110, 112–119, 122–126, 129–135
  presidential nomination, 1960, 193–194, 212, 230–231, 234
  vice presidential nomination, 1956, 109

Symington, Stuart, 156, 201, 204, 209, 216, 224–225, 231, 233

Taft, Robert A., 19–20, 83, 90–91, 98, 168
Taft-Hartley Act of 1947, 10, 18, 46, 52, 66–67
Teamsters, 142–143, 159, 162
Teamsters Union, 67–68
Time, 153–154
Tivnan, Robert X., 29
Tobin, Maurice, 6–7, 9, 41
tornado damage, 32, *plate 7*
Truman, Harry S.
  policy, foreign, 19
  and presidential election, 1956, 122–123, 125
  and presidential election, 1960, 33, 140, 209, 232–233, *plates 6, 26*
  St. Lawrence Seaway, 80–81, 84–85, 87–88

United Automobile Workers, 67, 143, 199

United Mine Workers, 68, 159, 162
United Steel Workers of America, 68
urban renewal, 63–66
U.S. Congress. *See* Congress
U.S. Senate. *See* Senate
The U.S. Senator John F. Kennedy Story, 172
U.S.A. Confidential, 5

Vandenberg, Arthur H., 81, 86
Verba, Sidney, 3

Wagner, Robert, 109
Walsh-Healey Act of 1936, 46, 52
Weeks, Sinclair, 43, 89–90, 106
While England Slept, 98
White, Theodore H., 1
Wilson, James Q., 3
Worcester Gazette, 51
Worcester Telegram, 32, 136, 187
Wright, John J., 32, 196, *plate 4*

Zablocki, Clement, 199